BARACK OBAMA

WHAT HE BELIEVES IN

FROM HIS OWN WORKS

Resolutions and Bills

Sponsored & Co-Sponsored By Senator Barack Obama

During the 110th Session (First Half) of the U.S. Congress

January 4, 2007 to December 19, 2007

MANOR

ROCKVILLE, MARYLAND

2008

ISBN: 978-1-60450-117-9

Publisher's Note: The Bills and Resolutions contained in this book are from the first session of the 110th Congress (calendar year, 2007) and do not include legislative action from earlier sessions of Congress that Senator Obama participated in.

Published by Arc Manor
P. O. Box 10339
Rockville, MD 20849-0339
www.ArcManor.com
Printed in the United States of America/United Kingdom

The Difference Between Various Forms of Legislative Actions

(excerpted from the Guide to Legislative Process in the House, US House of Representatives Committee on Rules)

BILLS

A bill is the form used for most legislation, whether permanent or temporary, general or special, public or private.

Bills may originate in either the House of Representatives or the Senate, with one notable exception provided for by the Constitution. Article I, Section 7, of the Constitution, provides that all bills for raising revenue shall originate in the House of Representatives but the Senate may propose or concur with amendments, as on other bills. By tradition, general appropriation bills also originate in the House of Representatives.

There are two types of bills—public and private. A public bill is one that affects the public generally. A bill of a private character, that is, a bill that affects an individual rather than the population at large, is called a private bill. A private bill is used for relief in matters such as immigration and naturalization and claims against the United States.

A Senate bill is designated by the letter "S." followed by its number. The term "companion bill" is used to describe a bill introduced in one House of Congress that is similar or identical to a bill introduced in the other House of Congress.

A bill that has been agreed to in identical form by both bodies becomes the law of the land only after—

1.   Presidential approval; or

2.   failure by the President to return it with objections to the House in which it originated within 10 days while Congress is in session; or

3.   the overriding of a Presidential veto by a two-thirds vote in each House.

It does not become law without the President's signature if Congress by their final adjournment prevent its return with objections. This is known as a "pocket veto."

JOINT RESOLUTIONS

Joint resolutions may originate either in the House of Representatives or in the Senate—not, as may be supposed, jointly in both Houses. There is little practical difference between a bill and a joint resolution and, although the latter are not as numerous as bills, the two forms are often used indiscriminately. Statutes that have been initiated as bills have later been amended by a joint resolution, and vice versa. Both are subject to the same procedure—with the exception of a joint resolution proposing an amendment to the Constitution. When a joint resolution amending the Constitution is approved by two-thirds of both Houses, it is not presented to the President for approval. Following congressional approval, a joint resolution to amend the Constitution is sent directly to the Archivist of the United States for submission to the several States where ratification by the legislatures of three-fourths of the States within the period of time prescribed in the joint resolution is necessary for the amendment to become part of the Constitution.

The term "joint" does not signify simultaneous introduction and consideration in both Houses.

A joint resolution originating in the House of Representatives is designated "H.J. Res." followed by its individual number which it retains throughout all its parliamentary stages. One originating in the Senate is designated "S.J. Res." followed by its number.

Joint resolutions, with the exception of proposed amendments to the Constitution, become law in the same manner as bills.

CONCURRENT RESOLUTIONS

Matters affecting the operations of both Houses are usually initiated by means of concurrent resolutions. In modern practice concurrent and simple resolutions normally are not legislative in character but are used merely for expressing facts, principles, opinions, and purposes of the two Houses. They are not equivalent to a bill and their use is narrowly limited within these bounds.

The term "concurrent" does not signify simultaneous introduction and consideration in both Houses.

A concurrent resolution originating in the House of Representatives is designated "H. Con. Res." followed by its individual number, while a Senate concurrent resolution is designated "S. Con. Res." together with its number. On approval by both Houses, they are signed by the Clerk of the House and the Secretary of the Senate and transmitted to the Archivist of the United States for publication in a special part of the Statutes at Large volume covering that session of Congress.

SIMPLE RESOLUTIONS

A matter concerning the rules, the operation or the opinion of either House alone is initiated by a simple resolution. A resolution affecting the House of Representatives is designated "H. Res." followed by its number, while a Senate resolution is designated "S. Res." together with its number. Simple resolutions are considered only by the body in which they were introduced and on adoption are attested to by the Clerk of the House of Representatives or the Secretary of the Senate, as the case may be, and are published in the Congressional Record.

CONTENTS

(Senate Resolutions and Bills Sponsored or Co-Sponsored by Senator Barack Obama during the 110th Congress)

SENATE CONCURRENT RESOLUTIONS

SENATE RESOLUTIONS

US SENATE BILL 1811   334
   Title: A bill to amend the Toxic Substances Control Act to assess and reduce the
   levels of lead found in child-occupied facilities in the United States, and for other
   purposes.
   7/18/2007

US SENATE BILL 1817   341
   Title: A bill to ensure proper administration of the discharge of members of the
   Armed Forces for personality disorder, and for other purposes.
   7/19/2007

US SENATE BILL 1818   343
   Title: A bill to amend the Toxic Substances Control Act to phase out the use of
   mercury in the manufacture of chlorine and caustic soda, and for other purposes.
   7/19/2007

US SENATE BILL 1824   351
   Title: A bill to amend title XVIII of the Social Security Act to establish a Hospital Quality Report Card Initiative under the Medicare program to assess and
   report on health care quality in hospitals.
   7/19/2007

US SENATE BILL 1873   357
   Title: A bill to amend the Public Health Service Act to establish demonstration
   programs on regionalized systems for emergency care, to support emergency medicine research, and for other purposes.
   7/25/2007

US SENATE BILL 1885   362
   Title: A bill to provide certain employment protections for family members who
   are caring for members of the Armed Forces recovering from illnesses and injuries
   incurred on active duty.
   7/26/2007

US SENATE BILL 1977   365
   Title: A bill to provide for sustained United States leadership in a cooperative
   global effort to prevent nuclear terrorism, reduce global nuclear arsenals, stop the
   spread of nuclear weapons and related material and technology, and support the
   responsible and peaceful use of nuclear technology.
   8/2/2007

US SENATE BILL 1989   376
   Title: A bill to provide a mechanism for the determination on the merits of the
   claims of claimants who met the class criteria in a civil action relating to racial
   discrimination by the Department of Agriculture but who were denied that
   determination.
   8/3/2007

US Senate Bill 2227   417
   Title: A bill to provide grants to States to ensure that all students in the middle
   grades are taught an academically rigorous curriculum with effective supports so
   that students complete the middle grades prepared for success in high school and
   postsecondary endeavors, to improve State and district policies and programs relating to the academic achievement of students in the middle grades, to develop and
   implement effective middle school models for struggling students, and for other
   purposes.
   10/24/2007

US Senate Bill 2330   435
   Title: A bill to authorize a pilot program within the Departments of Veterans Affairs and Housing and Urban Development with the goal of preventing at-risk veterans and veteran families from falling into homelessness, and for other purposes.
   11/8/2007

US Senate Bill 2347   444
   Title: A bill to restore and protect access to discount drug prices for university-
   based and safety-net clinics.
   11/13/2007

US Senate Bill 2392   447
   Title: A bill to direct the Secretary of Education to establish and maintain a
   public website through which individuals may find a complete database of available
   scholarships, fellowships, and other programs of financial assistance in the study of
   science, technology, engineering, and mathematics.
   11/16/2007

US Senate Bill 2428   450
   Title: A bill to direct the Secretary of Education to establish and maintain a
   public website through which individuals may find a complete database of available
   scholarships, fellowships, and other programs of financial assistance in the study of
   science, technology, engineering, and mathematics.
   12/6/2007

US Senate Bill 2433   453
   Title: A bill to require the President to develop and implement a comprehensive
   strategy to further the United States foreign policy objective of promoting the
   reduction of global poverty, the elimination of extreme global poverty, and the
   achievement of the Millennium Development Goal of reducing by one-half the
   proportion of people worldwide, between 1990 and 2015, who live on less than $1
   per day.
   12/7/2007

Title: A bill to prohibit the awarding of a contract or grant in excess of the simplified acquisition threshold unless the prospective contractor or grantee certifies in writing to the agency awarding the contract or grant that the contractor or grantee has no seriously delinquent tax debts, and for other purposes.

12/19/2007

US Senate Concurrent Resolution 5

Title: A concurrent resolution honoring the life of Percy Lavon Julian, a pioneer in the field of organic chemistry and the first and only African-American chemist to be inducted into the National Academy of Sciences.

Sponsor: Sen Obama, Barack [IL] (introduced 1/31/2007) Cosponsors (5)

Related Bills: H.CON.RES.34

Latest Major Action: 1/31/2007 Referred to Senate committee. Status: Referred to the Committee on the Judiciary.

Summary As Of:

1/31/2007—Introduced.

Honors the life of Percy Lavon Julian, a pioneer in the field of organic chemistry, and the first and only African American chemist to be inducted into the National Academy of Sciences.

Major Actions:

¤NONE¤

All Actions:

1/31/2007:

Referred to the Committee on the Judiciary. (text of measure as introduced: CR S1463)

Titles(s): (italics indicate a title for a portion of a bill)

¤NONE¤

Cosponsors(5), Alphabetical [followed by Cosponsors withdrawn]: (Sort: by date)

Sen Bayh, Evan [IN] - 1/31/2007

Sen Dodd, Christopher J. [CT] - 1/31/2007

Sen Durbin, Richard [IL] - 1/31/2007

Sen Lieberman, Joseph I. [CT] - 1/31/2007

Sen Lugar, Richard G. [IN] - 1/31/2007

Committee(s)

Committee/Subcommittee:

Activity:

Senate Judiciary

Referral, In Committee

Related Bill Details: (additional related bills may be indentified in Status)

Bill:

Relationship:

H.CON.RES.34

Related bill identified by CRS

Amendment(s)

¤NONE¤

In the Senate of the United States

January 31, 2007

Mr. OBAMA (for himself, Mr. DURBIN, Mr. DODD, Mr. LUGAR, Mr. LIE-BERMAN, and Mr. BAYH) submitted the following concurrent resolution; which was referred to the Committee on the Judiciary

CONCURRENT RESOLUTION

Honoring the life of Percy Lavon Julian, a pioneer in the field of organic chemistry and the first and only African-American chemist to be inducted into the National Academy of Sciences.

Whereas Percy Julian was born on April 11, 1899 in Montgomery, Alabama, the son of a railway clerk and the first member of his family to attend college;

Whereas Percy Julian graduated from DePauw University in 1920 and received an M.S. degree from Harvard University in 1923 and a Ph.D. from the University of Vienna in 1931;

Whereas, in 1935, Dr. Julian became the first to discover a process to synthesize physostigmine, the drug used in the treatment of glaucoma;

Whereas Dr. Julian later pioneered a commercial process to synthesize cortisone from soy beans, enabling the widespread use of cortisone as an affordable treatment for arthritis;

Whereas Dr. Julian was the first African-American chemist elected to the National Academy of Sciences in 1973 for his lifetime of scientific accomplishments, held over 130 patents at the time of his death in 1975, and dedicated much of his life to the advancement of African Americans in the sciences; and

Whereas Dr. Julian's life story has been documented in the Public Broadcasting Service NOVA film 'Forgotten Genius': Now, therefore, be it

Resolved by the Senate (the House of Representatives concurring), That the Congress honors the life of Percy Lavon Julian, a pioneer in the field of organic chemistry and the first and only African-American chemist to be inducted into the National Academy of Sciences.

US Senate Concurrent Resolution 25

Title: A concurrent resolution condemning the recent violent actions of the Government of Zimbabwe against peaceful opposition party activists and members of civil society.

Sponsor: Sen Obama, Barack [IL] (introduced 3/29/2007) Cosponsors (7)

Related Bills: H.CON.RES.100

Latest Major Action: 6/26/2007 Held at the desk.

Summary As Of:

6/26/2007—Passed Senate without amendment. (There are 2 other summaries)

(This measure has not been amended since it was introduced. The summary of that version is repeated here.)

Expresses the sense of Congress that: (1) the state-sponsored violence taking place in Zimbabwe represents a serious violation of fundamental human rights and the rule of law and should be condemned by all responsible governments, civic organizations, religious leaders, and international bodies; and (2) the government of Zimbabwe has not lived up to its commitments as a signatory to the Constitutive Act of the African Union and African Charter of Human and Peoples Rights.

Condemns: (1) the government of Zimbabwe's violent suppression of political and human rights; (2) the harassment and intimidation of lawyers attempting to carry out their professional obligations to their clients and repeated failure by police to comply with court decisions; and (3) the harassment of foreign officials, journalists, human rights workers, and others.

Commends U.S. Ambassador Christopher Dell and other U.S. officials and foreign officials for their support to political detainees and victims of torture and abuse while in police custody or in medical care centers.

Calls on the government of Zimbabwe to end: (1) its violent campaign against fundamental human rights, respect the courts and members of the legal profession, and restore the rule of law; and (2) illegitimate interference in travel abroad by its citizens, especially for humanitarian purposes.

Calls on the leaders of the Southern Africa Development Community (SADC) and the African Union (AU) to consult with all Zimbabwe stakeholders to intervene with the government of Zimbabwe while applying appropriate pressures to resolve the economic and political crisis.

MAJOR ACTIONS:

3/29/2007

Introduced in Senate

5/24/2007

Committee on Foreign Relations. Reported by Senator Biden without amendment and with a preamble. Without written report.

6/26/2007

Passed/agreed to in Senate: Resolution agreed to in Senate without amendment and with a preamble by Unanimous Consent.

6/26/2007

Held at the desk.

ALL ACTIONS:

3/29/2007:

Referred to the Committee on Foreign Relations. (text of measure as introduced: CR S4218)

5/24/2007:

Committee on Foreign Relations. Ordered to be reported without amendment favorably.

5/24/2007:

Committee on Foreign Relations. Reported by Senator Biden without amendment and with a preamble. Without written report.

5/24/2007:

Placed on Senate Legislative Calendar under General Orders. Calendar No. 176.

6/26/2007:

Resolution agreed to in Senate without amendment and with a preamble by Unanimous Consent. (consideration: CR S8519-8520; text as passed Senate: CR S8519-8520)

6/26/2007 7:51pm:

Received in the House.

6/26/2007:

Message on Senate action sent to the House.

6/26/2007 8:33pm:

Received in the House.

6/26/2007 8:33pm:

Held at the desk.

Titles(s): (italics indicate a title for a portion of a bill)

*** Official Title as Introduced:**

A concurrent resolution condemning the recent violent actions of the Government of Zimbabwe against peaceful opposition party activists and members of civil society.

Cosponsors(7), Alphabetical [followed by Cosponsors withdrawn]: (Sort: by date)

Sen Biden, Joseph R., Jr. [DE] - 3/29/2007

Sen Dodd, Christopher J. [CT] - 3/29/2007

Sen Durbin, Richard [IL] - 3/29/2007

Sen Feingold, Russell D. [WI] - 3/29/2007

Sen Hagel, Chuck [NE] - 5/24/2007

Sen Kerry, John F. [MA] - 3/29/2007

Sen Lieberman, Joseph I. [CT] - 4/11/2007

Committee(s)

Committee/Subcommittee:

Activity:

Senate Foreign Relations

Referral, Markup, Reporting

Related Bill Details: (additional related bills may be indentified in Status)

Bill:

Relationship:

H.CON.RES.100

Identical bill identified by CRS

Amendment(s)

¤NONE¤

Whereas in 2005 the Government of Zimbabwe launched Operation Murambatsvina ('Operation Throw Out the Trash') against citizens in major cities and suburbs throughout Zimbabwe, depriving... (Engrossed as Agreed to or Passed by Senate)

CONCURRENT RESOLUTION

Whereas in 2005 the Government of Zimbabwe launched Operation Murambatsvina ('Operation Throw Out the Trash') against citizens in major cities and suburbs throughout Zimbabwe, depriving over 700,000 people of their homes, businesses, and livelihoods;

Whereas on March 11, 2007, opposition party activists and members of civil society attempted to hold a peaceful prayer meeting to protest the economic and political crisis engulfing Zimbabwe, where inflation is running over 1,700 percent and unemployment stands at 80 percent and in response to President Robert Mugabe's announcement that he intends to seek reelection in 2008 if nominated;

Whereas opposition activist Gift Tandare died on March 11, 2007, as a result of being shot by police while attempting to attend the prayer meeting and Itai Manyeruke died on March 12, 2007, as a result of police beatings and was found in a morgue by his family on March 20, 2007;

Whereas under the direction of President Robert Mugabe and the ZANU-PF government, police officers, security forces, and youth militia brutally assaulted the peaceful demonstrators and arrested opposition leaders and hundreds of civilians;

Whereas Movement for Democratic Change (MDC) leader Morgan Tsvangarai was brutally assaulted and suffered a fractured skull, lacerations, and major bruising; MDC member Sekai Holland, a 64-year old grandmother, suffered ruthless attacks at Highfield Police Station, which resulted in the breaking of her leg, knee, arm, and three ribs; fellow activist Grace Kwinje, age 33, also was brutally beaten, while part of one ear was ripped off; and Nelson Chamisa was badly injured by suspected state agents at Harare airport on March 18, 2007, when trying to board a plane for a meeting of European Union and Africa, Caribbean, and Pacific Group of States lawmakers in Brussels, Belgium;

Whereas Zimbabwe's foreign minister warned Western diplomats that the Government of Zimbabwe would expel them if they gave support to the opposition, and said Western diplomats had gone too far by offering food and water to jailed opposition activists;

Whereas victims of physical assault by the Government of Zimbabwe have been denied emergency medical transfer to hospitals in neighboring South Africa, where their wounds can be properly treated;

Whereas those incarcerated by the Government of Zimbabwe were denied access to legal representatives and lawyers appearing at the jails to meet with detained clients were themselves threatened and intimidated;

Whereas at the time of Zimbabwe's independence, President Robert Mugabe was hailed as a liberator and Zimbabwe showed bright prospects for democracy, economic development, domestic reconciliation, and prosperity;

Whereas President Robert Mugabe and his ZANU-PF government continue to turn away from the promises of liberation and use state power to deny the people of Zimbabwe the freedom and prosperity they fought for and deserve;

Whereas the staggering suffering brought about by the misrule of Zimbabwe has created a large-scale humanitarian crisis in which 3,500 people die each week from a combination of disease, hunger, neglect, and despair;

Whereas the Chairman of the African Union, President Alpha Oumar Konare, expressed 'great concern' about Zimbabwe's crisis and called for the need for the scrupulous respect for human rights and democratic principles in Zimbabwe;

Whereas the Southern African Development Community (SADC) Council of Non-governmental Organizations stated that 'We believe that the crisis has reached a point where Zimbabweans need to be strongly persuaded and directly assisted to find an urgent solution to the crisis that affects the entire region.';

Whereas Zambian President, Levy Mwanawasa, has urged southern Africa to take a new approach to Zimbabwe instead of the failed 'quiet diplomacy', which he likened to a 'sinking Titanic,' and stated that 'quiet diplomacy has failed to help solve the political chaos and economic meltdown in Zimbabwe';

Whereas European Union and African, Caribbean, and Pacific lawmakers strongly condemned the latest attack on an opposition official in Zimbabwe and urged the government in Harare to cooperate with the political opposition to restore the rule of law; and

Whereas United States Ambassador to Zimbabwe, Christopher Dell, warned that opposition to President Robert Mugabe had reached a tipping point because the people no longer feared the regime and believed they had nothing left to lose: Now, therefore, be it

Resolved by the Senate (the House of Representatives concurring), That—

(1) it is the sense of Congress that

(A) the state-sponsored violence taking place in Zimbabwe represents a serious violation of fundamental human rights and the rule of law and should be condemned by all responsible governments, civic organizations, religious leaders, and international bodies; and

(B) the Government of Zimbabwe has not lived up to its commitments as a signatory to the Constitutive Act of the African Union and African Charter of Human and Peoples Rights which enshrine commitment to human rights and good governance as foundational principles of African states; and

(2) Congress—

(A) condemns the Government of Zimbabwe's violent suppression of political and human rights through its police force, security forces, and youth militia that deliberately inflict gross physical harm, intimidation, and abuse on those legitimately protesting the failing policies of the government;

(B) holds those individual police, security force members, and militia involved in abuse and torture responsible for the acts that they have committed;

(C) condemns the harassment and intimidation of lawyers attempting to carry out their professional obligations to their clients and repeated failure by police to comply promptly with court decisions;

(D) condemns the harassment of foreign officials, journalists, human rights workers, and others, including threatening their expulsion from the country if they continue to provide food and water to victims detained in prison and in police custody while in the hospital;

(E) commends United States Ambassador Christopher Dell and other United States Government officials and foreign officials for their support to political detainees and victims of torture and abuse while in police custody or in medical care centers and encourages them to continue providing such support;

(F) calls on the Government of Zimbabwe to cease immediately its violent campaign against fundamental human rights, to respect the courts and members of the legal profession, and to restore the rule of law while adhering to the principles embodied in an accountable democracy, including freedom of association and freedom of expression;

(G) calls on the Government of Zimbabwe to cease illegitimate interference in travel abroad by its citizens, especially for humanitarian purposes; and

(H) calls on the leaders of the Southern Africa Development Community (SADC) and the African Union to consult urgently with all Zimbabwe stakeholders to intervene with the Government of Zimbabwe while applying appropriate pressures to resolve the economic and political crisis.

Passed the Senate June 26, 2007.

US SENATE CONCURRENT RESOLUTION 44

TITLE: A concurrent resolution expressing the sense of Congress that a commemorative postage stamp should be issued honoring Rosa Louise McCauley Parks.

SPONSOR: Sen Obama, Barack [IL] (introduced 9/12/2007) Cosponsors (22)

RELATED BILLS: H.CON.RES.108

LATEST MAJOR ACTION: 10/19/2007 Referred to Senate subcommittee. Status: Committee on Homeland Security and Governmental Affairs referred to Subcommittee on Federal Financial Management, Government Information, Federal Services, and International Security.

SUMMARY As Of:

9/12/2007—Introduced.

Expresses the sense of Congress that: (1) a commemorative postage stamp honoring Rosa Louise McCauley Parks should be issued; (2) the provision requiring that an honoree must have died at least five years before this honor should be waived; and (3) the Citizens' Stamp Advisory Committee should recommend that such a stamp be issued.

Major Actions:

¤NONE¤

All Actions:

9/12/2007:

Referred to the Committee on Homeland Security and Governmental Affairs. (text of measure as introduced: CR S11514)

10/19/2007:

Committee on Homeland Security and Governmental Affairs referred to Subcommittee on Federal Financial Management, Government Information, Federal Services, and International Security.

Titles(s): (italics indicate a title for a portion of a bill)

¤NONE¤

Cosponsors(22), Alphabetical [followed by Cosponsors withdrawn]: (Sort: by date)

Sen Alexander, Lamar [TN] - 9/12/2007

Sen Bingaman, Jeff [NM] - 9/12/2007

Sen Boxer, Barbara [CA] - 9/12/2007

Sen Brown, Sherrod [OH] - 9/12/2007

Sen Cardin, Benjamin L. [MD] - 9/12/2007

Sen Clinton, Hillary Rodham [NY] - 9/12/2007

Sen Dodd, Christopher J. [CT] - 9/12/2007

Sen Durbin, Richard [IL] - 9/12/2007

Sen Harkin, Tom [IA] - 9/12/2007

Sen Kennedy, Edward M. [MA] - 9/12/2007

Sen Kerry, John F. [MA] - 9/12/2007

Sen Landrieu, Mary L. [LA] - 9/12/2007

Sen Levin, Carl [MI] - 9/12/2007

Sen Lieberman, Joseph I. [CT] - 9/12/2007

Sen Lugar, Richard G. [IN] - 9/12/2007

Sen Mikulski, Barbara A. [MD] - 9/12/2007

Sen Nelson, Bill [FL] - 12/7/2007

Sen Reid, Harry [NV] - 9/12/2007

Sen Schumer, Charles E. [NY] - 9/12/2007

Sen Stabenow, Debbie [MI] - 9/12/2007

Sen Voinovich, George V. [OH] - 9/12/2007

Sen Wyden, Ron [OR] - 9/12/2007

COMMITTEE(S)

Committee/Subcommittee:

Activity:

Senate Homeland Security and Governmental Affairs

Referral, In Committee

Subcommittee on Federal Financial Management, Government Information, Federal Services, and International Security

Referral

RELATED BILL DETAILS: (additional related bills may be indentified in Status)

Bill:

Relationship:

H.CON.RES.108

Related bill identified by CRS

AMENDMENT(S)

¤NONE¤

IN THE SENATE OF THE UNITED STATES

September 12, 2007

Mr. OBAMA (for himself, Mr. DURBIN, Mr. KERRY, Mrs. CLINTON, Mr. AL-EXANDER, Mr. CARDIN, Mr. LUGAR, Mr. LEVIN, Mr. HARKIN, Mr. LIE-BERMAN, Mr. REID, Mr. KENNEDY, Mr. BINGAMAN, Mrs. BOXER, Mr. DODD, Ms. LANDRIEU, Mr. SCHUMER, Ms. STABENOW, Mr. BROWN, Mr. VOINOVICH, Ms. MIKULSKI, and Mr. WYDEN) submitted the following concurrent resolution; which was referred to the Committee on Homeland Security and Governmental Affairs

CONCURRENT RESOLUTION

Expressing the sense of Congress that a commemorative postage stamp should be issued honoring Rosa Louise McCauley Parks.

Whereas Rosa Parks was born Rosa Louise McCauley in Tuskegee, Alabama, on February 4, 1913, and died on October 25, 2005;

Whereas Rosa Parks was an African American civil rights activist and seamstress whom Congress dubbed the 'Mother of the Modern-Day Civil Rights Movement';

Whereas Rosa Parks refused on December 1, 1955, to obey bus driver James Blake's demand that she relinquish her seat to a white man and her subsequent arrest and trial for this act of civil disobedience triggered the Montgomery Bus Boycott, one of the largest and most successful mass movements against racial segregation in history, and launched Martin Luther King, Jr., one of the organizers of the boycott, to the forefront of the civil rights movement;

Whereas Rosa Parks's role in American history earned her an iconic status in American culture, and her actions have left an enduring legacy for civil rights movements around the world;

Whereas through her role in sparking the boycott, Rosa Parks played an important part in internationalizing the awareness of the plight of African Americans and the civil rights struggle; and

Whereas Rosa Parks epitomized the struggle of everyday people trying to make a difference, as she took a stand against injustice and inequality: Now, therefore, be it

Resolved by the Senate (the House of Representatives concurring), That it is the sense of Congress that—

(1) a commemorative postage stamp should be issued by the United States Postal Service honoring Rosa Louise McCauley Parks;

(2) the provision requiring that an honoree must have died at least 5 years before this honor can be bestowed upon them, excepting Presidents of the United States, should be waived; and

(3) the Citizens' Stamp Advisory Committee should recommend to the Postmaster General that such a stamp be issued.

US Senate Concurrent Resolution 46

Title: A concurrent resolution supporting the goals and ideals of Sickle Cell Disease Awareness Month.

Sponsor: Sen Obama, Barack [IL] (introduced 9/17/2007) Cosponsors (None)

Related Bills: H.CON.RES.210

Latest Major Action: 9/17/2007 Referred to Senate committee. Status: Referred to the Committee on Health, Education, Labor, and Pensions.

Summary As Of:

9/17/2007—Introduced.

Expresses support for the goals and ideals of Sickle Cell Disease Awareness Month.

Major Actions:

¤NONE¤

All Actions:

9/17/2007:

Referred to the Committee on Health, Education, Labor, and Pensions. (text of measure as introduced: CR S11603)

TITLES(s): (italics indicate a title for a portion of a bill)

¤NONE¤

COSPONSOR(s):

¤NONE¤

COMMITTEE(s)

Committee/Subcommittee:

Activity:

Senate Health, Education, Labor, and Pensions

Referral, In Committee

RELATED BILL DETAILS: (additional related bills may be indentified in Status)

Bill:

Relationship:

H.CON.RES.210

Identical bill identified by CRS

AMENDMENT(s)

¤NONE¤

IN THE SENATE OF THE UNITED STATES

September 17, 2007

Mr. OBAMA submitted the following concurrent resolution; which was referred to the Committee on Health, Education, Labor, and Pensions

CONCURRENT RESOLUTION

Supporting the goals and ideals of Sickle Cell Disease Awareness Month.

Whereas Sickle Cell Disease is an inherited blood disorder that is a major health problem in the United States, primarily affecting African Americans;

Whereas Sickle Cell Disease causes the rapid destruction of sickle cells, which results in multiple medical complications, including anemia, jaundice, gallstones, strokes, and restricted blood flow, damaging tissue in the liver, spleen, and kidneys, and death;

Whereas Sickle Cell Disease causes episodes of considerable pain in one's arms, legs, chest, and abdomen;

Whereas Sickle Cell Disease affects over 70,000 Americans;

Whereas approximately 1,000 babies are born with Sickle Cell Disease each year in the United States, with the disease occurring in approximately 1 in 300 newborn African American infants;

Whereas more than 2,000,000 Americans have the sickle cell trait, and 1 in 12 African Americans carry the trait;

Whereas there is a 1 in 4 chance that a child born to parents who both have the sickle cell trait will have the disease;

Whereas the life expectancy of a person with Sickle Cell Disease is severely limited, with an average life span for an adult being 45 years;

Whereas, though researchers have yet to identify a cure for this painful disease, advances in treating the associated complications have occurred;

Whereas researchers are hopeful that in less than two decades, Sickle Cell Disease may join the ranks of chronic illnesses that, when properly treated, do not interfere with the activity, growth, or mental development of affected children;

Whereas Congress recognized the importance of researching, preventing, and treating Sickle Cell Disease by authorizing treatment centers to provide medical intervention, education, and other services and by permitting the Medicaid program to cover some primary and secondary preventative medical strategies for children and adults with Sickle Cell Disease;

Whereas the Sickle Cell Disease Association of America, Inc. remains the preeminent advocacy organization that serves the sickle cell community by focusing its efforts on public policy, research funding, patient services, public awareness, and education related to developing effective treatments and a cure for Sickle Cell Disease; and

Whereas the Sickle Cell Disease Association of America, Inc. has requested that the Congress designate September as Sickle Cell Disease Awareness Month in order to educate communities across the Nation about sickle cell and the need for research funding, early detection methods, effective treatments, and prevention programs: Now, therefore, be it

Resolved by the Senate (the House of Representatives concurring), That the Congress supports the goals and ideals of Sickle Cell Disease Awareness Month.

US Senate Resolution 133

Title: A resolution celebrating the life of Bishop Gilbert Earl Patterson.

Sponsor: Sen Obama, Barack [IL] (introduced 3/28/2007) Cosponsors (4)

Latest Major Action: 3/28/2007 Passed/agreed to in Senate. Status: Submitted in the Senate, considered, and agreed to without amendment and with a preamble by Unanimous Consent.

Summary As Of:

3/28/2007—Passed Senate without amendment. (There is 1 other summary)

(This measure has not been amended since it was introduced. The summary of that version is repeated here.)

Expresses the condolences of the nation to the family of Bishop Gilbert Earl Patterson, the Temple of Deliverance Congregation, and the Church of God in Christ.

Recognizes the life and accomplishments of Bishop Patterson.

MAJOR ACTIONS:

3/28/2007

Introduced in Senate

3/28/2007

Passed/agreed to in Senate: Submitted in the Senate, considered, and agreed to without amendment and with a preamble by Unanimous Consent.

ALL ACTIONS:

3/28/2007:

Submitted in the Senate, considered, and agreed to without amendment and with a preamble by Unanimous Consent. (consideration: CR S4078-4079; text as passed Senate: CR S4078-4079; text of measure as introduced: CR S4062-4063)

TITLES(s): (italics indicate a title for a portion of a bill)

* OFFICIAL TITLE AS INTRODUCED:

A resolution celebrating the life of Bishop Gilbert Earl Patterson.

COSPONSORS(4), ALPHABETICAL [FOLLOWED BY COSPONSORS WITHDRAWN]: (Sort: by date)

Sen Alexander, Lamar [TN] - 3/28/2007

Sen Corker, Bob [TN] - 3/28/2007

Sen Kerry, John F. [MA] - 3/28/2007

Sen Levin, Carl [MI] - 3/28/2007

COMMITTEE(s)

¤NONE¤

RELATED BILL DETAILS:

¤NONE¤

AMENDMENT(s)

¤NONE¤

IN THE SENATE OF THE UNITED STATES

March 28, 2007

Mr. OBAMA (for himself, Mr. LEVIN, Mr. KERRY, Mr. ALEXANDER, and Mr. CORKER) submitted the following resolution; which was considered and agreed to

RESOLUTION

Celebrating the life of Bishop Gilbert Earl Patterson.

Whereas Bishop Gilbert Earl Patterson was born in 1939 to Bishop W.A. and Mrs. Mary Patterson, Sr., in Humboldt, Tennessee;

Whereas Bishop Patterson was reared in Memphis, Tennessee, and Detroit, Michigan, and ordained as an elder in the Church of God in Christ in 1958 by Bishop J.S. Bailey;

Whereas Bishop Patterson grew in wisdom at the Detroit Bible Institute and LeMoyne Owen College in Memphis, Tennessee;

Whereas, in 1962, Bishop Patterson became co-pastor with his father of Holy Temple Church of God in Christ in Memphis, Tennessee;

Whereas, in 1975, Bishop Patterson founded Temple of Deliverance, the Cathedral of the Bountiful Blessings;

Whereas Temple of Deliverance is now a shining star of both the Church of God in Christ and all of the Nation's communities of faith;

Whereas Temple of Deliverance, under Bishop Patterson's wise leadership, continues to touch the entire Nation through its Bountiful Blessings Ministry;

Whereas Bishop Patterson reached millions across the globe with his direct and spirit-filled messages, encouraging the world to 'be healed, be delivered, and be set free';

Whereas Bishop Patterson served as the international leader of the Church of God in Christ since November 2000, ably leading this denomination of over 6,000,000 members;

Whereas Bishop Patterson passed away on Tuesday, March 20, 2007, in Memphis, Tennessee, surrounded by his wife, Mrs. Louise Patterson, and his family;

Whereas Bishop Patterson will be celebrated as an invigorating spiritual leader; and

Whereas the family of Bishop Patterson, the Temple of Deliverance congregation, the Church of God in Christ, and indeed the entire Nation are deeply saddened by the loss of this great man: Now, therefore, be it

Resolved, That the Senate—

(1) expresses the condolences of the Nation to the family of Bishop Gilbert Earl Patterson, the Temple of Deliverance Congregation, and the Church of God in Christ; and

(2) recognizes the life and accomplishments of Bishop Gilbert Earl Patterson, who guided a church, led a denomination, and influenced a nation.

US SENATE RESOLUTION 268

TITLE: A resolution designating July 12, 2007, as "National Summer Learning Day".

SPONSOR: Sen Obama, Barack [IL] (introduced 7/11/2007) Cosponsors (4)

LATEST MAJOR ACTION: 7/13/2007 Passed/agreed to in Senate. Status: Resolution agreed to in Senate without amendment and with a preamble by Unanimous Consent.

SUMMARY AS OF:

7/13/2007—Passed Senate without amendment. (There is 1 other summary)

(This measure has not been amended since it was introduced. The summary of that version is repeated here.)

Designates July 12, 2007, as National Summer Learning Day.

Urges people to promote summer learning activities to send youth back to school ready to learn, support working parents and their children, and keep children safe and healthy during the summer months.

MAJOR ACTIONS:

7/11/2007

Introduced in Senate

7/13/2007

Senate Committee on the Judiciary discharged by Unanimous Consent.

7/13/2007

Passed/agreed to in Senate: Resolution agreed to in Senate without amendment and with a preamble by Unanimous Consent.

ALL ACTIONS:

7/11/2007:

Referred to the Committee on the Judiciary. (text of measure as introduced: CR S9026)

7/13/2007:

Senate Committee on the Judiciary discharged by Unanimous Consent. (consideration: CR S9224-9225)

7/13/2007:

Resolution agreed to in Senate without amendment and with a preamble by Unanimous Consent. (text as passed Senate: CR S9224-9225)

TITLES(s): (italics indicate a title for a portion of a bill)

* OFFICIAL TITLE AS INTRODUCED:

A resolution designating July 12, 2007, as "National Summer Learning Day".

COSPONSORS(4), ALPHABETICAL [FOLLOWED BY COSPONSORS WITH-DRAWN]: (Sort: by date)

Sen Bunning, Jim [KY] - 7/11/2007

Sen Isakson, Johnny [GA] - 7/11/2007

Sen Mikulski, Barbara A. [MD] - 7/11/2007

Sen Sanders, Bernard [VT] - 7/11/2007

COMMITTEE(S)

Committee/Subcommittee:

Activity:

Senate Judiciary

Referral, Discharged

RELATED BILL DETAILS:

¤NONE¤

AMENDMENT(S)

¤NONE¤

IN THE SENATE OF THE UNITED STATES

July 11, 2007

Mr. OBAMA (for himself, Mr. ISAKSON, Ms. MIKULSKI, Mr. BUNNING, and Mr. SANDERS) submitted the following resolution; which was referred to the Committee on the Judiciary

July 13, 2007

Committee discharged; considered and agreed to

RESOLUTION

Designating July 12, 2007, as 'National Summer Learning Day'.

Whereas all students experience a measurable loss of mathematics and reading skills when they do not engage in educational activities during the summer months;

Whereas summer learning loss is greatest for low-income children, who often lack the academic enrichment opportunities available to their more affluent peers;

Whereas recent research indicates that 2/3 of the achievement gap between low-income children and their more affluent peers can be explained by unequal access to summer learning opportunities, which results in low-income youth being less likely to graduate from high school or enter college;

Whereas recent surveys indicate that low-income parents have considerable difficulty finding available summer opportunities for their children;

Whereas structured enrichment and education programs are proven to accelerate learning for students who participate in such programs for several weeks during the summer;

Whereas students who participate in the Building Educated Leaders for Life ('BELL') summer programs gain several months' worth of reading and mathematics skills through summer enrichment, and students who regularly attend the Teach Baltimore Summer Academy for 2 summers are 1/2 year ahead of their peers in reading skills;

Whereas thousands of students in similar programs make measurable gains in academic achievement;

Whereas recent research demonstrates that most children, particularly children at high risk of obesity, gain weight more rapidly when they are out of school during the summer;

Whereas Summer Learning Day is designed to highlight the need for more young people to be engaged in summer learning activities and to support local summer programs that benefit children, families, and communities;

Whereas a wide array of schools, public agencies, nonprofit organizations, universities, museums, libraries, and summer camps in many States across the United States, will celebrate annual Summer Learning Day on July 12, 2007: Now, therefore, be it

Resolved, That the Senate—

(1) designates July 12, 2007, as 'National Summer Learning Day', in order to raise public awareness about the positive impact of summer learning opportunities on the development and educational success of the children of our Nation;

(2) urges the people of the United States to promote summer learning activities, in order to send young people back to school ready to learn, to support working parents and their children, and to keep the children of our Nation safe and healthy during the summer months; and

(3) urges communities to celebrate, with appropriate ceremonies and activities, the importance of high quality summer learning opportunities in the lives of young students and their families.

US SENATE RESOLUTION 383

TITLE: A resolution honoring and recognizing the achievements of Carl Stokes, the first African-American mayor of a major American city, in the 40th year since his election as Mayor of Cleveland, Ohio.

SPONSOR: Sen Obama, Barack [IL] (introduced 11/15/2007) Cosponsors (2)

RELATED BILLS: H.RES.827

LATEST MAJOR ACTION: 11/15/2007 Referred to Senate committee. Status: Referred to the Committee on the Judiciary.

SUMMARY AS OF:

11/15/2007—Introduced.

Recognizes the pioneering career of Carl Stokes, who helped expand political opportunity for minorities by becoming the first African-American mayor of a major American city.

Commemorates the 40th anniversary of the election of Carl Stokes as the Mayor of Cleveland and the first African-American mayor of a major American city, one of the most significant events in the American Civil Rights movement.

Major Actions:

¤NONE¤

All Actions:

11/15/2007:

Referred to the Committee on the Judiciary. (text of measure as introduced: CR S14499-14500)

Titles(s): (italics indicate a title for a portion of a bill)

¤NONE¤

Cosponsors(2), Alphabetical [followed by Cosponsors withdrawn]: (Sort: by date)

Sen Brown, Sherrod [OH] - 11/15/2007

Sen Voinovich, George V. [OH] - 11/15/2007

Committee(s)

Committee/Subcommittee:

Activity:

Senate Judiciary

Referral, In Committee

Related Bill Details: (additional related bills may be indentified in Status)

Bill:

Relationship:

H.RES.827

Identical bill identified by CRS

Amendment(s)

¤NONE¤

IN THE SENATE OF THE UNITED STATES

November 15, 2007

Mr. REID (for Mr. OBAMA (for himself, Mr. BROWN, and Mr. VOINOVICH)) submitted the following resolution; which was referred to the Committee on the Judiciary

RESOLUTION

Honoring and recognizing the achievements of Carl Stokes, the first African-American mayor of a major American city, in the 40th year since his election as Mayor of Cleveland, Ohio.

Whereas Carl Stokes was a pioneer in cultivating a positive climate for African-Americans to seek election to public office and made great strides toward improving race relations in a tumultuous period of United States history;

Whereas Carl Stokes was born on June 27, 1927, in Cleveland, Ohio, to Charles and Louise Stokes;

Whereas Carl Stokes rose from poverty in Outhwaite Homes, Cleveland's first federally funded housing project for the poor, to be elected to the highest political office in Cleveland;

Whereas Carl Stokes earned his bachelor's degree from the University of Minnesota in 1954 and graduated from the Cleveland-Marshall College of Law in 1956, and was admitted to the Ohio State Bar in 1957;

Whereas, in 1962, Carl Stokes was elected to the Ohio General Assembly and served 3 terms as the first African-American Democrat to serve from Cuyahoga County;

Whereas, in 1967, relying on his ability to mobilize support that transcended racial divides, Carl Stokes was elected Mayor of Cleveland and became the first African-American mayor of a major American city;

Whereas, after declining to run for a 3rd term as Mayor of Cleveland, Carl Stokes became the first African-American to appear daily as an anchorman on a New York City television outlet, WNBC-TV;

Whereas Carl Stokes served as a municipal judge in Cleveland from 1983 to 1994, completing a political career encompassing each branch of government; and

Whereas Carl Stokes maintained his dedication to public service throughout his life, serving as Ambassador to the Seychelles and representing the White House on numerous goodwill trips abroad until his death in 1996: Now, therefore, be it

Resolved, That the Senate—

(1) recognizes the pioneering career of Carl Stokes, who helped expand political opportunity for minorities by becoming the first African-American mayor of a major American city; and

(2) commemorates the 40th anniversary of the election of Carl Stokes as the Mayor of Cleveland and the first African-American mayor of a major American city, one of the most significant events in the American Civil Rights movement.

US SENATE JOINT RESOLUTION 23

TITLE: A joint resolution clarifying that the use of force against Iran is not authorized by the Authorization for the Use of Military Force Against Iraq, any resolution previously adopted, or any other provision of law.

SPONSOR: Sen Obama, Barack [IL] (introduced 11/1/2007) Cosponsors (None)

RELATED BILLS: H.J.RES.64

LATEST MAJOR ACTION: 11/1/2007 Referred to Senate committee. Status: Read twice and referred to the Committee on Foreign Relations.

SUMMARY AS OF:

11/1/2007—Introduced.

States that nothing in the Authorization for the Use of Military Force Against Iraq of 2002 (P.L. 107-243), any act that serves as the statutory authority for Executive Order 13382 or Executive Order 13224, any resolution previously adopted, or any other provision of law including Executive Order 13382 or Executive Order 13224 shall be construed to authorize, encourage, or in any way address the use of the U.S. Armed Forces against Iran.

MAJOR ACTIONS:

¤NONE¤

ALL ACTIONS:

11/1/2007:

Read twice and referred to the Committee on Foreign Relations.

TITLES(s): (italics indicate a title for a portion of a bill)

¤NONE¤

COSPONSOR(s):

¤NONE¤

COMMITTEE(s)

Committee/Subcommittee:

Activity:

Senate Foreign Relations

Referral, In Committee

RELATED BILL DETAILS: (additional related bills may be indentified in Status)

Bill:

Relationship:

H.J.RES.64

Identical bill identified by CRS

AMENDMENT(S)

¤NONE¤

IN THE SENATE OF THE UNITED STATES

November 1, 2007

Mr. REID (for Mr. OBAMA) introduced the following joint resolution; which was read twice and referred to the Committee on Foreign Relations

JOINT RESOLUTION

Clarifying that the use of force against Iran is not authorized by the Authorization for the Use of Military Force Against Iraq, any resolution previously adopted, or any other provision of law.

Whereas the Authorization for the Use of Military Force Against Iraq (Public Law 107-243) authorized the President 'to use the Armed Forces of the United States as he determines to be necessary and appropriate in order to—(1) defend the national security of the United States against the continuing threat posed by Iraq; and (2) enforce all relevant United Nations Security Council resolutions regarding Iraq';

Whereas, on September 26, 2007, the Senate agreed to a provision, Senate Amendment 3017 to Senate Amendment 2011 to H.R. 1585, stating the sense of the Senate that 'the manner in which the United States transitions and structures its military presence in Iraq will have critical long-term consequences for the future of the Persian Gulf and the Middle East, in particular with regard to the capability of the Government of the Islamic Republic of Iran to pose a threat to the security of the region';

Whereas, on September 26, 2007, the Senate also stated the sense of the Senate 'that it is a critical national interest of the United States to prevent the Government of the Islamic Republic of Iran from turning Shi'a militia extremists in Iraq into a Hezbollah-like force that could serve its interests inside Iraq';

Whereas, on October 25, 2007, the Department of State designated the Islamic Revolutionary Guard Corps (IRGC) and the Ministry of Defense and Armed Forces Logistics (MODAFL) as proliferators of weapons of mass destruction under Executive Order 13382 in relation to concerns about their role in proliferation activities;

Whereas, on October 25, 2007, the Department of the Treasury also designated 9 IRGC-affiliated entities and 5 IRGC-affiliated individuals, as derivatives of the IRGC, as well as Iran's state-owned Bank Melli and Bank Mellat and 3 individuals affiliated with Iran's Aerospace Industries Organization (AIO), as proliferators of weapons of mass destruction or supporters of terrorism under Executive Order 13382;

Whereas, on October 25, 2007, the Department of the Treasury also designated the IRGC-Qods Force (IRGC-QF) as a supporter of terrorism for providing material support to the Taliban and other terrorist organizations, and designated Iran's state-owned Bank Saderat as a terrorist financier, under Executive Order 13224; and

Whereas any offensive military action taken by the United States against Iran must be explicitly authorized by Congress: Now, therefore, be it

Resolved by the Senate and House of Representatives of the United States of America in Congress assembled, That nothing in the Authorization for the Use of Military Force Against Iraq (Public Law 107-243), any act that serves as the statutory authority for Executive Order 13382 or Executive Order 13224, any resolution previously adopted, or any other provision of law including the terms of Executive Order 13382 or Executive Order 13224 shall be construed to authorize, encourage, or in any way address the use of the Armed Forces of the United States against Iran.

US Senate Bill 114

Title: A bill to authorize resources for a grant program for local educational agencies to create innovation districts.

Sponsor: Sen Obama, Barack [IL] (introduced 1/4/2007) Cosponsors (None)

Latest Major Action: 1/4/2007 Referred to Senate committee. Status: Read twice and referred to the Committee on Health, Education, Labor, and Pensions.

Summary As Of:

1/4/2007--Introduced.

Innovation Districts for School Improvement Act - Directs the Secretary of Education to award competitive grants to 10 urban and 10 non-urban local educational agencies (LEAs) for the creation of innovation districts.

Requires the LEAs to: (1) establish tests and longitudinal data systems to track the academic progress of each elementary and secondary school student and use such performance measures in evaluating and awarding school personnel and programs; (2) work with teacher representatives and other community partners to attain the administrative flexibility to staff more equitably all agency schools with effective personnel; (3) evaluate and award effective teachers on the basis of student progress and observations of teacher performance; (4) provide grants to recent college graduates and mid-career professionals to attend LEA-established Teacher Academies which provide classroom mentoring and concurrent teacher education from partner institutions in exchange for three years of service in hard-to-staff schools; (5) establish career ladders allowing teachers to progress from novice to master with a concomitant increase in compensation and responsibility for the development of fellow teachers; and (6) plan for the recruitment, training, and evaluation of school principals who are to serve as instructional leaders in the schools and hold significant responsiblity for teacher hiring and placement.

Allows the LEAs to support new schools or networks of public schools, serving predominantly disadvantaged students, which are sponsored by universities, education management organizations, or nonprofit organizations.

MAJOR ACTIONS:

¤NONE¤

ALL ACTIONS:

1/4/2007:

Read twice and referred to the Committee on Health, Education, Labor, and Pensions.

TITLE(S): (italics indicate a title for a portion of a bill)

¤NONE¤

COSPONSOR(S):

¤NONE¤

COMMITTEE(S):

Committee/Subcommittee:Activity:Senate Health, Education, Labor, and Pensions Referral, In Committee

RELATED BILL DETAILS:

¤NONE¤

AMENDMENT(S):

¤NONE¤

IN THE SENATE OF THE UNITED STATES

January 4, 2007

Mr. OBAMA introduced the following bill; which was read twice and referred to the Committee on Health, Education, Labor, and Pensions

A BILL

To authorize resources for a grant program for local educational agencies to create innovation districts.

Be it enacted by the Senate and House of Representatives of the United States of America in Congress assembled,

SECTION 1. SHORT TITLE.

This Act may be cited as the 'Innovation Districts for School Improvement Act'.

SEC. 2. FINDINGS.

Congress finds the following:

(1) Too many students emerge from secondary school unprepared for success in college or in the workforce. It is children of color and children of poverty who suffer most from a failure to provide them effective teachers and adequate resources.

(2) In urban elementary schools, African-American and Latino students are several times less likely than their white peers to be reading at even a basic level, and children living in poverty are several times less likely than their peers who are not poor to be proficient in reading or mathematics.

(3) These deficits continue on into higher levels of education, so that 6,000,000 middle school and secondary school students are reading with skills significantly below their grade level. Half of all teenagers are unable to understand basic mathematics.

(4) In New York City, only 35 percent of African-American students and 32 percent of Latino students graduate from secondary school. In Chicago, of every 100 African-American males, on average, only 38 graduate from secondary school by age 19, and less than 3 continue their education to earn a diploma from a 4-year college.

(5) The dropout problem is not limited to cities. Poor rural communities are also harmed by inadequate resources and low teacher quality. As a result, in some States, only 60 percent of white students graduate from secondary school; in others, there is a difference of 40 percentage points in the graduation rates of whites and students of color.

(6) Too many teachers and school leaders are not prepared adequately for their jobs, and too few States and local educational agencies have effective teacher induction or mentoring programs. Less-qualified teachers are concentrated in schools attended by African-American and Latino students, and in high-poverty areas, whether urban or rural.

(7) The effectiveness of teachers has a direct relationship to student academic achievement. Students who performed equally well in mathematics in second grade showed a significant performance gap 3 years later, depending on whether they had been assigned to the most effective or least effective teachers.

(8) Despite the numerous indicators that public schools are not adequately educating students, there are many pockets of innovation and success, where effective teachers work in schools where they support their students, with additional support from community organizations, foundations, and nonprofits. In high-poverty schools using the reforms of the Teacher Advancement Program, the most recent data shows that more that 70 percent of these schools increased the percentage of students achieving at proficient levels or above on standardized tests. In rural schools using the Teacher Advancement Program reforms, nearly two-thirds of schools increased the percentage of students at or above the proficient level.

(9) Lessons from the Teacher Advancement Program and other successes will form the basis for the expansion of successful efforts, used to positively transform education in school districts, and, in so doing, generate additional information on a group of effective practices that can be widely disseminated and applied.

SEC. 3. DEFINITIONS.

In this Act, the terms 'Department', 'elementary school', 'institution of higher education', 'local educational agency', 'secondary school', and 'Secretary' have the meanings given such terms in section 9101 of the Elementary and Secondary Education Act of 1965 (20 U.S.C. 7801).

SEC. 4. GRANT PROGRAM.

(a) Authorization-

(1) IN GENERAL- The Secretary shall establish a program to award grants, on a competitive basis, to 10 local educational agencies in urban areas and 10 local educational agencies in non-urban areas (which shall include a mix of rural and suburban areas), to enable such agencies to create innovation districts to implement systemic reforms in areas of teaching, assessment, school leadership, and administration, including the following:

(A) Implementation of data systems to evaluate student progress, identify and share best practices, and conduct rigorous, data-driven evaluations to determine the effect of reforms on student academic achievement.

(B) Recruitment and retention of highly-effective teachers, and allocation of such teachers into the classrooms of the students who need them most, using incentives, including differential pay to reward high-performing teachers, teachers who choose to work in the most challenging schools within a local educational agency, and teachers with expertise in needed subject areas, such as mathematics, science, and special education, and systems and schedules to support teacher collaboration and mentoring, and career ladders for teachers to work as mentor or master teachers.

(C) Support of teacher academies to recruit talented candidates, develop effective placement systems, and ensure that trainees receive both effective pre-service training and effective mentoring during induction as they enter the classroom.

(D) Placement of an outstanding principal in every school, including rigorous recruitment, selection, pre-service and in-service training, and placement of school leaders, and efforts to hold principals accountable for student academic achievement while providing the principals with the authority and autonomy needed especially regarding hiring and assigning teachers and staff.

(E) Support for new schools, including charter schools or contract schools, or for networks of public schools within the local educational agency, serving predominantly low-income populations, which are sponsored by universities, education management organizations, or other nonprofit entities. Such new schools shall--

(i) serve as demonstration sites for high-quality kindergarten through grade 12 schooling;

(ii) be the locus for training and support of aspiring, new and veteran teachers and school leaders; and

(iii) be designed to share best practices with other schools served by the local educational agency, and other local educational agencies, State and nationwide.

(2) FEWER GRANTS- If the amount appropriated for a fiscal year under subsection (h) is less than the amount authorized to be appropriated for such fiscal year, the Secretary may award fewer than 20 grants under this Act.

(b) Application-

(1) IN GENERAL- A local educational agency that desires to receive a grant under this Act shall submit an application to the Secretary at such time, in such manner, and accompanied by such information as the Secretary shall require.

(2) CONTENTS- An application submitted under paragraph (1) shall include how the local educational agency will carry out the activities described in subparagraphs (A) through (E) of subsection (a)(1) and a description of activities the local educational agency will undertake to--

(A) recruit and induct new professional employees into the schools served by the local educational agency, including establishment of residency-based teacher or leadership academies;

(B) provide mentoring and support for teachers who are not meeting standards for teacher effectiveness described in this Act;

(C) use the financial and human resources of the agency to meet the needs of students in a performance-based model focused on student learning;

(D) develop and use data systems and accountability to establish instructional plans to benefit students in schools served by the agency, with regular evaluation of agency-supported programs; and

(E) address how the agency will use funds available under title II of the Elementary and Secondary Education Act of 1965 (20 U.S.C. 6601 et seq.) to support the goals of this Act, including having effective teachers equitably placed in every classroom in every school served by the agency, and effective principals in every school served by the agency.

(c) Mandatory Uses of Funds- A local educational agency that receives a grant under this Act shall use the grant funds to carry out each of the following:

(1) ACCOUNTABILITY- The local educational shall improve accountability as follows:

(A) Work to establish longitudinal data systems that can monitor student progress as the students move from grade to grade, to determine the value-added and effectiveness of specific teachers, schools, and programs within the local educational agency. The data system may be designed and established in cooperation with institutions of higher education, regional educational laboratories (established pursuant to section 174 of the Education Sciences Reform Act of 2002 (20 U.S.C. 9564)), offices in the Department, or other entities with expertise in data acquisition and interpretation. Such a data system shall have the following attributes:

(i) A unique student identifier to track the progress of each individual student served by the local educational agency.

(ii) The ability to track the progress and assessment results of each individual student from year to year.

(iii) Enrollment, demographic, and program participation information for each student.

(iv) A teacher identifier system to match each student to each teacher within the system.

(v) Student-level graduation and dropout data.

(vi) Inclusion of data on risk factors for individual students, including such indicators as non-promotion mobility, interaction with the criminal justice system involving the school, eligibility for a free or reduced price lunch under the Richard B. Russell National School Lunch Act (42 U.S.C. 1751 et seq.), and such other factors as may be useful in targeting appropriate services, interventions, and supports for at-risk students.

(B) Devise or employ assessment tests to monitor the progress of all students in grade 1 through grade 12 in all the elementary schools and secondary schools served by the local educational agency.

(C) Rate the effectiveness of individual teachers, administrators, and schools within the local educational agency, using when feasible, as 1 measure, a value-added system, a statistical method to measure the influence of a teacher or school on the rate of academic progress of students. The local educational agency shall evaluate 1 year's worth of academic growth for each student using as the reference standard the national norm gain for each grade level, or the statewide or district-wide value-added gain.

(D) Assess the effectiveness of individual teachers, administrators, and schools, using when feasible, as 1 measure, the value-added system described in subparagraph (C), including a measure of progress toward the goal of every student becoming proficient in reading, writing, and mathematics, and a measure of the progress of students through coursework needed to gain the knowledge and skills necessary for eventual entrance into a postsecondary degree or certification program.

(E) Award incentives for effective teaching or school leadership that may be linked to the results of the assessments under subparagraph (D), including a measure of progress toward the goal of every student becoming proficient in reading, writing, and mathematics, and a measure of the progress of students through coursework needed to gain the knowledge and skills necessary for eventual entrance into a postsecondary degree or certification program.

(2) REMOVING OBSTACLES TO INNOVATION- The local educational agency shall work with local teacher representatives or unions and other community partners to achieve the following:

(A) Equitable distribution of effective teachers to all students within the agency to ensure that poor and minority students are not disproportionately taught by teachers who are--

(i) poorly trained in the subject being taught;

(ii) less likely to have significant teaching experience; and

(iii) less likely to excel in other measures of teacher effectiveness.

(B) Equitable distribution of expenditures to rectify policies and practices that guide teacher pay and have an adverse impact on disadvantaged students and schools. This may include the consideration of teacher salaries and policies of salary averaging in meeting agency-wide goals based on high expectations for student academic achievement.

(C) Modification of staffing procedures and collective bargaining rules to provide greater flexibility for agency and school leaders to establish effective school-level staffing, to fairly balance the distribution of experienced teachers, and to recruit, place, and retain new teachers within schools served by the agency, including the completion of staffing decisions in a timely fashion to provide effective planning for student academic achievement.

(3) TEACHERS- The local educational agency shall evaluate and reward teacher effectiveness as follows:

(A) TEACHER EFFECTIVENESS- The local educational agency shall evaluate teacher effectiveness by working with unions and other community stakeholders to establish a metric to determine the effectiveness of teachers, administrators, and schools served by the local educational agency. The metric may be used as the basis for systems of pay, incentives, and placement within the local educational agency. Such a metric may include the following items:

(i) STUDENT GROWTH- Teachers may be rated for meeting annual objectives that are monitored by evaluating student improvement in value-added assessments. These evaluations may include value-added data averaged for a period of several years.

(ii) MEASURING TEAMS OF TEACHERS- Measures may be used to track the progress and reward teams of teachers (such as a particular grade level or subject area) to encourage teamwork and sharing of best practices, and draw on similar effective approaches to financial rewards in the private sector.

(iii) PROFESSIONAL EVALUATION-

(I) IN GENERAL- Professional evaluation shall be based on formal and informal observations of teacher effectiveness. The ratings shall be prepared by the supervisor of each teacher, based on observations of such domains of teaching as the following:

(aa) Planning and preparation, including demonstrating knowledge of content, pedagogy, and assessment, including the use of formative assessment to improve student learning.

(bb) Classroom and school environment, which establishes a culture for learning, using when appropriate, schoolwide positive behavioral intervention and support.

(cc) Instruction, which clearly and accurately engages students in learning.

(dd) Professional responsibilities, including appropriate interaction with families of students, and with professional colleagues, which requires a demonstrated ability to work with mentors and instructional leaders to improve the teacher's teaching and resultant student learning.

(ee) Fair analysis of gains in student academic achievement over time.

(II) IMPROVEMENT PLAN- A teacher who receives an unsatisfactory professional evaluation under subclause (I) shall comply with an improvement plan, developed by the teacher and the school in which the teacher teaches or the local educational agency and provided by such school or agency.

(B) TEACHING INCENTIVES- Based on measures of teacher effectiveness and the needs of the school and the local educational agency, the local educational agency shall work with teacher and community representatives to develop a differentiated pay scale to provide incentives for effective teaching, teaching specific subject areas, and teaching in specific schools, including hard-to-staff schools or schools with high proportions of students who have been achieving at levels below the local educational agency or State average.

(4) TEACHER ACADEMIES-

(A) IN GENERAL- The local educational agency shall establish a Teacher Academy, based upon models of successful residency-based teacher training and induction programs, as a mechanism to train teachers for success in such local educational agency. Each Teacher Academy shall be headed by a director who shall award grants to eligible individuals to attend such Teacher Academy.

(B) ELIGIBLE INDIVIDUALS- An individual may be eligible for a grant to attend a Teacher Academy if the individual is a recent college graduate or mid-career professional from outside the field of education, possessing strong content knowledge or a record of achievement, or other such individual at the discretion of the Secretary.

(C) APPLICATION- An individual who is eligible under subparagraph (B) and who desires a grant under this paragraph shall submit an application to the Teacher Academy.

(D) SELECTION CRITERIA- The director of the Teacher Academy shall establish criteria for selection of individuals to receive grants under this paragraph, based on such domains of teaching as the following characteristics shared by highly-effective teachers:

(i) Comprehensive subject knowledge or record of accomplishment in an area outside of education.

(ii) Strong verbal and written communication skills.

(iii) Other attributes linked to effective teaching.

(E) RECEIPT OF GRANT- An individual who receives a grant under this paragraph shall enroll in the program of the Teacher Academy, which shall include the following:

(i) A 1-year residency-based program of teaching in a school served by the local educational agency, under the supervision of a mentor teacher who will instruct the resident in planning and preparation, instruction of students, management of the classroom environment, and other professional responsibilities. Alternatively, the first year of full-time teaching may be substituted for such residency-based program if all of the other requirements of this section are satisfied and if the full-time teaching is supported by a school, university, or nonprofit organization with a strong track record of helping new teachers get strong academic achievement results for students.

(ii) A living stipend or salary for the period of residency.

(iii) Concurrent instruction from a partner college, State-approved organization, or school of education at an institution of higher education in pedagogy classes necessary for certification as a teacher.

(iv) Ongoing mentoring and coaching during the first 2 years of induction into classroom teaching.

(F) PLACEMENT IN HARD-TO-STAFF SCHOOL-

(i) IN GENERAL- An eligible individual who receives a grant under this paragraph shall teach in a hard-to-staff school served by the local educational agency for a period of 3 years.

(ii) REPAYMENT- If an eligible individual does not complete the teaching requirement described in clause (i), such individual shall repay to the local educational agency a pro rata portion of the grant amount for the amount of teaching time the individual did not complete.

(5) TEACHER CAREERS-

(A) IN GENERAL- The local educational agency shall establish a career ladder for teachers in schools served by the local educational agency.

(B) PROGRESSION-

(i) IN GENERAL- In order to progress to higher rungs on the career ladder, a teacher or school leader shall prove effective at the teacher or school leader's current level under a set of criteria established by the local educational agency.

(ii) INCREASE IN ROLE AND COMPENSATION- In progressing to higher rungs on the career ladder, a teacher or school leader shall--

(I) accept an increasing role in assessing and helping to improve the teaching effectiveness of other teachers in the school; and

(II) be offered increased compensation.

(iii) COLLECTIVE BARGAINING AGREEMENT- The base salary and career ladder increments of increased compensation may be established in a collective bargaining agreement between the local educational agency and representatives of teachers.

(iv) STEPS- A career ladder may include the following steps:

(I) NOVICE TEACHERS- Novice teachers are teachers in their first years in the profession. This shall be the career entry stage and include professional employees with initial teaching certificates. Novice teachers shall receive induction and mentoring as described in subclause (III) until the novice teachers progress to become career teachers. Such induction and mentoring shall focus on improving the instructional and professional skills of the novice teachers. Novice teachers shall receive periodic performance reviews as a result of regular observations, using the criteria of teacher effectiveness set forth in paragraph (3)(A).

(II) CAREER TEACHERS- Career teachers are teachers who have served several years as novice teachers and have received an advanced teaching certification or master's degree, as determined by State certification requirements. Novice teachers may progress to this stage of the career ladder after receiving satisfactory reviews of teacher effectiveness as outlined in paragraph (3)(A) and receiving an advanced teaching certification or master's degree.

(III) MENTOR TEACHERS- Mentor teachers are teachers selected by local school administrators under clear criteria established at the local educational agency level, including superior assessment of their teaching effectiveness as described in paragraph (3)(A). Mentor teachers shall have extra responsibilities as teacher leaders and teacher coaches, including roles in induction and mentoring of novice teachers.

(IV) MASTER TEACHERS- Master teachers are mentor teachers who have received superior reviews of their mentoring and supervisory role and assume additional responsibilities and teacher mentoring and leadership roles.

(C) LEARNING COMMUNITY- The role of mentor and master teachers shall include establishing, within each school, a learning community in which all individuals are expected to continually improve their capacity to advance student learning, using a shared set of instructional principles or teaching strategies. The learning community shall require, in each school, continuing professional development, based on student academic achievement and behavioral outcomes, embedding in each school system for on-site coaching, mentoring, and study groups in which teachers work together to improve the instructional program for students.

(6) SCHOOL LEADERSHIP- The local educational agency shall include a specific plan to improve the school leadership in schools served by the agency, with the eventual goal of an effective principal in every school. The plan should include provisions to address the following topics:

(A) RESPONSIBILITY AND ROLE OF PRINCIPALS- A plan to support the primary role of the principal as the instructional leader in the school responsible for ensuring teaching effectiveness and student academic achievement schoolwide. Such plan shall include involving principals in planning systems and strategies for curricular, classroom, and schoolwide student behavioral interventions and supports, and for establishing mechanisms for using student academic achievement data to drive instructional decisions. The plan shall also address ways to give principals significant responsibility for decisions regarding teacher hiring and placement decisions.

(B) CREATING THE PIPELINE OF FUTURE PRINCIPALS- A plan for strategies and criteria for rigorous recruitment, selection, and pre-service training and induction for new principals who can effectively take on the responsibilities described in subparagraph (A). As with training teachers, the agency may establish a program for principal training, including a residency or internship with an exemplary principal in the agency. The program shall have explicit expectations and performance-based indicators of outcomes to ensure that each resident is competent in assuming instructional leadership responsibilities. In the case of an agency in which several principals are training as a cohort, the agency shall promote the use of cohort participant groups to discuss best practices and maintain focus on outcome assessments.

(C) SYSTEMATICALLY TRANSFORMING THE PRINCIPALSHIP DISTRICTWIDE- An assessment of how the agency currently handles each major policy and practice affecting the expectations set for the principalship and a plan for how the agency will align the principalship to the goals of this Act, including recruitment, selection, training, evaluation, compensation, management, and job design of the principalship and other school leadership roles.

(D) EVALUATION- A plan for an external evaluation to examine the impact of principals on driving measurable gains in student academic achievement.

(d) Flexibility for Small Rural Districts- The Secretary may give a local educational agency that is a small, rural local educational agency (as determined by the Secretary) that receives a grant under this Act flexibility in carrying out the activities required under subsection (c), including a waiver of the requirement to establish a Teacher Academy under subsection (c)(4).

(e) Permissible Use of Funds- The local educational agency may include a plan to support new schools, including charter schools or contract schools, or for networks of public schools within the local educational agency, serving predominantly low-income populations, which are sponsored by universities, education management organizations, or other nonprofit entities, using--

(1) funds appropriated to carry out this Act, in coordination with the charter school programs under subpart 1 of part B of title V of the Elementary and Secondary Education Act of 1965 (20 U.S.C. 7221 et seq.); or

(2) funds from State, local, or private sources.

(f) Reports- A local educational agency that receives a grant under this Act shall submit to the Secretary a report on the progress of such agency toward completion of the goals of the agency. Such report shall be available for public view on the website of the Department. Based on such reports, the Secretary may terminate grant funding to an agency for unsatisfactory performance.

(g) Peer Review Panel-

(1) IN GENERAL- There shall be established in accordance with paragraph (2), a peer review panel to--

(A) review applications submitted under subsection (b);

(B) submit to the Secretary evaluations of the applications reviewed under subparagraph (A); and

(C) evaluate reports described in subsection (f).

(2) SELECTION OF MEMBERS-

(A) IN GENERAL- Subject to subparagraph (B), members of the peer review panel shall be selected by the Secretary, in collaboration with the Majority Leader of the Senate, the Minority Leader of the Senate, the Majority Leader of the House of Representatives, and the Minority Leader of the House of Representatives and shall include representatives from foundations, universities, and other entities with a record of involvement in local educational agency reform efforts.

(B) NATIONAL GOVERNORS ASSOCIATION- Two members of the peer review panel shall be selected by the National Governors Association.

(h) Authorization of Appropriations-

(1) IN GENERAL- There are authorized to be appropriated to carry out this Act $1,500,000,000 for each of fiscal years 2008 through 2012.

(2) REDIRECT FUNDS- The Secretary shall redirect amounts appropriated to carry out programs under title II of the Elementary and Secondary Education Act of 1965 (20 U.S.C. 6601 et seq.) that the Secretary determines are ineffective, to carry out this Act.

US SENATE BILL 115

TITLE: A bill to suspend royalty relief, to repeal certain provisions of the Energy Policy Act of 2005, and to amend the Internal Revenue Code of 1986 to repeal certain tax incentives for the oil and gas industry.

SPONSOR: Sen Obama, Barack [IL] (introduced 1/4/2007) Cosponsors (None)

LATEST MAJOR ACTION: 1/4/2007 Referred to Senate committee. Status: Read twice and referred to the Committee on Finance.

SUMMARY AS OF:

1/4/2007—Introduced.

Oil Subsidy Elimination for New Strategies on Energy Act or the Oil SENSE Act - Repeals provisions of the Energy Policy Act of 2005 relating to: (1) incentives for production from marginal oil wells; (2) incentives for natural gas production in the Gulf of Mexico; (3) royalty relief for deep water production; (4) Alaska offshore royalty suspension; (5) the inventory of Outer Continental Shelf oil and natural gas resources; (6) management of federal oil and gas leasing programs; and (7) ultra-deepwater and unconventional natural gas and other petroleum resources.

Requires the Secretary of the Interior to: (1) suspend royalty relief for producers of oil or natural gas on federal lands during periods in which oil and natural gas production is at certain levels; and (2) renegotiate certain existing leases for oil and natural gas production on federal land.

Repeals provisions of the Internal Revenue Code relating to: (1) the election to expense certain costs associated with liquid fuel refineries; (2) accelerated depreciation of natural gas distribution lines and natural gas gathering lines; and (3) accelerated amortization of geological and geophysical expenditures. Reduces the daily barrel production requirement (from 75,000 to 50,000) applicable to small refiners eligible for the exemption from limitations on the oil and gas depletion allowance.

MAJOR ACTIONS:

¤NONE¤

ALL ACTIONS:

1/4/2007:

Read twice and referred to the Committee on Finance.

TITLES(s): (italics indicate a title for a portion of a bill)

¤NONE¤

Cosponsor(s):

¤NONE¤

Committee(s)

Committee/Subcommittee:

Activity:

Senate Finance

Referral, In Committee

Related Bill Details:

¤NONE¤

Amendment(s)

¤NONE¤

In the Senate of the United States

January 4, 2007

Mr. OBAMA introduced the following bill; which was read twice and referred to the Committee on Finance

A BILL

To suspend royalty relief, to repeal certain provisions of the Energy Policy Act of 2005, and to amend the Internal Revenue Code of 1986 to repeal certain tax incentives for the oil and gas industry.

Be it enacted by the Senate and House of Representatives of the United States of America in Congress assembled,

SECTION 1. SHORT TITLE; TABLE OF CONTENTS.

(a) Short Title- This Act may be cited as the 'Oil Subsidy Elimination for New Strategies on Energy Act' or the 'Oil SENSE Act'.

(b) Table of Contents- The table of contents for this Act is as follows:

TITLE III—REPEAL OF CERTAIN ENERGY TAX INCENTIVES

Sec. 301. Repeal of tax subsidies enacted by the Energy Policy Act of 2005 for oil and gas.

SEC. 2. FINDINGS.

Congress finds that—

(1) record highs in oil and natural gas prices have resulted in record profits for oil and natural gas producers and refiners;

(2) oil prices are projected to remain high for the foreseeable future;

(3) the Department of the Interior estimates that as much as $66,000,000,000 worth of oil and natural gas taken from the deep waters of the Gulf of Mexico over the next 5 years will be exempt from Government royalty payments, which could amount to the Government losing an estimated $7,000,000,000 to $9,500,000,000 based on anticipated production and current price projections for oil and gas, according to an analysis in the 5-year budget plan of the Department of the Interior;

(4) the chief executive officers of the top 5 oil companies stated at a November 9, 2005, joint hearing of the Committee on Energy and Natural Resource of the Senate and the Committee on Environment and Public Works of the Senate that their companies did not need the Federal tax incentives provided in the Energy Policy Act of 2005 (42 U.S.C. 15801 et seq.);

(5) the Statement of Administration Policy of June 14, 2005, on the energy bill that would become the Energy Policy Act of 2005 states, 'The President believes that additional taxpayer subsidies for oil-and-gas exploration are unwarranted in today's price environment, and urges the Senate to eliminate the Federal oil-and-gas subsidies and other exploration incentives contained in the bill.'; and

(6) incentives for the energy industry should be focused on the development of renewable energy resources in the United States that will also promote, jobs, investment, innovation, and economic development in rural, agriculture-dependent areas.

TITLE I—TERMINATION OF CERTAIN PROVISIONS OF THE ENERGY POLICY ACT OF 2005

SEC. 101. TERMINATION OF CERTAIN PROVISIONS OF THE ENERGY POLICY ACT OF 2005.

(a) In General- The following provisions of the Energy Policy Act of 2005 are repealed as of the date of enactment of this Act:

(1) Section 343 (42 U.S.C. 15903) (relating to marginal property production incentives).

(2) Section 344 (42 U.S.C. 15904) (relating to incentives for natural gas production from deep wells in the shallow waters of the Gulf of Mexico).

(3) Section 345 (42 U.S.C. 15905) (relating to royalty relief for deep water production).

(4) Section 346 (Public Law 109-58; 119 Stat. 794) (relating to Alaska offshore royalty suspension).

(5) Section 357 (42 U.S.C. 15912) (relating to comprehensive inventory of OCS oil and natural gas resources).

(6) Section 362 (42 U.S.C. 15921) (relating to management of Federal oil and gas leasing programs).

(7) Subtitle J of title IX (42 U.S.C. 16371 et seq.) (relating to ultra-deepwater and unconventional natural gas and other petroleum resources).

(b) Termination of Alaska Offshore Royalty Suspension-

(1) IN GENERAL- Section 8(a)(3)(B) of the Outer Continental Shelf Lands Act (43 U.S.C. 1337(a)(3)(B)) is amended by striking 'and in the Planning Areas offshore Alaska'.

(2) EFFECTIVE DATE- The amendment made by this subsection shall take effect as of the date of enactment of this Act.

TITLE II—SUSPENSION OF ROYALTY RELIEF

SEC. 201. SUSPENSION OF ROYALTY RELIEF.

(a) In General- Subject to subsection (c), the Secretary of the Interior (referred to in this title as the 'Secretary') shall suspend the application of any provision of Federal law under which a person would otherwise be provided relief from a requirement to pay a royalty for the production of oil or natural gas from Federal land (including submerged land) occurring after the date of enactment of this Act during any period in which—

(1) for the production of oil, the average price of crude oil in the United States during the 4-week period immediately preceding the suspension is greater than $34.71 per barrel; and

(2) for the production of natural gas, the average wellhead price of natural gas in the United States during the 4-week period immediately preceding the suspension is greater than $4.34 per 1,000 cubic feet.

(b) Determination of Average Prices- For purposes of subsection (a), the Secretary shall determine average prices, taking into consideration the most recent data reported by the Energy Information Administration.

(c) Required Adjustment- For fiscal year 2008 and each subsequent fiscal year, each dollar amount specified in subsection (a) shall be adjusted to reflect changes for the 1-year period ending the preceding November 30 in the Consumer Price Index for All Urban Consumers published by the Bureau of Labor Statistics of the Department of Labor.

SEC. 202. RENEGOTIATION OF EXISTING LEASES.

(a) Requirement- The Secretary shall renegotiate each lease authorizing production of oil or natural gas on Federal land (including submerged land) issued by the Secretary before the date of enactment of this Act as the Secretary determines to be necessary to modify the terms of the lease to ensure that a suspension of a requirement to pay royalties under the lease does not apply to production described in section 201(a).

(b) Failure to Renegotiate and Modify- Beginning on the date that is 1 year after the date of enactment of this Act, a lessee under a lease described in subsection (a) shall not be eligible—

(1) to enter into a new lease described in that subsection; or

(2) to obtain by sale or other transfer any lease issued before that date, unless the lessee—

(A) renegotiates the lease; and

(B) enters into an agreement with the Secretary to modify the terms of the lease in accordance with subsection (a).

TITLE III—REPEAL OF CERTAIN ENERGY TAX INCENTIVES

SEC. 301. REPEAL OF CERTAIN PROVISIONS OF THE ENERGY POLICY ACT OF 2005 PROVIDING TAX SUBSIDIES FOR THE OIL AND GAS INDUSTRY.

(a) Repeal of Election to Expense Certain Refineries-

(1) IN GENERAL- Subparagraph (B) of section 179C(c)(1) of the Internal Revenue Code of 1986 (relating to qualified refinery property) is amended by striking 'January 1, 2012' and inserting 'the date of the enactment of the Oil Subsidy Elimination for New Strategies on Energy Act'.

(2) EFFECTIVE DATE- The amendment made by paragraph (1) shall apply to property placed in service after the date of the enactment of this Act.

(b) Repeal of Treatment of Natural Gas Distribution Lines as 15-Year Property-

(1) IN GENERAL- Clause (viii) of section 168(e)(3)(E) of such Code (relating to 15-year property) is amended by striking 'January 1, 2011' and inserting 'the Oil Subsidy Elimination for New Strategies on Energy Act'.

(2) EFFECTIVE DATE- The amendment made by paragraph (1) shall apply to property placed in service after the date of the enactment of this Act.

(c) Repeal of Treatment of Natural Gas Gathering Lines as 7-Year Property-

(1) IN GENERAL- Clause (iv) of section 168(e)(3)(C) of such Code (relating to 7-year property) is amended by inserting 'and which is placed in service before the date of the enactment of the Oil Subsidy Elimination for New Strategies on Energy Act' after 'April 11, 2005,'.

(2) EFFECTIVE DATE- The amendment made by paragraph (1) shall apply to property placed in service after the date of the enactment of this Act.

(d) Repeal of New Rule for Determining Small Refiner Exception to Oil Depletion Deduction-

(1) IN GENERAL- Paragraph (4) of section 613A(d) of such Code (relating to certain refiners excluded) is amended to read as follows:

'(4) CERTAIN REFINERS EXCLUDED- If the taxpayer or a related person engages in the refining of crude oil, subsection (c) shall not apply to such taxpayer if on any day during the taxable year the refinery runs of the taxpayer and such person exceed 50,000 barrels.'.

(2) EFFECTIVE DATE- The amendment made by paragraph (1) shall apply to taxable years beginning after the date of the enactment of this Act.

(e) Repeal of Amortization of Geological and Geophysical Expenditures-

(1) IN GENERAL- Section 167 of such Code (relating to depreciation) is amended by striking subsection (h) and redesignating subsection (i) as subsection (h).

(2) CONFORMING AMENDMENT- Section 263A(c)(3) of such Code is amended by striking '167(h),'.

(3) EFFECTIVE DATE- The amendments made by this subsection shall apply to amounts paid or incurred after the date of the enactment of this Act.

US SENATE BILL 116

TITLE: A bill to authorize resources to provide students with opportunities for summer learning through summer learning grants.

SPONSOR: Sen Obama, Barack [IL] (introduced 1/4/2007) Cosponsors (3)

LATEST MAJOR ACTION: 1/4/2007 Referred to Senate committee. Status: Read twice and referred to the Committee on Health, Education, Labor, and Pensions.

SUMMARY AS OF:

1/4/2007—Introduced.

Summer Term Education Programs for Upward Performance Act of 2007, or the STEP UP Act of 2007 - Directs the Secretary of Education to make competitive demonstration grants to state educational agencies to pay the federal share of summer learning grants for eligible students to be summer scholars in summer learning opportunity programs primarily designed to increase the literacy and numeracy of such students.

MAJOR ACTIONS:

¤NONE¤

ALL ACTIONS:

1/4/2007:

Read twice and referred to the Committee on Health, Education, Labor, and Pensions.

4/26/2007:

Sponsor introductory remarks on measure. (CR S5177)

TITLES(s): (italics indicate a title for a portion of a bill)

¤NONE¤

Cosponsors(3), Alphabetical [followed by Cosponsors with-drawn]: (Sort: by date)

Sen Mikulski, Barbara A. [MD] - 1/4/2007

Sen Murray, Patty [WA] - 7/17/2007

Sen Sanders, Bernard [VT] - 6/13/2007

Committee(s)

Committee/Subcommittee:

Activity:

Senate Health, Education, Labor, and Pensions

Referral, In Committee

Related Bill Details:

¤NONE¤

Amendment(s)

¤NONE¤

In the Senate of the United States

January 4, 2007

Mr. OBAMA (for himself and Ms. MIKULSKI) introduced the following bill; which was read twice and referred to the Committee on Health, Education, Labor, and Pensions

A BILL

To authorize resources to provide students with opportunities for summer learning through summer learning grants.

Be it enacted by the Senate and House of Representatives of the United States of America in Congress assembled,

SECTION 1. SHORT TITLE.

This Act may be cited as the 'Summer Term Education Programs for Upward Performance Act of 2007' or the 'STEP UP Act of 2007'.

SEC. 2. FINDINGS.

Congress finds the following:

(1) All students experience learning losses when they do not engage in educational activities during the summer.

(2) Students on average lose more than 1 month's worth of academic skills, and 2 months or more in mathematics facts and skills, during the summer.

(3) The impact of summer learning loss is greatest for children living in poverty, for children with learning disabilities, and for children who do not speak English at home.

(4) While middle-class children's test scores plateau or even rise during the summer months, scores plummet for children living in poverty. Disparities grow, so that reading scores of disadvantaged students can fall more than 2 months behind the scores of their middle-class peers each summer during the elementary school years.

(5) Summer learning losses by children living in poverty accumulate over the elementary school years, so that their achievement scores fall further and further behind the scores of their more advantaged peers as the children progress through school.

(6) Analysis by Professor Karl Alexander and his colleagues demonstrates that summer learning differences during the elementary school years substantially account for achievement-related differences later in students' lives, including rates of secondary school completion.

(7) This summer slide is costly for American education. Analysis by Professor Harris Cooper and his colleagues demonstrates that over 2 months of instruction is lost each school year due to re-teaching material from the previous year.

(8) Analysis of summer learning programs using independent randomized controlled trials has demonstrated their impact and effectiveness. Students participating in the BELL summer programs in Boston, New York, and Washington, DC, improved their reading skills by approximately 1 month, took part in more academic activities, read more books, and were encouraged to read more by their parents. A randomized, 3-year longitudinal study of the Teach Baltimore Summer Academy, designed by the Center for Summer Learning, demonstrates that students attending a multi-year summer intervention return to school having gained close to 1/2 year in reading comprehension and vocabulary.

(9) Summer learning programs are proven to remedy, reinforce, and accelerate learning, and can serve to close the achievement gap in education.

SEC. 3. PURPOSE.

The purpose of this Act is to create opportunities for summer learning by providing summer learning grants to eligible students, in order to—

(1) provide the students with access to summer learning;

(2) facilitate the enrollment of students in elementary schools or youth development organizations during the summer;

(3) promote collaboration between teachers and youth development professionals in order to bridge gaps between schools and youth programs; and

(4) encourage teachers to try new techniques, acquire new skills, and mentor new colleagues.

SEC. 4. DEFINITIONS.

In this Act:

(1) EDUCATIONAL SERVICE AGENCY- The term 'educational service agency' has the meaning given the term in section 9101 of the Elementary and Secondary Education Act of 1965 (20 U.S.C. 7801).

(2) ELIGIBLE ENTITY- The term 'eligible entity' means an entity that—

(A) desires to participate in a summer learning grant program under this Act by providing summer learning opportunities described in section 6(d)(1)(B) to eligible students; and

(B) is—

(i) a local educational agency;

(ii) a for-profit educational provider, nonprofit organization, or summer enrichment camp, that has been approved by the State educational agency to provide the summer learning opportunity described in section 6(d)(1)(B), including an entity that is in good standing that has been previously approved by a State educational agency to provide supplemental educational services; or

(iii) a consortium consisting of a local educational agency and 1 or more of the following entities:

(I) Another local educational agency.

(II) A community-based youth development organization with a demonstrated record of effectiveness in helping students learn.

(III) An institution of higher education.

(IV) An educational service agency.

(V) A for-profit educational provider described in clause (ii).

(VI) A nonprofit organization described in clause (ii).

(VII) A summer enrichment camp described in clause (ii).

(3) ELIGIBLE STUDENT- The term 'eligible student' means a student who—

(A) is eligible for a free lunch under the Richard B. Russell National School Lunch Act (42 U.S.C. 1751 et seq.);

(B) is served by a local educational agency identified by the State educational agency in the application described in section 5(b); or

(C)(i) in the case of a summer learning grant program authorized under this Act for fiscal year 2008, 2009, or 2010, is eligible to enroll in any of the grades kindergarten through grade 3 for the school year following participation in the program; or

(ii) in the case of a summer learning grant program authorized under this Act for fiscal year 2011 or 2012, is eligible to enroll in any of the grades kindergarten through grade 5 for the school year following participation in the program.

(4) INSTITUTION OF HIGHER EDUCATION- The term 'institution of higher education' has the meaning given the term in section 101(a) of the Higher Education Act of 1965 (20 U.S.C. 1001(a)).

(5) LOCAL EDUCATIONAL AGENCY- The term 'local educational agency' has the meaning given the term in section 9101 of the Elementary and Secondary Education Act of 1965 (20 U.S.C. 7801).

(6) SECRETARY- The term 'Secretary' means the Secretary of Education.

(7) STATE- The term 'State' means each of the several States of the United States, the District of Columbia, the Commonwealth of Puerto Rico, Guam, American Samoa, the United States Virgin Islands, the Commonwealth of the Northern Mariana Islands, the Republic of the Marshall Islands, the Federated States of Micronesia, and the Republic of Palau.

(8) STATE EDUCATIONAL AGENCY- The term 'State educational agency' has the meaning given the term in section 9101 of the Elementary and Secondary Education Act of 1965 (20 U.S.C. 7801).

SEC. 5. DEMONSTRATION GRANT PROGRAM.

(a) Program Authorized-

(1) IN GENERAL- From the funds appropriated under section 8 for a fiscal year, the Secretary shall carry out a demonstration grant program in which the Secretary awards grants, on a competitive basis, to State educational agencies to enable the State educational agencies to pay the Federal share of summer learning grants for eligible students.

(2) NUMBER OF GRANTS- For each fiscal year, the Secretary shall award not more than 5 grants under this section.

(b) Application- A State educational agency that desires to receive a grant under this section shall submit an application to the Secretary at such time, in such manner, and accompanied by such information as the Secretary may require. Such application shall identify the areas in the State where the summer learning grant program will be offered and the local educational agencies that serve such areas.

(c) Award Basis-

(1) SPECIAL CONSIDERATION- In awarding grants under this section, the Secretary shall give special consideration to a State educational agency that agrees, to the extent possible, to enter into agreements under section 6(d) with eligible entities that are consortia described in section 4(2)(B)(iii) and that include 2 or more of the entities described in subclauses (I) through (VII) of such section 4(2)(B)(iii) as partners.

(2) GEOGRAPHIC DISTRIBUTION- In awarding grants under this section, the Secretary shall take into consideration an equitable geographic distribution of the grants.

SEC. 6. SUMMER LEARNING GRANTS.

(a) Use of Grants for Summer Learning Grants-

(1) IN GENERAL- Each State educational agency that receives a grant under section 5 for a fiscal year shall use the grant funds to provide summer learning grants for the fiscal year to eligible students in the State who desire to attend a summer learning opportunity offered by an eligible entity that enters into an agreement with the State educational agency under subsection (d)(1).

(2) AMOUNT; FEDERAL AND NON-FEDERAL SHARES-

(A) AMOUNT- The amount of a summer learning grant provided under this Act shall be—

(i) for each of the fiscal years 2008 through 2011, $1,600; and

(ii) for fiscal year 2012, $1,800.

(B) FEDERAL SHARE- The Federal share of each summer learning grant shall be not more than 50 percent of the amount of the summer learning grant determined under subparagraph (A).

(C) NON-FEDERAL SHARE- The non-Federal share of each summer learning grant shall be not less than 50 percent of the amount of the summer learning grant determined under subparagraph (A), and shall be provided from non-Federal sources, such as State or local sources.

(b) Designation of Summer Scholars- Eligible students who receive summer learning grants under this Act shall be known as 'summer scholars'.

(c) Selection of Summer Learning Opportunity-

(1) DISSEMINATION OF INFORMATION- A State educational agency that receives a grant under section 5 shall disseminate information about summer learning opportunities and summer learning grants to the families of eligible students in the State.

(2) APPLICATION- The parents of an eligible student who are interested in having their child participate in a summer learning opportunity and receive a summer learning grant shall submit an application to the State educational agency that includes a ranked list of preferred summer learning opportunities.

(3) PROCESS- A State educational agency that receives an application under paragraph (2) shall—

(A) process such application;

(B) determine whether the eligible student shall receive a summer learning grant;

(C) coordinate the assignment of eligible students receiving summer learning grants with summer learning opportunities; and

(D) if demand for a summer learning opportunity exceeds capacity—

(i) in a case where information on the school readiness (based on school records and assessments of student achievement) of the eligible students is available, give priority for the summer learning opportunity to eligible students with low levels of school readiness; or

(ii) in a case where such information on school readiness is not available, rely on randomization to assign the eligible students.

(4) FLEXIBILITY- A State educational agency may assign a summer scholar to a summer learning opportunity program that is offered in an area served by a local educational agency that is not the local educational agency serving the area where such scholar resides.

(5) REQUIREMENT OF ACCEPTANCE- An eligible entity shall accept, enroll, and provide the summer learning opportunity of such entity to, any summer scholar assigned to such summer learning opportunity by a State educational agency pursuant to this subsection.

(d) Agreement With Eligible Entity-

(1) IN GENERAL- A State educational agency shall enter into an agreement with the eligible entity offering a summer learning opportunity, under which—

(A) the State educational agency shall agree to make payments to the eligible entity, in accordance with paragraph (2), for a summer scholar; and

(B) the eligible entity shall agree to provide the summer scholar with a summer learning opportunity that—

(i) provides a total of not less than the equivalent of 30 full days of instruction (or not less than the equivalent of 25 full days of instruction, if the equivalent of an additional 5 days is devoted to field trips or other enrichment opportunities) to the summer scholar;

(ii) employs small-group, research-based educational programs, materials, curricula, and practices;

(iii) provides a curriculum that—

(I) emphasizes reading and mathematics;

(II) is primarily designed to increase the literacy and numeracy of the summer scholar; and

(III) is aligned with the standards and goals of the school year curriculum of the local educational agency serving the summer scholar;

(iv) applies assessments to measure the skills taught in the summer learning opportunity and disaggregates the results of the assessments for summer scholars by race and ethnicity, economic status, limited English proficiency status, and disability category, in order to determine the opportunity's impact on each subgroup of summer scholars;

(v) collects daily attendance data on each summer scholar; and

(vi) meets all applicable Federal, State, and local civil rights laws.

(2) AMOUNT OF PAYMENT-

(A) IN GENERAL- Except as provided in subparagraph (B), a State educational agency shall make a payment to an eligible entity for a summer scholar in the amount determined under subsection (a)(2)(A).

(B) ADJUSTMENT- In the case in which a summer scholar does not attend the full summer learning opportunity, the State educational agency shall reduce the amount provided to the eligible entity pursuant to subparagraph (A) by a percentage that is equal to the percentage of the summer learning opportunity not attended by such scholar.

(e) Use of School Facilities- State educational agencies are encouraged to require local educational agencies in the State to allow eligible entities, in offering summer learning opportunities, to make use of school facilities in schools served by such local educational agencies at reasonable or no cost.

(f) Access of Records- An eligible entity offering a summer learning opportunity under this Act is eligible to receive, upon request, the school records and any previous supplemental educational services assessment records of a summer scholar served by such entity.

(g) Administrative Costs- A State educational agency or eligible entity receiving funding under this Act may use not more than 5 percent of such funding for administrative costs associated with carrying out this Act.

SEC. 7. EVALUATIONS; REPORT; WEBSITE.

(a) Evaluation and Assessment- For each year that an eligible entity enters into an agreement under section 6(d), the eligible entity shall prepare and submit to the Secretary a report on the activities and outcomes of each summer learning opportunity that enrolled a summer scholar, including—

(1) information on the design of the summer learning opportunity;

(2) the alignment of the summer learning opportunity with State standards; and

(3) data from assessments of student mathematics and reading skills for the summer scholars and on the attendance of the scholars, disaggregated by the subgroups described in section 6(d)(1)(B)(iv).

(b) Report- For each year funds are appropriated under section 8 for this Act, the Secretary shall prepare and submit a report to Congress on the summer learning grant programs, including the effectiveness of the summer learning opportunities in improving student achievement.

(c) Summer Learning Grants Website- The Secretary shall make accessible, on the Department of Education website, information for parents and school personnel on successful programs and curricula, and best practices, for summer learning opportunities.

SEC. 8. AUTHORIZATION OF APPROPRIATIONS.

There are authorized to be appropriated to carry out this Act $100,000,000 for fiscal year 2008 and such sums as may be necessary for each of the fiscal years 2009 through 2012.

US SENATE BILL 117

TITLE: A bill to amend titles 10 and 38, United States Code, to improve benefits and services for members of the Armed Forces, veterans of the Global War on Terrorism, and other veterans, to require reports on the effects of the Global War on Terrorism, and for other purposes.

SPONSOR: Sen Obama, Barack [IL] (introduced 1/4/2007) Cosponsors (15)

RELATED BILLS: H.R.1354

Latest Major Action: 1/4/2007 Referred to Senate committee. Status: Read twice and referred to the Committee on Veterans' Affairs.

Summary As Of:

1/4/2007—Introduced.

Lane Evans Veterans Health and Benefits Improvement Act of 2007 - Makes a veteran who served on active duty during a period of war eligible for a mental health evaluation and hospital care, medical services, nursing home care, and family and marital counseling for any identified mental health condition, notwithstanding insufficient medical evidence to conclude that the condition is attributable to such service.

Requires: (1) post-deployment medical and mental health screenings to be conducted within 30 days after a deployment; (2) each member, upon discharge, to be provided an electronic copy of all military records of such member; and (3) the Secretary of Defense to ensure appropriate outreach to members of the National Guard and reserves concerning benefits and services available upon discharge or deactivation.

Directs the Secretary of Veterans Affairs to establish and maintain a Global War on Terrorism Veterans Information System.

Requires quarterly reports from the Secretaries of Veterans Affairs, Labor, and Defense on the effects on veterans and on each such department of participation in the Global War on Terrorism.

Major Actions:

¤NONE¤

All Actions:

1/4/2007:

Sponsor introductory remarks on measure. (CR S116-117)

1/4/2007:

Read twice and referred to the Committee on Veterans' Affairs.

8/2/2007:

Sponsor introductory remarks on measure. (CR S10781)

Titles(s): (italics indicate a title for a portion of a bill)

¤NONE¤

COSPONSORS(15), ALPHABETICAL [followed by Cosponsors withdrawn]: (Sort: by date)

Sen Biden, Joseph R., Jr. [DE] - 2/12/2007

Sen Brown, Sherrod [OH] - 2/12/2007

Sen Cantwell, Maria [WA] - 3/22/2007

Sen Durbin, Richard [IL] - 3/29/2007

Sen Kerry, John F. [MA] - 2/12/2007

Sen Lincoln, Blanche L. [AR] - 5/15/2007

Sen McCaskill, Claire [MO] - 3/19/2007

Sen Mikulski, Barbara A. [MD] - 2/12/2007

Sen Murray, Patty [WA] - 6/13/2007

Sen Rockefeller, John D., IV [WV] - 3/1/2007

Sen Salazar, Ken [CO] - 3/23/2007

Sen Schumer, Charles E. [NY] - 2/12/2007

Sen Snowe, Olympia J. [ME] - 1/4/2007

Sen Tester, Jon [MT] - 4/16/2007

Sen Wyden, Ron [OR] - 3/19/2007

Committee(s)

Committee/Subcommittee:

Activity:

Senate Veterans' Affairs

Referral, In Committee

Related Bill Details: (additional related bills may be indentified in Status)

Bill:

Relationship:

H.R.1354

Related bill identified by CRS

Amendment(s)

¤NONE¤

In the Senate of the United States

January 4, 2007

Mr. OBAMA (for himself and Ms. SNOWE) introduced the following bill; which was read twice and referred to the Committee on Veterans' Affairs

A BILL

To amend titles 10 and 38, United States Code, to improve benefits and services for members of the Armed Forces, veterans of the Global War on Terrorism, and other veterans, to require reports on the effects of the Global War on Terrorism, and for other purposes.

Be it enacted by the Senate and House of Representatives of the United States of America in Congress assembled,

SECTION 1. SHORT TITLE.

This Act may be cited as the 'Lane Evans Veterans Health and Benefits Improvement Act of 2007'.

TITLE I—BENEFITS AND SERVICES FOR MEMBERS OF THE ARMED FORCES AND VETERANS

SEC. 101. MEDICAL CARE AND SERVICES FOR VETERANS OF FUTURE CONFLICTS FOR MENTAL HEALTH CONDITIONS FOR WHICH EVIDENCE IS INSUFFICIENT TO ESTABLISH A SERVICE-CONNECTION.

(a) Eligibility- Paragraph (1) of section 1710(e) of title 38, United States Code, is amended by adding at the end the following new subparagraph:

'(F) Subject to paragraphs (2) and (3), a veteran who served on active duty as described in subparagraph (D) during a period of war, or after the date, specified in that subparagraph is also eligible for—

'(i) a mental health evaluation to be provided by the Secretary not later than 30 days after the date of the request of the veteran for such evaluation; and

'(ii) hospital care, medical services, nursing home care, and family and marital counseling for any mental health condition identified pursuant to such evaluation, notwithstanding that there is insufficient medical evidence to conclude that such condition is attributable to such service.'.

(b) Limitations-

(1) CAUSATION- Paragraph (2)(B) of such section is amended by striking 'or (E)' and inserting '(E), or (F)'.

(2) DURATION AFTER SERVICE- Paragraph (3) of such section is amended—

(A) in subparagraph (C), by striking 'and' at the end;

(B) in subparagraph (D), by striking the period at the end and inserting '; and'; and

(C) by adding at the end the following new subparagraph:

'(E) in the case of a veteran described in paragraph (1)(F)—

'(i) with respect to the evaluation described in clause (i) of that paragraph, after a period of 5 years beginning on the date of the veteran's discharge or release from active military, naval, or air service; and

'(ii) with respect to the care, services, and counseling described in clause (ii) of that paragraph, after a period of 2 years beginning on the date of the commencement of the provision of such care, services, and counseling to the veteran.'.

SEC. 102. POSTDEPLOYMENT MEDICAL AND MENTAL HEALTH SCREENINGS FOR MEMBERS OF THE ARMED FORCES.

Section 1074f(b) of title 10, United States Code, is amended—

(1) by inserting '(1)' before 'The system';

(2) by striking the second sentence; and

(3) by adding at the end the following new paragraph:

'(2) The postdeployment examination shall be conducted not later than 30 days after the date of the return of a member to the United States from a deployment as described in subsection (a). The examination shall include a comprehensive medical and mental health assessment conducted on an individualized basis by personnel qualified to conduct such examinations.'.

SEC. 103. PROVISION OF ELECTRONIC COPY OF MILITARY RECORDS ON DISCHARGE OR RELEASE OF MEMBERS FROM THE ARMED FORCES.

(a) In General- Each member of the Armed Forces shall be provided, upon discharge or release from the Armed Forces, a copy in an electronic format of the military records (including all medical, military service, and other military records) of such member. The copy of such records shall be provided through a portable, readily accessible, digital, read-only medium.

(b) Protection of Privacy- A copy of records shall be provided under subsection (a) in a manner, including the utilization of personal security codes for access, that ensures that access to such records is limited to the member of the Armed Forces concerned and such other individuals as may be authorized by such member.

(c) Report- Not later than 90 days after the date of the enactment of this Act, the Secretary of Defense shall submit to Congress a report on the actions being taken to comply with the requirements of this section. The report shall include a detailed discussion of the mechanisms to be utilized in order to assure the protection of privacy of military records of members of the Armed Forces as required by subsection (b).

SEC. 104. ENHANCED OUTREACH TO MEMBERS OF THE NATIONAL GUARD AND RESERVE ON AVAILABLE BENEFITS AND SERVICES.

(a) In General- The Secretary of Defense shall take appropriate actions to ensure that members of the National Guard and Reserve are provided comprehensive outreach on the following:

(1) The benefits and services available from and through the Federal Government to members of the National Guard and Reserve upon their deactivation from active duty service in the Armed Forces, including benefits under the Benefits Delivery at Discharge program and medical and mental health services.

(2) The benefits and services available from and through the Federal Government to members of the National Guard and Reserve upon their discharge or release from the Armed Forces, including benefits under the Benefits Delivery at Discharge program and medical and mental health services.

(b) Nature of Outreach- The outreach provided under subsection (a) shall be of the same nature, duration, and quality as outreach provided to members of the regular components of the Armed Forces at discharge or release from the Armed Forces, except that such outreach shall be tailored to the specific employment and other transition needs of members of the National Guard and Reserve who are being deactivated from active duty or discharged or released from the Armed Forces.

(c) Consultation- The Secretary of Defense shall provide outreach under subsection (a) in consultation with the following:

(1) The Secretary of Veterans Affairs, with respect to benefits and services available under the laws administered by the Secretary of Veterans Affairs.

(2) The Secretary of Labor, with respect to benefits and services available under the laws administered by the Secretary of Labor (including employment and reemployment benefits under chapter 43 of title 38, United States Code (commonly referred to as 'USERRA')).

(3) The Administrator of the Small Business Administration, with respect to benefits and services available under the laws administered by the Administrator.

(4) The Director of the Office of Personnel Management, with respect to eligibility for preferences in employment by the Federal Government.

(5) The head of any other department or agency of the Federal Government that provides benefits and services to former members of the Armed Forces, with respect to such benefits and services.

(d) Report- Not later than 90 days after the date of the enactment of this Act, the Secretary of Defense shall submit to Congress a report on the actions being taken to comply with the requirements of this section.

TITLE II—REPORTS ON EFFECTS OF GLOBAL WAR ON TERRORISM

SEC. 201. DEFINITIONAL MATTERS.

(a) General Definition of 'Global War on Terrorism'- Section 101 of title 38, United States Code, is amended by adding at the end the following new paragraph:

'(34) The term 'Global War on Terrorism' means the period beginning on September 11, 2001, and ending on the date thereafter prescribed by Presidential proclamation or by law.'.

(b) Specification of Locations of Global War on Terrorism- For purposes of this title, the geographic location of the Global War on Terrorism shall be the locations (including the airspace above) as follows: Afghanistan, Algeria, the Arabian Sea, Armenia, Bab el Mandeb, Bahrain, Bulgaria, Cyprus, Diego Garcia (United Kingdom Indian Ocean Territory), Djibouti, Egypt, Eritrea, Ethiopia, the Republic of Georgia, Greece, Guantanamo Bay, Cuba, the Gulf of Aden, the Gulf of Aqaba, the Gulf of Oman, the Gulf of Suez, Indonesia, the Ionian Sea, Iran, Iraq, Israel, Japan, Jordan, Kazakhstan, Kenya, Kyrgyzstan, Kuwait, Lebanon, the Mediterranean Sea, Oman, Pakistan, the Pentagon Reservation, Virginia (but only on September 11, 2001), the Persian Gulf, the Philippines, Qatar, the Red Sea, Romania, Saudi Arabia, Somalia, the Spratly Islands, the Strait of Hormuz, the Suez Canal, Syria, Tajikistan, Turkey, Turkmenistan, the United Arab Emirates, Uzbekistan, Yemen, and any other location specified for purposes of this Act by the Secretary of Veterans Affairs in consultation with the Secretary of Defense.

SEC. 202. GLOBAL WAR ON TERRORISM VETERANS INFORMATION SYSTEM.

(a) System Required- The Secretary of Veterans Affairs shall establish and maintain an information system designed to provide a comprehensive record of the following:

(1) The veterans of the Global War on Terrorism who seek benefits and services under the laws administered by the Secretary.

(2) The benefits and services provided by the Secretary to such veterans under the laws administered by the Secretary.

(b) Designation of System- The system required by subsection (a) shall be known as the 'Global War on Terrorism Veterans Information System'.

(c) Requirements for System-

(1) IN GENERAL- The system required by subsection (a) shall—

(A) permit the accumulation, storage, retrieval, and ready analysis of information on the veterans, and on the benefits and services, described by that subsection; and

(B) facilitate the preparation of the quarterly reports on the effects of participation in the Global War on Terrorism on veterans and the Department of Veterans Affairs as required by section 203.

(2) MODEL- The system may incorporate appropriate elements (or variations on such elements) of the Gulf War Veterans Information System.

(d) Information From Department of Defense-

(1) PROVISION OF INFORMATION IN GLOBAL WAR ON TERRORISM CONTINGENCY TRACKING SYSTEM- The Secretary of Defense shall provide to the Secretary of Veterans Affairs such information in the Global War on Terrorism Contingency Tracking System (CTS) of the Department of Defense as the Secretary of Defense and the Secretary of Veterans Affairs jointly determine appropriate for purposes of the system required by subsection (a), including the preparation and submittal of reports required by section 203.

(2) MEMORANDUM OF UNDERSTANDING- Information shall be provided under paragraph (1) pursuant to the terms of a memorandum of understanding entered into by the Secretary of Defense and the Secretary of Veterans Affairs for purposes of this section.

(3) COST OF PROVISION OF INFORMATION- The cost of the provision of information under paragraph (1) shall be borne by the Department of Defense in accordance with the provisions of section 5106 of title 38, United States Code.

SEC. 203. QUARTERLY REPORTS ON EFFECTS OF PARTICIPATION IN THE GLOBAL WAR ON TERRORISM ON VETERANS AND THE DEPARTMENT OF VETERANS AFFAIRS.

(a) Quarterly Reports Required- Not later than 90 days after the date of the enactment of this Act, and every fiscal year quarter thereafter, the Secretary of Veterans Affairs shall submit to the appropriate committees of Congress a report on the effects of participation in the Global War on Terrorism on veterans and on the Department of Veterans Affairs.

(b) Scope of Report- Each report required by subsection (a) shall provide the information specified in subsection (c), current as of the date of such report, separately for each of the following periods:

(1) The period of the fiscal year quarter for which such report is submitted.

(2) The period beginning on October 1, 2001, and ending on the last day of the most recent fiscal year completed on or before the date of such report, with such information set forth—

(A) in aggregate over such period; and

(B) separately for each complete fiscal year that falls within such period.

(c) Covered Information- The information specified in this subsection for a report under subsection (a) is information on the provision to veterans of the Global War on Terrorism of benefits and services under the laws administered by the Secretary of Veterans Affairs as follows:

(1) PERSONAL INFORMATION- Aggregated personal information on veterans of the Global War on Terrorism, including—

(A) the number of such veterans by race;

(B) the number of such veterans by sex;

(C) the number of such veterans by age;

(D) the number of such veterans by marital status (whether married, single, separated, or divorced); and

(E) the number of such veterans by residence (by State, territory, or country).

(2) INFORMATION ON MILITARY SERVICE- Aggregated information on the military service of veterans of the Global War on Terrorism, including information on the following:

(A) In the case of all veterans of the Global War on Terrorism—

(i) the number of such veterans by Armed Force, and by component of Armed Force, in which such veterans served in the Global War on Terrorism; and

(ii) the number of such veterans by duty status in which such veterans served in the Global War on Terrorism, including, in the case of veterans who were members of a reserve component of the Armed Forces, the number of such veterans who were members of the National Guard.

(B) In the case of veterans of the Global War on Terrorism who served only in Operation Enduring Freedom—

(i) the number of such veterans by Armed Force, and by component of Armed Force, in which such veterans served in Operation Enduring Freedom; and

(ii) the number of such veterans by duty status in which such veterans served in Operation Enduring Freedom, including, in the case of veterans who were members of a reserve component of the Armed Forces, the number of such veterans who were members of the National Guard.

(C) In the case of veterans of the Global War on Terrorism who served only in Operation Iraqi Freedom—

(i) the number of such veterans by Armed Force, and by component of Armed Force, in which such veterans served in Operation Iraqi Freedom; and

(ii) the number of such veterans by duty status in which such veterans served in Operation Iraqi Freedom, including, in the case of veterans who were members of a reserve component of the Armed Forces, the number of such veterans who were members of the National Guard.

(D) In the case of veterans of the Global War on Terrorism who served in both Operation Enduring Freedom and Operation Iraqi Freedom—

(i) the number of such veterans by Armed Force, and by component of Armed Force, in which such veterans served in each of Operation Enduring Freedom and Operation Iraqi Freedom; and

(ii) the number of such veterans by duty status in which such veterans served in Operation Enduring Freedom or Operation Iraqi Freedom, including, in the case of veterans who were members of a reserve component of the Armed Forces, the number of such veterans who were members of the National Guard.

(E) In the case of veterans of the Global War on Terrorism who served in neither Operation Enduring Freedom nor Operation Iraqi Freedom—

(i) the number of such veterans by Armed Force, and by component of Armed Force, in which such veterans served in the Armed Forces during the Global War on Terrorism; and

(ii) the number of such veterans by duty status in which such veterans served in the Armed Forces during the Global War on Terrorism, including, in the case of veterans who were members of a reserve component of the Armed Forces, the number of such veterans who were members of the National Guard.

(F) The number of veterans of the Global War on Terrorism by deployment location in the Global War on Terrorism, including the number of such veterans deployed to each location specified in section 201(b).

(G) The deployment history of veterans during the Global War on Terrorism, including—

(i) the number of veterans who were deployed more than once; and

(ii) for each number of veterans who were deployed twice, three times, four times, or more than four times, the number of such veterans who were deployed each such number of times.

(H) The number of veterans of the Global War on Terrorism by grade upon completion of military service in the Global War on Terrorism.

(I) The medical evacuation history of veterans during the Global War on Terrorism, including—

(i) the number of veterans who were evacuated once or more during the Global War on Terrorism; and

(ii) for each number of veterans who were evacuated twice, three times, four times, or more than four times, the number of such veterans who were evacuated each such number of times.

(3) HEALTH, COUNSELING, AND RELATED BENEFITS- Aggregated information on the health, counseling, and related benefits and services provided by the Department of Veterans Affairs to veterans of the Global War on Terrorism, including information on the following:

(A) The enrollment of such veterans in the patient enrollment system under section 1705 of title 38, United States Code, by priority of enrollment status.

(B) The number of inpatient stays of such veterans, and the cost of the provision of care and benefits to such veterans during such stays, set forth by—

(i) priority of enrollment status under the patient enrollment system; and

(ii) by condition, including traumatic brain injury, amputation, mental health condition, Post Traumatic Stress Disorder (PTSD), and other conditions.

(C) The number of outpatient visits of such veterans, and the cost of the provision of care and benefits to such veterans, set forth by—

(i) priority of enrollment status under the patient enrollment system; and

(ii) by condition, including traumatic brain injury, amputation, mental health condition, Post Traumatic Stress Disorder (PTSD), and other conditions.

(D) The number of visits of such veterans to a center for the provision of readjustment counseling and related mental health services under section 1712A of title 38, United States Code (commonly referred to as a 'vet center'), and the cost of the provision of such counseling and services.

(4) COMPENSATION, PENSION, AND OTHER BENEFITS- Aggregated information on the compensation, pension, and other benefits and services provided by the Department of Veterans Affairs to veterans of the Global War on Terrorism, including information on the following:

(A) The claims of such veterans for compensation under chapter 11 of title 38, United Stated Code, including—

(i) the number of claims received;

(ii) the number of claims granted;

(iii) the number of claims denied; and

(iv) the number of claims pending.

(B) The amount of compensation paid to such veterans, stated as an average monthly amount for each of the periods covered by such report and as a total amount for both such periods.

(C) The claims for dependency and indemnity compensation under chapter 13 of title 38, United States Code, with respect to such veterans, including—

(i) the number of claims received;

(ii) the number of claims granted;

(iii) the number of claims denied; and

(iv) the number of claims pending.

(D) The amount of dependency and indemnity compensation paid with respect to such veterans, stated as an average monthly amount for the periods covered by such report and as a total amount for such periods.

(E) The claims for pension under chapter 15 of title 38, United States Code, for or with respect to such veterans, including—

(i) the number of claims received;

(ii) the number of claims granted;

(iii) the number of claims denied; and

(iv) the number of claims pending.

(F) The education benefits provided to or with respect to such veterans or other individuals under chapter 30, 32, or 35 of title 38, United States Code, or chapter 1606 or 1607 of title 10, United States, including—

(i) the number of veterans or other individuals provided such benefits (set forth by chapter under which provided); and

(ii) the amount of such benefits (set forth by chapter under which provided).

(G) The vocational rehabilitation benefits and services provided to such veterans, including—

(i) the number of veterans submitting applications for such benefits or services;

(ii) the number of applications granted;

(iii) the number of applications denied;

(iv) the number of applications pending; and

(v) the type and amount of such benefits and services provided.

(H) The housing and small business loan guaranty benefits provided to such veterans under chapter 37 of title 38, United States Code, and other provisions of law, including—

(i) the number of veterans submitting applications for such benefits;

(ii) the type, and number and amount by type, of such benefits provided; and

(iii) the number and amount by type of loans in default.

(I) The specially adapted housing assistance provided to such veterans under chapter 21 of title 38, United States Code, including the type and amount of assistance provided.

(J) The insurance benefits provided to or with respect to such veterans under chapter 19 of title 38, United States Code, including the amount of benefits provided under each type of insurance offered by the Secretary.

(5) BURIAL AND CEMETERY BENEFITS- Aggregated information on the burial and cemetery benefits provided by the Department of Veterans Affairs with respect to veterans of the Global War on Terrorism, including information on the following:

(A) The number of burials in a cemetery of the National Cemetery System or Arlington National Cemetery.

(B) The number of flags furnished under section 2301 of title 38, United States Code.

(C) The amount of burial allowances paid under section 2302 of title 38, United States Code.

(D) The amount of plot allowances paid under section 2303 of title 38, United States Code.

(E) The number of headstones, markers, and burial receptacles furnished under section 2306 of title 38, United States Code, and the cost of furnishing such headstones, markers, and receptacles.

(F) The amount of burial and funeral expenses paid under section 2307 of title 38, United States Code, for veterans who die from a service-connected disability.

(G) The costs of the transportation of the remains of deceased veterans to a national cemetery under section 2308 of title 38, United States Code.

(d) Protection of Identities- The Secretary shall take appropriate actions in preparing and submitting reports under this section to ensure that no personally identifying information on any particular veteran is included or otherwise improperly released in such reports.

(e) Definitions- In this section:

(1) APPROPRIATE COMMITTEES OF CONGRESS- The term 'appropriate committees of Congress' means—

(A) the Committees on Armed Services, Appropriations and Veterans' Affairs of the Senate; and

(B) the Committees on Armed Services, Appropriations and Veterans' Affairs of the House of Representatives.

(2) GLOBAL WAR ON TERRORISM- The term 'Global War on Terrorism' has the meaning given that term in section 101(34) of title 38, United States Code (as added by section 201(a)).

(3) VETERAN OF THE GLOBAL WAR ON TERRORISM- The term 'veteran of the Global War on Terrorism' means a veteran of the Global War on Terrorism who served on active military, naval, or air service during the Global War on Terrorism in a location specified in section 201(b).

SEC. 204. QUARTERLY REPORTS ON EFFECTS OF PARTICIPATION IN THE GLOBAL WAR ON TERRORISM ON VETERANS AND THE DEPARTMENT OF LABOR.

(a) Quarterly Reports Required- Not later than 90 days after the date of the enactment of this Act, and every fiscal year quarter thereafter, the Secretary of Labor shall submit to the appropriate committees of Congress a report on the effects of participation in the Global War on Terrorism on veterans (under the laws administered by the Secretary of Labor) and on the Department of Labor.

(b) Scope of Report- Each report required by subsection (a) shall provide the information specified in subsection (c), current as of the date of such report, separately for each of the following periods:

(1) The period of the fiscal year quarter for which such report is submitted.

(2) The period beginning on October 1, 2001, and ending on the last day of the most recent fiscal year completed on or before the date of such report, with such information set forth—

(A) in aggregate over such period; and

(B) separately for each complete fiscal year that falls within such period.

(c) Covered Information- The information specified in this subsection for a report under subsection (a) is information on the provision to veterans of the Global War on Terrorism of employment and other benefits and services under the laws administered by the Secretary of Labor as follows:

(1) The number of veterans submitting applications for such benefits or services.

(2) The number of applications granted.

(3) The number of applications denied.

(4) The number of applications pending.

(5) The type and amount of such benefits and services provided.

(d) Protection of Identities- The Secretary shall take appropriate actions in preparing and submitting reports under this section to ensure that no personally identifying information on any particular veteran is included or otherwise improperly released in such reports.

(e) Definitions- In this section:

(1) APPROPRIATE COMMITTEES OF CONGRESS- The term 'appropriate committees of Congress' means—

(A) the Committees on Armed Services, Appropriations and Veterans' Affairs of the Senate; and

(B) the Committees on Armed Services, Appropriations and Veterans' Affairs of the House of Representatives.

(2) GLOBAL WAR ON TERRORISM- The term 'Global War on Terrorism' has the meaning given that term in section 101(34) of title 38, United States Code (as added by section 201(a)).

(3) VETERAN OF THE GLOBAL WAR ON TERRORISM- The term 'veteran of the Global War on Terrorism' means a veteran of the Global War on Terrorism who served on active military, naval, or air service during the Global War on Terrorism in a location specified in section 201(b).

SEC. 205. QUARTERLY REPORTS ON EFFECTS OF PARTICIPATION IN THE GLOBAL WAR ON TERRORISM ON MEMBERS OF THE ARMED FORCES AND THE DEPARTMENT OF DEFENSE.

(a) Quarterly Reports Required- Not later than 90 days after the date of the enactment of this Act, and every 90 days thereafter, the Secretary of Defense shall submit to the congressional defense committees a report on the effects of participation in the Global War on Terrorism on the members of the Armed Forces and on the Department of Defense.

(b) Scope of Report- Each report required by subsection (a) shall include the information specified in subsection (c), current as of the date of such report, separately for each of the following periods:

(1) The 90-day period ending on the date of such report.

(2) The period beginning on September 11, 2001, and ending on the date of such report.

(c) Covered Information- The information specified in this subsection for a report under subsection (a) is information on the participation of members of the Armed Forces in the Global War on Terrorism as follows:

(1) PERSONAL INFORMATION- Aggregated personal information on members of the Armed Forces participating in the Global War on Terrorism, including—

(A) the number of such members by race;

(B) the number of such members by sex;

(C) the number of such members by age;

(D) the number of such members by marital status (whether married, single, separated, or divorced); and

(E) the number of such members by home of record (by State or territory).

(2) INFORMATION ON MILITARY SERVICE- Aggregated information on the military service of members of the Armed Forces participating in the Global War on Terrorism, including information on the following:

(A) The number of such members by Armed Force, and by component of Armed Force, in which such members are serving in the Global War on Terrorism.

(B) The number of such members by duty status in which such members are serving in the Global War on Terrorism, including, in the case of members who are members of a reserve component of the Armed Forces, the number of such members who are members of the National Guard.

(C) The number of such members by deployment status in which such members are serving in the Global War on Terrorism, including the number of such members who—

(i) have served only in Operation Enduring Freedom;

(ii) have served only in Operation Iraqi Freedom;

(iii) have served in both Operation Enduring Freedom and Operation Iraqi Freedom; or

(iv) have served in neither Operation Enduring Freedom nor Operation Iraqi Freedom.

(D) The number of such members by deployment location in the Global War on Terrorism, including the number of such members deployed to each location specified in section 201(b).

(E) The deployment history of such members during the Global War on Terrorism, including—

(i) the number of members who have been deployed more than once; and

(ii) for each number of members who have been deployed twice, three times, four times, or more than four times, the number of such members who have been deployed each such number of times.

(F) The number of such members by grade.

(G) The medical evacuation history of such members during the Global War on Terrorism, including—

(i) the number of members who have been evacuated once or more during the Global War on Terrorism; and

(ii) for each number of members who have been evacuated twice, three times, four times, or more than four times, the number of such members who have been evacuated each such number of times.

(H) The number of such members whose enlistment or period of obligated service has been extended, or whose eligibility for retirement has been suspended, during the Global War on Terrorism under a provision of law (commonly referred to as a 'stop-loss authority') authorizing the President to extend an enlistment or period of obligated service, or suspend eligibility for retirement, of a member of the Armed Forces in a time of war or national emergency declared by Congress or the President, including—

(i) the number of such members who have been subject to the exercise of such authority; and

(ii) for each number of times being subject to the exercise of such authority, the number of such members who have been so subject to such authority each such number of times.

(I) The number of such members who have been discharged or released from the Armed Forces, including, for each category of condition of discharge, the number of members discharged under such category.

(3) INFORMATION ON ADMINISTRATION OF ARMED FORCES- Aggregated information on the administration of the Armed Forces participating in of the Global War on Terrorism, including information on the following:

(A) The number of members of the reserve components of the Armed Forces called or ordered to active duty for service in the Global War on Terrorism, including—

(i) the number of members of the National Guard and the number of Reserves so ordered;

(ii) for each number of times of being so called or ordered to active duty, the number of such members who have been so called or order to active duty each such number of times; and

(iii) the average number times being so called or ordered to active duty among all members of the National Guard and Reserve who have been so called or ordered to active duty.

(B) The number of members of the Armed Forces who have been subject to medical evacuation once or more in the Global War on Terrorism.

(C) The number of Purple Hearts awarded to members of the Armed Forces in the Global War on Terrorism.

(D) The number of Global War on Terrorism Expeditionary Medals awarded to members of the Armed Forces.

(E) The number of anthrax vaccinations performed on members of the Armed Forces for purposes of the Global War on Terrorism, stated for both of the periods covered by such report.

(F) The number of doses of the medication Larium issued to members of the Armed Forces for purposes of the Global War on Terrorism, stated for both of the period covered by such report.

(G) The number of members of the Armed Forces whose enlistment or period of obligated service has been extended, or whose eligibility for retirement has been suspended, for purposes of the Global War on Terrorism under a provision of law (commonly referred to as a 'stop-loss authority') authorizing the President to extend an enlistment or period of obligated service, or suspend eligibility for retirement, of a member of the Armed Forces in a time of war or national emergency declared by Congress or the President.

(H) The number of members of the Armed Forces participating in the Global War on Terrorism who have been discharged or released from the Armed Forces, including—

(i) the military status of such members at the time of discharge or release; and

(ii) the nature of such discharge or release, including less than honorable discharge for drug abuse, alcohol abuse, domestic violence, discipline problems, and other war-related reintegration problems.

(I) The number of members of the Armed Forces described in subparagraph (H) who have had their discharge upgraded, set forth by deployment status in the Global War on Terrorism and by nature of discharge upon discharge.

(d) Definitions- In this section:

(1) CONGRESSIONAL DEFENSE COMMITTEES- The term 'congressional defense committees' means—

(A) the Committees on Armed Services and Appropriations of the Senate; and

(B) the Committees on Armed Services and Appropriations of the House of Representatives.

(2) GLOBAL WAR ON TERRORISM- The term 'Global War on Terrorism' has the meaning given that term in section 101(34) of title 38, United States Code (as added by section 201(a)).

(3) MEMBER OF THE ARMED FORCES PARTICIPATING IN THE GLOBAL WAR ON TERRORISM- The term 'member of the Armed Forces participating in the Global War on Terrorism' means a member of the Armed Forces who served on active duty in the Global War on Terrorism at a location specified in section 201(b).

US SENATE BILL 133

TITLE: A bill to promote the national security and stability of the economy of the United States by reducing the dependence of the United States on oil through the use of alternative fuels and new technology, and for other purposes.

SPONSOR: Sen Obama, Barack [IL] (introduced 1/4/2007) Cosponsors (3)

RELATED BILLS: H.R.2354

LATEST MAJOR ACTION: 1/4/2007 Referred to Senate committee. Status: Read twice and referred to the Committee on Finance.

SUMMARY AS OF:

1/4/2007—Introduced.

American Fuels Act of 2007 - Establishes in the Executive Office of the President the Office of Energy Security to oversee all federal energy security programs, including coordination of all federal agency efforts to assist the United States in achieving full energy independence.

Amends the Internal Revenue Code to provide: (1) a tax credit, against both ordinary and alternative minimum tax, for production of qualified flexible fuel motor vehicles; and (2) an alternative fuel retail sales credit.

Amends the Clayton Act and the Petroleum Marketing Practices Act to prohibit restrictions on the installation of alternative fuel pumps within fuel franchise documents.

Amends the Clean Air Act to direct the Administrator of the Environmental Protection Agency to promulgate regulations to ensure that diesel sold or introduced into commerce in the United States, on an annual average basis, contains specified percentages of alternative diesel fuel.

Sets forth a credit program for the generation of diesel fuel.

Amends the Internal Revenue Code to allow an excise tax credit for: (1) production of cellulosic biomass ethanol; and (2) qualifying ethanol blending and processing equipment.

Amends the Energy Policy Act of 1992 (EPA) to treat a medium or heavy duty hybrid vehicle as an alternative fueled vehicle.

Sets a deadline by which: (1) any federal property with at least one fuel re-fueling station must include at least one alternative fuel refueling station; and (2) any alternative fuel refueling station on federally-owned property must permit full public access for the purpose of refueling using alternative fuel.

Amends federal transportation law to require that any bus purchased with funds from the Mass Transit Account of the Highway Trust Fund to be a clean fuel bus.

Amends armed forces law governing energy-related procurement to direct the Secretary of Defense to develop a strategy to use fuel produced from domestically produced fuel using starch, sugar, cellulosic biomass, plant or animal oils, or thermal chemical conversion, thermal depolymerization, or thermal conversion processes (covered fuel). Authorizes the Secretary to enter into contracts to: (1) develop and operate covered fuel production facilities; and (2) provide for construction or capital modification of such facilities.

Amends the EPA to include among alternative fueled vehicles any vehicle propelled by electric drive transportation, engine dominant hybrid electric, or plug-in hybrid technology.

MAJOR ACTIONS:

¤NONE¤

ALL ACTIONS:

1/4/2007:

Sponsor introductory remarks on measure. (CR S127-128)

1/4/2007:

Read twice and referred to the Committee on Finance. (text of measure as introduced: CR S128-133)

TITLES(s): (italics indicate a title for a portion of a bill)

¤NONE¤

COSPONSORS(3), ALPHABETICAL [FOLLOWED BY COSPONSORS WITHDRAWN]: (Sort: by date)

Sen Harkin, Tom [IA] - 1/4/2007

Sen Lugar, Richard G. [IN] - 1/4/2007

Sen Salazar, Ken [CO] - 2/26/2007

COMMITTEE(s)

Committee/Subcommittee:

Activity:

Senate Finance

Referral, In Committee

RELATED BILL DETAILS: (additional related bills may be indentified in Status)

BILL:

Relationship:

H.R.2354

Related bill identified by CRS

H.R.2354

Related bill as identified by House committee

AMENDMENT(S)

¤NONE¤

IN THE SENATE OF THE UNITED STATES

January 4, 2007

Mr. OBAMA (for himself, Mr. LUGAR, and Mr. HARKIN) introduced the following bill; which was read twice and referred to the Committee on Finance

A BILL

To promote the national security and stability of the economy of the United States by reducing the dependence of the United States on oil through the use of alternative fuels and new technology, and for other purposes.

Be it enacted by the Senate and House of Representatives of the United States of America in Congress assembled,

SECTION 1. SHORT TITLE; TABLE OF CONTENTS.

(a) Short Title- This Act may be cited as the 'American Fuels Act of 2007'.

(b) Table of Contents- The table of contents for this Act is as follows:

Sec. 8. Incentive for Federal and State fleets for medium and heavy duty hybrids.

Sec. 9. Credit for qualifying ethanol blending and processing equipment.

Sec. 10. Public access to Federal alternative refueling stations.

Sec. 11. Purchase of clean fuel buses.

Sec. 12. Domestic fuel production volumes to meet Department of Defense needs.

Sec. 13. Federal fleet energy conservation improvement.

SEC. 2. OFFICE OF ENERGY SECURITY.

(a) Definitions- In this section:

(1) DIRECTOR- The term 'Director' means the Director of Energy Security appointed under subsection (c)(1).

(2) OFFICE- The term 'Office' means the Office of Energy Security established by subsection (b).

(b) Establishment- There is established in the Executive Office of the President the Office of Energy Security.

(c) Director-

(1) IN GENERAL- The Office shall be headed by a Director, who shall be appointed by the President, by and with the advice and consent of the Senate.

(2) RATE OF PAY- The Director shall be paid at a rate of pay equal to level I of the Executive Schedule under section 5312 of title 5, United States Code.

(d) Responsibilities-

(1) IN GENERAL- The Office, acting through the Director, shall be responsible for overseeing all Federal energy security programs, including the coordination of efforts of Federal agencies to assist the United States in achieving full energy independence.

(2) SPECIFIC RESPONSIBILITIES- In carrying out paragraph (1), the Director shall—

(A) serve as head of the energy community;

(B) act as the principal advisor to the President, the National Security Council, the National Economic Council, the Domestic Policy Council, and the Homeland Security Council with respect to intelligence matters relating to energy security;

(C) with request to budget requests and appropriations for Federal programs relating to energy security—

(i) consult with the President and the Director of the Office of Management and Budget with respect to each major Federal budgetary decision relating to energy security of the United States;

(ii) based on priorities established by the President, provide to the heads of departments containing agencies or organizations within the energy community, and to the heads of such agencies and organizations, guidance for use in developing the budget for Federal programs relating to energy security;

(iii) based on budget proposals provided to the Director by the heads of agencies and organizations described in clause (ii), develop and determine an annual consolidated budget for Federal programs relating to energy security; and

(iv) present the consolidated budget, together with any recommendations of the Director and any heads of agencies and organizations described in clause (ii), to the President for approval;

(D) establish and meet regularly with a council of business and labor leaders to develop and provide to the President and Congress recommendations relating to the impact of energy supply and prices on economic growth;

(E) submit to Congress an annual report that describes the progress of the United States toward the goal of achieving full energy independence; and

(F) carry out such other responsibilities as the President may assign.

(e) Staff-

(1) IN GENERAL- The Director may, without regard to the civil service laws (including regulations), appoint and terminate such personnel as are necessary to enable the Director to carry out the responsibilities of the Director under this section.

(2) COMPENSATION-

(A) IN GENERAL- Except as provided in subparagraph (B), the Director may fix the compensation of personnel without regard to the provisions of chapter 51 and subchapter III of chapter 53 of title 5, United States Code, relating to classification of positions and General Schedule pay rates.

(B) MAXIMUM RATE OF PAY- The rate of pay for the personnel appointed by the Director shall not exceed the rate payable for level V of the Executive Schedule under section 5316 of title 5, United States Code.

(f) Authorization of Appropriations- There are authorized to be appropriated such sums as are necessary to carry out this section.

SEC. 3. CREDIT FOR PRODUCTION OF QUALIFIED FLEXIBLE FUEL MOTOR VEHICLES.

(a) In General- Subpart D of part IV of subchapter A of chapter 1 of the Internal Revenue Code of 1986 is amended by adding at the end the following new section:

'SEC. 45O. PRODUCTION OF QUALIFIED FLEXIBLE FUEL MOTOR VEHICLES.

'(a) Allowance of Credit- For purposes of section 38, in the case of a manufacturer, the qualified flexible fuel motor vehicle production credit determined under this section for any taxable year is an amount equal to the incremental flexible fuel motor vehicle cost for each qualified flexible fuel motor vehicle produced in the United States by the manufacturer during the taxable year.

'(b) Incremental Flexible Fuel Motor Vehicle Cost- With respect to any qualified flexible fuel motor vehicle, the incremental flexible fuel motor vehicle cost is an amount equal to the lesser of—

'(1) the excess of—

'(A) the cost of producing such qualified flexible fuel motor vehicle, over

'(B) the cost of producing such motor vehicle if such motor vehicle was not a qualified flexible fuel motor vehicle, or

'(2) $100.

'(c) Qualified Flexible Fuel Motor Vehicle- For purposes of this section, the term 'qualified flexible fuel motor vehicle' means a flexible fuel motor vehicle—

'(1) the production of which is not required for the manufacturer to meet—

'(A) the maximum credit allowable for vehicles described in paragraph (2) in determining the fleet average fuel economy requirements (as determined under section 32904 of title 49, United States Code) of the manufacturer for the model year ending in the taxable year, or

'(B) the requirements of any other provision of Federal law, and

'(2) which is designed so that the vehicle is propelled by an engine which can use as a fuel a gasoline mixture of which 85 percent (or another percentage of not less than 70 percent, as the Secretary may determine, by rule, to provide for requirements relating to cold start, safety, or vehicle functions) of the volume of consists of ethanol.

'(d) Other Definitions and Special Rules- For purposes of this section—

'(1) MOTOR VEHICLE- The term 'motor vehicle' has the meaning given such term by section 30(c)(2).

'(2) MANUFACTURER- The term 'manufacturer' has the meaning given such term in regulations prescribed by the Administrator of the Environmental Protection Agency for purposes of the administration of title II of the Clean Air Act (42 U.S.C. 7521 et seq.).

'(3) REDUCTION IN BASIS- For purposes of this subtitle, if a credit is allowed under this section for any expenditure with respect to any property, the increase in the basis of such property which would (but for this paragraph) result from such expenditure shall be reduced by the amount of the credit so allowed.

'(4) NO DOUBLE BENEFIT- The amount of any deduction or credit allowable under this chapter (other than the credits allowable under this section and section 30B) shall be reduced by the amount of credit allowed under subsection (a) for such vehicle for the taxable year.

'(5) ELECTION NOT TO TAKE CREDIT- No credit shall be allowed under subsection (a) for any vehicle if the taxpayer elects to not have this section apply to such vehicle.

'(6) TERMINATION- This section shall not apply to any vehicle produced after December 31, 2011.

'(7) CROSS REFERENCE- For an election to claim certain minimum tax credits in lieu of the credit determined under this section, see section 53(e).'.

(b) Credit Allowed Against the Alternative Minimum Tax- Section 38(c)(4)(B) of the Internal Revenue Code of 1986 (defining specified credits) is amended by striking the period at the end of clause (ii)(II) and inserting ', and', and by adding at the end the following new clause:

'(iii) the credit determined under section 45O.'.

(c) Election To Use Additional AMT Credit- Section 53 of the Internal Revenue Code of 1986 (relating to credit for prior year minimum tax liability) is amended by adding at the end the following new subsection:

'(e) Additional Credit in Lieu of Flexible Fuel Motor Vehicle Credit-

'(1) IN GENERAL- In the case of a taxpayer making an election under this subsection for a taxable year, the amount otherwise determined under subsection (c) shall be increased by any amount of the credit determined under section 45O for such taxable year which the taxpayer elects not to claim pursuant to such election.

'(2) ELECTION- A taxpayer may make an election for any taxable year not to claim any amount of the credit allowable under section 45O with respect to property produced by the taxpayer during such taxable year. An election under this subsection may only be revoked with the consent of the Secretary.

'(3) CREDIT REFUNDABLE- The aggregate increase in the credit allowed by this section for any taxable year by reason of this subsection shall for purposes of this title (other than subsection (b)(2) of this section) be treated as a credit allowed to the taxpayer under subpart C.'.

(d) Conforming Amendments- Section 38(b) of the Internal Revenue Code of 1986 is amended by striking 'plus' at the end of paragraph (30), by striking the period at the end of paragraph (31) and inserting ', plus', and by adding at the end the following new paragraph:

'(32) the qualified flexible fuel motor vehicle production credit determined under section 45N, plus'.

(e) Clerical Amendment- The table of sections for subpart D of part IV of subchapter A of chapter 1 of the Internal Revenue Code of 1986 is amended by adding at the end the following new item:

'Sec. 45O. Production of qualified flexible fuel motor vehicles.'.

(f) Effective Date- The amendments made by this section shall apply to motor vehicles produced in model years ending after the date of the enactment of this Act.

SEC. 4. INCENTIVES FOR THE RETAIL SALE OF ALTERNATIVE FUELS AS MOTOR VEHICLE FUEL.

(a) In General- Subpart D of part IV of subchapter A of chapter 1 of the Internal Revenue Code of 1986 (relating to business related credits) is amended by inserting after section 40A the following new section:

'SEC. 40B. CREDIT FOR RETAIL SALE OF ALTERNATIVE FUELS AS MOTOR VEHICLE FUEL.

'(a) General Rule- The alternative fuel retail sales credit for any taxable year is the applicable amount for each gallon of alternative fuel sold at retail by the taxpayer during such year.

'(b) Applicable Amount- For purposes of this section, the applicable amount shall be determined in accordance with the following table:

'In the case of any sale:	The applicable amount for each gallon is:
Before 2010	35 cents
During 2010 or 2011	20 cents
During 2012	10 cents.

'(c) Definitions- For purposes of this section—

'(1) ALTERNATIVE FUEL- The term 'alternative fuel' means any fuel at least 85 percent (or another percentage of not less than 70 percent, as the Secretary may determine, by rule, to provide for requirements relating to cold start, safety, or vehicle functions) of the volume of which consists of ethanol.

'(2) SOLD AT RETAIL-

'(A) IN GENERAL- The term 'sold at retail' means the sale, for a purpose other than resale, after manufacture, production, or importation.

'(B) USE TREATED AS SALE- If any person uses alternative fuel (including any use after importation) as a fuel to propel any qualified alternative fuel motor vehicle (as defined in this section) before such fuel is sold at retail, then such use shall be treated in the same manner as if such fuel were sold at retail as a fuel to propel such a vehicle by such person.

'(3) QUALIFIED ALTERNATIVE FUEL MOTOR VEHICLE- The term 'new qualified alternative fuel motor vehicle' means any motor vehicle—

'(A) which is capable of operating on an alternative fuel,

'(B) the original use of which commences with the taxpayer,

'(C) which is acquired by the taxpayer for use or lease, but not for resale, and

'(D) which is made by a manufacturer.

'(d) Election To Pass Credit- A person which sells alternative fuel at retail may elect to pass the credit allowable under this section to the purchaser of such fuel or, in the event the purchaser is a tax-exempt entity or otherwise declines to accept such credit, to the person which supplied such fuel, under rules established by the Secretary.

'(e) Pass-Thru in the Case of Estates and Trusts- Under regulations prescribed by the Secretary, rules similar to the rules of subsection (d) of section 52 shall apply.

'(f) Termination- This section shall not apply to any fuel sold at retail after December 31, 2012.'.

(b) Credit Treated as Business Credit- Section 38(b) of the Internal Revenue Code of 1986 (relating to current year business credit), as amended by section 4(d), is amended by striking 'plus' at the end of paragraph (31), by striking the period at the end of paragraph (32) and inserting ', plus', and by adding at the end the following new paragraph:

'(33) the alternative fuel retail sales credit determined under section 40B(a).'.

(c) Clerical Amendment- The table of sections for subpart D of part IV of subchapter A of chapter 1 of the Internal Revenue Code of 1986 is amended by inserting after the item relating to section 40A the following new item:

'Sec. 40B. Credit for retail sale of alternative fuels as motor vehicle fuel.'.

(d) Effective Date- The amendments made by this section shall apply to fuel sold at retail after the date of enactment of this Act, in taxable years ending after such date.

SEC. 5. FREEDOM FOR FUEL FRANCHISERS.

(a) Prohibition on Restriction of Installation of Alternative Fuel Pumps-

(1) IN GENERAL- Title I of the Petroleum Marketing Practices Act (15 U.S.C. 2801 et seq.) is amended by adding at the end the following:

'SEC. 107. PROHIBITION ON RESTRICTION OF INSTALLATION OF ALTERNATIVE FUEL PUMPS.

'(a) Definition- In this section:

'(1) ALTERNATIVE FUEL- The term 'alternative fuel' means any fuel—

'(A) at least 85 percent of the volume of which consists of ethanol, natural gas, compressed natural gas, liquefied natural gas, liquefied petroleum gas, hydrogen, or any combination of those fuels; or

'(B) any mixture of biodiesel (as defined in section 40A(d)(1) of the Internal Revenue Code of 1986) and diesel fuel (as defined in section 4083(a)(3) of the Internal Revenue Code of 1986), determined without regard to any use of kerosene and containing at least 20 percent biodiesel.

'(2) FRANCHISE-RELATED DOCUMENT- The term 'franchise-related document' means—

'(A) a franchise under this Act; and

'(B) any other contract or directive of a franchisor relating to terms or conditions of the sale of fuel by a franchisee.

'(b) Prohibitions-

'(1) IN GENERAL- Notwithstanding any provision of a franchise-related document in effect on the date of enactment of this section, no franchisee or affiliate of a franchisee shall be restricted from—

'(A) installing on the marketing premises of the franchisee an alternative fuel pump;

'(B) converting an existing tank and pump on the marketing premises of the franchisee for alternative fuel use;

'(C) advertising (including through the use of signage or logos) the sale of any alternative fuel; or

'(D) selling alternative fuel in any specified area on the marketing premises of the franchisee (including any area in which a name or logo of a franchisor or any other entity appears).

'(2) ENFORCEMENT- Any restriction described in paragraph (1) that is contained in a franchise-related document and in effect on the date of enactment of this section—

'(A) shall be considered to be null and void as of that date; and

'(B) shall not be enforced under section 105.

'(c) Exception to 3-Grade Requirement- No franchise-related document that requires that 3 grades of gasoline be sold by the applicable franchisee shall prevent the franchisee from selling an alternative fuel in lieu of 1 grade of gasoline.'.

(2) CONFORMING AMENDMENTS-

(A) IN GENERAL- Section 101(13) of the Petroleum Marketing Practices Act (15 U.S.C. 2801(13)) is amended by adjusting the indentation of subparagraph (C) appropriately.

(B) TABLE OF CONTENTS- The table of contents of the Petroleum Marketing Practices Act (15 U.S.C. 2801 note) is amended—

(i) by inserting after the item relating to section 106 the following:

'Sec. 107. Prohibition on restriction of installation of alternative fuel pumps.';

and

(ii) by striking the item relating to section 202 and inserting the following:

'Sec. 202. Automotive fuel rating testing and disclosure requirements.'.

(b) Application of Gasohol Competition Act of 1980- Section 26 of the Clayton Act (15 U.S.C. 26a) is amended—

(1) by redesignating subsection (c) as subsection (d);

(2) by inserting after subsection (b) the following:

'(c) Restriction Prohibited- For purposes of subsection (a), restricting the right of a franchisee to install on the premises of that franchisee qualified alternative fuel vehicle refueling property (as defined in section 30C(c) of the Internal Revenue Code of 1986) shall be considered an unlawful restriction.'; and

(3) in subsection (d) (as redesignated by paragraph (1)), by striking '(d) As used in this section,' and inserting the following:

SEC. 6. ALTERNATIVE DIESEL FUEL CONTENT OF DIESEL.

(a) Findings- Congress finds that—

(1) section 211(o) of the Clean Air Act (42 U.S.C. 7535(o)) (as amended by section 1501 of the Energy Policy Act of 2005 (Public Law 109-58)) established a renewable fuel program under which entities in the petroleum sector are required to blend renewable fuels into motor vehicle fuel based on the gasoline motor pool;

(2) the need for energy diversification is greater as of the date of enactment of this Act than it was only months before the date of enactment of the Energy Policy Act (Public Law 109-58; 119 Stat. 594); and

(3)(A) the renewable fuel program under section 211(o) of the Clean Air Act requires a small percentage of the gasoline motor pool, totaling nearly 140,000,000,000 gallons, to contain a renewable fuel; and

(B) the small percentage requirement described in subparagraph (A) does not include the 40,000,000,000-gallon diesel motor pool.

(b) Alternative Diesel Fuel Program for Diesel Motor Pool- Section 211 of the Clean Air Act (42 U.S.C. 7545) is amended by inserting after subsection (o) the following:

'(p) Alternative Diesel Fuel Program for Diesel Motor Pool-

'(1) DEFINITION OF ALTERNATIVE DIESEL FUEL-

'(A) IN GENERAL- In this subsection, the term 'alternative diesel fuel' means biodiesel (as defined in section 312(f) of the Energy Policy Act of 1992 (42 U.S.C. 13220(f))) and any blending components derived from alternative fuel (provided that only the alternative fuel portion of any such blending component shall be considered to be part of the applicable volume under the alternative diesel fuel program established by this subsection).

'(B) INCLUSIONS- The term 'alternative diesel fuel' includes a diesel fuel substitute produced from—

'(i) animal fat;

'(ii) plant oil;

'(iii) recycled yellow grease;

'(iv) single-cell or microbial oil;

'(v) thermal depolymerization;

'(vi) thermochemical conversion;

'(vii) a coal-to-liquid process (including the Fischer-Tropsch process) that provides for the sequestration of carbon emissions;

'(viii) a diesel-ethanol blend of not less than 7 percent ethanol; or

'(ix) sugar, starch, or cellulosic biomass.

'(2) ALTERNATIVE DIESEL FUEL PROGRAM-

'(A) REGULATIONS-

'(i) IN GENERAL- Not later than 1 year after the date of enactment of this subsection, the Administrator shall promulgate regulations to ensure that diesel sold or introduced into commerce in the United States (except in noncontiguous States or territories), on an annual average basis, contains the applicable volume of alternative diesel fuel determined in accordance with subparagraph (B).

'(ii) PROVISIONS OF REGULATIONS- Regardless of the date of promulgation, the regulations promulgated under clause (i)—

'(I) shall contain compliance provisions applicable to refineries, blenders, distributors, and importers, as appropriate, to ensure that the requirements of this paragraph are met; but

'(II) shall not—

'(aa) restrict geographic areas in which alternative diesel fuel may be used; or

'(bb) impose any per-gallon obligation for the use of alternative diesel fuel.

'(iii) REQUIREMENT IN CASE OF FAILURE TO PROMULGATE REGU-LATIONS- If the Administrator fails to promulgate regulations under clause (i), the percentage of alternative diesel fuel in the diesel motor pool sold or dispensed to consumers in the United States, on a volume basis, shall be 0.6 percent for calendar year 2009.

'(B) APPLICABLE VOLUME-

'(i) CALENDAR YEARS 2009 THROUGH 2016- For the purpose of subparagraph (A), the applicable volume for any of calendar years 2009 through 2016 shall be determined in accordance with the following table:

'Applicable volume of Alternative diesel fuel in diesel motor pool (in millions of gallons): Calendar year:

250	—	2009
500	—	2010
750	—	2011
1,000	—	2012
1,250	—	2013
1,500	—	2014
1,750	—	2015
2,000	—	2016.

'(ii) CALENDAR YEAR 2017 AND THEREAFTER- The applicable volume for calendar year 2017 and each calendar year thereafter shall be determined by the Administrator, in coordination with the Secretary of Agriculture and the Secretary of Energy, based on a review of the implementation of the program during calendar years 2009 through 2016, including a review of—

'(I) the impact of the use of alternative diesel fuels on the environment, air quality, energy security, job creation, and rural economic development; and

'(II) the expected annual rate of future production of alternative diesel fuels to be used as a blend component or replacement to the diesel motor pool.

'(iii) MINIMUM APPLICABLE VOLUME- For the purpose of subparagraph (A), the applicable volume for calendar year 2017 and each calendar year thereafter shall be equal to the product obtained by multiplying—

'(I) the number of gallons of diesel that the Administrator estimates will be sold or introduced into commerce during the calendar year; and

'(II) the ratio that—

'(aa) 2,000,000,000 gallons of alternative diesel fuel; bears to '(bb) the number of gallons of diesel sold or introduced into commerce during calendar year 2016.

'(3) APPLICABLE PERCENTAGES-

'(A) PROVISION OF ESTIMATE OF VOLUMES OF DIESEL SALES- Not later than October 31 of each of calendar years 2008 through 2016, the Administrator of the Energy Information Administration shall provide to the Administrator an estimate, with respect to the following calendar year, of the volumes of diesel projected to be sold or introduced into commerce in the United States.

'(B) DETERMINATION OF APPLICABLE PERCENTAGES-

'(i) IN GENERAL- Not later than November 30 of each of calendar years 2009 through 2016, based on the estimate provided under subparagraph (A), the Administrator shall determine and publish in the Federal Register, with respect to the following calendar year, the alternative diesel fuel obligation that ensures that the requirements of paragraph (2) are met.

'(ii) REQUIRED ELEMENTS- The alternative diesel fuel obligation determined for a calendar year under clause (i) shall—

'(I) be applicable to refineries, blenders, and importers, as appropriate;

'(II) be expressed in terms of a volume percentage of diesel sold or introduced into commerce in the United States; and

'(III) subject to subparagraph (C), consist of a single applicable percentage that applies to all categories of persons described in subclause (I).

'(C) ADJUSTMENTS- In determining the applicable percentage for a calendar year, the Administrator shall make adjustments to prevent the imposition of redundant obligations on any person described in subparagraph (B)(ii)(I).

'(4) CREDIT PROGRAM-

'(A) IN GENERAL- The regulations promulgated pursuant to paragraph (2)(A) shall provide for the generation of an appropriate amount of credits by any person that refines, blends, or imports diesel that contains a quantity of alternative diesel fuel that is greater than the quantity required under paragraph (2).

'(B) USE OF CREDITS- A person that generates a credit under subparagraph (A) may use the credit, or transfer all or a portion of the credit to another person, for the purpose of complying with regulations promulgated pursuant to paragraph (2).

'(C) DURATION OF CREDITS- A credit generated under this paragraph shall be valid during the 1-year period beginning on the date on which the credit is generated.

'(D) INABILITY TO GENERATE OR PURCHASE SUFFICIENT CREDITS- The regulations promulgated pursuant to paragraph (2)(A) shall include provisions allowing any person that is unable to generate or purchase sufficient credits under subparagraph (A) to meet the requirements of paragraph (2) by carrying forward a credit generated during a previous year on the condition that the person, during the calendar year following the year in which the alternative diesel fuel deficit is created—

'(i) achieves compliance with the alternative diesel fuel requirement under paragraph (2); and

'(ii) generates or purchases additional credits under subparagraph (A) to offset the deficit of the previous year.

'(5) WAIVERS-

'(A) IN GENERAL- The Administrator, in consultation with the Secretary of Agriculture and the Secretary of Energy, may waive the requirements of paragraph (2) in whole or in part on receipt of a petition of 1 or more States by reducing the national quantity of alternative diesel fuel for the diesel motor pool required under paragraph (2) based on a determination by the Administrator, after public notice and opportunity for comment, that—

'(i) implementation of the requirement would severely harm the economy or environment of a State, a region, or the United States; or

'(ii) there is an inadequate domestic supply of alternative diesel fuel.

'(B) PETITIONS FOR WAIVERS- Not later than 90 days after the date on which the Administrator receives a petition under subparagraph (A), the Administrator, in consultation with the Secretary of Agriculture and the Secretary of Energy, shall approve or disapprove the petition.

'(C) TERMINATION OF WAIVERS-

'(i) IN GENERAL- Except as provided in clause (ii), a waiver under subparagraph (A) shall terminate on the date that is 1 year after the date on which the waiver is provided.

'(ii) EXCEPTION- The Administrator, in consultation with the Secretary of Agriculture and the Secretary of Energy, may extend a waiver under subparagraph (A), as the Administrator determines to be appropriate.'.

(c) Penalties and Enforcement- Section 211(d) of the Clean Air Act (42 U.S.C. 7545(d)) is amended—

(1) in paragraph (1), by striking 'or (o)' each place it appears and inserting '(o), or (p)'; and

(2) in paragraph (2), by striking 'and (o)' each place it appears and inserting '(o), and (p)'.

(d) Technical Amendments- Section 211 of the Clean Air Act (42 U.S.C. 7545) is amended—

(1) in subsection (i)(4), by striking 'section 324' each place it appears and inserting 'section 325';

(2) in subsection (k)(10), by indenting subparagraphs (E) and (F) appropriately;

(3) in subsection (n), by striking 'section 219(2)' and inserting 'section 216(2)';

(4) by redesignating the second subsection (r) and subsection (s) as subsections (s) and (t), respectively; and

(5) in subsection (t)(1) (as redesignated by paragraph (4)), by striking 'this subtitle' and inserting 'this part'.

SEC. 7. EXCISE TAX CREDIT FOR PRODUCTION OF CELLULOSIC BIO-MASS ETHANOL.

(a) Allowance of Excise Tax Credit-

(1) IN GENERAL- Section 6426 of the Internal Revenue Code of 1986 (relating to credit for alcohol fuel, biodiesel, and alternative fuel mixtures) is amended by redesignating subsections (f) and (g) as subsections (g) and (h), respectively, and by inserting after subsection (e) the following new subsection:

'(f) Cellulosic Biomass Ethanol Credit-

'(1) IN GENERAL- For purposes of this section, in the case of a cellulosic biomass ethanol producer, the cellulosic biomass ethanol credit is the product of—

'(A) the product of 51 cents times the equivalent number of gallons of renewable fuel specified in section 211(o)(4) of the Clean Air Act, times

'(B) the number of gallons of qualified cellulosic biomass ethanol fuel production of such producer.

'(2) DEFINITIONS-

'(A) CELLULOSIC BIOMASS ETHANOL- The term 'cellulosic biomass ethanol' has the meaning given such term under section 211(o)(1)(A) of the Clean Air Act.

'(B) QUALIFIED CELLULOSIC BIOMASS ETHANOL FUEL PRODUCTION- The term 'qualified cellulosic biomass ethanol fuel production' means any alcohol which is cellulosic biomass ethanol which during the taxable year—

'(i) is sold by the producer to another person —

'(I) for use by such other person in the production of an alcohol fuel mixture in such other person's trade or business (other than casual off-farm production),

'(II) for use by such other person as a fuel in a trade or business, or

'(III) who sells such cellulosic biomass ethanol at retail to another person and places such ethanol in the fuel tank of such other person, or

'(ii) is used or sold by the producer for any purpose described in clause (i).

'(3) DENIAL OF DOUBLE BENEFIT- No credit shall be allowed under subsection (b) or (c) to any taxpayer with respect to any fuel to the extent that a credit has been allowed with respect to such fuel to any taxpayer under this subsection or a payment has been made with respect to such fuel under section 6427(e).

'(4) TERMINATION- This section shall not apply to any sale or use for any period after December 31, 2008.'.

(2) CONFORMING AMENDMENTS-

(A) Section 6426(a) of such Code is amended—

(i) by striking 'subsection (d)' in paragraph (2) and inserting 'subsections (d) and (f)', and

(ii) by striking 'and (e)' in the last sentence and inserting ', (e), and (f)'.

(B) The heading for section 6426 of such Code is amended to read as follows:

'SEC. 6426. CREDIT FOR CERTAIN FUELS AND FUEL MIXTURES.'.

(C) The table of section for subchapter B of chapter 65 of such Code is amended by striking the item relating to section 6426 and inserting the following new item:

'Sec. 6426. Credit for certain fuels and fuel mixtures.'.

(b) Cellulosic Biomass Ethanol Not Used for a Taxable Purpose-

(1) IN GENERAL- Section 6427(e) of the Internal Revenue Code of 1986 is amended by redesignating paragraphs (3) through (5) as paragraphs (4) through (6), respectively, and by inserting after paragraph (2) the following new paragraph:

'(3) CELLULOSIC BIOMASS ETHANOL- If any person sells or uses cellulosic biomass ethanol (as defined in section 6426(f)(2)(A)) for a purpose described in section 6426(f)(2)(B) in such person's trade or business, the Secretary shall pay (without interest) to such person an amount equal to the cellulosic biomass ethanol credit with respect to such fuel.'.

(2) DENIAL OF DOUBLE BENEFIT- Paragraph (4) of section 6427(e) of such Code, as redesignated by paragraph (1), is amended to read as follows:

'(4) COORDINATION WITH OTHER REPAYMENT PROVISIONS-

'(A) IN GENERAL- No amount shall be payable under paragraph (1), (2), or (3) with respect to any mixture, alternative fuel, or cellulosic biomass ethanol with respect to which an amount is allowed as a credit under section 6426.

'(B) CELLULOSIC BIOMASS ETHANOL- No amount shall be payable under paragraph (1) or (2) with respect to any cellulosic biomass ethanol if a payment has been made with respect to such ethanol under paragraph (3).'.

(3) TERMINATION- Paragraph (6) of section 6427(e) of such Code, as redesignated by paragraph (1), is amended by striking 'and' at the end of subparagraph (C), by striking the period at the end of subparagraph (D) and inserting ', and', and by adding at the end the following new subparagraph:

'(E) any cellulosic biomass ethanol credit (as defined in section 6426(f)(2)(A)) sold or used after December 31, 2008.'.

(4) CONFORMING AMENDMENT- Paragraph (5) of section 6427(e) of such Code, as redesignated by paragraph (1), is amended by striking 'or alternative fuel mixture credit' and inserting ', alternative fuel mixture credit, or cellulosic biomass ethanol credit'.

(c) Effective Date- The amendments made by this section shall apply to fuel sold or used after the date of the enactment of this Act.

SEC. 8. INCENTIVE FOR FEDERAL AND STATE FLEETS FOR MEDIUM AND HEAVY DUTY HYBRIDS.

Section 301 of the Energy Policy Act of 1992 (42 U.S.C. 13211) is amended—

(1) in paragraph (3), by striking 'or a dual fueled vehicle' and inserting ', a dual fueled vehicle, or a medium or heavy duty vehicle that is a hybrid vehicle';

(2) by redesignating paragraphs (11), (12), (13), and (14) as paragraphs (12), (14), (15), and (16), respectively;

(3) by inserting after paragraph (10) the following:

'(11) the term 'hybrid vehicle' means a vehicle powered both by a diesel or gasoline engine and an electric motor that is recharged as the vehicle operates;'; and

(4) by inserting after paragraph (12) (as redesignated by paragraph (2)) the following:

'(13) the term 'medium or heavy duty vehicle' means a vehicle that—

'(A) in the case of a medium duty vehicle, has a gross vehicle weight rating of more than 8,500 pounds but not more than 14,000 pounds; and

'(B) in the case of a heavy duty vehicle, has a gross vehicle weight rating of more than 14,000 pounds;'.

SEC. 9. CREDIT FOR QUALIFYING ETHANOL BLENDING AND PROCESSING EQUIPMENT.

(a) Allowance of Qualifying Ethanol Blending and Processing Equipment Credit- Section 46 of the Internal Revenue Code of 1986 (relating to amount of credit) is amended by striking 'and' at the end of paragraph (3), by striking the period at the end of paragraph (4) and inserting ', and', and by adding at the end the following new paragraph:

'(5) the qualifying ethanol blending and processing equipment credit.'.

(b) Amount of Qualifying Ethanol Blending and Processing Equipment Credit- Subpart E of part IV of subchapter A of chapter 1 of the Internal Revenue Code of 1986 (relating to rules for computing investment credit) is amended by inserting after section 48B the following new section:

'SEC. 48C. QUALIFYING ETHANOL BLENDING AND PROCESSING EQUIPMENT.

'(a) In General- For purposes of section 46, the qualifying ethanol blending and processing equipment credit for any taxable year is an amount equal to 50 percent of the basis of the qualifying ethanol blending and processing equipment placed in service at a qualifying facility during such taxable year.

'(b) Limitation- The credit allowed under subsection (a) for qualifying ethanol blending and processing equipment placed in service at any 1 qualifying facility during any taxable year shall not exceed $2,000,000.

'(c) Qualifying Ethanol Blending and Processing Equipment- For purposes of this section, the term 'qualifying ethanol blending and processing equipment' means any technology installed in or on a qualifying facility for blending ethanol with petroleum fuels for the purpose of direct retail sale, including in-line blending equipment, storage tanks, pumps and piping for denaturants, and load-out equipment.

'(d) Qualifying Facility- For purposes of this section, the term 'qualifying facility' means any facility which produces not less than 1,000,000 gallons of ethanol during the taxable year.

'(e) Special Rule for Certain Subsidized Property- Rules similar to section 48(a)(4) shall apply for purposes of this section.

'(f) Certain Qualified Progress Expenditures Rules Made Applicable- Rules similar to the rules of subsections (c)(4) and (d) of section 46 (as in effect on the day before the enactment of the Revenue Reconciliation Act of 1990) shall apply for purposes of this subsection.

'(g) Termination- This section shall not apply to property placed in service after December 31, 2014.'.

(c) Recapture of Credit Where Emissions Reduction Offset Is Sold- Paragraph (1) of section 50(a) of the Internal Revenue Code of 1986 is amended by redesignating subparagraph (B) as subparagraph (C) and by inserting after subparagraph (A) the following new subparagraph:

'(B) SPECIAL RULE FOR QUALIFYING ETHANOL BLENDING AND PROCESSING EQUIPMENT- For purposes of subparagraph (A), any investment property which is qualifying ethanol blending and processing equipment (as defined in section 48C(c)) shall cease to be investment credit property with respect to a taxpayer if such taxpayer receives a payment in exchange for a credit for emission reductions attributable to such qualifying pollution control equipment for purposes of an offset requirement under part D of title I of the Clean Air Act.'.

(d) Special Rule for Basis Reduction; Recapture of Credit- Paragraph (3) of section 50(c) of the Internal Revenue Code of 1986 (relating to basis adjustment to investment credit property) is amended by inserting 'or qualifying ethanol blending and processing equipment credit' after 'energy credit'.

(e) Certain Nonrecourse Financing Excluded From Credit Base- Section 49(a)(1)(C) of the Internal Revenue Code of 1986 (defining credit base) is amended by striking 'and' at the end of clause (iii), by striking the period at the end of clause (iv) and inserting ', and', and by adding at the end the following new clause:

'(v) the basis of any property which is part of any qualifying ethanol blending and processing equipment under section 48C.'.

(f) Effective Date- The amendments made by this section shall apply to property placed in service after December 31, 2007, in taxable years ending after such date, under rules similar to the rules of section 48(m) of the Internal Revenue Code of 1986 (as in effect on the day before the date of the enactment of the Revenue Reconciliation Act of 1990).

SEC. 10. PUBLIC ACCESS TO FEDERAL ALTERNATIVE REFUELING STATIONS.

(a) Definitions- In this section:

(1) ALTERNATIVE FUEL REFUELING STATION- The term 'alternative fuel refueling station' has the meaning given the term 'qualified alternative fuel vehicle refueling property' in section 30C(c)(1) of the Internal Revenue Code of 1986.

(2) SECRETARY- The term 'Secretary' means the Secretary of Energy.

(b) Access to Federal Alternative Refueling Stations- Not later than 18 months after the date of enactment of this Act—

(1) except as provided in subsection (d)(1), any Federal property that includes at least 1 fuel refueling station shall include at least 1 alternative fuel refueling station; and

(2) except as provided in subsection (d)(2), any alternative fuel refueling station located on property owned by the Federal government shall permit full public access for the purpose of refueling using alternative fuel.

(c) Duration- The requirements described in subsection (b) shall remain in effect until the sooner of—

(1) the date that is 7 years after the date of enactment of this Act; or

(2) the date on which the Secretary determines that not less than 5 percent of the commercial refueling infrastructure in the United States offers alternative fuels to the general public.

(d) Exceptions-

(1) WAIVER- Subsection (b)(1) shall not apply to any Federal property under the jurisdiction of a Federal agency if the Secretary determines that alternative fuel is not reasonably available to retail purchasers of the fuel, as certified by the head of the agency to the Secretary.

(2) NATIONAL SECURITY EXEMPTION- Subsection (b)(2) does not apply to property of the Federal government that the Secretary, in consultation with the Secretary of Defense, has certified must be exempt for national security reasons.

(e) Report- Not later than October 31 of each year beginning after the date of enactment of this Act, the President shall submit to Congress a report that describes the progress of the agencies of the Federal Government (including the Executive Office of the President) in complying with—

(1) the Energy Policy Act of 1992 (42 U.S.C. 13201 et seq.);

(2) Executive Order 13149 (65 Fed. Reg. 24595; relating to greening the government through Federal fleet and transportation efficiency); and

(3) the fueling center requirements of this section.

SEC. 11. PURCHASE OF CLEAN FUEL BUSES.

(a) In General- Chapter 53 of title 49, United States Code, is amended by inserting after section 5325 the following:

'Sec. 5326. Purchase of clean fuel buses

'(a) Definitions- In this section:

'(1) ALTERNATIVE DIESEL FUEL-

'(A) IN GENERAL- The term 'alternative diesel fuel' means—

'(i) biodiesel (as defined in section 312(f) of the Energy Policy Act of 1992 (42 U.S.C. 13220(f))); and '(ii) any blending components derived from alternative fuel.

'(B) INCLUSIONS- The term 'alternative diesel fuel' includes a diesel fuel substitute produced from—

'(i) animal fat;

'(ii) plant oil;

'(iii) recycled yellow grease;

'(iv) single-cell or microbial oil;

'(v) thermal depolymerization;

'(vi) thermochemical conversion;

'(vii) a coal-to-liquid process (including the Fischer-Tropsch process) that provides for the sequestration of carbon emissions; or

'(viii) a diesel-ethanol blend of not less than 7 percent ethanol.

'(2) CELLULOSIC BIOMASS ETHANOL- The term 'cellulosic biomass ethanol' means ethanol derived from any lignocellulosic or hemicellulosic matter that is available on a renewable or recurring basis, including—

'(A) dedicated energy crops and trees;

'(B) wood and wood residues;

'(C) plants;

'(D) grasses;

'(E) agricultural residues;

'(F) fibers;

'(G) animal wastes and other waste materials; and

'(H) municipal solid waste.

'(3) CLEAN FUEL BUS- The term 'clean fuel bus' means a vehicle that—

'(A) is capable of being powered by—

'(i) compressed natural gas;

'(ii) liquefied natural gas;

'(iii) 1 or more batteries;

'(iv) a fuel that is composed of at least 85 percent ethanol (or another percentage of not less than 70 percent, as the Secretary may determine, by rule, to provide for requirements relating to cold start, safety, or vehicle functions);

'(v) electricity (including a hybrid electric or plug-in hybrid electric vehicle);

'(vi) a fuel cell;

'(vii) a fuel that is composed of at least 22 percent biodiesel (as defined in section 312(f) of the Energy Policy Act of 1992 (42 U.S.C. 13220(f)) (or another percentage of not less than 10 percent, as the Secretary may determine, by rule, to provide for requirements relating to cold start, safety, or vehicle functions);

'(viii) ultra-low sulfur diesel; or

'(ix) liquid fuel manufactured with a coal feedstock; and

'(B) has been certified by the Administrator of the Environmental Protection Agency to significantly reduce harmful emissions, particularly in a nonattainment area (as defined in section 171 of the Clean Air Act (42 U.S.C. 7501)).

'(4) QUALIFIED ALTERNATIVE FUEL PRODUCER- The term 'qualified alternative fuel producer' means a producer of qualified fuels that, during the applicable taxable year—

'(A) are sold by the producer to another person—

'(i) for use by the person in the production of a mixture of qualified fuels in the trade or business of the person (other than casual off-farm production);

'(ii) for use by the other person as a fuel in a trade or business; or

'(iii) that—

'(I) sells to another person the qualified fuel at retail; and

'(II) places the qualified fuel in the fuel tank of the person that purchased the qualified fuel; or

'(B) are used or sold by the producer for any purpose described in subparagraph (A).

'(5) QUALIFIED FUEL- The term 'qualified fuel' includes—

'(A) cellulosic biomass ethanol;

'(B) ethanol produced in facilities in which animal waste or other waste materials are digested or otherwise used to displace at least 90 percent of the fossil fuels that would otherwise be used in the production of ethanol;

'(C) renewable fuels;

'(D) alternative diesel fuels;

'(E) sugar, starch, or cellulosic biomass; and

'(F) any other fuel that is not substantially petroleum.

'(6) RENEWABLE FUEL- The term 'renewable fuel' means fuel, at least 85 percent of the volume of which—

'(A)(i) is produced from grain, starch, oilseeds, vegetable, animal, or fish materials including fats, greases, and oils, sugarcane, sugar beets, sugar components, tobacco, potatoes, or other biomass; or

'(ii) is natural gas produced from a biogas source, including a landfill, sewage waste treatment plant, feedlot, or other place in which decaying organic material is found; and

'(B) is used to substantially replace or reduce the quantity of fossil fuel present in a fuel mixture used to operate a motor vehicle.

'(b) Purchase of Buses- Subject to subsections (c) and (d), beginning on the date that is 2 years after the date of enactment of this section, a bus purchased using funds made available from the Mass Transit Account of the Highway Trust Fund shall be a clean fuel bus.

'(c) Ultra-Low Sulfur Diesel-

'(1) IN GENERAL- Except as provided in paragraph (2), not more than 20 percent of the amount of the funds provided to a recipient to purchase buses under this section may be used by the recipient to purchase clean fuel buses that are capable of being powered by a fuel described in clause (iv), (vii), (viii), or (ix) of subsection (a)(3)(A).

'(2) EXCEPTION- Paragraph (1) shall not apply if the recipient enters into a 3-year purchase agreement with a qualified alternative fuel producer to acquire qualified fuels in a volume sufficient to power the clean fuel buses purchased using amounts made available under this section.

'(d) Use of Certain Alternative Fuels-

'(1) IN GENERAL- To be eligible to receive funds under subsection (c)(2) for the purchase of a clean fuel bus that is capable of being powered by a fuel described in clause (iv), (vii), or (ix) of subsection (a)(3)(A), an applicant or recipient shall submit to the Secretary—

'(A) a certification that the applicant will operate the clean fuel bus only with the fuel at all times in accordance with the fuel capacity and use of the fuel recommended by the manufacturer of the clean fuel bus; and

'(B) not later than 180 days after the purchase of the clean fuel bus and every 180 days thereafter, a report that documents that the fuel was used in accordance with subparagraph (A) during the 180-day period ending on the date of the report.

'(2) NONCOMPLIANCE- Failure of an applicant or recipient of funds to provide the certification or documentation required under paragraph (1) shall—

'(A) be considered a violation of the agreement to receive the funds; and

'(B) require the applicant or recipient to reimburse the Secretary the full amount of the funds not later than 90 days after the Secretary has determined that a violation has occurred.'.

(b) Conforming Amendment- The analysis for chapter 53 is amended by inserting after the item relating to section 5325 the following:

'5326. Clean fuel buses.'.

SEC. 12. DOMESTIC FUEL PRODUCTION VOLUMES TO MEET DEPARTMENT OF DEFENSE NEEDS.

Section 2922d of title 10, United States Code is amended—

(1) in the heading, by striking 'and tar sands' and inserting 'tar sands, and other sources';

(2) in subsection (a), by striking 'fuel produced, in whole or in part, from coal, oil shale, and tar sands (referred to in this section as a 'covered fuel') that are extracted by either mining or in-situ methods and refined or otherwise processed in the United

States' and inserting 'fuel produced, in whole or in part, from coal, oil shale, and tar sands that are extracted by either mining or in-situ methods and refined or otherwise processed in the United States and fuel produced in the United States using starch, sugar, cellulosic biomass, plant or animal oils, or thermal chemical conversion, thermal depolymerization, or thermal conversion processes (referred to in this section as a 'covered fuel')';

(3) in subsection (d), by striking '1 or more years' and inserting 'up to 5 years';

(4) in subsection (e), by striking the period at the end and inserting the following: ', with consideration given to military installations closed or realigned under a round of defense base closure and realignment.'; and

(5) by adding at the end the following new subsection:

'(f) Production Facilities for Covered Fuels- The Secretary of Defense may enter into contracts or other agreements with private companies or other entities to develop and operate production facilities for covered fuels, and may provide for the construction or capital modification of production facilities for covered fuels.'.

SEC. 13. FEDERAL FLEET ENERGY CONSERVATION IMPROVEMENT.

(a) Definitions- Section 301 of the Energy Policy Act of 1992 (42 U.S.C. 13211) is amended—

(1) in paragraph (3), by inserting before the semicolon at the end the following: ', including a vehicle that is propelled by electric drive transportation technology, engine dominant hybrid electric technology, or plug-in hybrid technology';

(2) in paragraph (13), by striking 'and' after the semicolon at the end;

(3) in paragraph (14), by striking the period at the end and inserting a semicolon; and

(4) by adding at the end the following:

'(15) the term 'electric drive transportation technology' means—

'(A) technology that uses an electric motor for all or part of the motive power of a vehicle (regardless of whether off-board electricity is used), including—

'(i) a battery electric vehicle;

'(ii) a fuel cell vehicle;

'(iii) an engine dominant hybrid electric vehicle;

'(iv) a plug-in hybrid electric vehicle;

'(v) a plug-in hybrid fuel cell vehicle; and

'(vi) an electric rail vehicle; or

'(B) technology that uses equipment for transportation (including transportation involving any mobile source of air pollution) that uses an electric motor to replace an internal combustion engine for all or part of the work of the equipment, including corded electric equipment that is linked to transportation or a mobile source of air pollution;

'(16) the term 'engine dominant hybrid electric vehicle' means an on-road or nonroad vehicle that—

'(A) is propelled by an internal combustion engine or heat engine using—

'(i) any combustible fuel; and

'(ii) an on-board, rechargeable storage device; and

'(B) has no means of using an off-board source of electricity; and

'(17) the term 'plug-in hybrid electric vehicle' means an on-road or nonroad vehicle that is propelled by an internal combustion engine or heat engine using—

'(A) any combustible fuel;

'(B) an on-board, rechargeable storage device; and

'(C) a means of using an off-board source of electricity.'.

(b) Minimum Federal Fleet Requirement- Section 303(b)(1) of the Energy Policy Act of 1992 (42 U.S.C. 13212(b)(1)) is amended—

(1) in subparagraph (C), by striking 'and' after the semicolon;

(2) in subparagraph (D), by striking 'fiscal year 1999 and thereafter,' and inserting 'each of fiscal years 1999 through 2013; and'; and

(3) by inserting after subparagraph (D) the following:

'(E) 100 percent in fiscal year 2014 and thereafter,'.

US Senate Bill 433

Title: A bill to state United States policy for Iraq, and for other purposes.

Sponsor: Sen Obama, Barack [IL] (introduced 1/30/2007) Cosponsors (3)

Related Bills: H.R.787

Latest Major Action: 1/30/2007 Referred to Senate committee. Status: Read twice and referred to the Committee on Foreign Relations.

Summary As Of:

1/30/2007—Introduced.

Iraq War De-Escalation Act of 2007 - States that: (1) U.S. Armed Forces levels in Iraq after the date of enactment of this Act shall not exceed January 10, 2007, levels without specific statutory authority enacted by Congress after the date of the enactment of this Act; and (2) except as otherwise provided, the phased redeployment of U.S. Armed Forces from Iraq shall begin by May 1, 2007.

Authorizes the President to temporarily suspend such redeployment upon certification to Congress that: (1) such action is in the U.S. national interest; and (2) the government of Iraq is taking specified actions. Resumes

redeployment if Congress enacts a joint resolution disapproving such suspension or suspension renewal.

Authorizes, upon certification by the President to Congress, post-deployment retention of certain forces in Iraq to: (1) protect U.S. personnel and facilities; (2) conduct targeted counter-terrorism operations; (3) provide training for Iraqi security forces; and (4) conduct Office of Defense Attache functions. Terminates retention if Congress enacts a joint resolution disapproving such retention.

Reaffirms provisions prohibiting the establishment of bases or installations providing for the permanent stationing of U.S. forces in Iraq.

States that it shall be U.S. policy to: (1) implement a plan to intensify training of Iraqi security forces; and (2) undertake diplomatic initiatives to restore peace in Iraq and prevent a regional conflict.

Conditions continued economic assistance (with exceptions for humanitarian, employment, and security assistance) to the government of Iraq after May 1, 2007, upon the President certifying to Congress that the government of Iraq is taking specified actions with respect to economic improvements and reducing sectarian violence.

MAJOR ACTIONS:

¤NONE¤

ALL ACTIONS:

1/30/2007:

Sponsor introductory remarks on measure. (CR S1322, S1343-1344)

1/30/2007:

Read twice and referred to the Committee on Foreign Relations.

TITLES(s): (italics indicate a title for a portion of a bill)

¤NONE¤

COSPONSORS(3), ALPHABETICAL [FOLLOWED BY COSPONSORS WITHDRAWN]: (Sort: by date)

Sen Durbin, Richard [IL] - 2/27/2007

Sen Leahy, Patrick J. [VT] - 2/1/2007

Sen Sanders, Bernard [VT] - 2/5/2007

COMMITTEE(s)

Committee/Subcommittee:

Activity:

Senate Foreign Relations

Referral, In Committee

RELATED BILL DETAILS: (additional related bills may be indentified in Status)

Bill:

Relationship:

H.R.787

Identical bill identified by CRS

AMENDMENT(S)

¤NONE¤

IN THE SENATE OF THE UNITED STATES

January 30, 2007

Mr. OBAMA introduced the following bill; which was read twice and referred to the Committee on Foreign Relations

A BILL

To state United States policy for Iraq, and for other purposes.

Be it enacted by the Senate and House of Representatives of the United States of America in Congress assembled,

SECTION 1. SHORT TITLE.

This Act may be cited as the 'Iraq War De-Escalation Act of 2007'.

SEC. 2. FINDINGS AND PURPOSES.

(a) Findings- Congress makes the following findings:

(1) Congress and the Nation honor the courage, sacrifices, and efforts of the members of the Armed Forces of the United States and their families.

(2) In his speech to the Nation on January 10, 2007, President George W. Bush said that 'I've made it clear to the Prime Minister and Iraq's other leaders that America's commitment is not open-ended. If the Iraqi government does not follow through on its promises, it will lose the support of the American people. . . The Prime Minister understands this'.

(3) In that speech, President George W. Bush also told the Nation that 'America will hold the Iraqi government to the benchmarks it has announced. . . [T]o take responsibility for security in all of Iraq's provinces by November. To give every Iraqi citizen a stake in the country's economy, Iraq will pass legislation to share oil revenues among all Iraqis. To show that it is committed to delivering a better life, the Iraqi government will spend $10,000,000,000 of its own money on reconstruction and infrastructure projects that will create new jobs. To empower local leaders, Iraqis plan to hold provincial elections later this year. And to allow more Iraqis to re-enter their nation's political life, the government will reform de-Baathification laws, and establish a fair process for considering amendments to Iraq's constitution'.

(4) In that speech, President George W. Bush also told the Nation that 'only Iraqis can end the sectarian violence and secure their people'.

(5) On December 18, 2006, former Secretary of State Colin Powell stated: '[s]o we have tried this surge of troops over the summer. I am not persuaded that another surge of troops in Baghdad for the purpose of suppressing this communitarian violence, this civil war, will work'.

(6) On November 15, 2006, General John Abizaid, Commander of the United States Central Command, stated before the Committee on Armed Services of the Senate that 'I met with every divisional commander, General Casey, the corps commander, General Dempsey. We all talked together. And I said, in your professional opinion, if we were to bring in more American troops now, does it add considerably to our ability to achieve success in Iraq? And they all said no. And the reason is, because we want the Iraqis to do more. It's easy for the Iraqis to rely upon us to do this work. I believe that more American forces prevent the Iraqis from doing more, from taking more responsibility for their own future'.

(7) In testimony before the Committee on Foreign Relations of the Senate on January 11, 2007, Secretary of State Condoleezza Rice stated that unless the Government of Iraq has met certain benchmarks and reestablishes the confidence of the Iraqi people over the next several months, 'this plan is not going to work'.

(8) In a statement on January 11, 2007, Secretary of Defense Robert Gates stated '[a]nd we will probably have a better view a couple of months from now in terms of whether we are making headway in terms of getting better control of Baghdad, with the Iraqis in the lead and with the Iraqis beginning to make better progress on the reconciliation process'.

(9) The bipartisan Iraq Study Group headed by former Secretary of State James Baker and former Representative Lee Hamilton reached a bipartisan consensus on 79 separate recommendations for a new approach in Iraq. Among those recommendations were calling for a new diplomatic offensive in the region and conditioning American economic assistance to Iraq on specific benchmarks, with the expectation that 'by the first quarter of 2008, subject to unexpected developments in the security situation on the ground, all combat brigades not necessary for force protection could be out of Iraq'.

(10) In reaction to the speech of President George W. Bush of January 10, 2007, former Secretary of State Baker and former Representative Hamilton wrote that '[t]he President did not suggest the possibility of a transition that could enable U.S. combat forces to begin to leave Iraq. The President did not state that political, military, or economic support for Iraq would be conditional on the Iraq government's ability to meet benchmarks. Within the region, the President did not announce an international support group for Iraq including all of Iraq's neighbors. . .'.

(b) Purposes- The purposes of this Act are as follows:

(1) To formulate and provide for the implementation of an effective United States policy towards Iraq and the Middle East region that employs military, political, diplomatic, and economic assets to promote and protect the national security interests of the United States.

(2) To provide for the implementation of a responsible, phased redeployment of the Armed Forces of the United States from Iraq in a substantial and gradual manner that places the highest priority on protecting the lives of members of the Armed Forces and civilian personnel of the United States and on promoting the national security interests of the United States in the Middle East region.

(3) To urge the political parties and leaders of Iraq to reach the political solution necessary to promote stability in Iraq and enhance the safety of innocent Iraqi civilians.

(4) To condition future economic assistance to the Government of Iraq on significant progress toward the achievement of political and economic measures to be taken by the Government of Iraq.

(5) To provide for the initiation of a wider and sustained diplomatic strategy aimed at promoting a political settlement in Iraq, thereby ending the civil war in Iraq, preventing a humanitarian catastrophe in Iraq, and preventing a wider regional conflict.

(6) To provide, through sections 4 through 7, for the implementation of key recommendations of the Iraq Study Group, a bipartisan panel of experts co-chaired by former Secretary of State James Baker and former Representative Lee Hamilton.

SEC. 3. APPROPRIATE FORCE LEVELS FOR UNITED STATES MILITARY FORCES IN IRAQ.

Notwithstanding any other provision of law, the levels of the Armed Forces of the United States in Iraq after the date of the enactment of this Act shall not exceed the levels of such forces in Iraq as of January 10, 2007, without specific authority in statute enacted by Congress after the date of the enactment of this Act.

SEC. 4. REDEPLOYMENT OF UNITED STATES MILITARY FORCES FROM IRAQ.

(a) Redeployment-

(1) DEADLINE FOR COMMENCEMENT OF REDEPLOYMENT- Except as otherwise provided in this section, the phased redeployment of the Armed Forces of the United States from Iraq shall commence not later than May 1, 2007.

(2) SCOPE AND MANNER OF REDEPLOYMENT- The redeployment of the Armed Forces under this section shall be substantial, shall occur in a gradual manner, and shall be executed at a pace to achieve the goal of the complete redeployment of all United States combat brigades from Iraq by March 31, 2008, consistent with the expectation of the Iraq Study Group, if all the matters set forth in subsection (b)(1) (B) are not met by such date, subject to the exceptions for retention of forces for force protection, counter-terrorism operations, training of Iraqi forces, and other purposes as contemplated by subsection (g).

(3) FORMULATION OF PLAN WITH MILITARY COMMANDERS- The redeployment of the Armed Forces under this section should be conducted pursuant to a plan formulated by United States military commanders that is developed, if practicable, in consultation with the Government of Iraq.

(4) PROTECTION OF UNITED STATES FORCES AND CIVILIAN PERSONNEL- In carrying out the redeployment of the Armed Forces under this section,

the highest priority shall be afforded to the safety of members of the Armed Forces and civilian personnel of the United States in Iraq.

(b) Suspension of Redeployment-

(1) IN GENERAL- The President may suspend, on a temporary basis as provided in paragraph (2), the redeployment of the Armed Forces under this section if the President certifies to the President pro tempore of the Senate and the Speaker of the House of Representatives that—

(A) doing so is in the national security interests of the United States; and

(B) the Government of Iraq—

(i) has lifted all restrictions concerning non-interference in operations of the Armed Forces of the United States in Iraq and does so on a continuing basis;

(ii) is making significant progress in reducing sectarian violence in Iraq and in reducing the size and operational effectiveness of sectarian militias in Iraq;

(iii) is making significant progress towards removing militia elements from the Iraqi Army, National Police, Facilities Protection Services, and other security forces of the Government of Iraq;

(iv) has enacted legislation or established other binding mechanisms to ensure the sharing of all Iraqi oil revenues among all segments of Iraqi society in an equitable manner;

(v) is making significant progress towards making available not less than $10,000,000,000 for reconstruction, job creation, and economic development in Iraq, with safeguards to prevent corruption, by January 10, 2008;

(vi) has deployed at least 18 Iraqi Army and National Police brigades to Baghdad and is effectively ensuring that such units are performing their security and police functions in all Baghdad neighborhoods, regardless of their sectarian composition;

(vii) has enacted legislation or established other binding mechanisms to revise its de-Baathification laws to encourage the employment in the Government of Iraq of qualified Iraqi professionals, irrespective of ethnic or political affiliation, including ex-Baathists who were not leading figures of the Saddam Hussein regime;

(viii) has established a fair process for considering amendments to the constitution of Iraq that promote lasting national reconciliation in Iraq;

(ix) is making significant progress towards assuming full responsibility for security in all the provinces of Iraq by November 30, 2007;

(x) is making significant progress towards holding free and fair provincial elections in Iraq at the earliest date practicable, but not later than December 31, 2007;

(xi) is making substantial progress towards increasing the size and effectiveness of Ministry of Defense forces as described on page 11 of 'Highlights of the Iraq Strategy Review' published by the National Security Council in January 2007;

(xii) is making significant progress in reforming and strengthening the civilian ministries and other government institutions that support the Iraqi Army and National Police; and

(xiii) is making significant progress towards reforming its civilian ministries to ensure that they are not administered on a sectarian basis and that government services are delivered in an even-handed and non-sectarian manner.

(2) PERIOD OF SUSPENSION- A suspension of the redeployment of the Armed Forces under this subsection, including any renewal of the suspension under paragraph (3), shall be for a period not to exceed 90 days.

(3) RENEWAL- A suspension of the redeployment of the Armed Forces under this subsection may be renewed. Any such renewal shall include a certification to the officers referred to in paragraph (1) on the matters set forth in clauses (i) through (xiii) of subparagraph (B) of that paragraph.

(c) Disapproval of Suspension-

(1) DISAPPROVAL- If Congress enacts a joint resolution disapproving the suspension of the redeployment of the Armed Forces under subsection (b), or any renewal of the suspension, the suspension shall be discontinued, and the redeployment of the Armed Forces from Iraq under this section shall resume.

(2) PROCEDURES FOR CONSIDERATION OF JOINT RESOLUTIONS-

(A) JOINT RESOLUTION DEFINED- For purposes of this subsection, the term 'joint resolution' means only a joint resolution introduced not later than 10 days after the date on which a certification of the President under subsection (b) is received by Congress, the matter after the resolving clause of which is as follows: 'That Congress disapproves the certification of the President submitted to Congress under section 4(b) of the Iraq War De-Escalation Act of 2007, on XXXXXXX.', the blank space being filled in with the appropriate date.

(B) PROCEDURES- A joint resolution described in paragraph (1) shall be considered in a House of Congress in accordance with the procedures applicable to joint resolutions under paragraphs (3) through (8) of section 8066(c) of the Department of Defense Appropriations Act, 1985 (as enacted by section 101(h) of Public Law 98-473; 98 Stat. 1936).

(d) Reports to Congress-

(1) IN GENERAL- Not later than 90 days after the date of the enactment of this Act, and every 90 days thereafter, the President shall submit to the President pro tempore of the Senate and the Speaker of the House of Representatives a report describing and assessing—

(A) the progress made by the Government of Iraq on each of the matters set forth in subsection (b)(1)(B); and

(B) the progress of the redeployment required by subsection (a).

(2) FORM- Each report under this subsection shall be submitted in unclassified form, but may include a classified annex.

(e) Sense of Congress on Location of Redeployment- It is the sense of Congress that, in redeploying the Armed Forces from Iraq under this section, appropriate units of the Armed Forces should be redeployed—

(1) to the United States;

(2) to Afghanistan, in order to enhance United States military operations in that country;

(3) elsewhere in the region, to serve as an over-the-horizon force to prevent the conflict in Iraq from becoming a wider war, to reassure allies of the United States of the commitment of the United States to remain engaged in the region, and to position troops to strike directly at al-Qaeda; and

(4) elsewhere, to meet urgent United States security needs.

(f) Political Solution in Iraq- The United States should use the redeployment of the Armed Forces under this section, and the possible suspension of such redeployment if the benchmarks set forth in subsection (b) are met, as a tool to press the Iraqi leaders to promote national reconciliation among ethnic and religious groups in Iraq in order to establish stability in Iraq.

(g) Retention of Certain Forces in Iraq-

(1) IN GENERAL- Notwithstanding the requirement for the redeployment of the Armed Forces under subsection (a) and subject to the provisions of this subsection, personnel of the Armed Forces of the United States may be in Iraq after the completion of the redeployment of the Armed Forces under this section for the following purposes:

(A) To protect United States personnel and facilities in Iraq.

(B) To conduct targeted counter-terrorism operations.

(C) To provide training for Iraqi security forces.

(D) To conduct the routine functions of the Office of Defense Attache.

(2) CERTIFICATION- Personnel of the Armed Forces may not be retained in Iraq under this subsection unless the President certifies to the President pro tempore of the Senate and the Speaker of the House of Representatives that—

(A) the retention of the Armed Forces in Iraq is necessary for one or more of the purposes set forth in paragraph (1); and

(B) the utilization of Armed Forces positioned outside Iraq could not result in the effective achievement of such purpose or purposes.

(3) DISAPPROVAL OF RETENTION- If Congress enacts a joint resolution disapproving the retention of personnel of the Armed Forces in Iraq under this subsection, or any renewal of the retention, the retention of such personnel in Iraq shall be discontinued, and such personnel shall be redeployed from Iraq.

(4) PROCEDURES FOR CONSIDERATION OF JOINT RESOLUTIONS-

(A) JOINT RESOLUTION DEFINED- For purposes of paragraph (3), the term 'joint resolution' means only a joint resolution introduced not later than 10 days after the date on which a certification of the President under paragraph (2) is received by Congress, the matter after the resolving clause of which is as follows: 'That Congress disapproves the certification of the President submitted to Congress under section 4(g)(2) of the Iraq War De-Escalation Act of 2007, on XXXXXXX.', the blank space being filled in with the appropriate date.

(B) PROCEDURES- A joint resolution described in subparagraph (A) shall be considered in a House of Congress in accordance with the procedures applicable to joint resolutions under paragraphs (3) through (8) of section 8066(c) of the Department of Defense Appropriations Act, 1985 (as enacted by section 101(h) of Public Law 98-473; 98 Stat. 1936).

(h) No Permanent Bases- Congress hereby reaffirms section 1519 of the John Warner National Defense Authorization Act for Fiscal Year 2007 (Public Law 109-364; 120 Stat. 2444), and related provisions of law, that prohibit the establishment of military installations or bases for the purpose of providing for the permanent stationing of United States Armed Forces in Iraq.

SEC. 5. INTENSIFICATION OF TRAINING OF IRAQI SECURITY FORCES.

It shall be the policy of the United States to immediately formulate and implement a plan that—

(1) with the Government of Iraq—

(A) removes militia elements from the Iraqi Army, National Police, and other security forces of the Government of Iraq; and

(B) puts such forces in charge of maintaining security in Iraq;

(2) focuses and intensifies United States efforts on training such forces; and

(3) presses the Government of Iraq to reform the civilian ministries and other government institutions that support the Iraqi Army, National Police, local police, and judicial system.

SEC. 6. AVAILABILITY OF ECONOMIC ASSISTANCE FOR IRAQ.

(a) Limitation- Except as provided in subsection (b), after May 1, 2007, economic assistance may be furnished to the Government of Iraq only if the President submits to the President pro tempore of the Senate and the Speaker of the House of Representatives a certification that the Government of Iraq—

(1) is making measurable progress toward providing not less than $10,000,000,000 of Iraqi funds for reconstruction, job creation, and economic development in Iraq, with safeguards to prevent corruption, by January 10, 2008;

(2) is making progress toward meeting the conditions set forth in the International Compact for Iraq and in the stand-by agreement with the International Monetary Fund; and

(3) is making progress toward reducing sectarian violence and promoting national reconciliation.

(b) Exceptions- The limitation in subsection (a) shall not apply to assistance for Iraq as follows:

(1) Humanitarian assistance.

(2) Assistance to address urgent security and employment needs.

(c) Assessment of Progress- Not later than 90 days after the date of the enactment of this Act, and every 90 days thereafter, the Special Inspector General for Iraq Reconstruction shall submit to Congress a report describing the progress of the Government of Iraq on each matter set forth in subsection (a).

SEC. 7. REGIONAL DIPLOMATIC INITIATIVES ON IRAQ.

(a) Policy of the United States- It shall be the policy of the United States to undertake comprehensive regional and international initiatives, involving key nations, that will assist the Government of Iraq in achieving the purposes of this Act, including promoting a political settlement among the Iraqi people, ending the civil war in Iraq, preventing a humanitarian catastrophe in Iraq, and preventing a regional conflict.

(b) Special Envoy- The President should, not later than 60 days after the date of the enactment of this Act, appoint a special envoy for Iraq to carry out the policy set forth in subsection (a).

(c) Strategy on Preventing Wider Regional War-

(1) STRATEGY- Not later than 90 days after the date of the enactment of this Act, the President shall submit to the President pro tempore of the Senate and the Speaker of the House of Representatives a report setting forth a strategy for preventing the conflict in Iraq from becoming a wider regional war.

(2) FORM- The report under paragraph (1) shall be submitted in unclassified form, but may include a classified annex.

US SENATE BILL 453

TITLE: A bill to prohibit deceptive practices in Federal elections.

SPONSOR: Sen Obama, Barack [IL] (introduced 1/31/2007) Cosponsors (20)

RELATED BILLS: H.R.1281

LATEST MAJOR ACTION: 10/4/2007 Placed on Senate Legislative Calendar under General Orders. Calendar No. 411.

SENATE REPORTS: 110-191

SUMMARY AS OF:

10/4/2007—Reported to Senate amended. (There is 1 other summary)

Deceptive Practices and Voter Intimidation Prevention Act of 2007 - (Sec. 3) Amends the Revised Statutes and federal criminal law to prohibit any person, whether acting under color of law or otherwise, from knowingly deceiving any other person regarding: (1) the time, place, or manner of conducting any federal election; or (2) the qualifications for or restrictions on voter eligibility for any such election. Makes intent to prevent another person from exercising the right to vote, or from voting for the candidate of such other person's choice, an essential element of the offense.

Prescribes a criminal penalty for such deceptive acts.

Directs the U.S. Sentencing Commission to review and, if appropriate, amend the federal sentencing guidelines and policy statements applicable to persons convicted of any offense under this Act.

(Sec. 4) Authorizes any person to report to the Attorney General false election information.

Requires the Attorney General, if a report provides a reasonable basis to find that an election violation has occurred, to pursue any appropriate criminal prosecution or civil action and refer the matter to the Civil Rights Division of the Department of Justice for criminal prosecution or civil action, but only if such matter is otherwise under the Division's jurisdiction.

Prohibits the commencement of any investigation or legal action relating to a report until after the election concerned has been completed, unless the Attorney General: (1) reasonably believes it is necessary to pursue such investigation or legal proceedings promptly; and (2) reasonably determines that such investigation or legal proceeding will not inhibit any person from exercising right to vote.

(Sec. 5) Requires the Attorney General, immediately after receiving such a report, to consider and review it and, if there is a reasonable basis to find that false information has been communicated, to undertake all effective measures necessary to provide correct information to voters affected by the false information.

Authorizes any person who has made such a report about which the Attorney General fails to take corrective action to apply to a U.S. district court for an order requiring the Attorney General to take such action.

Requires the Attorney General to report to Congress on the procedures and standards intended to be used to provide corrective action.

Directs the Attorney General to study the feasibility of providing such corrective information through public service announcements, the emergency alert system, or other forms of public broadcast.

Authorizes appropriations.

(Sec. 6) Directs the Attorney General to report to Congress on any allegations of false information submitted which relate to any federal general election or to any preceding primary or ensuing run-off election.

MAJOR ACTIONS:

1/31/2007

Introduced in Senate

10/4/2007

Committee on the Judiciary. Reported by Senator Leahy with an amendment in the nature of a substitute. With written report No. 110-191. Additional views filed.

10/4/2007

Placed on Senate Legislative Calendar under General Orders. Calendar No. 411.

ALL ACTIONS:

1/31/2007:

Sponsor introductory remarks on measure. (CR S1428)

1/31/2007:

Read twice and referred to the Committee on the Judiciary.

6/7/2007:

Committee on the Judiciary. Hearings held.

9/6/2007:

Committee on the Judiciary. Ordered to be reported with an amendment in the nature of a substitute favorably.

10/4/2007:

Committee on the Judiciary. Reported by Senator Leahy with an amendment in the nature of a substitute. With written report No. 110-191. Additional views filed.

10/4/2007:

Placed on Senate Legislative Calendar under General Orders. Calendar No. 411.

TITLES(s): (italics indicate a title for a portion of a bill)

* SHORT TITLE(s) AS INTRODUCED:

Deceptive Practices and Voter Intimidation Prevention Act of 2007

* SHORT TITLE(s) AS REPORTED TO SENATE:

Deceptive Practices and Voter Intimidation Prevention Act of 2007

* OFFICIAL TITLE AS INTRODUCED:

A bill to prohibit deceptive practices in Federal elections.

COSPONSORS(20), ALPHABETICAL [FOLLOWED BY COSPONSORS WITHDRAWN]: (Sort: by date)

Sen Boxer, Barbara [CA] - 1/31/2007

Sen Brown, Sherrod [OH] - 5/8/2007

Sen Cardin, Benjamin L. [MD] - 1/31/2007

Sen Clinton, Hillary Rodham [NY] - 1/31/2007

Sen Coburn, Tom [OK] - 9/6/2007

Sen Durbin, Richard [IL] - 9/6/2007

Sen Feingold, Russell D. [WI] - 1/31/2007

Sen Feinstein, Dianne [CA] - 1/31/2007

Sen Johnson, Tim [SD] - 6/4/2007

Sen Kennedy, Edward M. [MA] - 1/31/2007

Sen Kerry, John F. [MA] - 1/31/2007

Sen Landrieu, Mary L. [LA] - 3/19/2007

Sen Lautenberg, Frank R. [NJ] - 12/5/2007

Sen Leahy, Patrick J. [VT] - 1/31/2007

Sen Levin, Carl [MI] - 3/6/2007

Sen McCaskill, Claire [MO] - 6/4/2007

Sen Menendez, Robert [NJ] - 12/19/2007

Sen Schumer, Charles E. [NY] - 1/31/2007

Sen Whitehouse, Sheldon [RI] - 6/4/2007

Sen Wyden, Ron [OR] - 7/25/2007

COMMITTEE(S)

Committee/Subcommittee:

Activity:

Senate Judiciary

Referral, Hearings, Markup, Reporting

RELATED BILL DETAILS: (additional related bills may be indentified in Status)

Bill:

Relationship:

H.R.1281

Related bill identified by CRS

H.R.1281

Related bill as identified by the House Clerk's office

AMENDMENT(S)

¤NONE¤

IN THE SENATE OF THE UNITED STATES

January 31, 2007

Mr. OBAMA (for himself, Mr. SCHUMER, Mr. LEAHY, Mr. CARDIN, Mr. FEINGOLD, Mr. KERRY, Mrs. FEINSTEIN, Mrs. CLINTON, Mrs. BOXER, Mr. KENNEDY, Mr. LEVIN, Ms. LANDRIEU, Mr. BROWN, Mr. JOHNSON, Mrs. MCCASKILL, Mr. WHITEHOUSE, Mr. WYDEN, Mr. DURBIN, and Mr. COBURN) introduced the following bill; which was read twice and referred to the Committee on the Judiciary

October 4, 2007

Reported by Mr. LEAHY, with an amendment

A BILL

To prohibit deceptive practices in Federal elections.

Be it enacted by the Senate and House of Representatives of the United States of America in Congress assembled,

SECTION 1. SHORT TITLE.

This Act may be cited as the 'Deceptive Practices and Voter Intimidation Prevention Act of 2007'.

SEC. 2. FINDINGS.

Congress makes the following findings:

(1) The right to vote through casting a ballot for one's preferred candidate is a fundamental right accorded to United States citizens by the Constitution and the unimpeded exercise of this right is essential to the functioning of our democracy.

(2) Historically, certain citizens, especially racial minorities, were prevented from voting because of significant barriers such as literacy tests, poll taxes, and property requirements.

(3) Some of these barriers were removed by the 15th, 19th, and 24th Amendments to the Constitution.

(4) Despite the elimination of some of these barriers to the polls, the integrity of today's elections is threatened by newer tactics aimed at suppressing voter turnout. These tactics include 'deceptive practices', which involve the dissemination of false information intended to prevent voters from casting their ballots, prevent voters from voting for the candidate of their choice, intimidate the electorate, and undermine the integrity of the electoral process.

(5) Denials of the right to vote, and deceptive practices designed to prevent members of racial minorities from exercising that right, are an outgrowth of discriminatory history, including slavery. Measures to combat denials of that right are a legitimate exercise of congressional power under the 13th, 14th, and 15th Amendments to the United States Constitution.

(6) Shortly before the 1990 midterm Federal elections, 125,000 voters in North Carolina received postcards providing false information about voter eligibility and a warning about criminal penalties for voter fraud. Ninety-seven percent of the voters who received postcards were African American.

(7) In 2004, Native American voters in South Dakota were prevented from voting after they did not provide photographic identification upon request, despite the fact that they were not required to present such identification in order to vote under State or Federal law.

(8) In the 2006 midterm election, 14,000 Latino voters in Orange County, California received mailings from the California Coalition for Immigration Reform, warning them in Spanish that 'if you are an immigrant, voting in a federal election is a crime

that can result in incarceration...'. In fact, an immigrant who is a naturalized citizen of the United States has the same right to vote as any other citizen.

(9) In the same 2006 election, some Virginia voters received automated phone messages falsely warning them that the 'Virginia Elections Commission' had determined they were ineligible to vote and that they would face severe criminal penalties if they tried to cast a ballot.

(10) In 2006 in Maryland, certain campaigns for Governor and United States Senator distributed fliers in predominantly African-American neighborhoods falsely claiming that certain candidates had been endorsed by their opponents' party and by prominent figures who had actually endorsed the opponents of the candidates.

(11) Those responsible for these and similar efforts should be held accountable, and civil and criminal penalties should be available to punish anyone who seeks to keep voters away from the polls by providing false information.

(12) Moreover, the Federal Government should help correct such false information in order to assist voters in exercising their right to vote without confusion and to preserve the integrity of the electoral process.

(13) The Federal Government has a compelling interest in 'protecting voters from confusion and undue influence' and in 'preserving the integrity of its election process'. Burson v. Freeman, 504 U.S. 191, 199 (1992).

(14) The First Amendment does not preclude the regulation of some intentionally false speech, even if it is political in nature. As the Supreme Court of the United States has recognized, '[t]hat speech is used as a tool for political ends does not automatically bring it under the protective mantle of the Constitution. For the use of the known lie as a tool is at once at odds with the premises of democratic government and with the orderly manner in which economic, social, or political change is to be effected ... . Hence the knowingly false statement and the false statement made with reckless disregard of the truth, do not enjoy constitutional protection.'. Garrison v. Louisiana, 379 U.S. 64, 75 (1964).

SEC. 3. PROHIBITION ON DECEPTIVE PRACTICES IN FEDERAL ELECTIONS.

(a) Civil Action- Subsection (b) of section 2004 of the Revised Statutes (42 U.S.C. 1971(b)) is amended—

(1) by striking 'No person' and inserting the following:

'(1) No person'; and

(2) by inserting at the end the following new paragraph:

'(2)(A) No person, whether acting under color of law or otherwise, shall, within 60 days before an election described in subparagraph (B), communicate or cause to be communicated information described in subparagraph (C), or produce information described in subparagraph (C) with the intent that such information be communicated, if such person—

'(i) knows such information to be false; and

'(ii) has the intent to prevent another person from exercising the right to vote or from voting for the candidate of such other person's choice in an election described in subparagraph (B).

'(B) An election described in this subparagraph is any general, primary, run-off, or special election held solely or in part for the purpose of electing a candidate for the office of President, Vice President, presidential elector, Member of the Senate, Member of the House of Representatives, or Delegate or Commissioner from a territory or possession.

'(C) Information is described in this subparagraph if such information is regarding—

'(i) the time, place, or manner of any election described in subparagraph (B);

'(ii) the qualifications for or restrictions on voter eligibility for any such election, including—

'(I) any criminal penalties associated with voting in any such election; or

'(II) information regarding a voter's registration status or eligibility; or

'(iii) the explicit endorsement by any person or organization for the upcoming election of a candidate to any office described in subparagraph (B).'.

(b) Criminal Penalty-

(1) IN GENERAL- Section 594 of title 18, United States Code, is amended—

(A) by striking 'Whoever' and inserting the following:

'(a) Intimidation- Whoever';

(B) by striking 'at any election held solely or in part for the purpose of electing such a candidate' and inserting 'at any general, primary, run-off, or special election held solely or in part for the purpose of electing such a candidate'; and

(C) by adding at the end the following:

'(b) Deceptive Acts-

'(1) PROHIBITION-

'(A) IN GENERAL- It shall be unlawful for any person, within 60 days before an election described in subparagraph (B), to communicate or cause to be communicated information described in subparagraph (C), or produce information described in subparagraph (C) with the intent that such information be communicated, if such person—

'(i) knows such information to be false; and

'(ii) has the intent to prevent another person from exercising the right to vote or from voting for the candidate of such other person's choice in an election described in subparagraph (B).

'(B) ELECTION DESCRIBED- An election described in this subparagraph is any general, primary, run-off, or special election held solely or in part for the purpose of electing a candidate for the office of President, Vice President, presidential elector, Member of the Senate, Member of the House of Representatives, or Delegate or Commissioner from a territory or possession.

'(C) INFORMATION DESCRIBED- Information is described in this subparagraph if such information is regarding—

'(i) the time, place, or manner of any election described in subparagraph (B);

'(ii) the qualifications for or restrictions on voter eligibility for any such election, including—

'(I) any criminal penalties associated with voting in any such election; or

'(II) information regarding a voter's registration status or eligibility; or

'(iii) the explicit endorsement by any person or organization for the upcoming election of a candidate to any office described in subparagraph (B).

'(2) PENALTY- Any person who violates paragraph (1) shall be fined not more than $100,000, imprisoned not more than 5 years, or both.

'(c) Attempt- Any person who attempts to commit any offense described in subsection (a) or (b) shall be subject to the same penalties as those prescribed for the offense that the person attempted to commit.'.

(2) MODIFICATION OF PENALTY FOR VOTER INTIMIDATION- Section 594(a) of title 18, United States Code, as amended by paragraph (1), is amended—

(A) by inserting 'by any means, including by means of written, electronic, or telephonic communications,' after 'any other person'; and

(B) by striking 'one year' and inserting '5 years'.

(3) SENTENCING GUIDELINES-

(A) REVIEW AND AMENDMENT- Not later than 180 days after the date of enactment of this Act, the United States Sentencing Commission, pursuant to its authority under section 994 of title 28, United States Code, and in accordance with this section, shall review and, if appropriate, amend the Federal sentencing guidelines and policy statements applicable to persons convicted of any offense under section 594 of title 18, United States Code.

(B) AUTHORIZATION- The United States Sentencing Commission may amend the Federal sentencing guidelines in accordance with the procedures set forth in section 21(a) of the Sentencing Act of 1987 (28 U.S.C. 994 note) as though the authority under that section had not expired.

(c) Effective Date- The amendments made by this section shall take effect on the date of the enactment of this Act.

SEC. 4. REPORTING OF FALSE ELECTION INFORMATION.

(a) In General- Any person may report to the Attorney General any communication of, or the causation of any communication of, information, or the production of information with the intent that such information be communicated, if the information is—

(1) information that is described in—

(A) subparagraph (C) of section 2004(b)(2) of the Revised Statutes (42 U.S.C. 1971(b)(2)(C)); or

(B) subparagraph (C) of section 594(b)(1)(C) of title 18, United States Code; and

(2) false.

(b) Referral- If a report under subsection (a) provides a reasonable basis to find that a violation of section 2004(b) of the Revised Statutes (42 U.S.C. 1971(b)) or section 594(b) of title 18, United States Code, has occurred, the Attorney General shall pursue any appropriate criminal prosecution or civil action and shall refer the matter to the Civil Rights Division of the Department of Justice for criminal prosecution or civil action, but only if such matter is otherwise under the jurisdiction of such division.

(c) Delay of Investigation- No investigation or legal action relating to a report under subsection (a) may begin until after the election with respect to which such report relates has been completed, unless the Attorney General—

(1) reasonably believes that it is necessary to promptly pursue such investigation or legal proceedings; and

(2) reasonably determines that such investigation or legal proceeding will not inhibit any person from exercising the right to vote.

SEC. 5. CORRECTIVE ACTION.

(a) Action by Attorney General-

(1) IN GENERAL- Immediately after receiving a report under section 4(a), the Attorney General shall consider and review such report. If the report provides a reasonable basis to find that—

(A) false information relating to—

(i) the time or place of any general, primary, run-off, or special election held solely or in part for the purpose of electing a candidate for Federal office; or

(ii) the qualifications for or restrictions on voter eligibility for any such election;

has been communicated, caused to be communicated, or produced with the intent that such information be communicated; and

(B) the communication of such false information could materially hinder any citizen's right to vote;

the Attorney General shall undertake all effective measures necessary to correct such false information by providing correct information relating to the time or place of the election or the qualifications for or restrictions on voter eligibility to voters affected by the false information. The information provided by the Attorney General to affected voters under the preceding sentence shall only consist of information necessary to correct the false information described in the report.

(2) INVESTIGATION- In reviewing a report under paragraph (1), the Attorney General shall not undertake any investigation relating to the report unless—

(A) such an investigation is necessary to determine the need for, or the scope of, corrective action under paragraph (1); and

116

(B) the Attorney General reasonably determines that such investigation will not inhibit any person from exercising the right to vote.

(b) Right of Action- If a person has made a report under section 4(a) that provides a reasonable basis for finding that information described in subsection (a)(1)(A) has been communicated, caused to be communicated, or produced with the intent that such information be communicated, and the Attorney General fails to take corrective action required under subsection (a) within 72 hours of the filing of such report (or sooner if necessary to permit timely corrective action before an election), such person may apply to a United States district court for an order requiring the Attorney General to take such corrective action.

(c) Standards for Taking Corrective Action-

(1) IN GENERAL-

(A) BIANNUAL REPORT- Not later than January 1 of each year in which there is a regularly scheduled general election for Federal office, the Attorney General shall submit to the Committee on the Judiciary of the Senate and the Committee on the Judiciary of the House of Representatives a report on the procedures and standards intended to be used to provide corrective action under this subsection.

(B) SUPPLEMENTAL REPORTS- If the Attorney General revises or changes any procedures or standards contained in the most recent report submitted under subparagraph (A), the Attorney General shall promptly submit to the Committee on the Judiciary of the Senate and the Committee on the Judiciary of the House of Representatives a report on such revised or additional procedures.

(C) CONSULTATION- In developing or revising any standards or procedures for the methods and means of corrective actions under this subsection, the Attorney General shall consult with the Election Assistance Commission, civil rights organizations, voting rights groups, State and local election officials, voter protection groups, and other interested community organizations.

(2) STUDY-

(A) IN GENERAL- The Attorney General, in consultation with the Federal Communications Commission and the Election Assistance Commission, shall conduct a study on the feasibility of providing corrective information under subsection (a) through public service announcements, the emergency alert system, or other forms of public broadcast.

(B) REPORT- Not later than 90 days after the date of the enactment of this Act, the Attorney General shall submit to Congress a report detailing the results of the study conducted under subparagraph (A).

(d) Federal Office- For purposes of this section and section 6, the term 'Federal office' means the office of President, Vice President, presidential elector, Member of the Senate, Member of the House of Representatives, or Delegate or Commissioner from a territory or possession of the United States.

(e) Authorization of Appropriations- There are authorized to be appropriated to the Attorney General such sums as may be necessary to carry out this section.

SEC. 6. REPORTS TO CONGRESS.

(a) In General- Not later than 90 days after any general election for Federal office, the Attorney General shall submit to the appropriate committees of Congress a report compiling and detailing any allegations of false information submitted pursuant to section 4(a) which relate to such election or to any primary or run-off election held before such election and after the general election for Federal office preceding the general election to which the report relates.

(b) Contents-

(1) IN GENERAL- Each report submitted under subsection (a) shall include—

(A) detailed information on specific allegations of deceptive tactics;

(B) statistical compilations of how many allegations were made and of what type;

(C) the geographic locations of and the populations affected by the alleged deceptive information;

(D) the status of the investigations of such allegations;

(E) any corrective actions taken under section 5(a) in response to such allegations;

(F) the rationale used for any such corrective actions or for any refusal to pursue an allegation relating to information described in section 5(a)(1)(A);

(G) the effectiveness of any such corrective actions;

(H) any legal actions filed against the Attorney General under section 5(b), together with the outcome of each such legal action;

(I) any referrals of information to other Federal, State, or local agencies;

(J) any suit instituted under section 2004(b)(2) of the Revised Statutes (42 U.S.C. 1971(b)(2)) in connection with such allegations; and

(K) any criminal prosecution instituted under title 18, United States Code, in connection with such allegations.

(2) EXCEPTION- The Attorney General may withhold any nonpublic information that the Attorney General reasonably determines would infringe on the rights of a criminal suspect or defendant or would compromise an on-going investigation or prosecution.

(c) Report Made Public- On the date that the Attorney General submits the report required under subsection (a), the Attorney General shall also make the report publicly available through the Internet and other appropriate means.

SEC. 7. SEVERABILITY.

If any provision of this Act or any amendment made by this Act, or the application of a provision or amendment to any person or circumstance, is held to be unconstitutional, the remainder of this Act and the amendments made by this Act, and the application of the provisions and amendments to any person or circumstance, shall not be affected by the holding.

US SENATE BILL 674

TITLE: A bill to require accountability and enhanced congressional oversight for personnel performing private security functions under Federal contracts, and for other purposes.

SPONSOR: Sen Obama, Barack [IL] (introduced 2/16/2007) Cosponsors (4)

RELATED BILLS: H.R.369, H.R.2740

LATEST MAJOR ACTION: 2/16/2007 Referred to Senate committee. Status: Read twice and referred to the Committee on Armed Services.

SUMMARY AS OF:

2/16/2007—Introduced.

Transparency and Accountability in Military and Security Contracting Act of 2007 - Requires reports to Congress by specified federal officials on information with respect to federal military and security contracts being performed in Iraq and Afghanistan. Requires a separate report from the Secretary of Defense on Department of Defense (DOD) strategy and activities with respect to contractors and subcontractors in support of DOD missions in Iraq, Afghanistan, and the Global War on Terror.

Requires each contract, subcontract, or task order awarded or issued by a federal agency that includes private security functions (covered contract) to require the contractor to provide to the agency contracting officer specified information, including the number of persons to perform the security functions and the hiring and training process for such employees. Requires agency oversight in the performance of the covered contract.

Directs the Chairman of the Joint Chiefs of Staff (JCS) to issue rules of engagement regarding the circumstances under which force may be used by contractor personnel performing private security functions within the area covered by a contingency operation, and the types of force authorized. Provides for: (1) hiring, training, and equipment standards relating to private security contractors; and (2) coordination and communication between U.S. Armed Forces and contractor personnel.

Provides for the legal status of contractor personnel with respect to investigations and prosecution of abuses by private security contractors.

Requires the Federal Bureau of Investigation (FBI), for each theater of operations established in connection with a contingency operation in which contract personnel are carrying out work under a covered contract, to establish a Theater Investigative Unit to investigate allegations of contractor personnel criminal misconduct.

MAJOR ACTIONS:

¤NONE¤

ALL ACTIONS:

2/16/2007:

Read twice and referred to the Committee on Armed Services.

10/1/2007:

Sponsor introductory remarks on measure. (CR S12354-12355)

TITLES(s): (italics indicate a title for a portion of a bill)

¤NONE¤

COSPONSORS(4), ALPHABETICAL [FOLLOWED BY COSPONSORS WITHDRAWN]: (Sort: by date)

Sen Conrad, Kent [ND] - 12/6/2007

Sen Durbin, Richard [IL] - 6/7/2007

Sen Kerry, John F. [MA] - 9/19/2007

Sen Whitehouse, Sheldon [RI] - 6/4/2007

COMMITTEE(s)

Committee/Subcommittee:

Activity:

Senate Armed Services

Referral, In Committee

RELATED BILL DETAILS: (additional related bills may be indentified in Status)

Bill:

Relationship:

H.R.369

Related bill identified by CRS

H.R.2740

Related bill identified by CRS

AMENDMENT(s)

¤NONE¤

IN THE SENATE OF THE UNITED STATES

February 16, 2007

Mr. OBAMA introduced the following bill; which was read twice and referred to the Committee on Armed Services

A BILL

To require accountability and enhanced congressional oversight for personnel performing private security functions under Federal contracts, and for other purposes.

Be it enacted by the Senate and House of Representatives of the United States of America in Congress assembled,

SECTION 1. SHORT TITLE; TABLE OF CONTENTS.

(a) Short Title- This Act may be cited as the 'Transparency and Accountability in Military and Security Contracting Act of 2007'.

(b) Table of Contents- The table of contents for this Act is as follows:

SEC. 2. FINDINGS.

Congress makes the following findings:

(1) United States Government agencies, including the Department of Defense, the Department of State, the Department of the Interior, the United States Agency for International Development, and the intelligence community of the United States Government, are increasingly relying on private contractors to perform duties, including the provision of security and other traditionally military and governmental functions, in Iraq, Afghanistan, and other contingency operations.

(2) Estimates of the number of contract personnel in Iraq, including private security contractors, vary widely. The United States Central Command estimated the number to be 100,000 in 2006, and the Government Accountability Office concluded in 2005 that 'the Department of Defense (DOD) estimated at least 60 private security providers were working in Iraq with perhaps as many as 25,000 employees. In March 2006, the Director of the Private Security Company Association of Iraq estimated that approximately 181 private security companies were working in Iraq with just over 48,000 employees'.

(3) The various functions carried out by these personnel have entailed great danger to these personnel, but exact numbers of casualties are unknown. Estimates suggest that some 770 contractors have died, and thousands more have been wounded, in Iraq since 2003.

(4) The multinational character of private security contracting poses oversight and accountability challenges. In addition to Iraqi and United States security contractors working in Iraq, contractors also included citizens from Australia, Chile, Colombia, Croatia, Fiji, India, Nepal, New Zealand, Nicaragua, Russia, Serbia, South Africa, Sri Lanka, and the United Kingdom, among other countries.

(5) In June 2006, the Government Accountability Office reported that 'private security providers continue to enter the battle space without coordinating with the U.S. military, putting both the military and security providers at a greater risk for injury'.

(6) According to published accounts and government studies, the assignments being given private security contractors are often sensitive, including the protection of United States military bases, interrogation of detainees, maintenance and technical assistance to weapons systems, logistics and base operations functions, escort of United States convoys, and protection of key United States Government personnel.

(7) A recent report by the Congressional Research Service found that 'new [Department of Defense] contracts have characteristics that make oversight difficult'.

(8) Contractors are playing an expanded role in the national security operations of the United States and the manner in which the United States supports its troops in the field, especially in contingency operations, and therefore contracting practices and policies must be subject to improved and transparent oversight and management.

SEC. 3. REPORTS ON IRAQ AND AFGHANISTAN CONTRACTS.

(a) Reports Required- Not later than 90 days after the date of the enactment of this Act, the Secretary of Defense, the Secretary of State, the Secretary of the Interior, the Administrator of the United States Agency for International Development, and the Director of National Intelligence shall each submit to Congress a report that contains the information, current as of the date of the enactment of this Act, as follows:

(1) The number of persons performing work in Iraq and Afghanistan under contracts (and subcontracts at any tier) entered into by departments and agencies of the United States Government, including the Department of Defense, the Department of State, the Department of the Interior, the United States Agency for International Development. and the elements of the intelligence community, respectively.

(2) The companies awarded such contracts and subcontracts.

(3) The total cost of such contracts.

(4) The total number of persons who have been killed or wounded in performing work under such contracts.

(5) A description of the military equipment and safety equipment provided for the protection of contractors under such contracts, and an assessment of the adequacy of such equipment.

(6) The policies and procedures through which the departments and agencies of the United States Government instruct and inform contractors under such contracts of the applicability of law to their activities under such contracts, including the laws of the United States, Iraq, and Afghanistan, and other applicable laws.

(7) The policies and procedures through which the departments and agencies of the United States Government monitor contractors under such contracts on their adherence to applicable law, including the laws of the United States, Iraq, and Afghanistan.

(8) The laws, if any, determined to have been broken in the performance of such contracts, including laws of the United States, Iraq, and Afghanistan, and other applicable laws.

(9) A description of the disciplinary actions that have been taken against persons performing work under such contracts by the contractor concerned, the United States Government, or the Government of Iraq or the Government of Afghanistan.

(b) Elements of the Intelligence Community Defined- In this section, the term 'elements of the intelligence community' means the elements of the intelligence community specified in or designated under section 3(4) of the National Security Act of 1947 (50 U.S.C. 401a(4)).

SEC. 4. DEPARTMENT OF DEFENSE REPORT ON STRATEGY FOR AND APPROPRIATENESS OF ACTIVITIES OF CONTRACTORS UNDER DEPARTMENT OF DEFENSE CONTRACTS IN IRAQ, AFGHANISTAN, AND THE GLOBAL WAR ON TERROR.

(a) Report Required- Not later than 180 days after the date of the enactment of this Act, the Secretary of Defense shall submit to Congress a report setting forth the strategy of the Department of Defense for the use of, and a description of the activities being carried out by, contractors and subcontractors in support of Department missions in Iraq, Afghanistan, and the Global War on Terror, including its strategy for ensuring that such contracts do not—

(1) have private companies and their employees performing inherently governmental functions, emergency essential activities, or mission critical activities;

(2) place contractors in supervisory roles over United States Government personnel; or

(3) threaten the safety of contractor personnel or United States Government personnel.

(b) Emergency Essential Activities or Mission Critical Activities Defined- In this section, the term 'emergency essential activities or mission critical activities' means any activities as follows:

(1) Activities for which continued performance is considered essential to support combat systems and operational activities.

(2) Activities whose delay, absence, or failure of performance would significantly affect the broader success or failure of a military operation.

SEC. 5. REQUIREMENTS RELATED TO PERSONNEL PERFORMING PRIVATE SECURITY FUNCTIONS UNDER FEDERAL CONTRACTS DURING CONTINGENCY OPERATIONS.

(a) Accountability for Personnel Performing Private Security Functions Under Federal Contracts During Contingency Operations-

(1) PROVISION OF CERTAIN INFORMATION ABOUT PERSONNEL PERFORMING PRIVATE SECURITY FUNCTIONS- Each covered contract shall require the contractor to provide to the contracting officer for the contract, not later than 5 days after the award of the contract, the following information regarding private security functions to be performed under the contract:

(A) The approximate number of persons to be used to perform the private security functions.

(B) A description of the process used to hire such persons, including the method by which and the extent to which background checks regarding such persons are conducted.

(C) A description of how such persons are trained to carry out tasks specified under the contract relating to such functions.

(D) A description of each category of activity relating to such functions required by the contract.

(2) UPDATES OF INFORMATION- The information provided under paragraph (1) shall be updated by the contractor during contract performance as necessary.

(3) SAFEGUARDING INFORMATION- The head of each agency awarding a covered contract shall take such actions as are necessary to protect any information provided under paragraph (1) that is a trade secret, or commercial or financial information, from disclosure to persons outside the Government.

(4) ACCOUNTING- Each covered contract shall include the following requirements:

(A) Upon award of the contract, the contractor shall provide to the contracting officer cost estimates of salary, benefits, insurance, materials, logistics, travel, administrative costs, and other costs of carrying out private security functions under the contract.

(B) Before contract closeout (other than closeout of a firm, fixed price contract), the contractor shall provide to the contracting officer a report on the actual costs of carrying out private security functions under the contract, in the same categories as provided under subparagraph (A).

(5) QUARTERLY REPORTS ON STAFFING- Each covered contract shall require the contractor to submit to the contracting officer on a quarterly basis a report on the number of personnel performing private security functions under such contract during the preceding 90 days and on the location or locations in which such personnel performed such functions.

(6) OVERSIGHT- Before a covered contract is awarded, the head of the agency awarding the contract shall ensure that sufficient resources are available to enable contracting officers of the agency to perform oversight of the performance of private security functions under the contract, including oversight inspections of facilities and operations.

(7) WAIVER AUTHORITY-

(A) WAIVER- The head of the agency awarding a covered contract may waive a requirement of this subsection with respect to a contract in an emergency or exceptional situation, as determined by the head of the agency. Any such waiver shall be limited to the requirements that are impossible or impracticable to implement because of the emergency or exceptional situation.

(B) REPORT- Commencing 180 days after the date of the enactment of this Act, and continuing every 90 days thereafter, each head of an agency who has, during the preceding 90 days, waived a requirement under this subsection with respect to a covered contract shall submit to the committees of Congress referred to in subparagraph (C) a report that—

(i) describes each such waiver by the head of the agency, including the contract involved and the emergency or exceptional situation that justified such waiver; and

(ii) contains a plan for bringing each such contract into compliance with the waived requirements as soon as possible or an explanation of why such waiver needs to be permanent.

(C) COMMITTEES OF CONGRESS- The committees of Congress referred to in this subparagraph are the following:

(i) The Committees on Appropriations, Armed Services, Oversight and Government Reform, and Foreign Affairs of the House of Representatives.

(ii) The Committees on Appropriations, Armed Services, Homeland Security and Governmental Affairs, and Foreign Relations of the Senate.

(b) Reports Required-

(1) IN GENERAL- During a contingency operation, the head of each agency with any covered contracts in effect shall submit to Congress reports on such contracts in accordance with this subsection.

(2) MATTERS COVERED- Each report required by paragraph (1) shall include the following information:

(A) Total number of covered contracts awarded by the agency with respect to the contingency operation.

(B) The total number of contracting officers overseeing the covered contracts reported under subparagraph (A).

(C) The most current information available under subsection (a)(5) with respect to each covered contract.

(D) The number of covered contracts awarded since the last report.

(E) The total number of contract personnel working on the covered contracts reported under subparagraph (D).

(F) The total value of awards for covered contracts reported under subparagraph (D).

(G) A detailed catalogue of activities performed under covered contracts reported under subparagraph (D).

(3) DEADLINES- The head of an agency shall submit an initial report as required by paragraph (1) within 90 days after first awarding a covered contract, and shall issue additional reports thereafter every 90 days.

(4) COMMITTEES- The report required by paragraph (1) shall be submitted to the Committees on Appropriations and Armed Services of the House of Representatives and the Senate.

(5) FORM- The report required by paragraph (1) shall be submitted in unclassified form, but may include a classified annex.

SEC. 6. IMPROVED COORDINATION BETWEEN THE ARMED FORCES AND CONTRACTORS PERFORMING PRIVATE SECURITY FUNCTIONS IN CONTINGENCY OPERATIONS.

(a) Rules of Engagement-

(1) REQUIREMENT TO ISSUE- Not later than 15 days after the date on which a contingency operation is initiated, the Chairman of the Joint Chiefs of Staff shall issue rules of engagement regarding the circumstances under which force may be used by contract personnel performing private security functions within the area covered by the contingency operation and the types of force authorized. Each covered contract shall require contract personnel to adhere to the rules of engagement issued under this subsection.

(2) NOTIFICATION- The commander of the combatant command whose area of responsibility includes the theater of operations of a contingency operation shall communicate the rules of engagement for the contingency operation to contract personnel in accordance with subsection (c).

(3) EXCEPTIONS AND SPECIAL RULES- As appropriate, the Chairman of the Joint Chiefs of Staff may provide exceptions or special rules in the rules of engagement for specific contractors.

(b) Hiring, Training, and Equipment Standards Relating to Private Security Contractors-

(1) REGULATIONS- Not later than 30 days after the date on which a contingency operation is initiated, the head of each agency awarding a covered contract shall prescribe in regulations minimum standards (appropriate for the agency) for contract personnel performing private security functions within the area covered by the contingency operation, including minimum training and certification standards. The standards may vary based on the duties of personnel, but must address criminal records, security clearance requirements, and other issues that the head of the agency determines may lead to security or performance concerns.

(2) GUIDANCE FOR EQUIPMENT- The head of each agency awarding a covered contract shall issue guidance (appropriate for the agency) on equipment used for private security functions under covered contracts with the agency, including appropriate uniforms and levels of body armor and equipment armor, and a recommended list of re-armorers and weapons and armor manufacturers for complying with such guidelines.

(3) CONSULTATION WITH SECRETARY OF DEFENSE- The head of each agency shall consult with the Secretary of Defense in developing regulations and guidance under this subsection.

(c) Improved Coordination and Communication Between the Armed Forces and Contractors Performing Private Security Functions-

(1) DESIGNATION OF THEATER SECURITY CONTRACT COORDINATING OFFICER- For each contingency operation in which contract personnel performing private security functions are active, the Chairman of the Joint Chiefs of Staff shall designate a member of the Armed Forces or civilian employee of the Department to act as the coordinating officer on security contracts in the theater of operations of such contingency operation. The individual so designated shall be known as the 'Theater Security Contract Coordinating Officer' for the theater of operations of such contingency operation.

(2) RESPONSIBILITIES OF THEATER SECURITY CONTRACT COORDINATING OFFICER- The Theater Security Contract Coordinating Officer for a theater of operations of a contingency operation shall, for such theater of operations—

(A) establish regulations providing for reliable lines of communications between contract personnel performing private security functions and the Armed Forces;

(B) maintain a current database on the contract personnel performing such functions, including their employing contractors, nationalities, backgrounds, and training, and the nature of their activities;

(C) communicate the rules of engagement established under subsection (a) to contractors and contract personnel performing such functions;

(D) take any actions authorized by the Chairman of the Joint Chiefs of Staff for purposes of this subsection to ensure the compliance of contractors in the theater of operations with the requirements of paragraph (3);

(E) communicate other critical information, including guidance on Department of Defense responsibilities for force protection of contract personnel and guidance on equipment, to contractors and contract personnel; and

(F) as appropriate, communicate up-to-date information about the security environment that may be relevant to contract personnel.

(3) REQUIREMENTS FOR CONTRACTORS RELATING TO THEATER SECURITY CONTRACT COORDINATING OFFICER- Each contractor in a theater of operations of a contingency operation shall be required to—

(A) register with the Theater Security Contract Coordinating Officer for the theater of operations and keep the Officer currently informed on the number, nationality, background, and training of the contract personnel assigned to perform private security functions under a covered contract;

(B) report any incidents in which contract personnel performing such functions use force or are attacked by hostile forces;

(C) report to the Theater Security Contract Coordinating Officer any casualties suffered by covered contract personnel;

(D) communicate to the Theater Security Contract Coordinating Officer, in accordance with the regulations issued under paragraph (2)(A), tactical information, such

127

as information on the movement of contractor personnel performing such functions into and out of a battle space; and

(E) communicate to the Theater Security Contract Coordinating Officer relevant information, including intelligence, reports of hostile activity, or information relevant to military planning.

SEC. 7. LEGAL STATUS OF CONTRACT PERSONNEL.

(a) Clarification of Military Extraterritorial Jurisdiction Act-

(1) INCLUSION OF CONTRACTORS- Subsection (a) of section 3261 of title 18, United States Code, is amended—

(A) by striking 'or' at the end of paragraph (1);

(B) by striking the comma at the end of paragraph (2) and inserting '; or'; and

(C) by inserting after paragraph (2) the following:

'(3) while employed under a contract (or subcontract at any tier) awarded by any department or agency of the United States Government, where the work under such contract is carried out in a region outside the United States in which the Armed Forces are conducting a contingency operation,'.

(2) DEFINITION- Section 3267 of title 18, United States Code, is amended by adding at the end the following:

'(5) The term 'contingency operation' has the meaning given that term in section 101(a)(13) of title 10.'.

(b) Sense of Congress on Investigation and Prosecution of Abuses by Private Security Contractors and Others- It is the sense of Congress that—

(1) if there is probable cause to believe that an individual assigned to perform private security functions under a covered contract, any other contractor personnel, or any contractor has violated section 3261(a) of title 18, United States Code, except in situations in which the individual is prosecuted under chapter 47 of title 10, United States Code (the Uniform Code of Military Justice), or under other law, the Department of Defense should use the authority provided in section 3262 of title 18, United States Code, to arrest and detain such individual. personnel, or contractor and transfer such individual, personnel, or contractor to civilian authorities for prosecution; and

(2) the Secretary of Defense should issue guidance, as soon as possible after the date of the enactment of this Act, on how the amendment made by section 552 of the John Warner National Defense Authorization Act of 2007 (Public Law 109-364; 120 Stat. 2217) to section 802(a)(10) of title 10, United States Code (article 2(a)(10) of the Uniform Code of Military Justice), will be implemented.

(c) Department of Justice Inspector General Report-

(1) REPORT REQUIRED- Not later than 30 days after the date of the enactment of this Act, the Inspector General of the Department of Justice shall submit to Congress a report.

(2) CONTENT OF REPORT- The report shall include—

(A) a description of the status of Department of Justice investigations of abuses alleged to have been committed by contract personnel performing private security functions, other contract personnel, or contractors under covered contracts, which shall include—

(i) the number of complaints received by the Department of Justice;

(ii) the number of investigations into complaints opened by the Department of Justice;

(iii) the number of criminal cases opened by the Department of Justice; and

(iv) the number and result of criminal cases closed by the Department of Justice; and

(B) findings and recommendations about the capacity and effectiveness of the Department of Justice in prosecuting misconduct by such contract personnel.

(3) FORM- The report shall be submitted in unclassified form, but may include a classified annex.

SEC. 8. FEDERAL BUREAU OF INVESTIGATION INVESTIGATIVE UNIT FOR CONTINGENCY OPERATIONS.

(a) Establishment of Theater Investigative Unit- For each theater of operations established in connection with a contingency operation in which contract personnel are carrying out work under a covered contract, the Federal Bureau of Investigation shall establish a Theater Investigative Unit, which shall be responsible for investigating allegations of criminal misconduct under section 3261 of title 18, United States Code, by contract personnel.

(b) Responsibilities of Theater Investigative Unit- The Theater Investigative Unit established for a theater of operations shall—

(1) investigate reports that raise reasonable suspicion of criminal misconduct by contract personnel;

(2) investigate reports of fatalities resulting from the use of force by contract personnel; and

(3) upon conclusion of an investigation of alleged criminal misconduct, refer the case to the Attorney General of the United States for further action, as appropriate in the discretion of the Attorney General.

(c) Responsibilities of Federal Bureau of Investigation-

(1) RESOURCES- The Federal Bureau of Investigation shall ensure that each Theater Investigative Unit has adequate resources and personnel to carry out its responsibilities.

(2) NOTIFICATION- The Federal Bureau of Investigation shall notify Congress whenever a Theater Investigative Unit is established or terminated under this section.

(d) Responsibilities of Other Federal Agencies- An agency operating in a theater of operations in which a Theater Investigative Unit is established shall cooperate with and support the activities of the Theater Investigative Unit. Any investigation carried out by the Inspector General of an agency shall be coordinated with the activities of the unit as appropriate.

SEC. 9. DEFINITIONS.

In sections 5 through 8 of this Act:

(1) COVERED CONTRACT- The term 'covered contract' means—

(A) a prime contract awarded by an agency, if the work to be performed under the contract includes private security functions;

(B) a subcontract at any tier under any prime contract awarded by an agency, if the work to be performed under the subcontract includes private security functions; or

(C) a task order issued under a task or delivery order contract entered into by an agency, if the work to be performed under the task order includes private security functions.

(2) PRIVATE SECURITY FUNCTIONS- The term 'private security functions', with respect to activities carried out under a covered contract in a theater in which the United States is engaged in a contingency operation, means any activity as follows:

(A) Any activity for which personnel are allowed to carry weapons in the performance of the contract.

(B) The performance of—

(i) military logistics for operations;

(ii) maintenance or arming of weapons systems;

(iii) interrogation of prisoners;

(iv) convoy security;

(v) guarding vital facilities and personnel;

(vi) tactical security work; or

(vii) local force training.

(C) Any other activity in support of the contingency operation, as determined by the Theater Security Contract Coordinating Officer for the theater of operations of the contingency operation as designated under section 6(c)(1).

(3) AGENCY- The term 'agency' has the meaning given the term 'Executive agency' in section 105 of title 5, United States Code.

(4) CONTINGENCY OPERATION- The term 'contingency operation' has the meaning given the term section 101(13) of title 10, United States Code.

(5) CONTRACTOR- The term 'contractor' means an entity performing a covered contract (including a subcontract at any tier).

(6) CONTRACT PERSONNEL- The term 'contract personnel' means persons assigned by a contractor (including a subcontractor at any tier) to perform work under a covered contract.

SEC. 10. EFFECTIVE DATE.

(a) Applicability- The provisions of this Act shall apply to the following:

(1) All covered contracts and all covered contract personnel in which the work under the contract is carried out in a theater in which the United States is currently conducting contingency operations.

(2) In the event that the United States begins new contingency operations, all covered contracts and all covered contract personnel in which the work under the contract is carried out in a theater in which the United States is conducting such contingency operations.

(b) Immediate Effectiveness- The provisions of this Act shall enter into effect immediately upon the enactment of this Act.

(c) Implementation- With respect to covered contracts and covered contract personnel discussed in subsection (a)(1), the United States Government shall have 90 days following the enactment of this Act to ensure compliance with the provisions of this Act.

US SENATE BILL 692

TITLE: A bill to amend title 38, United States Code, to establish a Hospital Quality Report Card Initiative to report on health care quality in Veterans Affairs hospitals.

SPONSOR: Sen Obama, Barack [IL] (introduced 2/27/2007) Cosponsors (1)

RELATED BILLS: H.R.1448

LATEST MAJOR ACTION: 2/27/2007 Referred to Senate committee. Status: Read twice and referred to the Committee on Veterans' Affairs.

SUMMARY AS OF:

2/27/2007—Introduced.

VA Hospital Quality Report Card Act of 2007 - Directs the Secretary of Veterans Affairs to establish and implement a Hospital Quality Report Card Initiative to report on health care quality in Department of Veterans Affairs (VA) hospitals. Requires the Secretary, at least semiannually, to publish reports on VA hospital quality, including assessments of effectiveness, safety, timeliness, and efficiency.

MAJOR ACTIONS:

¤NONE¤

ALL ACTIONS:

2/27/2007:

Read twice and referred to the Committee on Veterans' Affairs.

TITLES(s): (italics indicate a title for a portion of a bill)

¤NONE¤

COSPONSORS(1), ALPHABETICAL [FOLLOWED BY COSPONSORS WITHDRAWN]: (Sort: by date)

Sen Wyden, Ron [OR] - 3/19/2007

COMMITTEE(S)

Committee/Subcommittee:

Activity:

Senate Veterans' Affairs

Referral, In Committee

RELATED BILL DETAILS: (additional related bills may be indentified in Status)

Bill:

Relationship:

H.R.1448

Related bill identified by CRS

AMENDMENT(S)

¤NONE¤

IN THE SENATE OF THE UNITED STATES

February 27, 2007

Mr. OBAMA introduced the following bill; which was read twice and referred to the Committee on Veterans' Affairs

A BILL

To amend title 38, United States Code, to establish a Hospital Quality Report Card Initiative to report on health care quality in Veterans Affairs hospitals.

Be it enacted by the Senate and House of Representatives of the United States of America in Congress assembled,

SECTION 1. SHORT TITLE.

This Act may be cited as the 'VA Hospital Quality Report Card Act of 2007'.

SEC. 2. PURPOSE.

The purpose of this Act is to establish the Hospital Quality Report Card Initiative under title 38, United States Code, to ensure that quality measures data for hospitals administered by the Secretary of Veterans Affairs are readily available and accessible in order to—

(1) inform patients and consumers about health care quality in such hospitals;

(2) assist Veterans Affairs health care providers in identifying opportunities for quality improvement and cost containment; and

(3) enhance the understanding of policy makers and public officials of health care issues, raise public awareness of hospital quality issues, and to help constituents of such policy makers and officials identify quality health care options.

SEC. 3. VA HOSPITAL QUALITY REPORT CARD INITIATIVE.

(a) In General- Subchapter III of chapter 17 of title 38, United States Code, is amended by adding at the end the following new section:

'Sec. 1730A. Hospital Quality Report Card Initiative

'(a) Not later than 18 months after the date of the enactment of the VA Hospital Quality Report Card Act of 2007, the Secretary shall establish and implement a Hospital Quality Report Card Initiative (in this section referred to as the 'Initiative') to report on health care quality in VA hospitals.

'(b) For purposes of this section, the term 'VA hospital' means a hospital administered by the Secretary.

'(c)(1)(A) Not less than 2 times each year, the Secretary shall publish reports on VA hospital quality. Such reports shall include quality measures data that allow for an assessment of health care—

'(i) effectiveness;

'(ii) safety;

'(iii) timeliness;

'(iv) efficiency;

'(v) patient-centeredness; and

'(vi) equity.

'(B) In collecting and reporting data as provided for under subparagraph (A), the Secretary shall include VA hospital information, as possible, relating to—

'(i) staffing levels of nurses and other health professionals, as appropriate;

'(ii) rates of nosocomial infections;

'(iii) the volume of various procedures performed;

'(iv) hospital sanctions and other violations;

'(v) the quality of care for various patient populations, including female, geriatric, disabled, rural, homeless, mentally ill, and racial and ethnic minority populations;

'(vi) the availability of emergency rooms, intensive care units, maternity care, and specialty services;

'(vii) the quality of care in various hospital settings, including inpatient, outpatient, emergency, maternity, and intensive care unit settings;

'(viii) ongoing patient safety initiatives; and

'(ix) other measures determined appropriate by the Secretary.

'(C)(i) In reporting data as provided for under subparagraph (A), the Secretary may risk adjust quality measures to account for differences relating to—

'(I) the characteristics of the reporting VA hospital, such as licensed bed size, geography, and teaching hospital status; and

'(II) patient characteristics, such as health status, severity of illness, and socioeconomic status.

'(ii) If the Secretary reports data under subparagraph (A) using risk-adjusted quality measures, the Secretary shall establish procedures for making the unadjusted data available to the public in a manner determined appropriate by the Secretary.

'(D) Under the Initiative, the Secretary may verify data reported under this paragraph to ensure accuracy and validity.

'(E) The Secretary shall disclose the entire methodology for the reporting of data under this paragraph to all relevant organizations and VA hospitals that are the subject of any such information that is to be made available to the public prior to the public disclosure of such information.

'(F)(i) The Secretary shall submit each report to the appropriate committees of Congress.

'(ii) The Secretary shall ensure that reports are made available under this section in an electronic format, in an understandable manner with respect to various populations (including those with low functional health literacy), and in a manner that allows health care quality comparisons to be made with local hospitals or regional hospitals, as appropriate.

'(iii) The Secretary shall establish procedures for making report findings available to the public, upon request, in a non-electronic format, such as through a toll-free telephone number.

'(G) The analytic methodologies and limitations on data sources utilized by the Secretary to develop and disseminate the comparative data under this section shall be identified and acknowledged as part of the dissemination of such data, and include the appropriate and inappropriate uses of such data.

'(H) On at least an annual basis, the Secretary shall compare quality measures data submitted by each VA hospital with data submitted in the prior year or years by the same hospital in order to identify and report actions that would lead to false or artificial improvements in the hospital's quality measurements.

'(2)(A) The Secretary shall develop and implement effective safeguards to protect against the unauthorized use or disclosure of VA hospital data that is reported under this section.

'(B) The Secretary shall develop and implement effective safeguards to protect against the dissemination of inconsistent, incomplete, invalid, inaccurate, or subjective VA hospital data.

'(C) The Secretary shall ensure that identifiable patient data shall not be released to the public.

'(d)(1) The Secretary shall evaluate and periodically submit a report to Congress on the effectiveness of the Initiative, including the effectiveness of the Initiative in meeting the purpose described in section 2 of the VA Hospital Quality Report Card Act of 2007. The Secretary shall make such reports available to the public.

'(2) The Secretary shall use the outcomes from the evaluation conducted pursuant to paragraph (1) to increase the usefulness of the Initiative.

'(e) There are authorized to be appropriated to carry out this section such sums as may be necessary for each of fiscal years 2008 through 2016.'.

(b) Clerical Amendment- The table of sections at the beginning of chapter 17, United States Code, is amended by inserting after the item relating to section 1730 the following new item:

'1730A. Hospital Quality Report Card Initiative.'.

US SENATE BILL 713

TITLE: A bill to ensure dignity in care for members of the Armed Forces recovering from injuries.

SPONSOR: Sen Obama, Barack [IL] (introduced 2/28/2007) Cosponsors (34)

RELATED BILLS: H.R.1268

LATEST MAJOR ACTION: 2/28/2007 Referred to Senate committee. Status: Read twice and referred to the Committee on Armed Services.

SUMMARY AS OF:

2/28/2007—Introduced.

Dignity for Wounded Warriors Act of 2007 - Requires each recovering servicemember who is assigned to a military barracks or dormitory to be assigned to one that is maintained at the highest service standard in effect for enlisted members of the Armed Forces. Requires at least semiannual inspections of, and appropriate repairs to, any such quarters, as well as alternate housing during periods of unremedied housing deficiencies.

Outlines requirements to be implemented for recovering servicemembers and their families, including: (1) physical disability evaluation system changes; (2) supervising officer and caseworker support; (3) increased training for caseworkers and social workers on particular servicemember conditions, including post-traumatic stress disorder (PTSD); (4) increased support services, including an Ombudsman for Recovering Servicemembers; (5) a prohibition on discrimination in employment of family members caring for such servicemembers; and (6) meal benefits for recovering servicemembers and family members caring for such servicemembers.

Establishes the Oversight Board for the Wounded.

MAJOR ACTIONS:

¤NONE¤

All Actions:

2/28/2007:

Sponsor introductory remarks on measure. (CR S2363-2364)

2/28/2007:

Read twice and referred to the Committee on Armed Services.

Titles(s): (italics indicate a title for a portion of a bill)

¤NONE¤

Cosponsors(34), Alphabetical [followed by Cosponsors withdrawn]: (Sort: by date)

Sen Baucus, Max [MT] - 2/28/2007

Sen Bayh, Evan [IN] - 2/28/2007

Sen Biden, Joseph R., Jr. [DE] - 2/28/2007

Sen Bingaman, Jeff [NM] - 2/28/2007

Sen Bond, Christopher S. [MO] - 2/28/2007

Sen Boxer, Barbara [CA] - 2/28/2007

Sen Brown, Sherrod [OH] - 2/28/2007

Sen Byrd, Robert C. [WV] - 3/8/2007

Sen Cantwell, Maria [WA] - 2/28/2007

Sen Cardin, Benjamin L. [MD] - 3/14/2007

Sen Carper, Thomas R. [DE] - 3/12/2007

Sen Conrad, Kent [ND] - 2/28/2007

Sen Dorgan, Byron L. [ND] - 2/28/2007

Sen Durbin, Richard [IL] - 2/28/2007

Sen Feingold, Russell D. [WI] - 2/28/2007

Sen Harkin, Tom [IA] - 3/6/2007

Sen Johnson, Tim [SD] - 5/11/2007

Sen Kerry, John F. [MA] - 2/28/2007

Sen Klobuchar, Amy [MN] - 2/28/2007

Sen Landrieu, Mary L. [LA] - 2/28/2007

Sen Lautenberg, Frank R. [NJ] - 3/12/2007

Sen Lieberman, Joseph I. [CT] - 3/1/2007

Sen Lincoln, Blanche L. [AR] - 3/7/2007

Sen McCaskill, Claire [MO] - 2/28/2007

Sen Mikulski, Barbara A. [MD] - 2/28/2007

Sen Murkowski, Lisa [AK] - 2/28/2007

Sen Pryor, Mark L. [AR] - 2/28/2007

Sen Rockefeller, John D., IV [WV] - 2/28/2007

Sen Sanders, Bernard [VT] - 2/28/2007

Sen Snowe, Olympia J. [ME] - 2/28/2007

Sen Stabenow, Debbie [MI] - 6/27/2007

Sen Tester, Jon [MT] - 6/12/2007

Sen Whitehouse, Sheldon [RI] - 4/19/2007

Sen Wyden, Ron [OR] - 3/19/2007

Committee(s)

Committee/Subcommittee:

Activity:

Senate Armed Services

Referral, In Committee

Related Bill Details: (additional related bills may be indentified in Status)

Bill:

Relationship:

H.R.1268

Related bill identified by CRS

Amendment(s)

¤NONE¤

In the Senate of the United States

February 28, 2007

Mr. OBAMA (for himself, Mrs. MCCASKILL, Mr. BAUCUS, Mr. BAYH, Mr. BIDEN, Mr. BINGAMAN, Mr. BOND, Mrs. BOXER, Mr. BROWN, Ms. CANTWELL, Mr. DORGAN, Mr. DURBIN, Mr. FEINGOLD, Mr. KERRY, Ms. KLOBUCHAR, Ms. LANDRIEU, Ms. MIKULSKI, Ms. MURKOWSKI, Mr. PRYOR, Mr. ROCKEFELLER, Mr. SANDERS, Ms. SNOWE, and Mr. CONRAD) introduced the following bill; which was read twice and referred to the Committee on Armed Services

A BILL

To ensure dignity in care for members of the Armed Forces recovering from injuries.

Be it enacted by the Senate and House of Representatives of the United States of America in Congress assembled,

SECTION 1. SHORT TITLE.

This Act may be cited as the 'Dignity for Wounded Warriors Act of 2007'.

SEC. 2. ACCESS OF RECOVERING SERVICEMEMBERS TO ADEQUATE OUTPATIENT RESIDENTIAL FACILITIES.

(a) Sufficiency of Residences-

(1) IN GENERAL- Each recovering servicemember who is assigned to a military barracks or dormitory shall be assigned to a barracks or dormitory that is maintained at a standard equal to the highest existing service standard in effect for quarters of the United States for enlisted members of the Armed Forces.

(2) INAPPLICABILITY TO CERTAIN FACILITIES- Facilities occupied by recovering servicemembers that are not funded with appropriated funds are not subject to the requirement under paragraph (1).

(b) Inspections and Repairs of Facilities-

(1) REQUIRED INSPECTIONS- All quarters of the United States and housing facilities under the jurisdiction of the Armed Forces that are occupied by at least 5 recovering servicemembers shall be inspected on a semiannual basis by the inspectors general of the regional medical commands.

(2) INSPECTOR GENERAL REPORTS- The inspector general for each regional medical command shall—

(A) submit a report on each inspection of a facility conducted under paragraph (1) to the post commander at such facility, the commanding officer of the hospital affiliated with such facility, the surgeon general of the military department that operates such hospital, the Secretary of the military department concerned, the Assistant Secretary of Defense for Health Affairs, the Oversight Board for the Wounded established pursuant to section 10, and the appropriate congressional committees; and

(B) post each such report on the Internet website of such regional medical command.

(3) ALTERNATE HOUSING-

(A) UNREMEDIED DEFICIENCIES- If a deficiency identified in a report submitted under paragraph (2) with respect to quarters or a facility is not remedied within 30 days after the submission of such report under that paragraph, each recovering servicemember occupying such quarters or facility and affected by the deficiency shall be provided the option of alternate quarters of the United States or housing facilities under the jurisdiction of the Armed Forces that meet the standard referred to in subsection (a)(1) until the deficiency is remedied.

(B) UNFULFILLED WORK ORDERS- If a work order issued to remedy a deficiency (including, but not limited to, deficiencies such as mold, leaking pipes, or rat, mouse, insect, or other pest infestation) in a room occupied by a recovering servicemember in quarters of the United States or a housing facility under the jurisdiction of the Armed Forces remains unfulfilled for more than 15 days after the date of the issuance of the work order, the servicemember shall be provided the option of alternate quarters of the United States or housing facilities under the jurisdiction of the Armed Forces that meet the standard referred to in subsection (a)(1) until the work order is fulfilled and the deficiency is remedied.

(c) Zero Tolerance for Chronic Infestations- If quarters of the United States or a housing facility under the jurisdiction of the Armed Forces that is occupied by a recovering servicemember is determined, whether pursuant to an inspection required by subsection (b)(1) or otherwise, to have a chronic infestation of rodents, insects, or other pests, the servicemember shall be provided the option of alternate quarters of the United States or housing facilities under the jurisdiction of the Armed Forces that meet the standard referred to in subsection (a)(1) until the deficiency is remedied.

SEC. 3. REDUCTION OF PAPERWORK AND BUREAUCRACY FOR RECOVERING SERVICEMEMBERS AND THEIR FAMILIES.

(a) Improvement of Physical Disability Evaluation Systems- Not later than one year after the date of the enactment of this Act, the Secretary of Defense shall implement appropriate improvements of the physical disability evaluation systems of the military departments, including the administrative and budgetary restructuring of such systems, in order to ensure their efficient and effective operation. The improvements shall include the requirement that, within each military department, a single command shall be responsible for the physical disability evaluation system of such military department, including any processing and military boards under such system.

(b) Electronic Clearing House-

(1) REQUIREMENT- In improving the physical disability evaluation system of a military department pursuant to this section, the Secretary of the military department shall establish and operate a single Internet site for the physical disability evaluation process under such system that enables recovering servicemembers to fully utilize such system through the Internet.

(2) ELEMENTS- Each Internet site operated under this subsection shall include the following:

(A) The availability of any forms required for the utilization of the applicable physical disability evaluation system by recovering servicemembers.

(B) Secure mechanisms for the submission of such forms by recovering servicemembers, and for the tracking of the acceptance and review of any forms so submitted.

(C) Secure mechanisms for advising recovering servicemembers of any additional information, forms, or other items that are required for the acceptance and review of any forms so submitted.

(D) The continuous availability of assistance to recovering servicemembers (including assistance through the caseworkers assigned to recovering servicemembers) in submitting and tracking such forms, including assistance in obtaining information, forms, or other items described by subparagraph (C).

(E) Secure mechanisms to request and receive personnel files or other personnel records of recovering servicemembers that are required for submission under the applicable physical disability evaluation system, including the capability to track requests for such files or records and to determine the status of such requests and of responses to such requests.

(3) DEADLINE FOR ESTABLISHMENT- Each Internet site required under this subsection shall be established not later than one year after the date of the enactment of this Act.

(4) NO REQUIREMENT FOR USE- This subsection may not be construed to require a recovering servicemember to utilize an Internet site established under this subsection as part of the physical disability evaluation process under a physical disability evaluation system.

(c) Co-Location of System Elements at Certain Facilities- In improving physical disability evaluation systems pursuant to this section, the Secretary of Defense shall—

(1) identify each military medical treatment facility covered by such system that serves, or is anticipated to serve, more than 100 recovering servicemembers simultaneously; and

(2) to the extent practicable, co-locate all elements of such system at a single location at each such facility.

(d) Report on Improvements-

(1) REPORT- Not later than 180 days after the date of the enactment of this Act, the Secretary of Defense shall submit to the appropriate congressional committees a report setting forth recommendations for the improvements required by subsection (a).

(2) RECOMMENDATIONS- The recommendations under paragraph (1) shall include recommendations for the following:

(A) Procedures to enable recovering servicemembers to interface with only one command while undergoing evaluation and care under a physical disability evaluation system.

(B) Procedures to allow clinical teams and the military chain of command to bypass significant parts of the applicable physical disability evaluation system in order to facilitate the prompt processing of cases under such system for specific injuries and illnesses.

(C) Specifications of the job requirements for every military occupational specialty (MOS) and grade.

(D) Means for retraining recovering servicemembers who are determined to be unfit for their assigned military occupational specialty for qualification for assignment to another military occupational specialty.

(E) Streamlining and reducing duplicative, unnecessary procedures and other obstacles to timely evaluations and decisions under a physical disability evaluation system.

(F) Such other matters with respect to the improvements required by subsection (a) as the Secretary and the Oversight Board for the Wounded consider appropriate.

(3) NO REDUCTION IN PERSONNEL AND RESOURCES- The requirements of this subsection may not be construed to authorize or require the reduction of staff,

or the closure of facilities, in order to achieve any improvements recommended under paragraph (1).

(e) Implementation- The Secretary of Defense shall commence the implementation of the recommendations submitted under subsection (d) not later than 90 days after the submission of the recommendations under that subsection.

(f) Retention of Certain Rights of Appeal- Nothing in the recommendations submitted and implemented under this section shall be construed to limit the ability of a recovering servicemember to appeal the following:

(1) The right of the recovering servicemember to remain a member of the Armed Forces.

(2) Any disability rating assigned the recovering servicemember.

(g) Consultation- The Secretary of Defense and the Secretaries of the military departments shall consult with and seek advice from the Oversight Board for the Wounded established pursuant to section 10 in carrying out this section.

SEC. 4. SUPERVISING OFFICER AND CASEWORKER SUPPORT FOR RECOVERING SERVICEMEMBERS.

(a) Provision of Adequate Support- Not later than one year after the date of the enactment of this Act, the Secretary of Defense shall work with officials from each military medical treatment facility—

(1) to assess whether the current ratio of supervising officers assigned to recovering servicemembers, and the current ratio of caseworkers assigned to recovering servicemembers, at such facility is adequate to meet the needs of recovering servicemembers at such facility; and

(2) to establish new ratios for such facility to increase such ratios where necessary, taking into account the needs of recovering servicemembers at such facility.

(b) Deadline for Achieving New Ratios- The Secretary shall ensure that the new ratios established pursuant to subsection (a)(2) are achieved not later than one year after the date of the enactment of this Act, and maintained each year thereafter.

(c) Annual Review of Ratios- The Secretary shall annually reevaluate the ratios established pursuant to subsection (a)(2), and shall monitor progress made in meeting such ratios.

(d) Employment of Additional Staff- Not later than 45 days after the date of the enactment of this Act, the Secretary shall hire such additional qualified staff as is necessary to achieve at each military medical treatment facility an interim ratio of one supervising officer, and one caseworker, for every 20 recovering servicemembers. Such ratios shall remain in effect until superseded under subsection (a)(2).

(e) Annual Report-

(1) REPORT REQUIRED- Not later than 90 days after the date of the enactment of this Act, and annually thereafter throughout the global war on terror, the Secretary shall submit to the appropriate congressional committees a report on current and planned ratios of supervising officers and caseworkers to recovering servicemembers at military medical treatment facilities under this section.

141

(2) ELEMENTS- Each report under paragraph (1) shall set forth the staff required to meet the new ratios established under subsection (a)(2), and include an estimate of the costs required to implement such plan.

(f) Consultation- The Secretary shall consult with and seek advice from the Oversight Board for the Wounded established pursuant to section 10 in carrying out this section.

SEC. 5. IMPROVED TRAINING FOR CASEWORKERS AND SOCIAL WORKERS ON PARTICULAR CONDITIONS OF RECOVERING SERVICEMEMBERS.

(a) Recommendations- Not later than 60 days after the date of the enactment of this Act, the Secretary of Defense shall submit to the appropriate congressional committees a report setting forth recommendations for the modification of the training provided to caseworkers and social workers who provide care for recovering servicemembers. The recommendations shall include, at a minimum, specific recommendations to ensure that such caseworkers and social workers are able to—

(1) detect early warning signs of post-traumatic stress disorder (PTSD) and suicidal tendencies among recovering servicemembers; and

(2) promptly devise appropriate treatment plans as such signs are detected.

(b) Annual Review of Training- Not later than 180 days after the date of the enactment of this Act and annually thereafter throughout the global war on terror, the Secretary shall submit to the appropriate congressional committees a report on the following:

(1) The progress made in providing the training recommended under subsection (a).

(2) The general state and quality of training provided to caseworkers and social workers who provide care for recovering servicemembers.

(c) Consultation- The Secretary shall consult with and seek advice from the Oversight Board for the Wounded established pursuant to section 10 in carrying out this section.

SEC. 6. SUPPORT SERVICES AND RIGHTS FOR RECOVERING SERVICEMEMBERS AND THEIR FAMILIES.

(a) Availability of Assistance for Recovering Servicemembers-

(1) NOTICE OF RIGHTS AND RESPONSIBILITIES- The Secretary of Defense shall clearly post, or provide for the posting, in all military medical treatment facilities, outpatient residences, and other hospital and residential care locations frequently utilized or visited by recovering servicemembers and their family members a notice of the rights and responsibilities of recovering servicemembers with respect to accessing quality and timely medical care and casework services and assistance during evaluation and care under a physical disability evaluation system.

(2) AVAILABILITY OF QUALIFIED PROFESSIONALS AT OUTPATIENT RESIDENTIAL FACILITIES- Each military outpatient residential facility at which at least 20 recovering servicemembers reside shall be staffed at all times with each of the following:

(A) At least one medical professional with the minimum qualifications of an emergency medical technician to provide care and services for recovering servicemembers at such facility.

(B) At least one clinical professional with the minimum qualifications of a certified clinical social worker or certified crisis counselor to provide care and services for recovering servicemembers at such facility.

(b) Assistance Hotlines-

(1) IN GENERAL- Not later than 90 days after the date of the enactment of this Act, the Secretaries of the military departments shall each establish and maintain for the military department concerned the following toll-free telephone assistance hotlines:

(A) A hotline for crisis counseling for recovering servicemembers and their family members.

(B) A hotline for recovering servicemembers and their family members (to be known as the 'Wounded Servicemember Rights and Family Respite Hotline') that—

(i) facilitates the reporting of delays and provides casework advocacy;

(ii) provides casework advice;

(iii) provides referrals to family and veteran support groups; and

(iv) facilitates the reporting of substandard conditions, casework services, or assistance during evaluation and care under a physical disability evaluation system.

(2) AVAILABILITY- The hotlines required by paragraph (1) shall operate at all times.

(3) BILINGUAL ASSISTANCE- The hotlines required by paragraph (1) shall be staffed at all times with operators fluent in English and Spanish.

(c) Ombudsmen for Recovering Servicemembers-

(1) IN GENERAL- The Secretary of Defense shall establish within each regional medical command of the Armed Forces the position of Ombudsman for Recovering Servicemembers (in this subsection referred to as the 'Ombudsman' or 'Ombudsmen').

(2) ASSIGNMENT- The Secretary shall assign to each position established under paragraph (1) a member of the Armed Forces or civilian employee of the Department of Defense who is qualified to discharge the duties of the position.

(3) DUTIES- Each Ombudsman shall act as a liaison for recovering servicemembers and their family members with respect to the evaluation and care of recovering servicemembers under the physical disability evaluation systems.

(4) OUTREACH- The Secretary shall make available to each recovering servicemember, and to the family members of all recovering servicemembers, information on contacting and utilizing the services of the Ombudsmen.

(d) Mechanisms for Obtaining Feedback on Outpatient Care- The Secretary of Defense shall establish the following mechanisms for obtaining feedback from recovering servicemembers and their family members on the quality of outpatient care available to recovering servicemembers through the Department of Defense:

(1) An anonymous feedback system that is available to recovering servicemembers and their family members in all military medical treatment facilities and all military out-patient residential facilities housing at least 5 recovering servicemembers and through the Internet.

(2) Convocations, town hall meetings, or other forums held at military medical treatment facilities at least once per month.

(e) Outpatient Care Manual- The Secretary of Defense shall publish and make available to all recovering servicemembers a single manual, in either English or Spanish, to guide them and their family members throughout the applicable physical disability evaluation system. The manual shall list all relevant locations and points of contact and shall include information on retrieving documentation required for medical processing.

(f) Consultation- The Secretary of Defense and the Secretaries of the military departments shall consult with and seek advice from the Oversight Board for the Wounded established pursuant to section 10 in carrying out this section.

SEC. 7. SUPPORT SERVICES FOR FAMILIES OF RECOVERING SERVICEMEMBERS.

(a) Medical Care- A family member of a recovering servicemember who is not otherwise eligible for medical care at a military medical treatment facility shall be eligible for such care if the family member is—

(1) on invitational orders while caring for the recovering servicemember;

(2) a non-medical attendee caring for the recovering servicemember; or

(3) receiving per diem payments from the Department of Defense while caring for the recovering servicemember.

(b) Job Placement Services- A family member who is on invitational orders or is a non-medical attendee while caring for a recovering servicemember for more than 45 days during a one-year period shall be eligible for job placement services otherwise offered by the Department of Defense.

SEC. 8. PROHIBITION ON DISCRIMINATION IN EMPLOYMENT AGAINST CERTAIN FAMILY MEMBERS CARING FOR RECOVERING SERVICEMEMBERS.

(a) Prohibition- A family member of a recovering servicemember described in subsection (b) shall not be denied retention in employment, promotion, or any benefit of employment by an employer on the basis of the person's absence from employment as described in that subsection.

(b) Covered Family Members- A family member described in this subsection is a family member of a recovering servicemember who is—

(1) on invitational orders while caring for the recovering servicemember;

(2) a non-medical attendee caring for the recovering servicemember; or

(3) receiving per diem payments from the Department of Defense while caring for the recovering servicemember.

(c) Treatment of Actions- An employer shall be considered to have engaged in an action prohibited by subsection (a) with respect to a person described in that subsection if the absence from employment of the person as described in that subsection is a motivating factor in the employer's action, unless the employer can prove that the action would have been taken in the absence of the absence of employment of the person.

(d) Definitions- In this section, the terms 'benefit of employment' and 'employer' have the meaning given such terms in section 4303 of title 38, United States Code.

SEC. 9. MEAL BENEFITS FOR RECOVERING SERVICEMEMBERS AND CERTAIN FAMILY MEMBERS CARING FOR RECOVERING SERVICEMEMBERS.

(a) Prohibition on Charges for Meals- Each individual described in subsection (b) shall not be required to pay any charge for meals provided such individual by the military medical treatment facility concerned as described in that subsection.

(b) Covered Individuals- An individual described in this subsection is any individual as follows:

(1) A recovering servicemember who is undergoing medical treatment, recuperation, or therapy, or is otherwise in medical hold or holdover status, in a military medical treatment facility for an injury, illness, or disease incurred or aggravated while on active duty in the Armed Forces.

(2) A family member of a recovering servicemember described in paragraph (1) who is—

(A) on invitational orders while caring for the recovering servicemember;

(B) a non-medical attendee caring for the recovering servicemember; or

(C) receiving per diem payments from the Department of Defense while caring for the recovering servicemember.

(c) Effective Date- The prohibition in subsection (a) shall take effect on the date of the enactment of this Act, and shall apply with respect to meals provided individuals covered by that subsection on or after that date.

SEC. 10. OVERSIGHT BOARD FOR THE WOUNDED.

(a) Establishment- There is hereby established a board to be known as the Oversight Board for the Wounded (in this section referred to as the 'Oversight Board').

(b) Composition- The Oversight Board shall be composed of 12 members, of whom—

(1) two shall be appointed by the majority leader of the Senate;

(2) two shall be appointed by the minority leader of the Senate;

(3) two shall be appointed by the Speaker of the House of Representatives;

(4) two shall be appointed by the minority leader of the House of Representatives;

(5) two shall be appointed by the President; and

(6) two shall be appointed by the Secretary of Defense.

(c) Qualifications-

(1) PARTICULAR QUALIFICATIONS- The Oversight Board shall include members with the following qualifications:

(A) One member shall be a veteran who served in Operation Enduring Freedom or Operation Iraqi Freedom.

(B) Two members shall have received treatment for injuries at a military medical treatment facility since September 11, 2001.

(C) One member shall be a former non-medical attendant for a recovering servicemember, such as a person who received and accepted invitational orders to care for a recovering servicemember.

(D) One member shall be a veteran who received treatment at a military medical treatment facility for injuries sustained in armed hostilities before Operation Enduring Freedom and Operation Iraqi Freedom.

(E) One member shall be a civilian expert in military healthcare.

(2) GENERAL QUALIFICATIONS- All members of the Oversight Board shall have sufficient knowledge of, or experience with, the military healthcare system or the experience of a recovering servicemember or family member of a recovering servicemember.

(d) Duties-

(1) ADVICE AND CONSULTATION- The Oversight Board shall provide advice and consultation to the Department of Defense and the appropriate congressional committees regarding—

(A) the process for streamlining the physical disability evaluation systems of the military departments under section 3;

(B) the process for correcting and improving the ratios of caseworkers and supervising officers to recovering servicemembers under section 4;

(C) the need to revise Department of Defense policies to improve the experience of recovering servicemembers while under Department of Defense care;

(D) the need to revise Department of Defense policies to improve counseling, outreach, and general services provided to family members of recovering servicemembers pursuant to sections 6 and 7;

(E) the need to revise Department of Defense policies regarding the provision of quality lodging to recovering servicemembers;

(F) progress made in implementing this Act; and

(G) such other matters relating to the evaluation and care of recovering servicemembers, including evaluation and care under physical disability evaluation systems, as the Board considers appropriate.

(2) VISITS TO MILITARY MEDICAL TREATMENT FACILITIES- In carrying out its duties, each member of the Oversight Board shall visit not less than three

military medical treatment facilities each year, and shall conduct each year at least one meeting of all the members of the Board at a military medical treatment facility.

(e) Staff- The Secretary shall make available the services of at least two officials or employees of the Department of Defense to provide support and assistance to members of the Oversight Board.

(f) Travel Expenses- Members of the Oversight Board shall be allowed travel expenses, including per diem in lieu of subsistence, at rates authorized for employees of agencies under subchapter I of chapter 57 of title 5, United States Code, while away from their homes or regular places of business in the performance of service for the Oversight Board.

(g) Access to Information-

(1) IN GENERAL- Except as provided in paragraph (2), the members of the Oversight Board shall have the right to access information related to the deliberations, processes, and documents of the Department of Defense pertaining to actions taken under this Act.

(2) NATIONAL SECURITY EXCEPTION- The Oversight Board shall not have the right to access information otherwise required under paragraph (1) if the Secretary—

(A) notifies the Oversight Board that disclosure of such information would compromise the national security of the United States; and

(B) upon request of the Oversight Board, provides the information in classified form to the appropriate congressional committees.

(h) Annual Reports- The Oversight Board shall submit to the Secretary of Defense and the appropriate congressional committees each year a report on its activities under this Act during the preceding year, including any findings and recommendations of the Oversight Board as a result of such activities.

SEC. 11. DEFINITIONS.

In this Act:

(1) APPROPRIATE CONGRESSIONAL COMMITTEES- The term 'appropriate congressional committees' means—

(A) the Committee on Armed Services of the Senate; and

(B) the Committee on Armed Services of the House of Representatives.

(2) FAMILY MEMBER- The term 'family member', with respect to a recovering servicemember, has the meaning given that term in section 411h(b) of title 37, United States Code.

(3) PHYSICAL DISABILITY EVALUATION SYSTEMS- The term 'physical disability evaluation systems' means the following:

(A) In the case of the Department of the Army, the Physical Disability Evaluation System (PDES) of the Army.

(B) In the case of any other military department, the physical disability evaluation system or similar system or process of such military departments that carries out functions equivalent to the function carried out for the Army by the Physical Disability Evaluation System of the Army.

(4) RECOVERING SERVICEMEMBER- The term 'recovering servicemember' means a member of the Armed Forces, including a member of the National Guard or a Reserve, who is undergoing medical treatment, recuperation, or therapy, or is otherwise in medical hold or holdover status, for an injury, illness, or disease incurred or aggravated while on active duty in the Armed Forces.

US SENATE BILL 737

TITLE: A bill to amend the Help America Vote Act of 2002 in order to measure, compare, and improve the quality of voter access to polls and voter services in the administration of Federal elections in the States.

SPONSOR: Sen Obama, Barack [IL] (introduced 3/1/2007) Cosponsors (1)

LATEST MAJOR ACTION: 3/1/2007 Referred to Senate committee. Status: Read twice and referred to the Committee on Rules and Administration.

SUMMARY AS OF:

3/1/2007—Introduced.

Voter Advocate and Democracy Index Act of 2007 - Amends the Help America Vote Act of 2002 to establish within the Election Assistance Commission an Office of the Voter Advocate to develop and administer a program to: (1) collect specified voter data from states with respect to each election for federal office; (2) develop, refine, and publish a Democracy Index; (3) make grants to eligible entities; and (4) make recommendations to states to improve their performance in the administration of federal elections (as determined based on a state-by-state comparison of the voter data collected under this Act.)

Directs the Office to establish a Democracy Index Pilot Program for calendar year 2008 to make grants to eligible entities for the purpose of creating a Democracy Index.

Requires each state to submit to the Office of the Voter Advocate specified voter data with respect to each election for federal office.

MAJOR ACTIONS:

¤NONE¤

ALL ACTIONS:

3/1/2007:

Sponsor introductory remarks on measure. (CR S2503)

3/1/2007:

Read twice and referred to the Committee on Rules and Administration.

TITLES(S): (italics indicate a title for a portion of a bill)

¤NONE¤

COSPONSORS(I), ALPHABETICAL [FOLLOWED BY COSPONSORS WITH-
DRAWN]: (Sort: by date)

Sen Feingold, Russell D. [WI] - 7/24/2007

COMMITTEE(S)

Committee/Subcommittee:

Activity:

Senate Rules and Administration

Referral, In Committee

RELATED BILL DETAILS:

¤NONE¤

AMENDMENT(S)

¤NONE¤

IN THE SENATE OF THE UNITED STATES

March 1, 2007

Mr. OBAMA introduced the following bill; which was read twice and referred to the Committee on Rules and Administration

A BILL

To amend the Help America Vote Act of 2002 in order to measure, compare, and improve the quality of voter access to polls and voter services in the administration of Federal elections in the States.

Be it enacted by the Senate and House of Representatives of the United States of America in Congress assembled,

SECTION 1. SHORT TITLE.

This Act may be cited as the 'Voter Advocate and Democracy Index Act of 2007'.

SEC. 2. OFFICE OF THE VOTER ADVOCATE AND STATE REQUIRE-
MENT TO REPORT VOTER DATA.

(a) Office of the Voter Advocate-

(1) IN GENERAL- Subtitle A of title II of the Help America Vote Act of 2002 (42 U.S.C. 15321 et seq.) is amended by adding at the end the following new part:

'PART 4—OFFICE OF THE VOTER ADVOCATE

'SEC. 223. OFFICE OF THE VOTER ADVOCATE.

Senate Bills and Resolutions Sponsored By

'(a) In General- There is established within the Commission an Office of the Voter Advocate (in this section referred to as the 'Office').

'(b) Duties- The Office shall develop and administer a program to—

'(1) collect the voter data described in subsection (c) from States with respect to each election for Federal office;

'(2) develop, refine, and publish a Democracy Index (as described in subsection (f));

'(3) make grants to eligible entities under section 224; and

'(4) provide recommendations to States to improve their performance in the administration of Federal elections (as determined based on a State-by-State comparison of the voter data collected under paragraph (1)).

'(c) Voter Data Described- The voter data described in this subsection includes any data the Office determines appropriate for developing or refining the Democracy Index published under subsection (b), which may include the following:

'(1) The amount of time spent by voters waiting in line.

'(2) The number of voters who appeared at, or were incorrectly directed to, the wrong polling place.

'(3) The rate of voter ballots discarded or not counted, and the reasons those voter ballots were discarded or not counted.

'(4) Provisional voting rates, including the percentage of provisional ballots that were cast and not counted and the reasons those provisional ballots were not counted.

'(5) The number and a description of registration and election day complaints, including any problems faced by individual voters in becoming involved and effectively participating in the process and the reasons given for such problems.

'(6) The rate of voting system malfunctions and the time required on average to put malfunctioning voting systems back online or otherwise correct the malfunction, or to replace them.

'(d) Consultation-

'(1) IN GENERAL- In developing and refining the Democracy Index published under subsection (b), the Office shall consult an independent Board of Advisors (as described in paragraph (2)).

'(2) INDEPENDENT BOARD OF ADVISORS- The Independent Board of Advisors consulted under paragraph (1) shall be composed of 20 members, selected by the Office from—

'(A) the academic, nonprofit, and election administration communities; and

'(B) Citizen Advisors nominated by the chief State election official of each State.

'(e) Coordination With States- The Office may, in coordination with a State, select precincts within the State on a sample basis from which to draw the information described in subsection (c) in order to form statistical conclusions. In forming such statistical conclusions, the Office may append the information collected from the

150

samples to other information provided by the State that was collected with respect to elections for Federal office in that State.

'(f) Democracy Index- The Democracy Index published under subsection (b) shall include the information described in subsection (c) with respect to each election for Federal office, presented on a State-by-State basis that allows for—

'(1) comparisons and rankings between States along each category of voter data collected under this section; and

'(2) an aggregate ranking of each State across all categories of such voter data.

'(g) Report- The Office shall submit an annual report to Congress and to chief State elections officials of each State that includes the voter data collected under subsection (b), together with any recommendations for—

'(1) improving the types of voter data that are collected and included in the Democracy Index published under such subsection; and

'(2) taking into consideration the voter data collected under such subsection, legislation or administrative action to improve State performance in the administration of Federal elections (as determined based on a State-by-State comparison of such voter data).

'SEC. 224. DEMOCRACY INDEX PILOT PROGRAM.

'(a) Establishment-

'(1) IN GENERAL- The Office shall establish a Democracy Index Pilot Program (in this section referred to as the 'pilot program') for calendar year 2008 to make grants to eligible entities for the purpose of creating a Democracy Index (consistent with the requirements of section 223).

'(2) ELIGIBLE ENTITY- In this section, the term 'eligible entity' means—

'(A) a State;

'(B) a nonprofit voting rights organization; and

'(C) any other organization the Office determines appropriate for the purpose of carrying out this section.

'(3) DURATION- The pilot program shall be conducted with respect to the general election for Federal office held in 2008.

'(b) Use of Funds- A grant awarded under subsection (a) shall be used for the following purposes:

'(1) For the collection of voter data described in section 223(c) through survey research.

'(2) The development and implementation of innovative proposals for adding—

'(A) to the types of voter data collected under such section; and

'(B) efficient mechanisms for collecting such voter data.

'(3) The development and use of methodologies to check such voter data for accuracy and uniformity.

'(c) Publication of Program Scope and Measures- Not later than 6 months before the general election held in 2008, the Commission shall publish a description of the scope of the program, including—

'(1) the voter data that will be included in the Democracy Index (consistent with the requirements of section 223); and

'(2) which States will receive a grant and participate in the pilot program under this section.

'(d) Report- Not later than 6 months after the regularly scheduled general election for Federal office held in 2008, the Office shall submit a report to Congress and each chief State election officials on the pilot program conducted under this section, together with recommendations for such legislation and administrative action as the Secretary determines appropriate.

'SEC. 225. FUNDING.

'There are authorized to be appropriated such sums as are necessary to carry out this part.'.

(2) CONFORMING AMENDMENT- The table of contents of the Help America Vote Act of 2002 is amended by inserting after the item relating to section 222 the following:

'PART 4—Office of the Voter Advocate

'Sec. 223. Office of the Voter Advocate.

'Sec. 224. Democracy Index Pilot Program.

'Sec. 225. Funding.'.

(b) State Requirement-

(1) IN GENERAL- Title III of the Help America Vote Act of 2002 is amended—

(A) by redesignating sections 304 and 305 as sections 305 and 306, respectively; and

(B) by inserting after section 303 the following new section:

'SEC. 304. REPORTING OF STATE VOTER DATA.

'(a) In General- Each State shall submit to the Office of the Voter Advocate the voter data described in section 223(c) with respect to each election for Federal office. Such voter data shall be submitted at the time and place, and in the manner, requested by the Office of the Voter Advocate.

'(b) Effective Date- This section shall apply with respect to general elections for Federal office held after 2008.'.

(2) ENFORCEMENT- Section 401 of the Help America Vote Act of 2002 is amended by striking 'and 303' and inserting '303, and 304'.

(3) CONFORMING AMENDMENT- The table of contents of the Help America Vote Act of 2002 is amended—

(A) by redesignating the items relating to sections 304 and 305 as relating to sections 305 and 306, respectively; and

(B) by inserting after the item relating to section 303 the following:

'Sec. 304. Reporting of State voter data.'.

US Senate Bill 767

Title: A bill to increase fuel economy standards for automobiles and for other purposes.

Sponsor: Sen Obama, Barack [IL] (introduced 3/6/2007) Cosponsors (6)

Related Bills: H.R.1506, S.768, S.875

Latest Major Action: 3/6/2007 Referred to Senate committee. Status: Read twice and referred to the Committee on Commerce, Science, and Transportation.

Summary As Of:

3/6/2007—Introduced.

Fuel Economy Reform Act - Amends federal transportation law to: (1) revise the definitions of automobile to require including all automobiles up to 10,000 pounds (currently, not all automobiles up to 10,000 pounds are required to be included in the definition) and passenger automobiles to eliminate the exclusion for automobiles capable of off-highway operation; and (2) continue applying the current minimum corporate average fuel economy (CAFE) standards for non-passenger and passenger automobiles to automobiles manufactured through model year 2012, but, for passenger automobiles, adds an increase of four percent per year in such standard for model years 2010 through 2012.

Requires an average fuel economy standard of 27.5 miles per gallon for all automobiles manufactured by all manufacturers for model year 2013, with an increase of four percent in the average fuel economy over the level of the prior model year for model year 2014 and beyond.

Subjects each manufacturer of passenger automobiles manufactured in a model year, in addition to such CAFE standards, to an average fuel economy standard equal to 92% of the average fuel economy projected by the Secretary for all passenger automobiles manufactured by all manufacturers in that model year.

Permits lower fuel economy standards if the minimum standards: (1) are technologically unachievable; (2) materially reduce auto safety and no offsetting safety improvements can be implemented; or (3) are not cost effective.

Allows, with specified exceptions, the selling of credits between manufacturers.

Allows a person who has been aggrieved by, or suffers a legal wrong because of (currently, adversely affected by), a CAFE standard to apply for judicial review.

153

MAJOR ACTIONS:

¤NONE¤

ALL ACTIONS:

3/6/2007:

Sponsor introductory remarks on measure. (CR S2700-2701)

3/6/2007:

Read twice and referred to the Committee on Commerce, Science, and Transportation. (text of measure as introduced: CR S2701-2703)

TITLES(s): (italics indicate a title for a portion of a bill)

¤NONE¤

COSPONSORS(6), ALPHABETICAL [FOLLOWED BY COSPONSORS WITH-DRAWN]: (Sort: by date)

Sen Biden, Joseph R., Jr. [DE] - 3/6/2007

Sen Bingaman, Jeff [NM] - 3/6/2007

Sen Coleman, Norm [MN] - 3/6/2007

Sen Lugar, Richard G. [IN] - 3/6/2007

Sen Smith, Gordon H. [OR] - 3/6/2007

Sen Specter, Arlen [PA] - 3/6/2007

COMMITTEE(s)

Committee/Subcommittee:

Activity:

Senate Commerce, Science, and Transportation

Referral, In Committee

RELATED BILL DETAILS: (additional related bills may be indentified in Status)

Bill:

Relationship:

H.R.1506

Related bill identified by CRS

S.768

Related bill identified by CRS

S.875

Related bill identified by CRS

Amendment(s)

¤NONE¤

In the Senate of the United States

March 6, 2007

Mr. OBAMA (for himself, Mr. LUGAR, Mr. BIDEN, Mr. SMITH, Mr. BINGA-MAN, Mr. COLEMAN, and Mr. SPECTER) introduced the following bill; which was read twice and referred to the Committee on Commerce, Science, and Transportation

A BILL

To increase fuel economy standards for automobiles and for other purposes.

Be it enacted by the Senate and House of Representatives of the United States of America in Congress assembled,

SECTION 1. SHORT TITLE.

This Act may be cited as the 'Fuel Economy Reform Act'.

SEC. 2. FINDINGS.

Congress makes the following findings:

(1) United States dependence on oil imports imposes tremendous burdens on the economy, foreign policy, and military of the United States.

(2) According to the Energy Information Administration, 60 percent of the crude oil and petroleum products consumed in the United States between April 2005 and March 2006 (12,400,000 barrels per day) were imported. At a cost of $75 per barrel of oil, people in the United States remit more than $600,000 per minute to other countries for petroleum.

(3) A significant percentage of these petroleum imports originate in countries controlled by regimes that are unstable or openly hostile to the interests of the United States. Dependence on production from these countries contributes to the volatility of domestic and global markets and the 'risk premium' paid by consumers in the United States.

(4) The Energy Information Administration projects that the total petroleum demand in the United States will increase by 23 percent between 2006 and 2026, while domestic crude production is expected to decrease by 11 percent, resulting in an anticipated 28 percent increase in petroleum imports. Absent significant action, the United States will become more vulnerable to oil price increases, more dependent upon foreign oil, and less able to pursue national interests.

(5) Two-thirds of all domestic oil use occurs in the transportation sector, which is 97 percent reliant upon petroleum-based fuels. Passenger vehicles, including light trucks under 10,000 pounds gross vehicle weight, represent over 60 percent of the oil used in the transportation sector.

(6) Corporate average fuel economy of all cars and trucks improved by 70 percent between 1975 and 1987. Between 1987 and 2006, fuel economy improvements have stagnated and the fuel economy of the United States is lower than many developed countries and some developing countries.

(7) Significant improvements in engine technology occurred between 1986 and 2006. These advances have been used to make vehicles larger and more powerful, and have not focused solely on increasing fuel economy.

(8) According to a 2002 fuel economy report by the National Academy of Sciences, fuel economy can be increased without negatively impacting the safety of cars and trucks in the United States. Some new technologies can increase both safety and fuel economy (such as high strength materials, unibody design, lower bumpers). Design changes related to fuel economy also present opportunities to reduce the incompatibility of tall, stiff, heavy vehicles with the majority of vehicles on the road.

(9) Significant change must occur to strengthen the economic competitiveness of the domestic auto industry. According to a recent study by the University of Michigan, a sustained gasoline price of $2.86 per gallon would lead Detroit's Big 3 automakers' profits to shrink by $7,000,000,000 as they absorb 75 percent of the lost vehicle sales. This would put nearly 300,000 people in the United States out of work.

(10) Opportunities exist to strengthen the domestic vehicle industry while improving fuel economy. A 2004 study performed by the University of Michigan concludes that providing $1,500,000,000 in tax incentives over a 10-year period to encourage domestic manufacturers and parts facilities to produce clean cars will lead to a gain of nearly 60,000 domestic jobs and pay for itself through the resulting increase in domestic tax receipts.

SEC. 3. DEFINITION OF AUTOMOBILE AND PASSENGER AUTOMOBILE.

(a) Definition of Automobile-

(1) IN GENERAL- Paragraph (3) of section 32901(a) of title 49, United States Code, is amended by striking 'rated at—' and all that follows through the period at the end and inserting 'rated at not more than 10,000 pounds gross vehicle weight.'.

(2) FUEL ECONOMY INFORMATION- Section 32908(a) of such title is amended, by striking 'section—' and all that follows through '(2)' and inserting 'section, the term'.

(3) EFFECTIVE DATE- The amendments made by paragraphs (1) and (2) shall apply to model year 2010 and each subsequent model year.

(b) Definition of Passenger Automobile-

(1) IN GENERAL- Paragraph (16) of section 32901(a) of such title is amended by striking ', but does not include' and all that follows through the end and inserting a period.

(2) EFFECTIVE DATE- The amendment made by paragraph (1) shall apply to model year 2012 and each subsequent model year.

SEC. 4. AVERAGE FUEL ECONOMY STANDARDS.

(a) Standards- Section 32902 of title 49, United States Code, is amended—

(1) in subsection (a)—

(A) in the heading, by inserting 'Manufactured Before Model Year 2013' after 'Non-Passenger Automobiles'; and

(B) by adding at the end the following: 'This subsection shall not apply to automobiles manufactured after model year 2012.';

(2) in subsection (b)—

(A) in the heading, by inserting 'Manufactured Before Model Year 2013' after 'Passenger Automobiles';

(B) by inserting 'and before model year 2010' after '1984'; and

(C) by adding at the end the following: 'Such standard shall be increased by 4 percent per year for model years 2010 through 2012 (rounded to the nearest 1/10 mile per gallon)';

(3) by amending subsection (c) to read as follows:

'(c) Automobiles Manufactured After Model Year 2012- (1)(A) Not later than 18 months before the beginning of each model year after model year 2012, the Secretary of Transportation shall prescribe, by regulation—

'(i) an average fuel economy standard for automobiles manufactured by a manufacturer in that model year; or

'(ii) based on 1 or more vehicle attributes that relate to fuel economy—

'(I) separate average fuel economy standards for different classes of automobiles; or

'(II) average fuel economy standards expressed in the form of a mathematical function.

'(B)(i) Except as provided under paragraphs (3) and (4) and subsection (d), average fuel economy standards under subparagraph (A) shall attain a projected aggregate level of average fuel economy of 27.5 miles per gallon for all automobiles manufactured by all manufacturers for model year 2013.

'(ii) The projected aggregate level of average fuel economy for model year 2014 and each model year thereafter shall be increased by 4 percent over the level of the prior model year (rounded to the nearest 1/10 mile per gallon).

'(2) In addition to the average fuel economy standards under paragraph (1), each manufacturer of passenger automobiles shall be subject to an average fuel economy standard for passenger automobiles manufactured by a manufacturer in a model year that shall be equal to 92 percent of the average fuel economy projected by the Secretary for all passenger automobiles manufactured by all manufacturers in that model year. An average fuel economy standard under this subparagraph for a model year shall be promulgated at the same time as the standard under paragraph (1) for such model year.

'(3) If the actual aggregate level of average fuel economy achieved by manufacturers for each of 3 consecutive model years is 5 percent or more less than the projected aggregate level of average fuel economy for such model year, the Secretary may make appropriate adjustments to the standards prescribed under this subsection.

'(4)(A) Notwithstanding paragraphs (1) through (3) and subsection (b), the Secretary of Transportation may prescribe a lower average fuel economy standard for 1 or more model years if the Secretary of Transportation, in consultation with the Secretary of Energy, finds, by clear and convincing evidence, that the minimum standards prescribed under paragraph (1)(B) or (3) or subsection (b) for each model year—

'(i) are technologically not achievable;

'(ii) cannot be achieved without materially reducing the overall safety of automobiles manufactured or sold in the United States and no offsetting safety improvements can be practicably implemented for that model year; or

'(iii) is shown not to be cost effective.

'(B) If a lower standard is prescribed for a model year under subparagraph (A), such standard shall be the maximum standard that—

'(i) is technologically achievable;

'(ii) can be achieved without materially reducing the overall safety of automobiles manufactured or sold in the United States; and

'(iii) is cost effective.

'(5) In determining cost effectiveness under paragraph (4)(A)(iii), the Secretary of Transportation shall take into account the total value to the United States of reduced petroleum use, including the value of reducing external costs of petroleum use, using a value for such costs equal to 50 percent of the value of a gallon of gasoline saved or the amount determined in an analysis of the external costs of petroleum use that considers—

'(A) value to consumers;

'(B) economic security;

'(C) national security;

'(D) foreign policy;

'(E) the impact of oil use—

'(i) on sustained cartel rents paid to foreign suppliers;

'(ii) on long-run potential gross domestic product due to higher normal-market oil price levels, including inflationary impacts;

'(iii) on import costs, wealth transfers, and potential gross domestic product due to increased trade imbalances;

'(iv) on import costs and wealth transfers during oil shocks;

'(v) on macroeconomic dislocation and adjustment costs during oil shocks;

'(vi) on the cost of existing energy security policies, including the management of the Strategic Petroleum Reserve;

'(vii) on the timing and severity of the oil peaking problem;

'(viii) on the risk, probability, size, and duration of oil supply disruptions;

'(ix) on OPEC strategic behavior and long-run oil pricing;

'(x) on the short term elasticity of energy demand and the magnitude of price increases resulting from a supply shock;

'(xi) on oil imports, military costs, and related security costs, including intelligence, homeland security, sea lane security and infrastructure, and other military activities;

'(xii) on oil imports, diplomatic and foreign policy flexibility, and connections to geopolitical strife, terrorism, and international development activities;

'(xiii) on all relevant environmental hazards under the jurisdiction of the Environmental Protection Agency; and

'(xiv) on well-to-wheels urban and local air emissions of 'pollutants' and their uninternalized costs;

'(F) the impact of the oil or energy intensity of the United States economy on the sensitivity of the economy to oil price changes, including the magnitude of gross domestic product losses in response to short term price shocks or long term price increases;

'(G) the impact of United States payments for oil imports on political, economic, and military developments in unstable or unfriendly oil exporting countries;

'(H) the uninternalized costs of pipeline and storage oil seepage, and for risk of oil spills from production, handling, and transport, and related landscape damage; and

'(I) additional relevant factors, as determined by the Secretary.

'(6) When considering the value to consumers of a gallon of gasoline saved, the Secretary of Transportation may not use a value that is less than the greatest of—

'(A) the average national cost of a gallon of gasoline sold in the United States during the 12-month period ending on the date on which the new fuel economy standard is proposed;

'(B) the most recent weekly estimate by the Energy Information Administration of the Department of Energy of the average national cost of a gallon of gasoline (all grades) sold in the United States; or

'(C) the gasoline prices projected by the Energy Information Administration for the 20-year period beginning in the year following the year in which the standards are established.

'(7) In prescribing standards under this subsection, the Secretary may prescribe standards for 1 or more model years.

'(8)(A) Not later than December 31, 2016, the Secretary of Transportation, the Secretary of Energy, and the Administrator of the Environmental Protection Agency shall submit a joint report to Congress on the state of global automotive efficiency technology development, and on the accuracy of tests used to measure fuel economy of automobiles under section 32904(c), utilizing the study and assessment of the National Academy of Sciences referred to in subparagraph (B).

'(B) The Secretary of Transportation shall enter into appropriate arrangements with the National Academy of Sciences to conduct a comprehensive study of the technological opportunities to enhance fuel economy and an analysis and assessment of the accuracy of fuel economy tests used by the Administrator of the Environmental Protection Agency to measure fuel economy for each model under section 32904(c). Such analysis and assessment shall identify any additional factors or methods that should be included in tests to measure fuel economy for each model to more accurately reflect actual fuel economy of automobiles. The Secretary of Transportation and the Administrator of the Environmental Protection Agency shall furnish, at the request of the Academy, any information that the Academy determines to be necessary to conduct the study, analysis, and assessment under this subparagraph.

'(C) The report submitted under subparagraph (A) shall include—

'(i) the study of the National Academy of Sciences referred to in subparagraph (B); and

'(ii) an assessment by the Secretary of Transportation of technological opportunities to enhance fuel economy and opportunities to increase overall fleet safety.

'(D) The report submitted under subparagraph (A) shall identify and examine additional opportunities to reform the regulatory structure under this chapter, including approaches that seek to merge vehicle and fuel requirements into a single system that achieves equal or greater reduction in petroleum use and environmental benefits than the amount of petroleum use and environmental benefits that have been achieved as of the date of the enactment of this Act.

'(E) The report submitted under subparagraph (A) shall—

'(i) include conclusions reached by the Administrator of the Environmental Protection Agency, as a result of detailed analysis and public comment, on the accuracy of fuel economy tests as in use during the period beginning on the date that is 5 years before the completion of the report and ends on the date of such completion;

'(ii) identify any additional factors that the Administrator determines should be included in tests to measure fuel economy for each model to more accurately reflect actual fuel economy of automobiles; and

'(iii) include a description of options, formulated by the Secretary of Transportation and the Administrator, to incorporate such additional factors in fuel economy tests in a manner that will not effectively increase or decrease average fuel economy for any automobile manufacturer.'; and

(4) in subsection (g)(2), by striking '(and submit the amendment to Congress when required under subsection (c)(2) of this section)'.

(b) Conforming Amendments-

(1) IN GENERAL- Chapter 329 of title 49, United States Code, is amended—

(A) in section 32903—

(i) by striking 'passenger' each place it appears;

(ii) by striking 'section 32902(b)-(d) of this title' each place it appears and inserting 'subsection (c) or (d) of section 32902';

(iii) by striking subsection (e); and

(iv) by redesignating subsection (f) as subsection (e); and

(B) in section 32904—

(i) in subsection (a)—

(I) by striking 'passenger' each place it appears; and

(II) in paragraph (1), by striking 'subject to' and all that follows through 'section 32902(b)-(d) of this title' and inserting 'subject to subsection (c) or (d) of section 32902'; and

(ii) in subsection (b)(1)(B), by striking 'under this chapter' and inserting 'under section 32902(c)(2)'.

(2) EFFECTIVE DATE- The amendments made by this section shall apply to automobiles manufactured after model year 2012.

SEC. 5. CREDIT TRADING, COMPLIANCE, AND JUDICIAL REVIEW.

(a) Credit Trading- Section 32903(a) of title 49, United States Code, is amended—

(1) by inserting 'Credits earned by a manufacturer under this section may be sold to any other manufacturer and used as if earned by that manufacturer, except that credits earned by a manufacturer described in clause (i) of section 32904(b)(1)(A) may only be sold to a manufacturer described such clause (i) and credits earned by a manufacturer described in clause (ii) of such section may only be sold to a manufacturer described in such clause (ii).' after 'earns credits.';

(2) by striking '3 consecutive model years immediately' each place it appears and inserting 'model years'; and

(3) effective for model years after 2012, the sentence added by paragraph (1) of this subsection is amended by inserting 'for purposes of compliance with section 32902(c)(2)' after 'except that'.

(b) Multi-Year Compliance Period- Section 32904(c) of such title is amended—

(1) by inserting '(1)' before 'The Administrator'; and

(2) by adding at the end the following:

'(2) The Secretary, by rule, may allow a manufacturer to elect a multi-year compliance period of not more than 4 consecutive model years in lieu of the single model year compliance period otherwise applicable under this chapter.'.

(c) Judicial Review of Regulations- Section 32909(a)(1) of such title is amended by striking out 'adversely affected by' and inserting 'aggrieved or adversely affected by, or suffering a legal wrong because of,'.

US Senate Bill 768

Title: A bill to increase fuel economy standards for automobiles and for other purposes.

Sponsor: Sen Obama, Barack [IL] (introduced 3/6/2007) Cosponsors (6)

Related Bills: H.R.1506, S.767, S.875

Latest Major Action: 3/6/2007 Referred to Senate committee. Status: Read twice and referred to the Committee on Finance.

Summary As Of:

3/6/2007—Introduced.

Fuel Economy Reform Act - Amends federal transportation law to: (1) revise the definitions of automobile to require including all automobiles up to 10,000 pounds (currently, not all automobiles up to 10,000 pounds are required to be included in the definition) and passenger automobile to eliminate the exclusion of automobiles capable of off-highway operation; and (2) continue applying the current minimum corporate average fuel economy (CAFE) standards for non-passenger and passenger automobiles to automobiles manufactured through model year 2012, but, for passenger automobiles, adds an increase of four percent per year in such standard for model years 2010 through 2012.

Requires an average fuel economy standard of 27.5 miles per gallon for all automobiles manufactured by all manufacturers for model year 2013, with an increase of four percent in the average fuel economy from the level for the prior model year for model year 2014 and beyond.

Subjects each manufacturer of passenger automobiles manufactured in a model year, in addition to such CAFE standards, to an average fuel economy standard equal to 92% of the average fuel economy projected by the Secretary for all passenger automobiles manufactured by all manufacturers in that model year.

Permits lower fuel economy standards if the minimum standards: (1) are technologically unachievable; (2) materially reduce auto safety and no offsetting safety improvements can be implemented; or (3) are not cost effective.

Allows, with specified exceptions, the selling of credits between manufacturers.

Allows a person who has been aggrieved by, or suffers a legal wrong because of (currently, adversely affected by), a CAFE standard to apply for judicial review.

Amends the Internal Revenue Code to: (1) terminate the limitation on the number of new qualified hybrid and advanced lean burn technology vehicles eligible for the alternative motor vehicle credit; (2) extend, through 2011, the alternative vehicle credit for certain new qualified hybrid motor

vehicles; and (3) allow an advanced technology motor vehicles manufacturing credit.

Major Actions:

¤NONE¤

All Actions:

3/6/2007:

Sponsor introductory remarks on measure. (CR S2700-2701)

3/6/2007:

Read twice and referred to the Committee on Finance. (consideration: CR S2703-2706)

Titles(s): (italics indicate a title for a portion of a bill)

¤NONE¤

Cosponsors(6), Alphabetical [followed by Cosponsors withdrawn]: (Sort: by date)

Sen Biden, Joseph R., Jr. [DE] - 3/6/2007

Sen Bingaman, Jeff [NM] - 3/6/2007

Sen Coleman, Norm [MN] - 3/6/2007

Sen Lugar, Richard G. [IN] - 3/6/2007

Sen Smith, Gordon H. [OR] - 3/6/2007

Sen Specter, Arlen [PA] - 3/6/2007

Committee(s)

Committee/Subcommittee:

Activity:

Senate Finance

Referral, In Committee

Related Bill Details: (additional related bills may be indentified in Status)

Bill:

Relationship:

H.R.1506

Related bill identified by CRS

S.767

Related bill identified by CRS

S.875

Related bill identified by CRS

AMENDMENT(S)

¤NONE¤

IN THE SENATE OF THE UNITED STATES

March 6, 2007

Mr. OBAMA (for himself, Mr. LUGAR, Mr. BIDEN, Mr. SMITH, Mr. BINGA-MAN, Mr. COLEMAN, and Mr. SPECTER) introduced the following bill; which was read twice and referred to the Committee on Finance

A BILL

To increase fuel economy standards for automobiles and for other purposes.

Be it enacted by the Senate and House of Representatives of the United States of America in Congress assembled,

SECTION 1. SHORT TITLE.

This Act may be cited as the 'Fuel Economy Reform Act'.

SEC. 2. FINDINGS.

Congress makes the following findings:

(1) United States dependence on oil imports imposes tremendous burdens on the economy, foreign policy, and military of the United States.

(2) According to the Energy Information Administration, 60 percent of the crude oil and petroleum products consumed in the United States between April 2005 and March 2006 (12,400,000 barrels per day) were imported. At a cost of $75 per barrel of oil, people in the United States remit more than $600,000 per minute to other countries for petroleum.

(3) A significant percentage of these petroleum imports originate in countries controlled by regimes that are unstable or openly hostile to the interests of the United States. Dependence on production from these countries contributes to the volatility of domestic and global markets and the 'risk premium' paid by consumers in the United States.

(4) The Energy Information Administration projects that the total petroleum demand in the United States will increase by 23 percent between 2006 and 2026, while domestic crude production is expected to decrease by 11 percent, resulting in an anticipated 28 percent increase in petroleum imports. Absent significant action, the United States will become more vulnerable to oil price increases, more dependent upon foreign oil, and less able to pursue national interests.

(5) Two-thirds of all domestic oil use occurs in the transportation sector, which is 97 percent reliant upon petroleum-based fuels. Passenger vehicles, including light trucks

under 10,000 pounds gross vehicle weight, represent over 60 percent of the oil used in the transportation sector.

(6) Corporate average fuel economy of all cars and trucks improved by 70 percent between 1975 and 1987. Between 1987 and 2006, fuel economy improvements have stagnated and the fuel economy of the United States is lower than many developed countries and some developing countries.

(7) Significant improvements in engine technology occurred between 1986 and 2006. These advances have been used to make vehicles larger and more powerful, and have not focused solely on increasing fuel economy.

(8) According to a 2002 fuel economy report by the National Academies of Science, fuel economy can be increased without negatively impacting the safety of cars and trucks in the United States. Some new technologies can increase both safety and fuel economy (such as high strength materials, unibody design, lower bumpers). Design changes related to fuel economy also present opportunities to reduce the incompatibility of tall, stiff, heavy vehicles with the majority of vehicles on the road.

(9) Significant change must occur to strengthen the economic competitiveness of the domestic auto industry. According to a recent study by the University of Michigan, a sustained gasoline price of $2.86 per gallon would lead Detroit's Big 3 automakers' profits to shrink by $7,000,000,000 as they absorb 75 percent of the lost vehicle sales. This would put nearly 300,000 people in the United States out of work.

(10) Opportunities exist to strengthen the domestic vehicle industry while improving fuel economy. A 2004 study performed by the University of Michigan concludes that providing $1,500,000,000 in tax incentives over a 10-year period to encourage domestic manufacturers and parts facilities to produce clean cars will lead to a gain of nearly 60,000 domestic jobs and pay for itself through the resulting increase in domestic tax receipts.

SEC. 3. DEFINITION OF AUTOMOBILE AND PASSENGER AUTOMOBILE.

(a) Definition of Automobile-

(1) IN GENERAL- Paragraph (3) of section 32901(a) of title 49, United States Code, is amended by striking 'rated at—' and all that follows through the period at the end and inserting 'rated at not more than 10,000 pounds gross vehicle weight.'.

(2) FUEL ECONOMY INFORMATION- Section 32908(a) of such title is amended, by striking 'section—' and all that follows through '(2)' and inserting 'section, the term'.

(3) EFFECTIVE DATE- The amendments made by paragraphs (1) and (2) shall apply to model year 2010 and each subsequent model year.

(b) Definition of Passenger Automobile-

(1) IN GENERAL- Paragraph (16) of section 32901(a) of such title is amended by striking ', but does not include' and all that follows through the end and inserting a period.

(2) EFFECTIVE DATE- The amendment made by paragraph (1) shall apply to model year 2012 and each subsequent model year.

SEC. 4. AVERAGE FUEL ECONOMY STANDARDS.

(a) Standards- Section 32902 of title 49, United States Code, is amended—

(1) in subsection (a)—

(A) in the heading, by inserting 'Manufactured Before Model Year 2013' after 'Non-Passenger Automobiles'; and

(B) by adding at the end the following: 'This subsection shall not apply to automobiles manufactured after model year 2012.';

(2) in subsection (b)—

(A) in the heading, by inserting 'Manufactured Before Model Year 2013' after 'Passenger Automobiles';

(B) by inserting 'and before model year 2010' after '1984'; and

(C) by adding at the end the following: 'Such standard shall be increased by 4 percent per year for model years 2010 through 2012 (rounded to the nearest 1/10 mile per gallon)';

(3) by amending subsection (c) to read as follows:

'(c) Automobiles Manufactured After Model Year 2012- (1)(A) Not later than 18 months before the beginning of each model year after model year 2012, the Secretary of Transportation shall prescribe, by regulation—

'(i) an average fuel economy standard for automobiles manufactured by a manufacturer in that model year; or

'(ii) based on 1 or more vehicle attributes that relate to fuel economy—

'(I) separate average fuel economy standards for different classes of automobiles; or

'(II) average fuel economy standards expressed in the form of a mathematical function.

'(B)(i) Except as provided under paragraphs (3) and (4) and subsection (d), average fuel economy standards under subparagraph (A) shall attain a projected aggregate level of average fuel economy of 27.5 miles per gallon for all automobiles manufactured by all manufacturers for model year 2013.

'(ii) The projected aggregate level of average fuel economy for model year 2014 and each model year thereafter shall be increased by 4 percent over the level of the prior model year (rounded to the nearest 1/10 mile per gallon).

'(2) In addition to the average fuel economy standards under paragraph (1), each manufacturer of passenger automobiles shall be subject to an average fuel economy standard for passenger automobiles manufactured by a manufacturer in a model year that shall be equal to 92 percent of the average fuel economy projected by the Secretary for all passenger automobiles manufactured by all manufacturers in that model year. An average fuel economy standard under this subparagraph for a model year shall be promulgated at the same time as the standard under paragraph (1) for such model year.

'(3) If the actual aggregate level of average fuel economy achieved by manufacturers for each of 3 consecutive model years is 5 percent or more less than the projected aggregate level of average fuel economy for such model year, the Secretary may make appropriate adjustments to the standards prescribed under this subsection.

'(4)(A) Notwithstanding paragraphs (1) through (3) and subsection (b), the Secretary of Transportation may prescribe a lower average fuel economy standard for 1 or more model years if the Secretary of Transportation, in consultation with the Secretary of Energy, finds, by clear and convincing evidence, that the minimum standards prescribed under paragraph (1)(B) or (3) or subsection (b) for each model year—

'(i) are technologically not achievable;

'(ii) cannot be achieved without materially reducing the overall safety of automobiles manufactured or sold in the United States and no offsetting safety improvements can be practicably implemented for that model year; or

'(iii) is shown not to be cost effective.

'(B) If a lower standard is prescribed for a model year under subparagraph (A), such standard shall be the maximum standard that—

'(i) is technologically achievable;

'(ii) can be achieved without materially reducing the overall safety of automobiles manufactured or sold in the United States; and

'(iii) is cost effective.

'(5) In determining cost effectiveness under paragraph (4)(A)(iii), the Secretary of Transportation shall take into account the total value to the United States of reduced petroleum use, including the value of reducing external costs of petroleum use, using a value for such costs equal to 50 percent of the value of a gallon of gasoline saved or the amount determined in an analysis of the external costs of petroleum use that considers—

'(A) value to consumers;

'(B) economic security;

'(C) national security;

'(D) foreign policy;

'(E) the impact of oil use—

'(i) on sustained cartel rents paid to foreign suppliers;

'(ii) on long-run potential gross domestic product due to higher normal-market oil price levels, including inflationary impacts;

'(iii) on import costs, wealth transfers, and potential gross domestic product due to increased trade imbalances;

'(iv) on import costs and wealth transfers during oil shocks;

'(v) on macroeconomic dislocation and adjustment costs during oil shocks;

'(vi) on the cost of existing energy security policies, including the management of the Strategic Petroleum Reserve;

'(vii) on the timing and severity of the oil peaking problem;

'(viii) on the risk, probability, size, and duration of oil supply disruptions;

'(ix) on OPEC strategic behavior and long-run oil pricing;

'(x) on the short term elasticity of energy demand and the magnitude of price increases resulting from a supply shock;

'(xi) on oil imports, military costs, and related security costs, including intelligence, homeland security, sea lane security and infrastructure, and other military activities;

'(xii) on oil imports, diplomatic and foreign policy flexibility, and connections to geopolitical strife, terrorism, and international development activities;

'(xiii) on all relevant environmental hazards under the jurisdiction of the Environmental Protection Agency; and

'(xiv) on well-to-wheels urban and local air emissions of 'pollutants' and their uninternalized costs;

'(F) the impact of the oil or energy intensity of the United States economy on the sensitivity of the economy to oil price changes, including the magnitude of gross domestic product losses in response to short term price shocks or long term price increases;

'(G) the impact of United States payments for oil imports on political, economic, and military developments in unstable or unfriendly oil exporting countries;

'(H) the uninternalized costs of pipeline and storage oil seepage, and for risk of oil spills from production, handling, and transport, and related landscape damage; and

'(I) additional relevant factors, as determined by the Secretary.

'(6) When considering the value to consumers of a gallon of gasoline saved, the Secretary of Transportation may not use a value that is less than the greatest of—

'(A) the average national cost of a gallon of gasoline sold in the United States during the 12-month period ending on the date on which the new fuel economy standard is proposed;

'(B) the most recent weekly estimate by the Energy Information Administration of the Department of Energy of the average national cost of a gallon of gasoline (all grades) sold in the United States; or

'(C) the gasoline prices projected by the Energy Information Administration for the 20-year period beginning in the year following the year in which the standards are established.

'(7) In prescribing standards under this subsection, the Secretary may prescribe standards for 1 or more model years.

'(8)(A) Not later than December 31, 2016, the Secretary of Transportation, the Secretary of Energy, and the Administrator of the Environmental Protection Agency shall submit a joint report to Congress on the state of global automotive efficiency technology development, and on the accuracy of tests used to measure fuel economy of automobiles under section 32904(c), utilizing the study and assessment of the National Academy of Sciences referred to in subparagraph (B).

'(B) The Secretary of Transportation shall enter into appropriate arrangements with the National Academy of Sciences to conduct a comprehensive study of the technological opportunities to enhance fuel economy and an analysis and assessment of the accuracy of fuel economy tests used by the Administrator of the Environmental Protection Agency to measure fuel economy for each model under section 32904(c). Such analysis and assessment shall identify any additional factors or methods that should be included in tests to measure fuel economy for each model to more accurately reflect actual fuel economy of automobiles. The Secretary of Transportation and the Administrator of the Environmental Protection Agency shall furnish, at the request of the Academy, any information that the Academy determines to be necessary to conduct the study, analysis, and assessment under this subparagraph.

'(C) The report submitted under subparagraph (A) shall include—

'(i) the study of the National Academy of Sciences referred to in subparagraph (B); and

'(ii) an assessment by the Secretary of Transportation of technological opportunities to enhance fuel economy and opportunities to increase overall fleet safety.

'(D) The report submitted under subparagraph (A) shall identify and examine additional opportunities to reform the regulatory structure under this chapter, including approaches that seek to merge vehicle and fuel requirements into a single system that achieves equal or greater reduction in petroleum use and environmental benefits than the amount of petroleum use and environmental benefits that have been achieved as of the date of the enactment of this Act.

'(E) The report submitted under subparagraph (A) shall—

'(i) include conclusions reached by the Administrator of the Environmental Protection Agency, as a result of detailed analysis and public comment, on the accuracy of fuel economy tests as in use during the period beginning on the date that is 5 years before the completion of the report and ends on the date of such completion;

'(ii) identify any additional factors that the Administrator determines should be included in tests to measure fuel economy for each model to more accurately reflect actual fuel economy of automobiles; and

'(iii) include a description of options, formulated by the Secretary of Transportation and the Administrator, to incorporate such additional factors in fuel economy tests in a manner that will not effectively increase or decrease average fuel economy for any automobile manufacturer.'; and

(4) in subsection (g)(2), by striking '(and submit the amendment to Congress when required under subsection (c)(2) of this section)'.

(b) Conforming Amendments-

(1) IN GENERAL- Chapter 329 of title 49, United States Code, is amended—

(A) in section 32903—

(i) by striking 'passenger' each place it appears;

(ii) by striking 'section 32902(b)-(d) of this title' each place it appears and inserting 'subsection (c) or (d) of section 32902';

(iii) by striking subsection (e); and

(iv) by redesignating subsection (f) as subsection (e); and

(B) in section 32904—

(i) in subsection (a)—

(I) by striking 'passenger' each place it appears; and

(II) in paragraph (1), by striking 'subject to' and all that follows through 'section 32902(b)-(d) of this title' and inserting 'subject to subsection (c) or (d) of section 32902'; and

(ii) in subsection (b)(1)(B), by striking 'under this chapter' and inserting 'under section 32902(c)(2)'.

(2) EFFECTIVE DATE- The amendments made by this section shall apply to automobiles manufactured after model year 2012.

SEC. 5. CREDIT TRADING, COMPLIANCE, AND JUDICIAL REVIEW.

(a) Credit Trading- Section 32903(a) of title 49, United States Code, is amended—

(1) by inserting 'Credits earned by a manufacturer under this section may be sold to any other manufacturer and used as if earned by that manufacturer, except that credits earned by a manufacturer described in clause (i) of section 32904(b)(1)(A) may only be sold to a manufacturer described such clause (i) and credits earned by a manufacturer described in clause (ii) of such section may only be sold to a manufacturer described in such clause (ii).' after 'earns credits.';

(2) by striking '3 consecutive model years immediately' each place it appears and inserting 'model years'; and

(3) effective for model years after 2012, the sentence added by paragraph (1) of this subsection is amended by inserting 'for purposes of compliance with section 32902(c)(2)' after 'except that'.

(b) Multi-Year Compliance Period- Section 32904(c) of such title is amended—

(1) by inserting '(1)' before 'The Administrator'; and

(2) by adding at the end the following:

'(2) The Secretary, by rule, may allow a manufacturer to elect a multi-year compliance period of not more than 4 consecutive model years in lieu of the single model year compliance period otherwise applicable under this chapter.'.

(c) Judicial Review of Regulations- Section 32909(a)(1) of such title is amended by striking out 'adversely affected by' and inserting 'aggrieved or adversely affected by, or suffering a legal wrong because of,'.

SEC. 6. CONSUMER TAX CREDIT.

(a) Elimination on Number of New Qualified Hybrid and Advanced Lean Burn Technology Vehicles Eligible for Alternative Motor Vehicle Credit-

(1) IN GENERAL- Section 30B of the Internal Revenue Code of 1986 is amended—

(A) by striking subsection (f); and

(B) by redesignating subsections (g) through (j) as subsections (f) through (i), respectively.

(2) CONFORMING AMENDMENTS-

(A) Paragraphs (4) and (6) of section 30B(h) of such Code are each amended by striking '(determined without regard to subsection (g))' and inserting 'determined without regard to subsection (f))'.

(B) Section 38(b)(25) of such Code is amended by striking 'section 30B(g)(1)' and inserting 'section 30B(f)(1)'.

(C) Section 55(c)(2) of such Code is amended by striking 'section 30B(g)(2)' and inserting 'section 30B(f)(2)'.

(D) Section 1016(a)(36) of such Code is amended by striking 'section 30B(h)(4)' and inserting 'section 30B(g)(4)'.

(E) Section 6501(m) of such Code is amended by striking 'section 30B(h)(9)' and inserting 'section 30B(g)(9)'.

(b) Extension of Alternative Vehicle Credit for New Qualified Hybrid Motor Vehicles- Paragraph (3) of section 30B(i) of such Code (as redesignated by subsection (a)) is amended by striking 'December 31, 2009' and inserting 'December 31, 2011'.

(c) Computation of Credit- Section 30B of such Code is amended by striking 'city' each place it appears and inserting 'combined'.

(d) Effective Dates- The amendments made by subsections (a) and (b) of this section shall apply to property placed in service after December 31, 2007, in taxable years ending after such date. The amendments made by subsection (c) shall apply to vehicles acquired after the date of the enactment of this Act.

SEC. 7. ADVANCED TECHNOLOGY MOTOR VEHICLES MANUFAC-TURING CREDIT.

(a) In General- Subpart B of part IV of subchapter A of chapter 1 of the Internal Revenue Code of 1986 (relating to foreign tax credit, etc.) is amended by adding at the end the following new section:

'SEC. 30D. ADVANCED TECHNOLOGY MOTOR VEHICLES MANUFAC-TURING CREDIT.

'(a) Credit Allowed- There shall be allowed as a credit against the tax imposed by this chapter for the taxable year an amount equal to 35 percent of the qualified investment of an eligible taxpayer for such taxable year.

'(b) Qualified Investment- For purposes of this section—

'(1) IN GENERAL- The qualified investment for any taxable year is equal to the incremental costs incurred during such taxable year—

'(A) to re-equip, expand, or establish any manufacturing facility in the United States of the eligible taxpayer to produce advanced technology motor vehicles or to produce eligible components,

'(B) for engineering integration performed in the United States of such vehicles and components as described in subsection (d),

'(C) for research and development performed in the United States related to advanced technology motor vehicles and eligible components, and

'(D) for employee retraining with respect to the manufacturing of such vehicles or components (determined without regard to wages or salaries of such retrained employees).

'(2) ATTRIBUTION RULES- In the event a facility of the eligible taxpayer produces both advanced technology motor vehicles and conventional motor vehicles, or eligible and non-eligible components, only the qualified investment attributable to production of advanced technology motor vehicles and eligible components shall be taken into account.

'(c) Definitions- In this section:

'(1) ADVANCED TECHNOLOGY MOTOR VEHICLE- The term 'advanced technology motor vehicle' means—

'(A) any qualified electric vehicle (as defined in section 30(c)(1)),

'(B) any new qualified fuel cell motor vehicle (as defined in section 30B(b)(3)),

'(C) any new advanced lean burn technology motor vehicle (as defined in section 30B(c)(3)),

'(D) any new qualified hybrid motor vehicle (as defined in section 30B(d)(2)(A) and determined without regard to any gross vehicle weight rating),

'(E) any new qualified alternative fuel motor vehicle (as defined in section 30B(e)(4), including any mixed-fuel vehicle (as defined in section 30B(e)(5)(B)), and

'(F) any other motor vehicle using electric drive transportation technology (as defined in paragraph (3)).

'(2) ELECTRIC DRIVE TRANSPORTATION TECHNOLOGY- The term 'electric drive transportation technology' means technology used by vehicles that use an electric motor for all or part of their motive power and that may or may not use off-board electricity, such as battery electric vehicles, fuel cell vehicles, engine dominant hybrid electric vehicles, plug-in hybrid electric vehicles, and plug-in hybrid fuel cell vehicles.

'(3) ELIGIBLE COMPONENTS- The term 'eligible component' means any component inherent to any advanced technology motor vehicle, including—

'(A) with respect to any gasoline or diesel-electric new qualified hybrid motor vehicle—

'(i) electric motor or generator;

'(ii) power split device;

'(iii) power control unit;

'(iv) power controls;

'(v) integrated starter generator; or

'(vi) battery;

'(B) with respect to any hydraulic new qualified hybrid motor vehicle—

'(i) accumulator or other energy storage device;

'(ii) hydraulic pump;

'(iii) hydraulic pump-motor assembly;

'(iv) power control unit; and

'(v) power controls;

'(C) with respect to any new advanced lean burn technology motor vehicle—

'(i) diesel engine;

'(ii) turbo charger;

'(iii) fuel injection system; or

'(iv) after-treatment system, such as a particle filter or NOx absorber; and

'(D) with respect to any advanced technology motor vehicle, any other component submitted for approval by the Secretary.

'(4) ELIGIBLE TAXPAYER- The term 'eligible taxpayer' means any taxpayer if more than 20 percent of the taxpayer's gross receipts for the taxable year is derived from the manufacture of motor vehicles or any component parts of such vehicles.

'(d) Engineering Integration Costs- For purposes of subsection (b)(1)(B), costs for engineering integration are costs incurred prior to the market introduction of advanced technology vehicles for engineering tasks related to—

'(1) establishing functional, structural, and performance requirements for component and subsystems to meet overall vehicle objectives for a specific application,

'(2) designing interfaces for components and subsystems with mating systems within a specific vehicle application,

'(3) designing cost effective, efficient, and reliable manufacturing processes to produce components and subsystems for a specific vehicle application, and

'(4) validating functionality and performance of components and subsystems for a specific vehicle application.

'(e) Limitation Based on Amount of Tax- The credit allowed under subsection (a) for the taxable year shall not exceed the excess of—

'(1) the sum of—

'(A) the regular tax liability (as defined in section 26(b)) for such taxable year, plus

'(B) the tax imposed by section 55 for such taxable year and any prior taxable year beginning after 1986 and not taken into account under section 53 for any prior taxable year, over

'(2) the sum of the credits allowable under subpart A and sections 27, 30, and 30B for the taxable year.

'(f) Reduction in Basis- For purposes of this subtitle, if a credit is allowed under this section for any expenditure with respect to any property, the increase in the basis of such property which would (but for this paragraph) result from such expenditure shall be reduced by the amount of the credit so allowed.

'(g) No Double Benefit-

'(1) COORDINATION WITH OTHER DEDUCTIONS AND CREDITS- Except as provided in paragraph (2), the amount of any deduction or other credit allowable under this chapter for any cost taken into account in determining the amount of the credit under subsection (a) shall be reduced by the amount of such credit attributable to such cost.

'(2) RESEARCH AND DEVELOPMENT COSTS-

'(A) IN GENERAL- Except as provided in subparagraph (B), any amount described in subsection (b)(1)(C) taken into account in determining the amount of the credit under subsection (a) for any taxable year shall not be taken into account for purposes of determining the credit under section 41 for such taxable year.

'(B) COSTS TAKEN INTO ACCOUNT IN DETERMINING BASE PERIOD RESEARCH EXPENSES- Any amounts described in subsection (b)(1)(C) taken into account in determining the amount of the credit under subsection (a) for any taxable year which are qualified research expenses (within the meaning of section 41(b)) shall be taken into account in determining base period research expenses for purposes of applying section 41 to subsequent taxable years.

'(h) Business Carryovers Allowed- If the credit allowable under subsection (a) for a taxable year exceeds the limitation under subsection (e) for such taxable year, such excess (to the extent of the credit allowable with respect to property subject to the allowance for depreciation) shall be allowed as a credit carryback to each of the 15 taxable years immediately preceding the unused credit year and as a carryforward to each of the 20 taxable years immediately following the unused credit year.

'(i) Special Rules- For purposes of this section, rules similar to the rules of section 179A(e)(4) and paragraphs (1) and (2) of section 41(f) shall apply.

'(j) Allocation of Credit to Purchasers-

'(1) ELECTION TO ALLOCATE-

'(A) IN GENERAL- In the case of an eligible taxpayer, any portion of the credit determined under subsection (a) for the taxable year may, at the election of such taxpayer, be apportioned among purchasers of qualifying vehicles from the taxpayer in the taxable year (or in any year in which the credit may be carried over).

'(B) QUALIFYING VEHICLES- For purposes of this subsection, the term 'qualifying vehicle' means an advanced technology vehicle manufactured at a facility described in subsection (b)(1)(A).

'(C) FORM AND EFFECT OF ELECTION- An election under subparagraph (A) for any taxable year shall be made on a timely filed return for such year. Such election, once made, shall be irrevocable for such taxable year.

'(2) TREATMENT OF TAXPAYER AND PURCHASERS- The amount of the credit apportioned to any purchaser under paragraph (1)—

'(A) shall not be included in the amount determined under subsection (a) with respect to the eligible taxpayer for the taxable year; and

'(B) shall be treated as an amount determined under subsection (a) for the taxable year of the purchaser which ends in the calendar year of purchase.

'(3) SPECIAL RULES FOR DECREASE IN CREDITS FOR TAXABLE YEAR- If the amount of the credit of an eligible taxpayer determined under subsection (a) for a taxable year is less than the amount of such credit shown on the return of the taxpayer for such year, an amount equal to the excess of—

'(A) such reduction, over

'(B) the amount not apportioned to such purchasers under paragraph (1) for the taxable year,

shall be treated as an increase in tax imposed by this chapter on the eligible taxpayer.

'(4) WRITTEN NOTICE TO PURCHASERS- If any portion of the credit available under subsection (a) is allocated to purchasers under paragraph (1), the eligible taxpayer shall provide any purchaser receiving an allocation written notice of the amount of the allocation. Such notice may be provided either at the time of purchase or at any time not later than 60 days after the close of the calendar year in which the vehicle is purchased.

'(k) Election Not To Take Credit- No credit shall be allowed under subsection (a) for any property if the taxpayer elects not to have this section apply to such property.

'(l) Regulations- The Secretary shall prescribe such regulations as necessary to carry out the provisions of this section.

'(m) Termination- This section shall not apply to any qualified investment after December 31, 2011.'.

(b) Conforming Amendments-

(1) Section 1016(a) of the Internal Revenue Code of 1986 is amended by striking 'and' at the end of paragraph (36), by striking the period at the end of paragraph (37) and inserting ', and', and by adding at the end the following new paragraph:

'(38) to the extent provided in section 30D(g).'.

(2) Section 6501(m) of such Code is amended by inserting '30D(k),' after '30C(e)(5),'.

(3) The table of sections for subpart B of part IV of subchapter A of chapter 1 of such Code is amended by inserting after the item relating to section 30C the following new item:

'Sec. 30D. Advanced technology motor vehicles manufacturing credit.'.

(c) Effective Date- The amendments made by this section shall apply to amounts incurred in taxable years beginning after December 31, 1999.

US SENATE BILL 795

TITLE: A bill to assist aliens who have been lawfully admitted in becoming citizens of the United States, and for other purposes.

SPONSOR: Sen Obama, Barack [IL] (introduced 3/7/2007) Cosponsors (5)

RELATED BILLS: H.R.1379

LATEST MAJOR ACTION: 3/7/2007 Referred to Senate committee. Status: Read twice and referred to the Committee on the Judiciary.

SUMMARY AS OF:

3/7/2007—Introduced.

Citizenship Promotion Act of 2007 - Amends the Immigration and Nationality Act to revise provisions respecting: (1) immigration service fees; and (2) naturalization testing.

Prohibits an applicant or petitioner for U.S. permanent residence or citizenship from being required to use an electronic method to file any application to, or access a customer account.

Requires: (1) a Government Accountability Office (GAO) study and report on naturalization background checks; and (2) the Attorney General to make reasonable efforts to complete background checks of applicants for temporary or permanent residence or citizenship within 90 days.

Directs the Secretary of Homeland Security to establish a national citizenship promotion program to assist lawful permanent resident aliens become citizens.

MAJOR ACTIONS:

¤NONE¤

ALL ACTIONS:

3/7/2007:

Sponsor introductory remarks on measure. (CR S2803-2804)

3/7/2007:

Read twice and referred to the Committee on the Judiciary.

TITLES(s): (italics indicate a title for a portion of a bill)

¤NONE¤

COSPONSORS(5), ALPHABETICAL [FOLLOWED BY COSPONSORS WITHDRAWN]: (Sort: by date)

Sen Bingaman, Jeff [NM] - 3/7/2007

Sen Durbin, Richard [IL] - 4/11/2007

Sen Lieberman, Joseph I. [CT] - 4/16/2007

Sen Menendez, Robert [NJ] - 3/7/2007

Sen Salazar, Ken [CO] - 3/7/2007

COMMITTEE(s)

Committee/Subcommittee:

Activity:

Senate Judiciary

Referral, In Committee

RELATED BILL DETAILS: (additional related bills may be indentified in Status)

Bill:

Relationship:

H.R.1379

Related bill identified by CRS

AMENDMENT(s)

¤NONE¤

IN THE SENATE OF THE UNITED STATES

March 7, 2007

Mr. OBAMA (for himself, Mr. MENENDEZ, Mr. SALAZAR, and Mr. BINGA-MAN) introduced the following bill; which was read twice and referred to the Committee on the Judiciary

A BILL

To assist aliens who have been lawfully admitted in becoming citizens of the United States, and for other purposes.

Be it enacted by the Senate and House of Representatives of the United States of America in Congress assembled,

SECTION 1. SHORT TITLE; TABLE OF CONTENTS.

(a) Short Title- This Act may be cited as the 'Citizenship Promotion Act of 2007'.

(b) Table of Contents- The table of contents for this Act is as follows:

Sec. 1. Short title; table of contents.

Sec. 2. Immigration service fees.

Sec. 3. Administration of tests for naturalization.

Sec. 4. Voluntary electronic filing of applications.

Sec. 5. Timely background checks.

Sec. 6. National citizenship promotion program.

SEC. 2. IMMIGRATION SERVICE FEES.

(a) In General- Subsection (m) of section 286 of the Immigration and Nationality Act (8 U.S.C. 1356(m)) is amended to read as follows:

'(m) Immigration Service Fees-

'(1) IN GENERAL- Except as provided in paragraph (2) and notwithstanding any other provision of law, all adjudication fees as are designated by the Secretary of Homeland Security in regulations shall be deposited as offsetting receipts into a separate account entitled 'Immigration Examinations Fee Account' in the Treasury of the United States, whether collected directly by the Secretary or through clerks of courts.

'(2) VIRGIN ISLANDS AND GUAM- All fees received by the Secretary of Homeland Security from applicants residing in the Virgin Islands of the United States, or in Guam, under this subsection shall be paid over to the treasury of the Virgin Islands or to the treasury of Guam, respectively.

'(3) FEES FOR IMMIGRATION SERVICES-

'(A) IN GENERAL- Subject to subparagraph (B), the Secretary of Homeland Security may set fees for providing immigration services at a level that will—

'(i) ensure recovery of the full costs of providing such services, or a portion thereof, including the costs of similar services provided without charge to asylum applicants or other immigrants; and

'(ii) recover the full cost of administering the collection of fees under this paragraph, or a portion thereof.

'(B) REPORT REQUIREMENT- The Secretary of Homeland Security may not increase any fee under this paragraph above the level of such fee on the day before the date of the introduction of the Citizenship Promotion Act of 2007, until—

'(i) the Secretary submits to the Committee on the Judiciary of the Senate and the Committee on the Judiciary of the House of Representatives a report that—

'(I) identifies the direct and indirect costs associated with providing immigration services, and distinguishes such costs from immigration enforcement and national security costs; and

'(II) contains information regarding the amount the fee will be increased; and

'(ii) a period of 45 days has expired beginning on the date that the report in clause (i) is received by the committees described in such clause.'.

(b) Sense of Congress- It is the sense of Congress that—

(1) the Secretary of Homeland Security should set fees under section 286(m)(3) of the Immigration and Nationality Act (8 U.S.C. 1356(m)(3)), as amended by subsection (a) of this section, at a level that ensures recovery of only the direct costs associated with the services described in such section 286(m)(3); and

(2) Congress should appropriate to the Secretary of Homeland Security such funds as may be necessary to cover the indirect costs associated with the services described in such section 286(m)(3).

(c) Technical Amendment- Section 286 of the Immigration and Nationality Act (8 U.S.C. 1356) is amended—

(1) in subsections (d), (e), (f), (h), (i), (j), (k), (l), (n), (o), (q), (t), and (u), by striking 'Attorney General' each place it appears and inserting 'Secretary of Homeland Security';

(2) in subsection (i) of such section, by striking 'Attorney General's' and inserting 'Secretary's'; and

(3) in subsection (r)—

(A) in paragraph (2), by striking 'Department of Justice' and inserting 'Department of Homeland Security'; and

(B) in paragraphs (3) and (4), by striking 'Attorney General' each place it appears and inserting 'Secretary of Homeland Security'.

(d) Authorization of Appropriations- For each fiscal year, there is authorized to be appropriated to the Secretary of Homeland Security an amount equal to the difference between the fees collected under section 286(m)(3) of the Immigration and Nationality Act (8 U.S.C. 1356(m)(3)), as amended by subsection (a) of this section, and the cost of providing the services referred to in such section 286(m)(3).

SEC. 3. ADMINISTRATION OF TESTS FOR NATURALIZATION.

(a) In General- Subsection (a) of section 312 of the Immigration and Nationality Act (8 U.S.C. 1423) is amended to read as follows:

'(a) Naturalization Test-

'(1) REQUIREMENTS- Except as otherwise provided in this title, a person may not be naturalized as a citizen of the United States upon the application of such person if such person cannot demonstrate the following:

'(A) A proficiency in the English language.

'(B) A knowledge and understanding of—

'(i) the fundamentals of the history of the United States; and

'(ii) the principles and form of government of the United States.

'(2) TESTING-

'(A) IN GENERAL- The Secretary of Homeland Security, in administering any test that the Secretary uses to determine whether an applicant for naturalization as a citizen of the United States has the proficiency and knowledge sufficient to meet the requirements of paragraph (1), shall administer such test uniformly throughout the United States.

'(B) CONSIDERATION- In selecting and phrasing items in the administration of a test described in subparagraph (A) and in evaluating the performance of an applicant on such test, the Secretary shall consider the following:

'(i) The age of the applicant.

'(ii) The education level of the applicant.

'(iii) The amount of time the applicant has resided in the United States.

'(iv) The efforts made by the applicant, and the opportunities available to the applicant, to acquire the knowledge and proficiencies required by paragraph (1).

'(v) Such other factors as the Secretary considers appropriate.

'(C) ENGLISH LANGUAGE TESTING- The requirement in paragraph (1)(A) shall be satisfactorily met if an applicant can—

'(i) speak words in ordinary usage in the English language; and

'(ii) read or write simple words and phrases in ordinary usage in the English language.

'(D) PROHIBITION ON EXTRAORDINARY AND UNREASONABLE CONDITIONS- The Secretary may not impose any extraordinary or unreasonable condition on any applicant seeking to meet the requirements of paragraph (1).'.

(b) Conforming Amendments- Subsection (b) of such section is amended—

(1) in paragraph (1), by striking 'subsection (a)' and inserting 'subsection (a)(1)';

(2) in paragraph (2), by striking 'subsection (a)(1)' and inserting 'subsection (a)(1)(A)'; and

(3) in paragraph (3)—

(A) by striking 'subsection (a)(2)' and inserting 'subsection (a)(1)(B)';

(B) by striking 'The Attorney General' and inserting 'The Secretary of Homeland Security'; and

(C) by striking 'determined by the Attorney General' and inserting 'determined by the Secretary'.

SEC. 4. VOLUNTARY ELECTRONIC FILING OF APPLICATIONS.

The Secretary of Homeland Security may not require that an applicant or petitioner for permanent residence or citizenship of the United States use an electronic method to file any application to, or access a customer account.

SEC. 5. TIMELY BACKGROUND CHECKS.

(a) Study-

(1) IN GENERAL- The Comptroller General of the United States shall conduct a study on the process used by the Department of Justice on the day before the date of the enactment of this Act to conduct a background check on an applicant for citizenship of the United States.

(2) REPORT- Not later than 1 year after the date of the enactment of this Act and annually thereafter, the Comptroller General of the United States shall report to Congress on the findings of the study required by paragraph (1).

(3) CONTENTS OF REPORT- The report required by paragraph (2) shall include the following information with respect to the calendar year preceding the date on which the report is filed:

(A) The number of background checks conducted by the Department of Justice on applicants for citizenship of the United States.

(B) The types of such background checks conducted.

(C) The average time spent on each such type of background check.

(D) A description of the obstacles that impede the timely completion of such background checks.

(b) Timely Completion of Background Checks-

(1) IN GENERAL- With respect to a request submitted to the Attorney General by the Secretary of Homeland Security for a background check on an applicant for temporary or permanent residence or citizenship of the United States, the Attorney General shall make a reasonable effort to complete a background check on such applicant not later than 90 days after the Attorney General receives such request from the Secretary of Homeland Security.

(2) DELAYS ON BACKGROUND CHECKS- If a background check described in paragraph (1) is not completed by the Attorney General before the date that is 91 days after the date that the Attorney General receives a request described in paragraph (1)—

(A) the Attorney General shall document the reason why such background check was not completed before such date; and

(B) if such background check is not completed before the date that is 181 days after the date of such receipt, then the Attorney General shall, not later than 210 days after the date of such receipt, submit to the appropriate congressional committees and the Secretary of Homeland Security a report that describes—

(i) the reason that such background check was not completed within 180 days; and

(ii) the earliest date on which the Attorney General is certain the background check will be completed.

(3) ANNUAL REPORT ON DELAYED BACKGROUND CHECKS- Not later than the end of each fiscal year, the Attorney General shall submit to the appropriate congressional committees a report containing, with respect to that fiscal year—

(A) the number of background checks described in subparagraph (B) or (C) of paragraph (2);

(B) the time taken to complete each such background check;

(C) a statistical analysis of the causes of the delays in completing such background checks; and

(D) a description of the efforts being made by the Attorney General to address each such cause.

(4) NOTIFICATION TO APPLICANT- If, with respect to a background check on an applicant described in paragraph (1), the Secretary of Homeland Security receives a report under paragraph (2)(C), then the Secretary shall provide to such applicant a copy of such report, redacted to remove any classified information contained therein.

(5) APPROPRIATE CONGRESSIONAL COMMITTEES- In this subsection, the term 'appropriate congressional committees' means the following:

(A) The Committee on the Judiciary of the Senate.

(B) The Committee on Homeland Security and Governmental Affairs of the Senate.

(C) The Committee on the Judiciary of the House of Representatives.

(D) The Committee on Homeland Security of the House of Representatives.

(6) AUTHORIZATION OF APPROPRIATIONS- There is authorized to be appropriated to the Attorney General such funds as may be necessary to carry out the provisions of this subsection.

SEC. 6. NATIONAL CITIZENSHIP PROMOTION PROGRAM.

(a) Establishment-

(1) IN GENERAL- Not later than January 1, 2008, the Secretary of Homeland Security shall establish a program to assist aliens who have been lawfully admitted for permanent residence in becoming citizens of the United States.

(2) DESIGNATION- The program required by paragraph (1) shall be known as the 'New Americans Initiative' (in this section referred to as the 'Program').

(b) Program Activities- As part of the Program required by subsection (a), the Secretary of Homeland Security shall—

(1) award grants in accordance with subsection (c); and

(2) carry out outreach activities in accordance with subsection (d).

(c) Grants-

(1) IN GENERAL- The Secretary of Homeland Security shall award grants to eligible entities to assist aliens who have been lawfully admitted for permanent residence in becoming citizens of the United States.

(2) ELIGIBLE ENTITY DEFINED- In this subsection, the term 'eligible entity' means a not-for-profit organization that has experience working with immigrant communities.

(3) USE OF FUNDS- Grants awarded under this subsection shall be used for activities to assist aliens who have been lawfully admitted for permanent residence in becoming citizens of the United States, including—

(A) conducting English language and citizenship classes for such aliens;

(B) providing legal assistance, by attorneys or entities accredited by the Board of Immigration Appeals, to such aliens to assist such aliens in becoming citizens of the United States;

(C) carrying out outreach activities and providing education to immigrant communities to assist such aliens in becoming citizens of the United States; and

(D) assisting such aliens with applications to become citizens of the United States, as allowed by Federal and State law.

(4) APPLICATION FOR GRANT-

(A) IN GENERAL- Each eligible entity seeking a grant under this subsection shall submit an application to the Secretary of Homeland Security at such time, in such manner, and accompanied by such information as the Secretary shall require.

(B) CONTENTS- Each application submitted pursuant to subparagraph (A) shall include a description of—

(i) the activities for which a grant under this section is sought;

(ii) the manner in which the entity plans to leverage available private and State and local government resources to assist aliens who have been lawfully admitted for permanent residence in becoming citizens of the United States;

(iii) the experience of the entity in carrying out the activities for which a grant under this section is sought, including the number of aliens and geographic regions served by such entity; and

(iv) the manner in which the entity plans to employ best practices developed by adult educators, State and local governments, and community organizations—

(I) to promote citizenship and civic participation by such aliens; and

(II) to provide assistance to such aliens with the process of becoming citizens of the United States.

(d) Outreach- The Secretary of Homeland Security shall—

(1) develop outreach materials targeted to aliens who have been lawfully admitted for permanent residence to encourage such aliens to apply to become citizens of the United States; and

(2) make such outreach materials available through—

(A) public service announcements;

(B) advertisements; and

(C) such other media as the Secretary determines is appropriate.

(e) Authorization of Appropriations- There are authorized to be appropriated to the Secretary of Homeland Security, $80,000,000 to carry out this section.

US Senate Bill 823

Title: A bill to amend the Public Health Service Act with respect to facilitating the development of microbicides for preventing transmission of HIV/AIDS and other diseases, and for other purposes.

Sponsor: Sen Obama, Barack [IL] (introduced 3/8/2007) Cosponsors (18)

RELATED BILLS: H.R.1420

LATEST MAJOR ACTION: 3/8/2007 Referred to Senate committee. Status: Read twice and referred to the Committee on Health, Education, Labor, and Pensions.

SUMMARY AS OF:

3/8/2007—Introduced.

Microbicide Development Act - Amends the Public Health Service Act to require the Director of the Office of AIDS Research to: (1) expedite the implementation of the federal strategic plan for the conduct and support of microbicide research and development; and (2) expand, intensify, and coordinate all activities with respect to research and development of microbicides to prevent the transmission of HIV and other sexually transmitted diseases.

Requires the Director of the National Institute of Allergy and Infectious Diseases to: (1) establish within the Division of AIDS an organizational branch to carry out microbicide research and development; and (2) assign priority to ensuring adequate funding and support for the Microbicide Trials Network and other programs for supporting microbicides clinical trials.

Requires the Director of the Centers for Disease Control and Prevention (CDC) to fully implement the CDC's microbicide agenda to support microbicide research and development.

Directs the head of the Office of HIV/AIDS of the U.S. Agency for International Development (USAID) to develop and implement a program to support the development of microbicides products for the prevention of the transmission of HIV/AIDS and other diseases, and facilitate wide-scale availability of such products.

Requires the Secretary of State to report to Congress on advance market commitments of microbicides to prevent HIV infection as a means of creating private sector investment incentives.

MAJOR ACTIONS:

¤NONE¤

ALL ACTIONS:

3/8/2007:

Sponsor introductory remarks on measure. (CR S2919-2920)

3/8/2007:

Read twice and referred to the Committee on Health, Education, Labor, and Pensions.

TITLES(s): (italics indicate a title for a portion of a bill)

¤NONE¤

Cosponsors(18), Alphabetical [followed by Cosponsors withdrawn]: (Sort: by date)

Sen Bingaman, Jeff [NM] - 3/12/2007

Sen Boxer, Barbara [CA] - 3/8/2007

Sen Brown, Sherrod [OH] - 3/22/2007

Sen Cantwell, Maria [WA] - 5/24/2007

Sen Clinton, Hillary Rodham [NY] - 3/8/2007

Sen Dodd, Christopher J. [CT] - 3/8/2007

Sen Durbin, Richard [IL] - 3/8/2007

Sen Feinstein, Dianne [CA] - 5/14/2007

Sen Kennedy, Edward M. [MA] - 5/14/2007

Sen Kerry, John F. [MA] - 3/8/2007

Sen Lautenberg, Frank R. [NJ] - 6/4/2007

Sen Leahy, Patrick J. [VT] - 3/12/2007

Sen Mikulski, Barbara A. [MD] - 3/27/2007

Sen Murray, Patty [WA] - 4/26/2007

Sen Sanders, Bernard [VT] - 4/25/2007

Sen Schumer, Charles E. [NY] - 3/8/2007

Sen Smith, Gordon H. [OR] - 3/20/2007

Sen Snowe, Olympia J. [ME] - 3/8/2007

Committee(s)

Committee/Subcommittee:

Activity:

Senate Health, Education, Labor, and Pensions

Referral, In Committee

Related Bill Details: (additional related bills may be indentified in Status)

Bill:

Relationship:

H.R.1420

Related bill identified by CRS

Amendment(s)

¤NONE¤

IN THE SENATE OF THE UNITED STATES

March 8, 2007

Mr. OBAMA (for himself, Ms. SNOWE, Mr. DURBIN, Mr. DODD, Mrs. CLINTON, Mrs. BOXER, Mr. SCHUMER, and Mr. KERRY) introduced the following bill; which was read twice and referred to the Committee on Health, Education, Labor, and Pensions

A BILL

To amend the Public Health Service Act with respect to facilitating the development of microbicides for preventing transmission of HIV/AIDS and other diseases, and for other purposes.

Be it enacted by the Senate and House of Representatives of the United States of America in Congress assembled,

SECTION 1. SHORT TITLE.

This Act may be cited as the 'Microbicide Development Act'.

SEC. 2. FINDINGS.

Congress makes the following findings:

(1) Women and girls are the new face of HIV/AIDS, and are increasingly affected by the disease in every region of the world. As of 2006, nearly half of the 37,200,000 adults living with HIV and AIDS worldwide were women. In sub-Saharan Africa, that proportion was 59 percent.

(2) Because of their social and biological vulnerabilities, young women are particularly at risk of HIV infection. In sub-Saharan Africa, the prevalence of HIV/AIDS is three times higher among women ages 15 to 24 than it is among men in that same age group.

(3) Women infected with HIV can transmit the infection to their infants during pregnancy, labor, delivery, or breast-feeding. The most effective way to interrupt mother-to-child transmission is to ensure that mothers are not infected in the first place.

(4) Many women who become infected with HIV have just one sexual partner—their husband. Marriage is not necessarily effective protection against HIV, because to protect themselves from HIV, women have to rely on their male partners to be faithful or to use condoms. Many women, especially in the developing world, are unable to insist on mutual monogamy or negotiate condom use, particularly in long-term relationships.

(5) Scientists are working on a promising new prevention tool that could slow down the spread of the HIV/AIDS epidemic—microbicides. Formulated as gels, creams, tablets or rings, microbicides are being designed to stop the transmission of the pathogens that cause AIDS and other sexually transmitted infections (referred to in this section as 'STIs'). Microbicides could allow a woman to protect herself from disease.

(6) Couples need a method of HIV protection that will allow them to conceive a child and start a family. No existing HIV prevention method also allows conception. Some

microbicides in development may allow women to become pregnant while at the same time protecting them from infection.

(7) According to UNICEF, worldwide, the lack of HIV/AIDS prevention and treatment has left over 15,000,000 children as orphans. Of these, more than 12,000,000 live in sub-Saharan Africa. The number of AIDS orphans in sub-Saharan Africa alone is expected to grow to nearly 16,000,000 by 2010.

(8) HIV prevention tools like microbicides could also be valuable for women in the United States, who account for an increasing proportion of new HIV and AIDS cases among Americans. Minority women in the United States are particularly affected. Both African-American and Latina women account for a disproportionate number of new AIDS cases, and HIV/AIDS was the leading cause of death in 2002 for African-American women ages 25 to 34.

(9) With nearly 20,000,000 new cases of sexually transmitted infections occurring every year, the United States has the highest STI rates of any industrialized nation. Like HIV, STIs pose significant health threats and costs, with young people and women bearing a disproportionate burden. Nearly half of new STI cases each year occur in people under 25 years of age with women both more vulnerable to infection and more likely to experience serious and lasting health consequences when they do become infected. Some microbicides could help prevent STIs.

(10) HIV/AIDS threatens national and global security. Beyond its burdens on individuals, families, and communities, the pandemic reduces economic growth, decimates health budgets, undermines civil society, and burdens the armed forces of many nations, including the United States military.

(11) The microbicide field has gained considerable scientific momentum. Several first-generation products are in large-scale human trials to measure effectiveness, and new products based on recent advances in HIV treatment are well into safety trials.

(12) Microbicides are a public health good with potential for large social benefits but limited economic incentives for private investment, so that public funding is required to fill the gap. As is the case for vaccines and other public goods, microbicide development must depend heavily on government leadership and investment.

(13) The Federal Government needs to make a strong commitment to microbicide research and development. Three agencies, the National Institutes of Health, Centers for Disease Control and Prevention, and United States Agency for International Development, have played important roles in the progress to date, and each makes a valuable and unique contribution. As the primary federal agency for conducting and supporting medical research and the largest single Federal Government contributor to microbicide research, the National Institutes of Health supports the Microbicide Trials Network as well as other important research activities. The United States Agency for International Development sustains strong partnerships with public and private organizations working on microbicide research, including trials in developing countries where its experience is extensive, and is well positioned to facilitate introduction of microbicides once available. The Centers for Disease Control and Prevention has a long history of conducting field trials in developing countries, but the extent of its current engagement remains quite limited.

(14) According to the National Institutes of Health's strategic plan, microbicides may provide 'one of the most promising primary preventative interventions that could be safe, effective, readily available, affordable, and widely acceptable.' In a recent report to Congress, the United States Agency for International Development states that 'the US government is firmly committed to accelerating the development of safe and effective microbicides to prevent HIV.' In addition, the President's Emergency Plan for AIDS Relief recognizes the urgency of developing safe and effective microbicides.

(15) The National Institutes of Health, United States Agency for International Development, and the Centers for Disease Control and Prevention have expanded their microbicide portfolios, but overall Federal leadership and coordination is required to eliminate costly inefficiencies and unproductive duplication of effort.

(16) HIV prevention options available as of 2006 are insufficient in general. Most critically, they fail to recognize women's particular needs and vulnerabilities. If women are to have a genuine opportunity to protect themselves, their best option is the rapid development of new HIV-prevention technologies like microbicides, which women can initiate.

TITLE I—MICROBICIDE RESEARCH AT THE NATIONAL INSTITUTES OF HEALTH

SEC. 101. OFFICE OF AIDS RESEARCH; PROGRAM REGARDING MICROBICIDES FOR PREVENTING TRANSMISSION OF HIV/AIDS AND OTHER DISEASES.

Subpart I of part D of title XXIII of the Public Health Service Act (42 U.S.C. 300cc-40 et seq.) is amended by inserting after section 2351 the following:

'SEC. 2351A. MICROBICIDES FOR PREVENTING TRANSMISSION OF HIV/AIDS AND OTHER DISEASES.

'(a) Federal Strategic Plan-

'(1) IN GENERAL- The Director of the Office of AIDS Research shall—

'(A) expedite the implementation of Federal strategic plans for the conduct and support of microbicide research and development; and

'(B) annually review and, as appropriate, revise such plan, to prioritize funding and activities in terms of their scientific urgency.

'(2) COORDINATION- In implementing, reviewing, and prioritizing elements of the plan described under paragraph (1), the Director of the Office of AIDS Research shall coordinate with—

'(A) other Federal agencies, including the Director of the Centers for Disease Control and Prevention and the Administrator of the United States Agency for International Development, involved in microbicide research;

'(B) the microbicide research and development community; and

'(C) health advocates.

'(b) Expansion and Coordination of Activities- The Director of the Office of AIDS Research, acting in coordination with relevant institutes and offices, shall expand, intensify, and coordinate the activities of all appropriate institutes and components of the National Institutes of Health with respect to research and development of microbicides to prevent the transmission of the human immunodeficiency virus ('HIV') and other sexually transmitted infections.

'(c) Microbicide Development Branch- In carrying out subsection (b), the Director of the National Institute of Allergy and Infectious Diseases shall establish within the Division of AIDS in the Institute, a clearly defined organizational branch charged with carrying out microbicide research and development. In establishing such branch, the Director shall ensure that there are a sufficient number of employees dedicated to carrying out its mission.

'(d) Microbicide Clinical Trials- In carrying out subsection (c), the Director of the National Institute of Allergy and Infectious Diseases shall assign priority to ensuring adequate funding and support for the Microbicide Trials Network and other programs for supporting microbicides clinical trials, with particular emphasis on implementation of trials leading to product licensure.

'(e) Reports to Congress-

'(1) IN GENERAL- Not later than 6 months after the date of enactment of the Microbicide Development Act, and annually thereafter, the Director of the Office of AIDS Research shall submit to the appropriate committees of Congress a report that describes the strategies being implemented by the Federal Government regarding microbicide research and development.

'(2) CONTENTS OF REPORTS- Each report submitted under paragraph (1) shall include—

'(A) a description of activities with respect to microbicide research and development conducted and supported by the Federal Government;

'(B) a summary and analysis of the expenditures made by the Director of the Office of AIDS Research during the preceding year for activities with respect to microbicide-specific research and development, including basic research, preclinical product development, clinical trials, and behavioral science; and

'(C) a description and evaluation of the progress made, during the preceding year, toward the development of effective microbicides.

'(3) APPROPRIATE COMMITTEES OF CONGRESS DEFINED- In this subsection, the term 'appropriate committees of Congress' means the Committee on Health, Education, Labor, and Pensions and the Committee on Appropriations of the Senate and the Committee on Energy and Commerce and the Committee on Appropriations of the House of Representatives.

'(f) Authorization of Appropriations- There are authorized to be appropriated such sums as may be necessary for each fiscal year to carry out this section.'.

TITLE II—MICROBICIDE RESEARCH AT THE CENTERS FOR DISEASE CONTROL AND PREVENTION

SEC. 201. MICROBICIDES FOR PREVENTING TRANSMISSION OF HIV/AIDS AND OTHER DISEASES.

Part B of title III of the Public Health Service Act (42 U.S.C. 243 et seq.) is amended—

(1) by transferring section 317R so as to appear after section 317Q; and

(2) by inserting after section 317R (as so transferred) the following:

'SEC. 371S. MICROBICIDES FOR PREVENTING TRANSMISSION OF HIV/AIDS AND OTHER DISEASES.

'(a) Development and Implementation of the Centers for Disease Control and Prevention's Microbicide Agenda- The Director of the Centers for Disease Control and Prevention shall fully implement such Centers' microbicide agenda to support microbicide research and development. Such an agenda shall include—

'(1) conducting laboratory research in preparation for, and support of, clinical microbicide trials; and

'(2) conducting behavioral research in preparation for, and support of, clinical microbicide trials.

'(b) Personnel- The Centers for Disease Control and Prevention shall ensure that there are sufficient numbers of dedicated employees for carrying out the microbicide agenda under subsection (a).

'(c) Report to Congress-

'(1) IN GENERAL- Not later than 1 year after the date of enactment of the Microbicide Development Act, and annually thereafter, the Director of the Centers for Disease Control and Prevention shall submit to the appropriate committees of Congress, a report on the strategies being implemented by the Centers for Disease Control and Prevention with respect to microbicide research and development. Such report shall be submitted alone or as part of the overall Federal strategic plan on microbicides compiled annually by the National Institutes of Health Office of AIDS Research as required under section 2351A.

'(2) CONTENTS OF REPORT- Such report shall include—

'(A) a description of activities with respect to microbicides conducted or supported by the Director of the Centers for Disease Control and Prevention;

'(B) a summary and analysis of the expenditures made by such Director during the preceding year, for activities with respect to microbicide-specific research and development, including the number of employees of such Centers involved in such activities; and

'(C) a description and evaluation of the progress made, during the preceding year, toward the development of effective microbicides.

'(3) APPROPRIATE COMMITTEES OF CONGRESS DEFINED- For the purposes of this subsection, the term 'appropriate committees of Congress' means the Committee on Health, Education, Labor, and Pensions and the Committee on Appropriations of the Senate and the Committee on Energy and Commerce and the Committee on Appropriations of the House of Representatives.

'(d) Authorization of Appropriations- There are authorized to be appropriated such sums as may be necessary for each fiscal year to carry out this section.'.

TITLE III—MICROBICIDE RESEARCH AND DEVELOPMENT AT THE UNITED STATES AGENCY FOR INTERNATIONAL DEVELOPMENT

SEC. 301. MICROBICIDES FOR PREVENTING TRANSMISSION OF HIV/ AIDS AND OTHER DISEASES.

Section 104A of the Foreign Assistance Act of 1961 (22 U.S.C. 2151b-2) is amended by adding at the end the following new subsection:

'(h) Microbicides for Preventing Transmission of HIV/AIDS and Other Diseases-

'(1) DEVELOPMENT AND IMPLEMENTATION OF THE MICROBICIDE AGENDA- The head of the Office of HIV/AIDS of the United States Agency for International Development, in conjunction with other offices of such Agency, shall develop and implement a program to support the development of microbicides for the prevention of the transmission of HIV/AIDS and other diseases, and facilitate wide-scale availability of such products after such development.

'(2) STAFFING- The head of the Office of HIV/AIDS shall ensure that the Agency has a sufficient number of dedicated employees to carry out the microbicide agenda.

'(3) REPORTS TO CONGRESS-

'(A) IN GENERAL- Not later than 1 year after the date of enactment of the Microbicide Development Act, and annually thereafter, the Administrator of the Agency shall submit to the appropriate committees of Congress a report on the activities of the Administrator to carry out the microbicide agenda and on any other activities carried out by the Administrator related to microbicide research and development.

'(B) CONTENTS OF REPORT- Each report submitted under subparagraph (A) shall include—

'(i) a description of activities with respect to microbicides conducted or supported by the Administrator;

'(ii) a summary and analysis of the expenditures made by the Administrator during the preceding year for activities with respect to microbicide-specific research and development, including the number of employees of the Agency who are involved in such activities; and

'(iii) a description and evaluation of the progress made during the preceding year toward the development of effective microbicides, including activities in support of eventual product access.

'(C) CONSULTATION- The Administrator shall consult with the Director of the Office of AIDS Research of the National Institutes of Health in preparing a report required by subparagraph (A).

'(D) APPROPRIATE COMMITTEES OF CONGRESS DEFINED- In this paragraph, the term 'appropriate committees of Congress' means the Committee on Foreign Relations and the Committee on Appropriations of the Senate and the Committee on Foreign Affairs and the Committee on Appropriations of the House of Representatives.

'(4) AUTHORIZATION OF APPROPRIATIONS- There are authorized to be appropriated such sums as may be necessary for each fiscal year to carry out this subsection.'.

TITLE IV—ADVANCE MARKET COMMITMENTS

SEC. 401. REPORT ON ADVANCE MARKET COMMITMENTS AS INCENTIVES FOR MICROBICIDE DEVELOPMENT.

(a) Report- Not later than 180 days after the date of the enactment of this Act, the Secretary of State shall submit to the appropriate committees of Congress a report on the feasibility and impediments to the Government of the United States entering into advanced market commitments of microbicides to prevent HIV infection as a means of creating incentives for the private sector to invest in research, development, and manufacturing of microbicides.

(b) Appropriate Committees of Congress Defined- In this section, the term 'appropriate committees of Congress' means the Committee on Health, Education, Labor, and Pensions and the Committee on Foreign Relations of the Senate, and the Committee on Energy and Commerce and the Committee on Foreign Affairs of the House of Representatives.

US SENATE BILL 906

TITLE: A bill to prohibit the sale, distribution, transfer, and export of elemental mercury, and for other purposes.

SPONSOR: Sen Obama, Barack [IL] (introduced 3/15/2007) Cosponsors (3)

RELATED BILLS: H.R.1534

LATEST MAJOR ACTION: 3/15/2007 Referred to Senate committee. Status: Read twice and referred to the Committee on Environment and Public Works.

SUMMARY AS OF:

3/15/2007—Introduced.

Mercury Market Minimization Act of 2007 - Amends the Toxic Substances Control Act to: (1) prohibit any federal agency from conveying, selling, or distributing to any other federal, state, or local agency, or any private individual or entity, any elemental mercury under the control or jurisdiction of such agency; (2) prohibit the export of elemental mercury from the United States effective January 1, 2010; (3) require the Administrator of the Environmental Protection Agency to report to Congress on mercury compounds that may currently be used in products or processes; and (4) establish the Excess Mercury Storage Advisory Committee.

MAJOR ACTIONS:

¤NONE¤

ALL ACTIONS:

3/15/2007:

Sponsor introductory remarks on measure. (CR S3213)

3/15/2007:

Read twice and referred to the Committee on Environment and Public Works. (text of measure as introduced: CR S3213-3215)

TITLES(s): (italics indicate a title for a portion of a bill)

¤NONE¤

COSPONSORS(3), ALPHABETICAL [FOLLOWED BY COSPONSORS WITHDRAWN]: (Sort: by date)

Sen Biden, Joseph R., Jr. [DE] - 6/5/2007

Sen Murkowski, Lisa [AK] - 3/15/2007

Sen Salazar, Ken [CO] - 10/25/2007

COMMITTEE(S)

Committee/Subcommittee:

Activity:

Senate Environment and Public Works

Referral, In Committee

RELATED BILL DETAILS: (additional related bills may be indentified in Status)

Bill:

Relationship:

H.R.1534

Related bill identified by CRS

AMENDMENT(S)

¤NONE¤

IN THE SENATE OF THE UNITED STATES

March 15, 2007

Mr. OBAMA (for himself and Ms. MURKOWSKI) introduced the following bill; which was read twice and referred to the Committee on Environment and Public Works

A BILL

To prohibit the sale, distribution, transfer, and export of elemental mercury, and for other purposes.

Be it enacted by the Senate and House of Representatives of the United States of America in Congress assembled,

SECTION 1. SHORT TITLE.

This Act may be cited as the 'Mercury Market Minimization Act of 2007'.

SEC. 2. FINDINGS.

Congress finds that—

(1) mercury and mercury compounds are highly toxic to humans, ecosystems, and wildlife;

(2) as many as 10 percent of women in the United States of childbearing age have mercury in the blood at a level that could put a baby at risk;

(3) as many as 630,000 children born annually in the United States are at risk of neurological problems related to mercury;

(4) the most significant source of mercury exposure to people in the United States is ingestion of mercury-contaminated fish;

(5) the Environmental Protection Agency reports that, as of 2004—

(A) 44 States have fish advisories covering over 13,000,000 lake acres and over 750,000 river miles;

(B) in 21 States the freshwater advisories are statewide; and

(C) in 12 States the coastal advisories are statewide;

(6) the long-term solution to mercury pollution is to minimize global mercury use and releases to eventually achieve reduced contamination levels in the environment, rather than reducing fish consumption since uncontaminated fish represents a critical and healthy source of nutrition worldwide;

(7) mercury pollution is a transboundary pollutant, depositing locally, regionally, and globally, and affecting water bodies near industrial sources (including the Great Lakes) and remote areas (including the Arctic Circle);

(8) the free trade of mercury and mercury compounds on the world market, at relatively low prices and in ready supply, encourages the continued use of mercury outside of the United States, often involving highly dispersive activities such as artisinal gold mining;

(9) the intentional use of mercury is declining in the United States as a consequence of process changes to manufactured products (including batteries, paints, switches, and measuring devices), but those uses remain substantial in the developing world where releases from the products are extremely likely due to the limited pollution control and waste management infrastructures in those countries;

(10) the member countries of the European Union collectively are the largest source of mercury exports globally;

(11) the European Union is in the process of enacting legislation that will prohibit mercury exports by not later than 2011;

(12) the United States is a net exporter of mercury and, according to the United States Geologic Survey, exported 506 metric tons of mercury more than the United States imported during the period of 2000 through 2004; and

(13) banning exports of mercury from the United States will have a notable affect on the market availability of mercury and switching to affordable mercury alternatives in the developing world.

SEC. 3. PROHIBITION ON SALE, DISTRIBUTION, OR TRANSFER OF MERCURY BY DEPARTMENT OF DEFENSE OR DEPARTMENT OF ENERGY.

Section 6 of the Toxic Substances Control Act (15 U.S.C. 2605) is amended by adding at the end the following:

'(f) Mercury-

'(1) PROHIBITION ON SALE, DISTRIBUTION, OR TRANSFER OF MERCURY BY FEDERAL AGENCIES- Except as provided in paragraph (2), effective beginning on the date of enactment of this subsection, no Federal agency shall convey, sell, or distribute to any other Federal agency, any State or local government agency, or any private individual or entity any elemental mercury under the control or jurisdiction of the Federal agency.

'(2) EXCEPTION- Paragraph (1) shall not apply to a transfer between Federal agencies of elemental mercury for the sole purpose of facilitating storage of mercury to carry out this Act.'.

SEC. 4. PROHIBITION ON EXPORT OF MERCURY.

Section 12 of the Toxic Substances Control Act (15 U.S.C. 2611) is amended—

(1) in subsection (a) by striking 'subsection (b)' and inserting 'subsections (b) and (c)'; and

(2) by adding at the end the following:

'(c) Prohibition on Export of Mercury-

'(1) ELEMENTAL MERCURY- Effective January 1, 2010, the export of elemental mercury from the United States is prohibited.

'(2) REPORT TO CONGRESS ON MERCURY COMPOUNDS-

'(A) REPORT-

'(i) IN GENERAL- Not later than 1 year after the date of enactment of the Mercury Market Minimization Act of 2007, the Administrator shall publish and submit to Congress a report on mercuric chloride, mercurous chloride or calomel, mercuric oxide, and other mercury compounds, if any, that may currently be used in significant quantities in products or processes.

'(ii) INCLUSIONS- The report shall include an analysis of—

'(I) the sources and amounts of each mercury compound produced annually in, or imported into, the United States;

'(II)(aa) the purposes for which each of the compounds are used domestically;

'(bb) the quantity of the compounds currently consumed annually for each purpose; and '(cc) the estimated quantity of the compounds to be consumed for each purpose during calendar year 2010 and thereafter;

'(III) the sources and quantities of each mercury compound exported from the United States during each of the preceding 3 calendar years;

'(IV) the potential for the compounds to be processed into elemental mercury after export from the United States; and

'(V) other information that Congress should consider in determining whether to extend the export prohibition to include 1 or more of those mercury compounds.

'(B) PROCEDURE-

'(i) IN GENERAL- Except as provided in clause (ii), for the purpose of preparing the report under this paragraph, the Administrator may use the information gathering authorities of this title, including sections 10 and 11.

'(ii) EXCEPTION- Subsection (b)(2) of section 11 shall not apply to activities under this subparagraph.

'(3) EXCESS MERCURY STORAGE ADVISORY COMMITTEE-

'(A) ESTABLISHMENT- There is established an advisory committee, to be known as the 'Excess Mercury Storage Advisory Committee' (referred to in this paragraph as the 'Committee').

'(B) MEMBERSHIP-

'(i) IN GENERAL- The Committee shall be composed of 9 members, of whom—

'(I) 2 members shall be jointly appointed by the Speaker of the House of Representatives and the Majority Leader of the Senate—

'(aa) 1 of whom shall be designated to serve as Chairperson of the Committee; and

'(bb) 1 of whom shall be designated to serve as Vice-Chairperson of the Committee;

'(II) 1 member shall be the Administrator;

'(III) 1 member shall be the Secretary of Defense;

'(IV) 1 member shall be a representative of State environmental agencies;

'(V) 1 member shall be a representative of State attorneys general;

'(VI) 1 member shall be a representative of the chlorine industry;

'(VII) 1 member shall be a representative of the mercury waste treatment industry; and

'(VIII) 1 member shall be a representative of a nonprofit environmental organization.

'(ii) APPOINTMENTS- Not later than 45 days after the date of enactment of this subsection, the Administrator, in consultation with the appropriate congressional committees, shall appoint the members of the Committee described in subclauses (IV) through (VIII) of clause (i).

'(C) INITIAL MEETING- Not later than 30 days after the date on which all members of the Committee have been appointed, the Committee shall hold the initial meeting of the Committee.

'(D) MEETINGS- The Committee shall meet at the call of the Chairperson.

'(E) QUORUM- A majority of the members of the Committee shall constitute a quorum.

'(F) REPORT- Not later than 1 year after the date of enactment of this subsection, the Committee shall submit to Congress a report describing the findings and recommendations of the Committee, if any, relating to—

'(i) the environmental, health, and safety requirements necessary to prevent—

'(I) the release of elemental mercury into the environment; and

'(II) worker exposure from the storage of elemental mercury;

'(ii) the estimated annual cost of storing elemental mercury on a per-pound or per-ton basis;

'(iii) for the 40-year period beginning on the date of submission of the report, the optimal size, number, and other characteristics of Federal facilities required to store elemental mercury under current and anticipated jurisdictions of each Federal agency;

'(iv) the estimated quantity of—

'(I) elemental mercury that will result from the decommissioning of mercury cell chlor-alkali facilities in the United States; and

'(II) any other supplies that may require storage to carry out this Act;

'(v) for the 40-year period beginning on the date of submission of the report, the estimated quantity of elemental mercury generated from the recycling of unwanted products and other wastes that will require storage to comply with the export prohibitions under this Act;

'(vi) any legal, technical, economic, or other barrier that may prevent the private sector from storing elemental mercury produced by the private sector during the 40-year period beginning on the date of submission of the report, including a description of measures to address the barriers;

'(vii) the advantages and disadvantages of consolidating the storage of mercury produced by public and private sources under the management of the public or private sector;

'(viii) the optimal plan of the Committee for storing excess mercury produced by public and private sources; and

'(ix) additional research, if any, required to determine a long-term disposal option for the storage of excess mercury.

'(G) COMPENSATION OF MEMBERS-

'(i) IN GENERAL-

'(I) NON-FEDERAL EMPLOYEES- A member of the Committee who is not an officer or employee of the Federal Government shall be compensated at a rate equal to the daily equivalent of the annual rate of basic pay prescribed for level V of the Executive Schedule under section 5316 of title 5, United States Code, for each day (including travel time) during which the member is engaged in the performance of the duties of the Committee.

'(II) FEDERAL EMPLOYEES- A member of the Committee who is an officer or employee of the Federal Government shall serve without compensation in addition to the compensation received for the services of the member as an officer or employee of the Federal Government.

'(ii) TRAVEL EXPENSES- A member of the Committee shall be allowed travel expenses, including per diem in lieu of subsistence, at rates authorized for an employee of an agency under subchapter I of chapter 57 of title 5, United States Code, while away from the home or regular place of business of the member in the performance of the duties of the Committee.

'(H) STAFF AND FUNDING- The Administrator shall provide to the Committee such funding and additional personnel as are necessary to enable the Committee to perform the duties of the Committee.

'(I) TERMINATION- The Committee shall terminate 180 days after the date on which the Committee submits the report of the Committee under subparagraph (F).

'(4) INAPPLICABILITY OF UNREASONABLE RISK REQUIREMENT- Subsection (a) shall not apply to this subsection.'.

US SENATE BILL 976

TITLE: A bill to secure the promise of personalized medicine for all Americans by expanding and accelerating genomics research and initiatives to improve the accuracy of disease diagnosis, increase the safety of drugs, and identify novel treatments.

SPONSOR: Sen Obama, Barack [IL] (introduced 3/23/2007) Cosponsors (1)

LATEST MAJOR ACTION: 3/23/2007 Referred to Senate committee. Status: Read twice and referred to the Committee on Health, Education, Labor, and Pensions.

SUMMARY AS OF:

3/23/2007—Introduced.

Genomics and Personalized Medicine Act of 2007 - Directs the Secretary of Health and Human Services to: (1) establish the Genomics and Personalized Medicine Interagency Working Group (IWG) to facilitate collaboration, coordination, and integration of activities among federal agencies relating to genomic research and initiatives; (2) establish a national biobanking distributed database for the collection and integration of genomic data and associated environmental and clinical health information; (3) establish a grant program for academic medical centers and other

entities to develop or expand biobanking initiatives; (4) improve genetics and genomics training for diagnosis, treatment, and counseling of adults and children for both rare and common disorders; (5) contract with the National Academy of Sciences to study incentives to encourage companion diagnostic test development; and (6) make information available on the safety and efficacy of genetic tests and commission a study for improving federal oversight and regulation of such tests.

Requires the Director of the Centers for Disease Control and Prevention to: (1) conduct an analysis of the public health impact of direct-to-consumer marketing of genetic tests; and (2) expand efforts to educate the public about genomics and its health applications.

MAJOR ACTIONS:

¤NONE¤

ALL ACTIONS:

3/23/2007:

Sponsor introductory remarks on measure. (CR S3708-3710)

3/23/2007:

Read twice and referred to the Committee on Health, Education, Labor, and Pensions.

TITLES(s): (italics indicate a title for a portion of a bill)

¤NONE¤

COSPONSORS(1), ALPHABETICAL [followed by Cosponsors withdrawn]: (Sort: by date)

Sen Burr, Richard [NC] - 3/23/2007

COMMITTEE(s)

Committee/Subcommittee:

Activity:

Senate Health, Education, Labor, and Pensions

Referral, In Committee

RELATED BILL DETAILS:

¤NONE¤

AMENDMENT(s)

¤NONE¤

IN THE SENATE OF THE UNITED STATES

March 23, 2007

Mr. OBAMA (for himself and Mr. BURR) introduced the following bill; which was read twice and referred to the Committee on Health, Education, Labor, and Pensions

A BILL

To secure the promise of personalized medicine for all Americans by expanding and accelerating genomics research and initiatives to improve the accuracy of disease diagnosis, increase the safety of drugs, and identify novel treatments.

Be it enacted by the Senate and House of Representatives of the United States of America in Congress assembled,

SECTION 1. SHORT TITLE.

This Act may be cited as the 'Genomics and Personalized Medicine Act of 2007'.

SEC. 2. FINDINGS.

Congress makes the following findings:

(1) The completion of the Human Genome Project in 2003 paved the way for a more sophisticated understanding of diseases and drug responses, which has contributed to the advent of 'personalized medicine'.

(2) Personalized medicine is the application of genomic and molecular data to better target the delivery of health care, facilitate the discovery and clinical testing of new products, and help determine a person's predisposition to a particular disease or condition.

(3) Many commonly-used drugs are typically effective in only 40 to 60 percent of the patient population.

(4) In the United States, up to 15 percent of hospitalized patients experience a serious adverse drug reaction, and more than 100,000 deaths are attributed annually to such reactions.

(5) Pharmacogenomics has the potential to dramatically increase the efficacy and safety of drugs and reduce health care costs, and is fundamental to the practice of genome-based personalized medicine.

(6) Pharmacogenomics is the study of how genetic variation affects a person's response to drugs. This relatively new field combines pharmacology (the science of drugs) and genomics (the study of genes and their functions) to develop safer and more effective medications and dosing regimens that will be tailored to an individual's genetic makeup.

(7) The cancer drug Gleevec was developed based on knowledge of the chromosomal translocation that causes chronic myelogenous leukemia, which is characterized by an abnormal growth in the number of white blood cells. The mean 5-year survival for affected patients who are treated with Gleevec is 95 percent, which contrasts to a 5-year survival of 50 percent for patients treated with older therapies.

(8) The ERBB2 gene helps cells grow, divide and repair themselves. One in 4 breast cancers are characterized by extra copies of this gene, which causes uncontrolled and rapid tumor growth. Pharmacogenomics research led to both the development of the test for this type of breast cancer as well as an effective biologic, Herceptin.

(9) Warfarin, a blood thinner used to prevent the formation of life-threatening clots, significantly elevates patient risk for bleeding in the head or gastrointestinal tract, both of which are associated with increased rates of hospitalization, disability and death. Pharmacogenomic researchers have identified and developed tests for genetic variants in the cytochrome P450 metabolizing enzyme (CYP2C9) and vitamin K epoxide reductase complex that increase risk for these adverse events. By using a companion diagnostic test for these two genes, physicians can modify the dosing regimen and decrease the likelihood of adverse events.

(10) Although the cancer drug 6-mercaptopurine (6-MP) cures 85 percent of children with acute lymphoblastic leukemia, historically, a significant number of patients would die inexplicably from the drug. Researchers later discovered that 1 in 300 individuals inherit an inactive version of the gene encoding the metabolizing enzyme thiopurine methyltransferase (TPMT) from both their mother and father and, as a result, should receive only a fraction of the standard dose of purine drugs. In addition, 1 in 10 individuals have only 1 copy of the gene with variable function, and the dosage of 6-MP must be adjusted for a subset of these patients. Physicians now are able to screen for TPMT gene variants before administering these drugs.

(11) Research into the genetics of breast cancer identified two pivotal genes, BRCA1 and BRCA2, mutations in which correspond to a significantly increased lifetime risk of developing breast and ovarian cancer. Individuals in affected families or with specific risk factors may use genetic testing to identify whether they carry mutations in these genes and to inform their decisions about treatment options, including prophylatic mastectomy and oophorectomy.

(12) Realizing the promise of personalized medicine will require continued Federal leadership and agency collaboration, expansion and acceleration of genomics research, a capable genomics workforce, incentives to encourage development and collection of data on the analytic and clinical validity and clinical utility of genomic tests and therapies, and improved regulation over the quality of genetic tests, direct-to-consumer advertising of genetic tests, and use of personal genomic information.

SEC. 3. DEFINITIONS.

In this Act:

(1) BIOBANK- The term 'biobank' means a shared repository of human biological specimens that may also include data associated with such specimens collected for medical or research purposes. Human biological specimens may include body fluids, tissues, blood, cells, or materials derived from these sources, and data associated with such specimens may include health information or environmental data.

(2) BIOMARKER- The term 'biomarker' means an analyte found in or derived from a patient specimen that is objectively measured and evaluated as an indicator of normal biologic processes, pathogenic processes, or pharmacologic responses to a therapeutic intervention.

(3) CLIA- The term 'CLIA' means the Clinical Laboratory Improvement Amendments of 1988 (42 U.S.C. 263a).

(4) ENVIRONMENT- The term 'environment' means conditions or circumstances that are nongenetic but may have a health impact.

(5) GENETIC TEST- The term 'genetic test' means an analysis of human DNA, RNA, chromosomes, proteins, or metabolites, that detects genotypes, mutations, or chromosomal and biochemical changes.

(6) LABORATORY-DEVELOPED GENETIC TEST- The term 'laboratory-developed genetic test' means a genetic test that is designed, validated, conducted, and offered as a service by a clinical laboratory subject to CLIA using either commercially available analyte specific reagents (FDA-regulated) or reagents prepared by the laboratory (not FDA-regulated), or some combination thereof.

(7) PHARMACOGENETIC TEST- The term 'pharmacogenetic test' means a genetic test intended to identify individual variations in DNA sequence related to drug absorption and disposition (pharmacokinetics) or drug action (pharmacodynamics), including polymorphic variation in the genes that encode the functions of transporters, receptors, metabolizing enzymes, and other proteins.

(8) PHARMACOGENOMIC TEST-

(A) IN GENERAL- The term 'pharmacogenomic test' means a genetic test intended to identify individual variations in single-nucleotide polymorphisms, haplotype markers, or alterations in gene expression or inactivation, that may be correlated with pharmacological function and therapeutic response.

(B) VARIATIONS AND ALTERATIONS- For purposes of this paragraph, the variations or alterations referred to in subparagraph (A) may be a pattern or profile of change, rather than a change in an individual marker.

(9) SECRETARY- The term 'Secretary' means the Secretary of Health and Human Services.

SEC. 4. GENOMICS AND PERSONALIZED MEDICINE INTERAGENCY WORKING GROUP.

(a) In General- Not later than 90 days after the date of enactment of this Act, the Secretary shall establish within the Department of Health and Human Services the Genomics and Personalized Medicine Interagency Working Group (referred to in this Act as the 'IWG').

(b) Duties- The IWG shall facilitate collaboration, coordination, and integration of activities within the Department of Health and Human Services and other Federal agencies, and among such agencies and relevant public and private entities, by—

(1) reviewing current and proposed genomic initiatives, in order to identify shared interests and leverage resources;

(2) prioritizing new genomic initiatives, based on areas of need as measured by public health impact;

(3) reaching consensus on standardized genomic terminology, definitions, and data code sets for adoption and use in Federally conducted or supported programs;

(4) establishing and disseminating quality standards and guidelines for the collection, processing, archiving, storage, and dissemination of genomic samples and data for research and clinical purposes;

(5) developing and promulgating guidelines regarding procedures, protocols, and policies for the safeguarding of the privacy of biobank subjects, in accordance with the Office for Human Research Protection and Clinical Research Policy Analysis and Coordination Program at the National Institutes of Health, and other guidelines as appropriate;

(6) reviewing and making recommendations to address ownership and patient access issues with respect to genomic samples and analyses;

(7) developing and promulgating guidelines regarding procedures, protocols, and policies for access to patient data, genomic samples, and associated health information by non-governmental entities for research purposes;

(8) developing and disseminating guidelines for constructing informed consent forms that ensure patient privacy and confidentiality of associated clinical data and information, understanding of research procedures, benefits, risks, rights, and responsibilities, and continuous voluntary participation; and

(9) providing recommendations for the establishment of a distributed database, pursuant to section 5.

(c) IWG Chairperson- The Secretary, or his or her designee, shall serve as chairperson of the IWG.

(d) Members- In addition to the Secretary, the IWG shall include members from the—

(1) National Institutes of Health;

(2) Centers for Disease Control and Prevention;

(3) Food and Drug Administration;

(4) Health Resources and Services Administration;

(5) Office of Minority Health;

(6) Agency for Healthcare Research and Quality;

(7) Centers for Medicare & Medicaid Services;

(8) Veterans Health Administration;

(9) Office of the National Coordinator for Health Information Technology;

(10) Department of Energy;

(11) Armed Forces Institute of Pathology;

(12) Indian Health Service; and

(13) other Federal departments and agencies as determined appropriate by the Secretary.

(e) Public Input- The IWG shall solicit input from relevant stakeholders with respect to meeting the duties described in subsection (b).

(f) Report- Not later than 18 months after the date of enactment of this Act, the Secretary shall prepare and submit a report to the appropriate committees of Congress and to the public on IWG deliberations, activities, and recommendations with respect to meeting the duties described in subsection (b).

(g) Termination- The IWG shall terminate after submitting the report described in subsection (f), or later at the discretion of the Secretary.

(h) Authorization of Appropriations- There are authorized to be appropriated to carry out this section, $1,000,000 for fiscal years 2008 and 2009.

SEC. 5. NATIONAL BIOBANKING INITIATIVE.

(a) In General- The Secretary shall advance the field of genomics and personalized medicine through establishment of a national biobanking distributed database for the collection and integration of genomic data, and associated environmental and clinical health information, which shall facilitate synthesis and pooled analysis of such data.

(b) Database- With respect to the national biobanking distributed database, the Secretary shall—

(1) adhere to relevant guidelines, policies, and recommendations of the IWG, pursuant to section 4;

(2) establish, directly or by contract, a single point of authority to manage operations of the database;

(3) incorporate biobanking data from Federally conducted or supported genomics initiatives, as feasible;

(4) encourage voluntary submission of biobanking data obtained or analyzed with private or non-Federal funds;

(5) facilitate submission of data, including secure and efficient electronic submission;

(6) allow public use of data only—

(A) with appropriate privacy safeguards in place; and

(B) for health research purposes;

(7) determine appropriate procedures for access by nongovernmental entities to biobank data for research and development of new or improved tests and treatments, and submission of data generated from such samples to the Food and Drug Administration as part of the approval process for drugs and devices;

(8) conduct, directly or by contract, analytical research, including clinical, epidemiological, and social research, using biobank data; and

(9) make analytic findings from biobanking initiatives supported by Federal funding publicly available within an appropriate timeframe to be determined by the Secretary.

(c) Rule of Construction- Nothing in this section shall be construed to require the submission or acceptance of biological specimens.

(d) Biobank Initiatives Grants-

(1) IN GENERAL- The Secretary shall establish a grant program for eligible entities to develop or expand biobanking initiatives to increase understanding of how genomics interacts with environmental factors to cause disease, and to accelerate the development of genomic-based tests and treatments.

(2) ELIGIBLE ENTITIES-

(A) IN GENERAL- For purposes of this subsection, eligible entities include academic medical centers and other entities determined appropriate by the Secretary. Eligible entities desiring a grant under this subsection shall submit an application to the Secretary in accordance with this subsection, at such time, in such manner, and containing such additional information as the Secretary may require.

(B) PRIORITY- Academic medical centers that partner with health care professionals within their communities in order to obtain diverse genomic samples shall be given priority for awards made under this subsection.

(3) REQUIREMENTS- The Secretary shall ensure that biobanks supported by grant awards under this section—

(A) adhere to guidelines and recommendations developed pursuant to section 4;

(B) are established to complement activities related to the implementation of current Federal biobanking research initiatives, as feasible;

(C) are based on well-defined populations, including population-based registries of disease and family-based registries;

(D) collect data from participants with diverse genomic profiles, demographics, environmental exposures, and presence or absence of health conditions and diseases, as appropriate;

(E) meet quality standards for the collection, processing, archiving, storage, and dissemination of data, which shall be developed by the IWG;

(F) have practical experience and demonstrated expertise in genomics and its clinical and public health applications;

(C) establish mechanisms to ensure patient privacy and protection of information from non-health applications and, as feasible, patient access to genomic samples for clinical testing purposes; and

(H) contribute genomic and associated clinical and environmental data and analyses to the national biobanking distributed database, pursuant to subsection (b).

(4) USE OF FUNDS- An eligible entity that receives a grant under this subsection shall use the grant funds to develop or expand a biobanking initiative, which may include the following activities:

(A) Support for scientific and community advisory committees.

(B) Recruitment and education of participants.

(C) Development of consent protocols.

(D) Obtaining genetic samples and associated environmental and clinical information.

(E) Establishment and maintenance of secure storage for genetic samples and clinical information.

(F) Conduct of data analyses and evidence-based systemic reviews that allow for the following:

(i) Identification of biomarkers and other surrogate markers to improve predictions of onset of disease, response to therapy, and clinical outcomes.

(ii) Increased understanding of gene-environment interactions.

(iii) Development of genetic screening, diagnostic, and therapeutic interventions.

(iv) Genotypic characterization of tissue samples.

(G) Other activities, as determined appropriate by the Secretary.

(5) QUALITY ASSURANCE- The Secretary may enter into a contract with an external entity to evaluate grantees under this subsection to ensure that quality standards are met.

(e) Application of Privacy Rules- Nothing in this Act shall be construed to supercede the requirements for the protection of patient privacy under—

(1) the Federal regulations promulgated under section 264(c) of the Health Insurance Portability and Accountability Act of 1996 (42 U.S.C. 1320d-2 note); or

(2) sections 552 and 552a of title 5, United States Code (5 U.S.C. App.).

(f) Authorization of Appropriations- There are authorized to be appropriated to carry out this section, $75,000,000 for fiscal year 2009, and such sums as may be necessary for each of fiscal years 2010 through 2014.

SEC. 6. GENOMICS WORKFORCE AND TRAINING.

(a) Genetics and Genomics Training- The Secretary, directly or through contracts or grants to eligible entities, which shall include professional genetics and genomics societies, academic institutions, and other entities as determined appropriate by the Secretary, shall improve the adequacy of genetics and genomics training for diagnosis, treatment, and counseling of adults and children for both rare and common disorders, through support of efforts to—

(1) develop and disseminate model training program and residency curricula and teaching materials that reflect the new knowledge and evolving practice of genetics and genomics;

(2) assist the review of board and other certifying examinations by professional societies and accreditation bodies to ensure adequate focus on the fundamental principles of genomics; and

(3) identify and evaluate options for distance or on-line learning for degree or continuing education programs.

(b) Integration- The Secretary, in collaboration with medical professional societies and accreditation bodies and associations of health professional schools, shall support initiatives to increase the integration of genetics and genomics into all aspects of clinical and public health practice by promoting genetics and genomics competency across all clinical, public health, and laboratory disciplines through the development and dissemination of health professional guidelines which shall—

(1) include focus on appropriate techniques for collection and storage of genomics samples, administration and interpretation of genetic and genomic tests, and subsequent clinical and public health decisionmaking; and

(2) specifically target health professionals without formal training or experience in the field of genomics.

(c) Authorization of Appropriations- There are authorized to be appropriated to carry out this section $5,000,000 for fiscal year 2008 and such sums as may be necessary for each of fiscal years 2009 through 2013.

SEC. 7. REALIZING THE POTENTIAL OF PERSONALIZED MEDICINE.

(a) National Academy of Sciences Study- Not later than 180 days after the date of enactment of this Act, the Secretary shall enter into a contract with the National Research Council of the National Academy of Sciences to study and recommend appropriate incentives to encourage—

(1) codevelopment of companion diagnostic testing by a drug sponsor;

(2) development of companion diagnostic testing for already-approved drugs by the drug sponsor;

(3) companion diagnostic test development by device companies that are not affiliated with the drug sponsor; and

(4) action on other issues determined appropriate by the Secretary.

(b) Genetic Test Quality-

(1) IN GENERAL- The Secretary shall improve the availability of information on, and safety and efficacy of, genetic tests, including pharmacogenetic and pharmacogenomic tests.

(2) INSTITUTE OF MEDICINE STUDY- Not later than 30 days after the date of enactment of this Act, the Secretary shall enter into a contract with the Institute of Medicine to conduct a study and prepare a report that includes recommendations to improve Federal oversight and regulation of genetic tests, with specific recommendations on the implementation of the decision matrix under paragraph (3). Such study shall take into consideration relevant reports by the Secretary's Advisory Committee on Genetic Testing and other groups and shall be completed not later than 1 year after the date on which the Secretary entered into such contract.

(3) DECISION MATRIX-

(A) IN GENERAL- Not later than 18 months after the date of enactment of this Act, the Secretary, taking into consideration the recommendations of the Institute of Medicine report under paragraph (2), shall implement a decision matrix (referred to in this section as the 'matrix') to improve the oversight and regulation of genetic tests, including pharmacogenomic and pharmacogenetic tests by determining—

(i) the classification of all genetic tests;

(ii) which categories of tests, including laboratory-developed tests, require review and the level of review needed for such categories of tests;

(iii) which agency shall have oversight over the review process of such categories of tests that are determined to require review; and

(iv) to the extent practicable, which requirements the agency shall apply to the types of tests identified in clause (ii).

(B) LEVEL OF REVIEW- In determining the level of review needed by a genetic test, the Secretary shall take into consideration—

(i) performance characteristics of the test and its target disease or condition;

(ii) intended use of the test;

(iii) potential for improved medical conditions and patient harms; and

(iv) social consequences of the test.

(C) COMPARATIVE ANALYSIS- To inform implementation of the matrix, the Secretary shall undertake a comparative analysis of laboratory review requirements under CLIA and those of the Food and Drug Administration to—

(i) assess and reduce unnecessary differences in such requirements;

(ii) eliminate redundancies and decrease burden of review, as practicable; and

(iii) specify which elements of the test constitute a device that may be regulated by the Food and Drug Administration and which elements comprise a service that may be regulated under CLIA.

(D) REGULATIONS- The Secretary shall promulgate regulations to implement the matrix not later than the date specified under subparagraph (A).

(E) TRANSITION PERIOD- The Secretary may not require a laboratory to submit a report under section 510(k) or an application under section 515 of the Federal Food, Drug and Cosmetic Act (21 U.S.C. 301 et seq.) until 180 days after the regulations promulgated under subparagraph (D) take effect.

(4) ADVERSE EVENTS- The Secretary, acting through the Commissioner of Food and Drugs and the Administrator of the Centers for Medicare & Medicaid Services, shall—

(A) develop or expand adverse event reporting systems to encompass reports of adverse events resulting from genetic testing;

(B) respond appropriately to any adverse events resulting from such testing; and

(C) facilitate the use of genetic and genomic approaches, as feasible, to assess risk for, and reduce incidence of, adverse drug reactions.

(5) AUTHORIZATION OF APPROPRIATIONS- There are authorized to be appropriated to carry out this subsection, $6,000,000 for fiscal year 2008, and such sums as may be necessary for each of fiscal years 2009 through 2013.

(c) Food and Drug Administration-

(1) IN GENERAL-

(A) SUMMARY INFORMATION- If a genetic test that is determined to be within the jurisdiction of the Food and Drug Administration but that does not require review as determined under the matrix, the sponsor of such test shall provide the Secretary with summary information on how such test was validated and its performance characteristics. Such information shall be in a standardized format and with standardized content as specified by the Food and Drug Administration, and shall be made easily accessible to the public.

(B) SOURCE OF INFORMATION- The information described under subparagraph (A) may be obtained from the labeling submitted for CLIA complexity categorization.

(2) ENCOURAGEMENT OF COMPANION DIAGNOSTIC TESTING- The Secretary may encourage the sponsor of a drug or biological product—

(A) to codevelop a companion diagnostic test, after filing an investigational new drug application or a new drug application to address significant safety concerns of the drug or biological product;

(B) to develop a companion diagnostic test if phase IV data demonstrate significant safety or effectiveness concerns with use of the drug or biological product; and

(C) to relabel the drug or biological product to require validated companion diagnostic testing when evidence of improved outcomes has been established in practice or if data demonstrate significant safety concerns with use of such drug or biological product.

(3) PHARMACOGENOMIC DATA SUBMISSION- The Secretary shall encourage and facilitate voluntary pharmacogenomic data submission from drug sponsors, which may include—

(A) the development and dissemination of guidance on relevant policies, procedure and practice regarding such submission;

(B) the provision of technical assistance;

(C) the establishment of a mechanism to store, maintain and analyze such data, in collaboration with the National Institutes of Health and the Centers for Disease Control and Prevention;

(D) determining when such data may be used to support an investigational new drug or a new drug application;

(E) the conduct of a study of the use of genomic approaches to understand and reduce adverse drug reactions; and

(F) other activities determined appropriate by the Commissioner.

(4) TERMINATION OF CERTAIN ADVERTISING CAMPAIGNS- The Food and Drug Administration shall collaborate with the Federal Trade Commission to identify and terminate, pursuant to section 5 of the Federal Trade Commission Act (15 U.S.C. 45), advertising campaigns that make false, misleading, deceptive, or unfair claims about the benefits or risks of genetic tests.

(d) Centers for Medicare & Medicaid Services-

(1) IN GENERAL- If a genetic test that is determined to be within the jurisdiction of the Centers for Medicare & Medicaid Services but that does not require review as determined under the matrix, the sponsor of such test shall provide the Administrator of the Centers for Medicare & Medicaid Services with summary information on how the test was validated and its performance characteristics. Such information shall be in a standardized format and with standardized content as specified by the Centers for Medicare & Medicaid Services, and shall be made easily accessible to the public.

(2) SPECIALTY AREA- To ensure the accuracy, validity, and reliability of clinical genetic tests that do not require premarket approval by or notification to the Food and Drug Administration, and to improve oversight of genetic test laboratories, the Director of the Division of Laboratory Services of the Survey and Certification Group of the Center for Medicaid and State Operations of the Centers for Medicare & Medicaid Services, in collaboration with the Clinical Laboratory Improvement Advisory Committee at the Centers for Disease Control and Prevention, shall establish a specialty area for molecular and biochemical genetic tests, in order to—

(A) develop criteria for establishing analytic and clinical validity for genetic tests that are determined to require review under the matrix;

(B) specify requirements for proficiency testing for laboratories;

(C) provide guidance regarding the scope of duty for laboratory directors;

(D) make information easily accessible to the public about—

(i) laboratory certification; and

(ii) analytic and clinical validity for genetic tests that are determined to require high level review under the matrix; and

(E) conduct other activities at the discretion of the Administrator of the Centers for Medicare & Medicaid Services.

(3) REIMBURSEMENT-

(A) CODING- To foster adoption of genetic screening tools, the Administrator of the Centers for Medicare & Medicaid Services shall—

(i) assess and update current procedure terminology codes to encourage the rapid review and coverage of novel tests through the creation of new HCPCS codes and adoption of new CPT codes and without undue reliance on national coverage determinations; and

(ii) determine and implement fair and reasonable coverage policies and reimbursement rates for medically necessary genetic and genomic treatments and services, including laboratory testing.

(B) BUDGET NEUTRALITY- Before enhancing payment for a year pursuant to this paragraph, the Secretary shall, if necessary, provide for an adjustment to payments made under part B of title XVIII of the Social Security Act (42 U.S.C. 1395j et seq.) in that year to ensure that such payments shall be equal to aggregate payments that would have been made under such part in that year if this paragraph had not been enacted.

(e) Centers for Disease Control and Prevention-

(1) DIRECT-TO-CONSUMER MARKETING- Not later than 2 years after the date of enactment of this Act, the Director of the Centers for Disease Control and Prevention, with respect to genetic tests for which consumers have direct access, shall—

(A) conduct an analysis of the public health impact of direct-to-consumer marketing to the extent possible from available data sources;

(B) analyze the validity of claims made in direct-to-consumer marketing to determine whether such claims are substantiated by competent and reliable scientific evidence; and

(C) make recommendations to the Secretary regarding necessary interventions to protect the public from potential harms of direct-to-consumer marketing and access to genetic tests.

(2) PUBLIC AWARENESS- The Director shall expand efforts to educate and increase awareness of the general public about genomics and its applications to improve health, prevent disease and eliminate health disparities. Such efforts shall include the—

(A) ongoing collection of data on the awareness, knowledge and use of genetic tests through public health surveillance systems, and analysis of the impact of such tests on population health; and

(B) integration of the use of validated genetic and genomic tests in public health programs as appropriate.

(3) AUTHORIZATION OF APPROPRIATIONS- There are authorized to be appropriated to carry out this subsection, $10,000,000 for fiscal year 2008, and such sums as may be necessary for each of fiscal years 2009 through 2013.

(f) Agency for Healthcare Research and Quality- The Director of the Agency for Healthcare Research and Quality, after consultation with the IWG and other public and private organizations based in the United States and abroad, as appropriate, shall support the assessment of the clinical utility and cost-effectiveness of companion diagnostic tests that guide prescribing decisions, through research that—

(1) develops standardized tools and methodologies to assess the clinical utility and cost-effectiveness of such tests, as well as criteria for use;

(2) establishes and validates drug dosing algorithms for which such tests can improve outcomes, taking into consideration—

(A) a reduction in toxicity, adverse events, and mortality;

(B) improved clinical outcomes and quality of life, including decreased requirements for monitoring and laboratory testing; and

(C) the impact on the direct and indirect costs of health care, which may include costs due to length of hospital stay, length of time to identify safe and effective dosing for patients, toxicity and adverse events, and other measures of health care utilization and outcomes;

(3) supports and expedites the development of clinical decision tools for clinical use of genetic tests, as warranted; and

(4) prioritizes the development of such tests for diseases and health conditions that have a significant public health impact because of prevalence, risk of complications from treatment, and other factors determined appropriate by the Director.

(g) Authorization of Appropriations- There are authorized to be appropriated to carry out this section, $10,000,000 for fiscal year 2008, and such sums as may be necessary for each of fiscal years 2009 through 2013.

US SENATE BILL 1067

TITLE: A bill to require Federal agencies to support health impact assessments and take other actions to improve health and the environmental quality of communities, and for other purposes.

SPONSOR: Sen Obama, Barack [IL] (introduced 3/29/2007) Cosponsors (3)

RELATED BILLS: H.R.398

LATEST MAJOR ACTION: 3/29/2007 Referred to Senate committee. Status: Read twice and referred to the Committee on Health, Education, Labor, and Pensions.

SUMMARY AS OF:

3/29/2007—Introduced.

Healthy Places Act of 2007 - Requires the Secretary of Health and Human Services to establish an interagency working group to discuss environmental health concerns, particularly concerns disproportionately affecting disadvantaged populations.

Requires the Secretary, acting through the Director of the Centers for Disease Control and Prevention (CDC), to establish a program at the National Center of Environmental Health at CDC focused on advancing the field of health impact assessment.

Requires the Director to develop guidance for the assessment of potential health effects of land use, housing, and transportation policy and plans.

Requires the Secretary, acting through the Director, to: (1) establish a program to provide funding and technical assistance to state or local governments affected or potentially affected by an activity or proposed activity to prepare health impact assessments; and (2) establish and maintain a health impact assessment database.

Requires the Director to establish a grant program to award grants to state or local communities for environmental health improvement activities. Requires grantees to: (1) establish a planning and prioritizing council; and (2) conduct environmental health assessment.

Requires the Secretary to provide grants to public or private nonprofit institutions to conduct and coordinate research on the built environment and its influence on individual and population-based health.

Major Actions:

¤NONE¤

All Actions:

3/29/2007:

Sponsor introductory remarks on measure. (CR S4207-4208)

3/29/2007:

Read twice and referred to the Committee on Health, Education, Labor, and Pensions.

Titles(s): (italics indicate a title for a portion of a bill)

¤NONE¤

Cosponsors(3), Alphabetical [followed by Cosponsors withdrawn]: (Sort: by date)

Sen Clinton, Hillary Rodham [NY] - 3/29/2007

Sen Durbin, Richard [IL] - 3/29/2007

Sen Kerry, John F. [MA] - 3/29/2007

Committee(s)

Committee/Subcommittee:

Activity:

Senate Health, Education, Labor, and Pensions

Referral, In Committee

Related Bill Details: (additional related bills may be indentified in Status)

Bill:

Relationship:

H.R.398

Related bill identified by CRS

Amendment(s)

¤NONE¤

In the Senate of the United States

March 29, 2007

Mr. OBAMA (for himself, Mr. KERRY, Mrs. CLINTON, and Mr. DURBIN) introduced the following bill; which was read twice and referred to the Committee on Health, Education, Labor, and Pensions

A BILL

To require Federal agencies to support health impact assessments and take other actions to improve health and the environmental quality of communities, and for other purposes.

Be it enacted by the Senate and House of Representatives of the United States of America in Congress assembled,

SECTION 1. SHORT TITLE.

This Act may be cited as the 'Healthy Places Act of 2007'.

SEC. 2. DEFINITIONS.

In this Act:

(1) ADMINISTRATOR- The term 'Administrator' means the Administrator of the Environmental Protection Agency.

(2) BUILT ENVIRONMENT- The term 'built environment' means an environment consisting of all buildings, spaces, and products that are created or modified by people, including—

(A) homes, schools, workplaces, parks and recreation areas, greenways, business areas, and transportation systems;

(B) electric transmission lines;

(C) waste disposal sites; and

(D) land-use planning and policies that impact urban, rural, and suburban communities.

(3) DIRECTOR- The term 'Director' means the Director of the Centers for Disease Control and Prevention.

(4) ENVIRONMENTAL HEALTH- The term 'environmental health' means the health and well-being of a population as affected by—

(A) the direct pathological effects of chemicals, radiation, and some biological agents; and

(B) the effects (often indirect) of the broad physical, psychological, social, and aesthetic environment.

(5) HEALTH IMPACT ASSESSMENT- The term 'health impact assessment' means any combination of procedures, methods, tools, and means used under section 4 to analyze the actual or potential effects of a policy, program, or project on the health of a population (including the distribution of those effects within the population).

(6) SECRETARY- The term 'Secretary' means the Secretary of Health and Human Services.

SEC. 3. INTERAGENCY WORKING GROUP ON ENVIRONMENTAL HEALTH.

(a) Definitions- In this section:

(1) INSTITUTE- The term 'Institute' means the Institute of Medicine of the National Academies of Science.

(2) IWG- The term 'IWG' means the interagency working group established under subsection (b).

(b) Establishment- The Secretary, in coordination with the Administrator, shall establish an interagency working group to discuss environmental health concerns, particularly concerns disproportionately affecting disadvantaged populations.

(c) Membership- The IWG shall be composed of a representative from each Federal agency (as appointed by the head of the agency) that has jurisdiction over, or is affected by, environmental policies and projects, including—

(1) the Council on Environmental Quality;

(2) the Department of Agriculture;

(3) the Department of Commerce;

(4) the Department of Defense;

(5) the Department of Education;

(6) the Department of Energy;

(7) the Department of Health and Human Services;

(8) the Department of Housing and Urban Development;

(9) the Department of the Interior;

(10) the Department of Justice;

(11) the Department of Labor;

(12) the Department of State;

(13) the Department of Transportation;

(14) the Environmental Protection Agency; and

(15) such other Federal agencies as the Administrator and the Secretary jointly determine to be appropriate.

(d) Duties- The IWG shall—

(1) facilitate communication and partnership on environmental health-related projects and policies—

(A) to generate a better understanding of the interactions between policy areas; and

(B) to raise awareness of the relevance of health across policy areas to ensure that the potential positive and negative health consequences of decisions are not overlooked;

(2) serve as a centralized mechanism to coordinate a national effort—

(A) to discuss and evaluate evidence and knowledge on the relationship between the general environment and the health of the population of the United States;

(B) to determine the range of effective, feasible, and comprehensive actions to improve environmental health; and

(C) to examine and better address the influence of social and environmental determinants of health;

(3) survey Federal agencies to determine which policies are effective in encouraging, and how best to facilitate outreach without duplicating, efforts relating to environmental health promotion;

(4) establish specific goals within and across Federal agencies for environmental health promotion, including determinations of accountability for reaching those goals;

(5) develop a strategy for allocating responsibilities and ensuring participation in environmental health promotions, particularly in the case of competing agency priorities;

(6) coordinate plans to communicate research results relating to environmental health to enable reporting and outreach activities to produce more useful and timely information;

(7) establish an interdisciplinary committee to continue research efforts to further understand the relationship between the built environment and health factors (including air quality, physical activity levels, housing quality, access to primary health care practitioners and health care facilities, injury risk, and availability of nutritional, fresh food) that coordinates the expertise of the public health, urban planning, and transportation communities;

(8) develop an appropriate research agenda for Federal agencies—

(A) to support—

(i) longitudinal studies;

(ii) rapid-response capability to evaluate natural conditions and occurrences; and

(iii) extensions of national databases; and

(B) to review evaluation and economic data relating to the impact of Federal interventions on the prevention of environmental health concerns;

(9) initiate environmental health impact demonstration projects to develop integrated place-based models for addressing community quality-of-life issues;

(10) provide a description of evidence-based best practices, model programs, effective guidelines, and other strategies for promoting environmental health;

(11) make recommendations to improve Federal efforts relating to environmental health promotion and to ensure Federal efforts are consistent with available standards and evidence and other programs in existence as of the date of enactment of this Act;

(12) monitor Federal progress in meeting specific environmental health promotion goals;

(13) assist in ensuring, to the maximum extent practicable, integration of the impact of environmental policies, programs, and activities on the areas under Federal jurisdiction;

216

(14) assist in the implementation of the recommendations from the reports of the Institute of Medicine entitled 'Does the Built Environment Influence Physical Activity? Examining the Evidence' and dated January 11, 2005, and 'Rebuilding the Unity of Health and the Environment: A New Vision of Environmental Health for the 21st Century' and dated January 22, 2001, including recommendations for—

(A) the expansion of national public health and travel surveys to provide more detailed information about the connection between the built environment and health, including expansion of such surveys as—

(i) the Behavioral Risk Factor Surveillance System, the National Health and Nutrition Examination Survey, and the National Health Interview Survey conducted by the Centers for Disease Control and Prevention;

(ii) the American Community survey conducted by the Census Bureau;

(iii) the American Time Use Survey conducted by the Bureau of Labor Statistics;

(iv) the Youth Risk Behavior Survey conducted by the Centers for Disease Control and Prevention; and

(v) the National Longitudinal Cohort Survey of American Children (the National Children's Study) conducted by the National Institute of Child Health and Human Development;

(B) collaboration with national initiatives to learn from natural experiments such as observations from changes in the built environment and the consequent effects on health;

(C) development of a program of research with a defined mission and recommended budget, concentrating on multiyear projects and enhanced data collection;

(D) development of interdisciplinary education programs—

(i) to train professionals in conducting recommended research; and

(ii) to prepare practitioners with appropriate skills at the intersection of physical activity, public health, transportation, and urban planning;

(15) not later than 2 years after the date of enactment of this Act, submit to Congress a report that describes the extent to which recommendations from the Institute of Medicine reports described in paragraph (14) were executed; and

(16) assist the Director with the development of guidance for the assessment of the potential health effects of land use, housing, and transportation policy and plans.

(e) Meetings-

(1) IN GENERAL- The IWG shall meet at least 3 times each year.

(2) ANNUAL CONFERENCE- The Secretary, acting through the Director and in collaboration with the Administrator, shall sponsor an annual conference on environmental health and health disparities to enhance coordination, build partnerships, and share best practices in environmental health data collection, analysis, and reporting.

(f) Authorization of Appropriations- There are authorized to be appropriated such sums as are necessary to carry out this section.

SEC. 4. HEALTH IMPACT ASSESSMENTS.

(a) Definition of Eligible Entity- In this section, the term 'eligible entity' means any unit of State or local government the jurisdiction of which includes individuals or populations the health of which are or will be affected by an activity or a proposed activity.

(b) Establishment- The Secretary, acting through the Director and in collaboration with the Administrator, shall—

(1) establish a program at the National Center of Environmental Health at the Centers for Disease Control and Prevention focused on advancing the field of health impact assessment, including—

(A) collecting and disseminating best practices;

(B) administering capacity building grants, in accordance with subsection (d);

(C) providing technical assistance;

(D) providing training;

(E) conducting evaluations; and

(F) awarding competitive extramural research grants;

(2) in accordance with subsection (f), develop guidance to conduct health impact assessments; and

(3) establish a grant program to allow eligible entities to conduct health impact assessments.

(c) Guidance- The Director, in collaboration with the IWG, shall—

(1) develop guidance for the assessment of the potential health effects of land use, housing, and transportation policy and plans, including—

(A) background on international efforts to bridge urban planning and public health institutions and disciplines, including a review of health impact assessment best practices internationally;

(B) evidence-based causal pathways that link urban planning, transportation, and housing policy and objectives to human health objectives;

(C) data resources and quantitative and qualitative forecasting methods to evaluate both the status of health determinants and health effects; and

(D) best practices for inclusive public involvement in planning decision-making;

(2) not later than 1 year after the date of enactment of this Act, promulgate the guidance; and

(3) present the guidance to the public at the annual conference described in section 3(e)(2).

(d) Grant Program- The Secretary, acting through the Director and in collaboration with the Administrator, shall establish a program under which the Secretary shall provide funding and technical assistance to eligible entities to prepare health impact assessments—

(1) to ensure that appropriate health factors are taken into consideration as early as practicable during any planning, review, or decision-making process; and

(2) to evaluate the effect on the health of individuals and populations, and on social and economic development, of decisions made outside of the health sector that result in modifications of a physical or social environment.

(e) Applications-

(1) IN GENERAL- To receive a grant under this section, an eligible entity shall submit to the Secretary an application in accordance with this subsection, in such time, in such manner, and containing such additional information as the Secretary may require.

(2) INCLUSION-

(A) IN GENERAL- An application under this subsection shall include an assessment by the eligible entity of the probability that an applicable activity or proposed activity will have at least 1 significant, adverse health effect on an individual or population in the jurisdiction of the eligible entity, based on the criteria described in subparagraph (B).

(B) CRITERIA- The criteria referred to in subparagraph (A) include, with respect to the applicable activity or proposed activity—

(i) any substantial adverse effect on—

(I) existing air quality, ground or surface water quality or quantity, or traffic or noise levels;

(II) a significant habitat area;

(III) physical activity;

(IV) injury;

(V) mental health;

(VI) social capital;

(VII) accessibility;

(VIII) the character or quality of an important historical, archeological, architectural, or aesthetic resource (including neighborhood character) of the community of the eligible entity; or

(IX) any other natural resource;

(ii) any increase in—

(I) solid waste production; or

(II) problems relating to erosion, flooding, leaching, or drainage;

(iii) any requirement that a large quantity of vegetation or fauna be removed or destroyed;

(iv) any conflict with the plans or goals of the community of the eligible entity;

(v) any major change in the quantity or type of energy used by the community of the eligible entity;

(vi) any hazard presented to human health;

(vii) any substantial change in the use, or intensity of use, of land in the jurisdiction of the eligible entity, including agricultural, open space, and recreational uses;

(viii) the probability that the activity or proposed activity will result in an increase in tourism in the jurisdiction of the eligible entity;

(ix) any substantial, adverse aggregate impact on environmental health resulting from—

(I) changes caused by the activity or proposed activity to 2 or more elements of the environment; or

(II) 2 or more related actions carried out under the activity or proposed activity; and

(x) any other significant change of concern, as determined by the eligible entity.

(C) FACTORS FOR CONSIDERATION- In making an assessment under subparagraph (A), an eligible entity may take into consideration any reasonable, direct, indirect, or cumulative effect relating to the applicable activity or proposed activity, including the effect of any action that is—

(i) included in the long-range plan relating to the activity or proposed activity;

(ii) likely to be carried out in coordination with the activity or proposed activity;

(iii) dependent on the occurrence of the activity or proposed activity; or

(iv) likely to have a disproportionate impact on disadvantaged populations.

(f) Use of Funds-

(1) IN GENERAL- An eligible entity shall use assistance received under this section to prepare and submit to the Secretary a health impact assessment in accordance with this subsection.

(2) PURPOSES- The purposes of a health impact assessment are—

(A) to facilitate the involvement of State and local health officials in community planning and land use decisions to identify any potential health concern relating to an activity or proposed activity;

(B) to provide for an investigation of any health-related issue addressed in an environmental impact statement or policy appraisal relating to an activity or a proposed activity;

(C) to describe and compare alternatives (including no-action alternatives) to an activity or a proposed activity to provide clarification with respect to the costs and benefits of the activity or proposed activity; and

(D) to contribute to the findings of an environmental impact statement with respect to the terms and conditions of implementing an activity or a proposed activity, as necessary.

(3) REQUIREMENTS- A health impact assessment prepared under this subsection shall—

(A) describe the relevance of the applicable activity or proposed activity (including the policy of the activity) with respect to health issues;

(B) assess each health impact of the applicable activity or proposed activity;

(C) provide recommendations of the eligible entity with respect to—

(i) the mitigation of any adverse impact on health of the applicable activity or proposed activity; or

(ii) the encouragement of any positive impact of the applicable activity or proposed activity;

(D) provide for monitoring of the impacts on health of the applicable activity or proposed activity, as the eligible entity determines to be appropriate; and

(E) include a list of each comment received with respect to the health impact assessment under subsection (e).

(4) METHODOLOGY- In preparing a health impact assessment under this subsection, an eligible entity—

(A) shall follow guidelines developed by the Director, in collaboration with the IWG, that—

(i) are consistent with subsection (c);

(ii) will be established not later than 1 year after the date of enactment of this Act; and

(iii) will be made publicly available at the annual conference described in section 3(e)(2); and

(B) may establish a balance, as the eligible entity determines to be appropriate, between the use of—

(i) rigorous methods requiring special skills or increased use of resources; and

(ii) expedient, cost-effective measures.

(g) Public Participation-

(1) IN GENERAL- Before preparing and submitting to the Secretary a final health impact assessment, an eligible entity shall request and take into consideration public and agency comments, in accordance with this subsection.

(2) REQUIREMENT- Not later than 30 days after the date on which a draft health impact assessment is completed, an eligible entity shall submit the draft health impact assessment to each Federal agency, and each State and local organization, that—

(A) has jurisdiction with respect to the activity or proposed activity to which the health impact assessment applies;

(B) has special knowledge with respect to an environmental or health impact of the activity or proposed activity; or

(C) is authorized to develop or enforce any environmental standard relating to the activity or proposed activity.

(3) COMMENTS REQUESTED-

(A) REQUEST BY ELIGIBLE ENTITY- An eligible entity may request comments with respect to a health impact assessment from—

(i) affected Indian tribes;

(ii) interested or affected individuals or organizations; and

(iii) any other State or local agency, as the eligible entity determines to be appropriate.

(B) REQUEST BY OTHERS- Any interested or affected agency, organization, or individual may—

(i) request an opportunity to comment on a health impact assessment; and

(ii) submit to the appropriate eligible entity comments with respect to the health impact assessment by not later than—

(I) for a Federal, State, or local government agency or organization, the date on which a final health impact assessment is prepared; and

(II) for any other individual or organization, the date described in subclause (I) or another date, as the eligible entity may determine.

(4) RESPONSE TO COMMENTS- A final health impact assessment shall describe the response of the eligible entity to comments received within a 90-day period under this subsection, including—

(A) a description of any means by which the eligible entity, as a result of such a comment—

(i) modified an alternative recommended with respect to the applicable activity or proposed activity;

(ii) developed and evaluated any alternative not previously considered by the eligible entity;

(iii) supplemented, improved, or modified an analysis of the eligible entity; or

(iv) made any factual correction to the health impact assessment; and

(B) for any comment with respect to which the eligible entity took no action, an explanation of the reasons why no action was taken and, if appropriate, a description of the circumstances under which the eligible entity would take such an action.

(h) Health Impact Assessment Database- The Secretary, acting through the Director and in collaboration with the Administrator, shall establish and maintain a health impact assessment database, including—

(1) a catalog of health impact assessments received under this section;

(2) an inventory of tools used by eligible entities to prepare draft and final health impact assessments; and

(3) guidance for eligible entities with respect to the selection of appropriate tools described in paragraph (2).

(i) Authorization of Appropriations- There are authorized to be appropriated to carry out this section such sums as are necessary.

SEC. 5. GRANT PROGRAM.

(a) Definitions- In this section:

(1) DIRECTOR- The term 'Director' means the Director of the Centers for Disease Control and Prevention, acting in collaboration with the Administrator and the Director of the National Institute of Environmental Health Sciences.

(2) ELIGIBLE ENTITY- The term 'eligible entity' means a State or local community that—

(A) bears a disproportionate burden of exposure to environmental health hazards;

(B) has established a coalition—

(i) with not less than 1 community-based organization; and

(ii) with not less than 1—

(I) public health entity;

(II) health care provider organization; or

(III) academic institution;

(C) ensures planned activities and funding streams are coordinated to improve community health; and

(D) submits an application in accordance with subsection (c).

(b) Establishment- The Director shall establish a grant program under which eligible entities shall receive grants to conduct environmental health improvement activities.

(c) Application- To receive a grant under this section, an eligible entity shall submit an application to the Director at such time, in such manner, and accompanied by such information as the Director may require.

(d) Cooperative Agreements- An eligible entity may use a grant under this section—

(1) to promote environmental health; and

(2) to address environmental health disparities.

(e) Amount of Cooperative Agreement-

(1) IN GENERAL- The Director shall award grants to eligible entities at the 2 different funding levels described in this subsection.

(2) LEVEL 1 COOPERATIVE AGREEMENTS-

(A) IN GENERAL- An eligible entity awarded a grant under this paragraph shall use the funds to identify environmental health problems and solutions by—

(i) establishing a planning and prioritizing council in accordance with subparagraph (B); and

(ii) conducting an environmental health assessment in accordance with subparagraph (C).

(B) PLANNING AND PRIORITIZING COUNCIL-

(i) IN GENERAL- A prioritizing and planning council established under subparagraph (A)(i) (referred to in this paragraph as a 'PPC') shall assist the environmental health assessment process and environmental health promotion activities of the eligible entity.

(ii) MEMBERSHIP- Membership of a PPC shall consist of representatives from various organizations within public health, planning, development, and environmental services and shall include stakeholders from vulnerable groups such as children, the elderly, disabled, and minority ethnic groups that are often not actively involved in democratic or decision-making processes.

(iii) DUTIES- A PPC shall—

(I) identify key stakeholders and engage and coordinate potential partners in the planning process;

(II) establish a formal advisory group to plan for the establishment of services;

(III) conduct an in-depth review of the nature and extent of the need for an environmental health assessment, including a local epidemiological profile, an evaluation of the service provider capacity of the community, and a profile of any target populations; and

(IV) define the components of care and form essential programmatic linkages with related providers in the community.

(C) ENVIRONMENTAL HEALTH ASSESSMENT-

(i) IN GENERAL- A PPC shall carry out an environmental health assessment to identify environmental health concerns.

(ii) ASSESSMENT PROCESS- The PPC shall—

(I) define the goals of the assessment;

(II) generate the environmental health issue list;

(III) analyze issues with a systems framework;

(IV) develop appropriate community environmental health indicators;

(V) rank the environmental health issues;

(VI) set priorities for action;

(VII) develop an action plan;

(VIII) implement the plan; and

(IX) evaluate progress and planning for the future.

(D) EVALUATION- Each eligible entity that receives a grant under this paragraph shall evaluate, report, and disseminate program findings and outcomes.

(E) TECHNICAL ASSISTANCE- The Director may provide such technical and other non-financial assistance to eligible entities as the Director determines to be necessary.

(3) LEVEL 2 COOPERATIVE AGREEMENTS-

(A) ELIGIBILITY-

(i) IN GENERAL- The Director shall award grants under this paragraph to eligible entities that have already—

(I) established broad-based collaborative partnerships; and

(II) completed environmental assessments.

(ii) NO LEVEL 1 REQUIREMENT- To be eligible to receive a grant under this paragraph, an eligible entity is not required to have successfully completed a Level 1 Cooperative Agreement (as described in paragraph (2).

(B) USE OF GRANT FUNDS- An eligible entity awarded a grant under this paragraph shall use the funds to further activities to carry out environmental health improvement activities, including—

(i) addressing community environmental health priorities in accordance with paragraph (2)(C)(ii), including—

(I) air quality;

(II) water quality;

(III) solid waste;

(IV) land use;

(V) housing;

(VI) food safety;

(VII) crime;

(VIII) injuries; and

(IX) healthcare services;

(ii) building partnerships between planning, public health, and other sectors, to address how the built environment impacts food availability and access and physical activity to promote healthy behaviors and lifestyles and reduce obesity and related co-morbidities;

(iii) establishing programs to address—

(I) how environmental and social conditions of work and living choices influence physical activity and dietary intake; or

(II) how those conditions influence the concerns and needs of people who have impaired mobility and use assistance devices, including wheelchairs and lower limb prostheses; and

(iv) convening intervention programs that examine the role of the social environment in connection with the physical and chemical environment in—

(I) determining access to nutritional food; and

(II) improving physical activity to reduce morbidity and increase quality of life.

(f) Authorization of Appropriations- There are authorized to be appropriated to carry out this section—

(1) $25,000,000 for fiscal year 2007; and

(2) such sums as are necessary for the period of fiscal years 2008 through 2011.

SEC. 6. ADDITIONAL RESEARCH ON THE RELATIONSHIP BETWEEN THE BUILT ENVIRONMENT AND THE HEALTH OF COMMUNITY RESIDENTS.

(a) Definition of Eligible Institution- In this section, the term 'eligible institution' means a public or private nonprofit institution that submits to the Secretary and the Administrator an application for a grant under the grant program authorized under subsection (b)(2) at such time, in such manner, and containing such agreements, assurances, and information as the Secretary and Administrator may require.

(b) Research Grant Program-

(1) DEFINITION OF HEALTH- In this section, the term 'health' includes—

(A) levels of physical activity;

(B) consumption of nutritional foods;

(C) rates of crime;

(D) air, water, and soil quality;

(E) risk of injury;

(F) accessibility to healthcare services; and

(G) other indicators as determined appropriate by the Secretary.

(2) GRANTS- The Secretary, in collaboration with the Administrator, shall provide grants to eligible institutions to conduct and coordinate research on the built environment and its influence on individual and population-based health.

(3) RESEARCH- The Secretary shall support research that—

(A) investigates and defines the causal links between all aspects of the built environment and the health of residents;

(B) examines—

(i) the extent of the impact of the built environment (including the various characteristics of the built environment) on the health of residents;

(ii) the variance in the health of residents by—

(I) location (such as inner cities, inner suburbs, and outer suburbs); and

(II) population subgroup (such as children, the elderly, the disadvantaged); or

(iii) the importance of the built environment to the total health of residents, which is the primary variable of interest from a public health perspective;

(C) is used to develop—

(i) measures to address health and the connection of health to the built environment; and

(ii) efforts to link the measures to travel and health databases;

(D) distinguishes carefully between personal attitudes and choices and external influences on observed behavior to determine how much an observed association between the built environment and the health of residents, versus the lifestyle preferences of the people that choose to live in the neighborhood, reflects the physical characteristics of the neighborhood; and

(E)(i) identifies or develops effective intervention strategies to promote better health among residents with a focus on behavioral interventions and enhancements of the built environment that promote increased use by residents; and

(ii) in developing the intervention strategies under clause (i), ensures that the intervention strategies will reach out to high-risk populations, including low-income urban and rural communities.

(4) PRIORITY- In providing assistance under the grant program authorized under paragraph (2), the Secretary and the Administrator shall give priority to research that incorporates—

(A) interdisciplinary approaches; or

(B) the expertise of the public health, physical activity, urban planning, and transportation research communities in the United States and abroad.

(c) Authorization of Appropriations- There are authorized to be appropriated such sums as are necessary to carry out this section.

US SENATE BILL 1068

TITLE: A bill to promote healthy communities.

SPONSOR: Sen Obama, Barack [IL] (introduced 3/29/2007) Cosponsors (2)

LATEST MAJOR ACTION: 3/29/2007 Referred to Senate committee. Status: Read twice and referred to the Committee on Health, Education, Labor, and Pensions.

SUMMARY AS OF:

3/29/2007—Introduced.

Healthy Communities Act of 2007 - Requires the Secretary of Health and Human Services to establish the Advisory Committee on Environmental Health to review environmental health data and studies to: (1) assess the impact of federal laws, policies, and practices on environmental health and justice; and (2) identify and recommend ways to change or ensure compliance with federal laws, address gaps in federal environmental health research, and prevent or mitigate harm from federal policies, programs, and practices that may adversely affect environmental health or justice.

Requires the Director of the Centers for Disease Control and Prevention (CDC) and the Administrator of the Environmental Protection Agency (EPA) to prepare a biennial Environmental Health Report Card for the nation and for each state.

Requires the Secretary to: (1) establish the Health Action Zone Program to award grants to at-risk communities for comprehensive environmental health improvement activities; and (2) expand and intensify environmental health research.

Requires the Secretary, acting through the Director, to provide grants and technical assistance to enable states to develop or expand activities related to biomonitoring of exposure to environmental toxicants and pollutants. Requires the Secretary to: (1) promote translation and dissemination of findings; and (2) incorporate the data collected under this Act with existing data collection efforts.

Requires the Director to expand training and educational activities relating to environmental health and justice for health professionals and public health practitioners.

MAJOR ACTIONS:

¤NONE¤

ALL ACTIONS:

3/29/2007:

Sponsor introductory remarks on measure. (CR S4207-4208)

3/29/2007:

Read twice and referred to the Committee on Health, Education, Labor, and Pensions.

TITLES(s): (italics indicate a title for a portion of a bill)

¤NONE¤

COSPONSORS(2), ALPHABETICAL [FOLLOWED BY COSPONSORS WITHDRAWN]: (Sort: by date)

Sen Clinton, Hillary Rodham [NY] - 3/29/2007

Sen Kerry, John F. [MA] - 3/29/2007

COMMITTEE(S)

Committee/Subcommittee:

Activity:

Senate Health, Education, Labor, and Pensions

Referral, In Committee

RELATED BILL DETAILS:

¤NONE¤

AMENDMENT(S)

¤NONE¤

IN THE SENATE OF THE UNITED STATES

March 29, 2007

Mr. OBAMA (for himself, Mr. KERRY, and Mrs. CLINTON) introduced the following bill; which was read twice and referred to the Committee on Health, Education, Labor, and Pensions

A BILL

To promote healthy communities.

Be it enacted by the Senate and House of Representatives of the United States of America in Congress assembled,

SECTION 1. SHORT TITLE.

This Act may be cited as the 'Healthy Communities Act of 2007'.

SEC. 2. FINDINGS.

Congress finds as follows:

(1) Environmental quality is a leading health indicator. An estimated 25 percent of preventable illnesses worldwide can be attributed to poor environmental quality.

(2) Many diseases are caused or exacerbated by environmental hazards, including cancer, heart disease, asthma, birth defects, behavioral disorders, infertility, and obesity.

(3) Of the chemicals produced in the United States annually in quantities greater than 10,000 pounds, only 43 percent have been tested for their potential human toxicity and only 7 percent have been studied to assess effects on development.

(4) Approximately 126,000,000 people in the United States live in areas of non-attainment for pollutants that have health-based standards. In 1997, approximately 43 percent of the population of the United States lived in areas designated as non-attainment areas for established health-based standards for ozone.

(5) In the United States, air pollution alone is estimated to be associated with 50,000 premature deaths and an estimated $50,000,000,000 in health-related costs annually.

(6) In children, environmental toxins are estimated to cause up to 35 percent of asthma cases, up to 10 percent of cancer cases, and up to 20 percent of neurobehavioral disorders.

(7) Almost 400,000 children have elevated blood lead levels. In 2002, researchers reported that 100 percent of childhood lead poisoning resulted from environmental lead exposure. If not detected early, lead poisoning in children is associated with behavioral and learning problems, slowed growth, impaired hearing, and damage to the kidneys, brain, and bone marrow.

(8) Studies have found that the reduction of blood lead levels in children from 1976 to 1999 led to an economic benefit of approximately $319,000,000,000.

(9) Elevated lead levels can also harm adults by causing difficulties during pregnancy, high blood pressure, digestive problems, nerve disorders, memory and concentration problems, and muscle and joint pain.

(10) Minority Americans are at greater risk of exposure to environmental toxins. Research has shown that 3 of every 5 individuals of African-American or Latino background live in communities with 1 or more toxic waste sites. More than 15,000,000 African-Americans, more than 8,000,000 Hispanics, and about 50 percent of Asian and Pacific Islanders and Native Americans are living in communities with 1 or more abandoned or uncontrolled toxic waste sites.

(11) Communities with existing incinerators are significantly more likely to have a large percentage of minorities. Communities where incinerators are proposed to be located have minority populations that are 60 percent higher and property values 35 percent lower than other communities.

SEC. 3. ADVISORY COMMITTEE ON ENVIRONMENTAL HEALTH.

(a) In General- The Secretary of Health and Human Services (referred to in this section as the 'Secretary'), in collaboration with the Administrator of the Environmental Protection Agency (referred to in this section as the 'Administrator'), shall establish an independent, 5-year Advisory Committee on Environmental Health (referred to in this section as the 'Committee').

(b) Membership-

(1) IN GENERAL- The Committee shall be composed of members with academic training and practical experience in—

(A) the areas of—

(i) environmental health and public health;

(ii) environmental justice;

(iii) community-based participatory research;

(iv) adult and child health and development;

(v) data collection, analysis, and reporting;

(vi) health and health care disparities;

(vii) community engagement and mobilization, including grassroots organizing and community-level activism in communities with health disparity populations; and

(viii) urban, suburban, rural, and regional planning; and

(B) other areas determined appropriate by the Secretary.

(2) TERM- Members of the Committee shall serve on the Committee for the life of the Committee.

(3) SELECTION- The Secretary shall appoint members of the Committee from health disparity populations. No candidate for appointment on the Committee shall

be asked to provide non-relevant information, such as voting record, political party affiliation, or position on particular policies.

(4) PROHIBITION AGAINST FEDERAL EMPLOYEES- No member of the Committee may be a Federal employee.

(c) Chairperson- Members of the Committee shall select a chairperson from among the members of the Committee, who shall serve a 1-year term.

(d) Meetings- The Committee shall meet not less frequently than 3 times per year.

(e) Duties of the Committee- The Committee shall review environmental health data and studies, as well as Federal environmental health research and programmatic initiatives, in order to—

(1) assess the impact of Federal laws, policies, programs, and practices on environmental health and environmental justice;

(2) identify and recommend ways to—

(A) draft new or modify existing Federal laws needed to improve environmental health;

(B) ensure compliance with Federal laws related to environmental health;

(C) address gaps in environmental health research or programs at the Federal level, particularly research or programs that address the needs of health-disparity populations;

(D) prevent or mitigate harm from Federal policies and federally operated or supported programs and practices, that may adversely affect environmental health and environmental justice;

(E) increase coordination and integration of interagency environmental health and environmental justice initiatives; and

(F) promote efforts to meet Healthy People 2010 goals and objectives relating to environmental health;

(3) assist in the development of the Environmental Health Report Card;

(4) assist in the development of the Health Action Zone Program, including identification of eligible communities; and

(5) conduct other activities at the request of the Secretary.

(f) Vulnerable Populations- The Committee shall include specific focus on health disparity populations in completion of all duties of the Committee.

(g) Collaboration- To the extent possible, the Committee shall seek input from new or existing Federal committees on environmental health and environmental justice issues, including the Federal Interagency Working Group on Environmental Justice and the National Environmental Justice Advisory Council.

(h) Public Input-

(1) PUBLIC NOTICE- The Chairperson of the Committee shall provide public notice of the availability of draft recommendations not less than 90 days prior to the date of finalization of such recommendations.

(2) CONSIDERATION- The Committee shall solicit and take into consideration public review and comment on draft recommendations pursuant to this section.

(i) Personnel-

(1) DETAIL OF GOVERNMENT EMPLOYEES- Any Federal Government employee may be detailed to the Committee without reimbursement, and such detail shall be without interruption or loss of civil service status or privilege.

(2) STAFF, INFORMATION, OR OTHER ASSISTANCE- The Secretary and the Administrator of the Environmental Protection Agency shall provide to the Committee such staff, information, and other assistance as may be necessary to carry out the duties of the Committee.

(j) Reports- On an annual basis, the Committee shall compile and submit the Committee's findings and recommendations to the public and Congress.

(k) Federal Response- Not later than 1 year after the date the Committee submits a report under subsection (j), the Secretary and the Administrator shall propose a plan to implement relevant recommendations of the Committee included in such report.

(l) Authorization of Appropriations- There is authorized to be appropriated to the Committee such sums as may be necessary to carry out the objectives of this section.

SEC. 4. ENVIRONMENTAL HEALTH REPORT CARD.

(a) In General- The Director of the Centers for Disease Control and Prevention (referred to in this section as the 'Director'), in collaboration with the Administrator of the Environmental Protection Agency (referred to in this section as the 'Administrator'), shall assess and report the environmental health of the Nation and, to the extent possible, for each State.

(b) Environmental Health Report Card- The Director and the Administrator shall prepare an Environmental Health Report Card (referred to in this section as a 'Report Card') for the Nation and, to the extent possible, for each State on a biennial basis, that includes the—

(1) potential risk of high or cumulative exposure to environmental toxicants and pollutants—

(A) taking into consideration the prevalence and health effect;

(B) including those measured in the National Report on Human Exposure to Environmental Chemicals;

(C) including those that are man-made, natural, and biogenic; and

(D) that are present in the air, water, or soil;

(2) burden of acute and chronic disease empirically shown to be associated with or exacerbated by exposure to environmental toxicants or pollutants;

(3) demographic characteristics of populations that are most affected by overexposure to environmental toxicants or pollutants; and

(4) environmental health resources and initiatives, including national and State health tracking and biomonitoring activities.

(c) Report- The Director, in collaboration with the Administrator, shall—

(1) submit each Report Card to Congress; and

(2) make each Report Card readily available in print and electronically to each State and to the public.

(d) Adaptable- Each Report Card shall be able to be adapted by local agencies in order to rate or report local environmental quality.

(e) Consultation- In developing a Report Card, the Director, in collaboration with the Administrator, shall consult with the Advisory Committee on Environmental Health established under section 3 and incorporate the recommendations set forth by the Committee.

(f) Updated Report- Each Report Card that is prepared after the initial Report Card shall include trend analysis for the Nation, and, to the extent possible, for each State, in order to track progress in meeting established national goals and objectives for improving environmental health (including Healthy People 2010), and to inform policy and program development.

SEC. 5. HEALTH ACTION ZONES.

(a) Purpose- The Secretary of Health and Human Services (referred to in this section as the 'Secretary'), in collaboration with the Administrator of the Environmental Protection Agency, shall establish the Health Action Zone Program for comprehensive environmental health improvement activities.

(b) Health Action Zone Program-

(1) IN GENERAL- The Secretary shall award not less than 10 Health Action Zone Program grants to eligible communities each year. The duration of each grant shall be 5 years.

(2) ELIGIBLE COMMUNITIES-

(A) IDENTIFICATION- The Advisory Committee on Environmental Health, established under section 3, shall identify eligible communities under this section, pursuant to subparagraph (B), and report such identifications to the Secretary and the public.

(B) TYPES OF COMMUNITIES- Eligible communities under this section shall be communities that are most at risk, or at greatest disproportionate risk, for adverse health outcomes from environmental toxicants and pollutants, as measured by—

(i) proximity to sites with high levels of environmental toxicants or pollutants, or high levels of exposure to environmental toxicants or pollutants, including those that are—

(I) measured in the National Report on Human Exposure to Environmental Chemicals;

(II) man-made, natural, or biogenic; or

(III) in air, water, or soil;

(ii) burden of disease and health conditions that may be caused or exacerbated by environmental toxicants or pollutants;

(iii) level of community health and economic resources available; and

(iv) other factors determined appropriate by the Advisory Committee on Environmental Health.

(3) NOTIFICATION- The Secretary shall solicit applications for Health Action Zone Program grants from communities identified by the Advisory Committee on Environmental Health pursuant to paragraph (2).

(4) APPLICATIONS-

(A) IN GENERAL- An eligible community that desires to receive a Health Action Zone Program grant shall submit an application to the Secretary at such time, in such manner, and accompanied by such information as the Secretary may require, including a strategic plan described in subparagraph (B) and a description of the community advisory board under subparagraph (C).

(B) STRATEGIC PLAN-

(i) IN GENERAL- An eligible community shall include in an application under subparagraph (A) a strategic plan that shall—

(I) describe the proposed activities pursuant to subsection (c);

(II) report the extent to which local institutions and organizations and community residents have participated in the strategic plan development;

(III) identify State, local, and private resources that will be available;

(IV) describe the private and public partnerships to be used, which may include partnerships with community-based organizations and advocacy groups, institutions of higher education, federally qualified health centers, academic medical centers, hospitals, health plans, public health departments, elected officials, and other public and private entities;

(V) identify Federal funding needed to support the proposed activities; and

(VI) report the baselines, methods, and benchmarks for measuring the success of activities proposed in the strategic plan, including health and environmental health outcomes and community engagement and participation.

(ii) TECHNICAL ASSISTANCE- The Secretary shall provide technical assistance, as needed, for the development and implementation of strategic plans in—

(I) the areas of—

(aa) public health;

(bb) environmental health;

(cc) environmental justice;

(dd) community-based participatory research;

(ee) health tracking, biomonitoring, and other relevant exposure technologies;

(ff) health and health care disparities; and

(gg) human disease genetics; and

(II) other areas determined appropriate by the Secretary.

(C) COMMUNITY ADVISORY BOARD-

(i) IN GENERAL- In order to receive a Health Action Zone Program grant under this section, a community shall have a community advisory board.

(ii) MEMBERS-

(I) FROM COMMUNITY- The majority of the members of a community advisory board under clause (i) shall be individuals that will benefit from the activities or services provided by the grants under this section.

(II) REPRESENTATIVES- A community advisory board shall include representatives from the respective State health department and county or local health department, community-based organizations, environmental and public health experts, health care professionals and providers, nonprofit leaders, community organizers, and elected officials.

(iii) DUTIES- A community advisory board shall—

(I) oversee the functions and operations of Health Action Zone Program grant activities;

(II) assist in the evaluation of such activities; and

(III) prepare an annual report that—

(aa) describes the progress towards achieving stated goals; and

(bb) recommends future courses of action.

(c) Use of Funds- An eligible community that receives a grant under this section may use the grant funding to—

(1) promote disease prevention and health promotion, particularly for health disparity populations;

(2) facilitate partnerships between health care providers, public and environmental health agencies, academic institutions, community based or advocacy organizations, elected officials, professional societies, and other stakeholder groups;

(3) enhance the local capacity for environmental health data collection and reporting, which may include using information from health tracking and biomonitoring;

(4) coordinate and integrate economic development, healthcare and social services, transportation, education, community, and physical development plans, as well as policymaking and other related activities at the local level to comprehensively address environmental health concerns;

(5) mobilize financial and other resources from the public and private sector to increase local capacity to address environmental health issues;

(6) build upon existing environmental and economic efforts to address contaminated sites through the Department of Health and Human Services, the Environmental

Protection Agency, and other Federal and State programs that address public health and the environment;

(7) identify and assess factors relating to the historical contamination of the community, in order to mitigate ongoing or prevent future occurrences, including examining—

(A) the historical use of planning mechanisms such as zoning practices;

(B) noncompliance with environmental laws and public health codes; and

(C) abuse of extraterritorial jurisdiction or redlining;

(8) support the training of staff in communication and outreach to the general public, particularly those at disproportionate risk from environmental health hazards;

(9) assist eligible communities in meeting Healthy People 2010 objectives relating to environmental health; and

(10) aid eligible communities in developing environmental management systems to improve the processes and actions that an organization undertakes to meet its business and environmental goals.

(d) Planning Grant-

(1) IN GENERAL- At the discretion of the Secretary, an eligible community may receive a 1-time planning grant to—

(A) establish or strengthen State or local partnerships;

(B) identify Federal, State, or local resources;

(C) research promising health practices and models;

(D) develop a strategic plan for community intervention;

(E) create necessary data collection systems or linkages to facilitate baseline and follow-up data assessment and evaluation;

(F) engage target communities in all planning activities, including formation of a community advisory board; and

(G) prepare a Health Action Zone Program grant application.

(2) DURATION- The duration of each planning grant shall be 1 year.

(3) ELIGIBLE COMMUNITIES NOT RECEIVING PLANNING GRANTS- An eligible community that does not receive a planning grant under this subsection shall still be eligible to receive a Health Action Zone Program grant under this section.

(e) Evaluation-

(1) IN GENERAL- The Secretary, directly or through contract, shall conduct an evaluation of the Health Action Zone Program in order to determine success in achieving the purpose of such program.

(2) REPORTS- Findings from the evaluation under paragraph (1) shall be reported to Congress and the public annually.

(f) Supplement, Not Supplant- Grant funds received under this section shall be used to supplement, and not supplant, funding that would otherwise be used for activities described under this section.

(g) Priority- In awarding grants under this section, the Secretary—

(1) shall give priority to communities that do not have sites already listed on the National Priorities List for which remediation activities are actively ongoing, as determined by the Environmental Protection Agency; and

(2) may give priority to empowerment zones and enterprise communities designated pursuant to section 1391 of the Internal Revenue Code of 1986.

(h) Authorization of Appropriations- There are authorized to be appropriated to carry out this section $50,000,000 for fiscal year 2008 and $50,000,000 for each of the fiscal years 2009 through 2012.

SEC. 6. ENVIRONMENTAL HEALTH RESEARCH.

(a) In General- The Secretary of Health and Human Services (referred to in this section as the 'Secretary'), in collaboration with the Administrator of the Environmental Protection Agency, the Director of the Centers for Disease Control and Prevention, and the Director of the National Institutes of Health, shall expand and intensify environmental health research.

(b) Areas of Focus- The Secretary shall expand research on the following:

(1) The health effects of environmental toxins, which shall include expansion and intensification of biomonitoring, in order to—

(A) monitor the presence and concentration of designated chemicals;

(B) measure toxic chemical exposure levels by testing blood, tissue, saliva, exhaled breath, and urine samples from nationwide volunteers;

(C) identify the role of genetic and nongenetic susceptibility factors such as underlying disease rates, social demographics, psychosocial factors, community access to nutritional food and opportunities for recreational exercise, and other factors in modifying health outcomes from environmental pollutants; and

(D) determine the availability of and compliance with ethical guidelines when collecting samples and conducting research.

(2) The contribution of differential exposure to environmental toxicants and pollutants to racial, ethnic, age, gender, and socioeconomic position disparities in health.

(3) The methods to assess the cumulative risk of exposure or cumulative exposure to multiple pollutants from a variety of sources over time.

(4) The methods and tools to assess overall environmental community health, including—

(A) the presence, level, and type of environmental contaminants;

(B) the burden of disease and other health conditions;

(C) predisposing factors such as race, ethnicity, socioeconomic position, access to healthcare, geography, and cultural practices;

(D) available local health care resources; and

(E) other factors determined appropriate by the Secretary.

(c) State Biomonitoring Capacity-

(1) IN GENERAL- The Secretary, acting through the Director of the Centers for Disease Control and Prevention (referred to in this subsection as the 'Director'), shall provide grants to States to enable the States to develop or expand the capacity of such States to conduct biomonitoring in order to, with respect to environmental toxicants and pollutants—

(A) detect and monitor exposure;

(B) assess or predict population and individual health risk as a result of exposure;

(C) develop and implement interventions to reduce exposure;

(D) evaluate the effectiveness of interventions to reduce exposure;

(E) monitor trends in exposure over time; and

(F) conduct other biomonitoring-related activities, as determined appropriate by the Director.

(2) REPORT- Each State that receives a grant under this subsection shall report to the Director and to the public, information on the biomonitoring findings and activities pursuant to paragraph (1).

(3) COORDINATION- The Director shall ensure, to the extent possible, that each State that receives a grant under this subsection demonstrates the—

(A) coordination and integration of biomonitoring activities throughout the State; and

(B) interoperability of data collection and reporting systems with neighboring States for the formation of regional networks.

(4) TECHNICAL ASSISTANCE- The Secretary, acting through the Director, shall directly or through grants or contracts, or both, provide technical assistance to States in the establishment and operation of the State biomonitoring system, including providing—

(A) training for environmental health personnel and for other appropriate personnel to develop environmental health leadership capacity at the State and local level, including investigative, diagnostic, analytical, risk communication, and response and prevention capabilities;

(B) assistance in improving relevant regional and State laboratory capacity and other activities to complement State and local investigative capabilities;

(C) assistance in establishing a computerized data collection, reporting, and processing system; and

(D) any other technical assistance the Secretary or Director determines to be necessary.

(5) AUTHORIZATION OF APPROPRIATIONS- There is authorized to be appropriated to carry out this subsection $50,000,000 for fiscal year 2008 and such sums as may be necessary for the 4 succeeding fiscal years.

(d) Translation- The Secretary shall promote translation and dissemination of findings to—

(1) inform the public; and

(2) facilitate use by States and communities to address environmental health concerns.

(e) Integration of Efforts- The Secretary shall incorporate the data collected pursuant to this section with existing data collection efforts, including the following surveys and registries as appropriate:

(1) The National Electronic Disease Surveillance System.

(2) State birth defects surveillance systems.

(3) Surveillance Epidemiology and End Results and State cancer registries.

(4) State asthma surveillance systems.

(5) The National Health and Nutrition Examination Survey.

(6) The Behavioral Risk Factor Surveillance System.

(7) The Substance Release/Health Effects Database.

(8) State blood lead surveillance systems.

(9) The Hazardous Substances Emergency Events Surveillance System.

(10) The Health Alert Network.

(11) The National Hospital Discharge Survey.

(12) The National Ambulatory Medical Care Survey.

(13) The National Health Interview Survey.

(14) The Environmental Public Health Tracking Network.

(15) The National Report on Human Exposure to Environmental Chemicals.

(16) Other data and surveillance systems, registries, and surveys as considered appropriate by the Secretary and the Administrator of the Environmental Protection Agency.

SEC. 7. ENVIRONMENTAL HEALTH WORKFORCE DEVELOPMENT.

(a) In General- The Director of the Centers for Disease Control and Prevention, in collaboration with the Director of the National Institutes of Health and national and professional organizations, shall expand training and educational activities relating to environmental health and environmental justice for health professionals and public health practitioners, including those from health disparity populations.

(b) Authorization of Appropriations- There is authorized to be appropriated to carry out this section such sums as may be necessary.

SEC. 8. DEFINITIONS.

In this Act:

(1) ENVIRONMENTAL HEALTH- The term 'environmental health', as defined by the World Health Organization, includes both the direct pathological effects of chemicals, radiation, and some biological agents, and the effects (often indirect) on health and well-being of the broad physical, psychological, social, and aesthetic environment.

(2) ENVIRONMENTAL JUSTICE- The term 'environmental justice', as defined by the Environmental Protection Agency, includes the fair treatment and meaningful involvement of all people regardless of race, color, national origin, or income with respect to the development, implementation, and enforcement of environmental laws, regulations, and policies.

(3) HEALTH DISPARITY POPULATION- The term 'health disparity population' means a health disparity population as described in section 485E(d) of the Public Health Service Act (42 U.S.C. 287c-31(d)).

(4) STATE- The term 'State' means each of the 50 States, the District of Columbia, the Commonwealth of Puerto Rico, the United States Virgin Islands, Guam, American Samoa, the Commonwealth of the Northern Mariana Islands, the Republic of the Marshall Islands, the Federated States of Micronesia, the Republic of Palau, and any Indian country (as defined in section 1151 of title 18, United States Code).

US SENATE BILL 1084

TITLE: A bill to provide housing assistance for very low-income veterans.

SPONSOR: Sen Obama, Barack [IL] (introduced 4/10/2007) Cosponsors (10)

RELATED BILLS: H.R.3329

LATEST MAJOR ACTION: 4/10/2007 Referred to Senate committee. Status: Read twice and referred to the Committee on Banking, Housing, and Urban Affairs.

SUMMARY AS OF:

4/10/2007—Introduced.

Homes for Heroes Act of 2007 - Amends the Department of Housing and Urban Development Act to establish in the Department of Housing and Urban Development (HUD) a Special Assistant for Veterans Affairs to: (1) ensure veteran access to HUD housing and homeless assistance programs; (2) coordinate all HUD programs and activities relating to veterans; and (3) serve as a HUD liaison with the Department of Veterans Affairs.

Directs the HUD Secretary to provide assistance to private nonprofit organizations and consumer cooperatives to expand the supply of supportive housing for very low-income veteran families (that is, families with incomes not exceeding 50% of the area median income).

Amends the United States Housing Act of 1937 to: (1) make housing rental vouchers available to homeless veterans; and (2) include veterans in public housing planning.

Excludes veterans' benefits from income for purposes of HUD assisted housing rental determinations.

Requires the Secretary to: (1) make grants to nonprofit entities for technical assistance in sponsoring HUD housing projects for veterans; and (2) report annually to specified congressional committees and the Secretary of Veterans Affairs on HUD activities relating to veterans.

MAJOR ACTIONS:

¤NONE¤

ALL ACTIONS:

4/10/2007:

Sponsor introductory remarks on measure. (CR S4310)

4/10/2007:

Read twice and referred to the Committee on Banking, Housing, and Urban Affairs.

TITLES(s): (italics indicate a title for a portion of a bill)

¤NONE¤

COSPONSORS(10), ALPHABETICAL [FOLLOWED BY COSPONSORS WITH-DRAWN]: (Sort: by date)

Sen Akaka, Daniel K. [HI] - 2/6/2008

Sen Brown, Sherrod [OH] - 4/10/2007

Sen Cantwell, Maria [WA] - 4/10/2007

Sen Durbin, Richard [IL] - 9/19/2007

Sen Harkin, Tom [IA] - 4/24/2007

Sen Kerry, John F. [MA] - 4/16/2007

Sen Lautenberg, Frank R. [NJ] - 5/22/2007

Sen McCaskill, Claire [MO] - 4/16/2007

Sen Menendez, Robert [NJ] - 4/10/2007

Sen Schumer, Charles E. [NY] - 4/10/2007

COMMITTEE(S)

Committee/Subcommittee:

Activity:

Senate Banking, Housing, and Urban Affairs

Referral, In Committee

RELATED BILL DETAILS: (additional related bills may be indentified in Status)

Bill:

Relationship:

H.R.3329

Related bill identified by CRS

AMENDMENT(S)

¤NONE¤

IN THE SENATE OF THE UNITED STATES

April 10, 2007

Mr. REID (for Mr. OBAMA (for himself, Mr. SCHUMER, Mr. MENENDEZ, Mr. BROWN, and Ms. CANTWELL)) introduced the following bill; which was read twice and referred to the Committee on Banking, Housing, and Urban Affairs

A BILL

To provide housing assistance for very low-income veterans.

Be it enacted by the Senate and House of Representatives of the United States of America in Congress assembled,

SECTION 1. SHORT TITLE.

This Act may be cited as the 'Homes for Heroes Act of 2007'.

SEC. 2. SPECIAL ASSISTANT FOR VETERANS AFFAIRS IN OFFICE OF SECRETARY OF HOUSING AND URBAN DEVELOPMENT.

Section 4 of the Department of Housing and Urban Development Act (42 U.S.C. 3533) is amended by adding at the end the following new subsection:

'(g) Special Assistant for Veterans Affairs-

'(1) ESTABLISHMENT- There shall be in the Department a Special Assistant for Veterans Affairs, who shall be in the Office of the Secretary.

'(2) APPOINTMENT- The Special Assistant for Veterans Affairs shall be appointed based solely on merit and shall be covered under the provisions of title 5, United States Code, governing appointments in the competitive service.

'(3) RESPONSIBILITIES- The Special Assistant for Veterans Affairs shall be responsible for—

'(A) ensuring veterans have access to housing and homeless assistance under each program of the Department providing either such assistance;

'(B) coordinating all programs and activities of the Department relating to veterans;

'(C) serving as a liaison for the Department with the Department of Veterans Affairs, including establishing and maintaining relationships with the Secretary of Veterans Affairs;

'(D) serving as a liaison for the Department, and establishing and maintaining relationships with officials of State, local, regional, and nongovernmental organizations concerned with veterans;

'(E) providing information and advice regarding—

'(i) sponsoring housing projects for veterans assisted under programs administered by the Department; or

'(ii) assisting veterans in obtaining housing or homeless assistance under programs administered by the Department;

'(F) administering the technical assistance grants program under section 7 of the Homes for Heroes Act of 2006;

'(G) preparing the annual report under section 8 of such Act; and

'(H) carrying out such other duties as may be assigned to the Special Assistant by the Secretary or by law.'.

SEC. 3. SUPPORTIVE HOUSING FOR VERY LOW-INCOME VETERAN FAMILIES.

(a) Purpose- The purposes of this section are—

(1) to expand the supply of permanent housing for very low-income veteran families; and

(2) to provide supportive services through such housing to support the needs of such veteran families.

(b) Authority-

(1) IN GENERAL- The Secretary of Housing and Urban Development shall, to the extent amounts are made available for assistance under this section and the Secretary receives approvable applications for such assistance, provide assistance to private non-profit organizations and consumer cooperatives to expand the supply of supportive housing for very low-income veteran families.

(2) NATURE OF ASSISTANCE- The assistance provided under paragraph (1)—

(A) shall be available for use to plan for and finance the acquisition, construction, reconstruction, or moderate or substantial rehabilitation of a structure or a portion of a structure to be used as supportive housing for very low-income veteran families in accordance with this section; and

(B) may also cover the cost of real property acquisition, site improvement, conversion, demolition, relocation, and other expenses that the Secretary determines are necessary to expand the supply of supportive housing for very low-income veteran families.

(3) CONSULTATION- In meeting the requirement of paragraph (1), the Secretary shall consult with—

(A) the Secretary of Veterans Affairs; and

(B) the Special Assistant for Veterans Affairs, as such Special Assistant was established under section 4(g) of the Department of Housing and Urban Development Act.

(c) Forms of Assistance- Assistance under this section shall be made available in the following forms:

(1) Assistance may be provided as a grant for costs of planning a project to be used as supportive housing for very low-income veteran families.

(2) Assistance may be provided as a capital advance under this paragraph for a project, such advance shall—

(A) bear no interest;

(B) not be required to be repaid so long as the housing remains available for occupancy by very low-income veteran families in accordance with this section; and

(C) be in an amount calculated in accordance with the development cost limitation established pursuant to subsection (j).

(3) Assistance may be provided as project rental assistance, under an annual contract that—

(A) obligates the Secretary to make monthly payments to cover any part of the costs attributed to units occupied (or, as approved by the Secretary, held for occupancy) by very low-income veteran families that is not met from project income;

(B) provides for the project not more than the sum of the initial annual project rentals for all units so occupied and any initial utility allowances for such units, as approved by the Secretary;

(C) any contract amounts not used by a project in any year shall remain available to the project until the expiration of the contract; and

(D) provides that the Secretary shall, to the extent appropriations for such purpose are made available, adjust the annual contract amount if the sum of the project income and the amount of assistance payments available under this paragraph are inadequate to provide for reasonable project costs.

(d) Tenant Rent Contribution- A very low-income veteran family shall pay as rent for a dwelling unit assisted under this section the highest of the following amounts, rounded to the nearest dollar:

(1) 30 percent of the veteran family's adjusted monthly income.

(2) 10 percent of the veteran family's monthly income.

(3) If the veteran family is receiving payments for welfare assistance from a public agency and a part of such payments, adjusted in accordance with the veteran family's actual housing costs, is specifically designated by such agency to meet the veteran family's housing costs, the portion of such payments which is so designated.

(e) Term of Commitment-

(1) USE LIMITATIONS- All units in housing assisted under this section shall be made available for occupancy by very low-income veteran families for not less than 15 years.

(2) CONTRACT TERMS-

(A) INITIAL TERM- The initial term of a contract entered into under subsection (c) (2) shall be 60 months.

(B) EXTENSION- The Secretary shall, to the extent approved in appropriation Acts, extend any expiring contract for a term of not less than 12 months.

(C) AUTHORITY OF SECRETARY TO MAKE EARLY COMMITMENTS- In order to facilitate the orderly extension of expiring contracts, the Secretary may make commitments to extend expiring contracts during the year prior to the date of expiration.

(f) Applications-

(1) IN GENERAL- Amounts made available under this section shall be allocated by the Secretary among approvable applications submitted by private nonprofit organizations and consumer cooperatives.

(2) CONTENT OF APPLICATION-

(A) IN GENERAL- Applications for assistance under this section shall be submitted by an applicant in such form and in accordance with such procedures as the Secretary shall establish.

(B) REQUIRED CONTENT- Applications for assistance under this section shall contain—

(i) a description of the proposed housing;

(ii) a description of the assistance the applicant seeks under this section;

(iii) a description of—

(I) the supportive services to be provided to the persons occupying such housing;

(II) the manner in which such services will be provided to such persons, including, in the case of frail elderly persons (as such term is defined in section 202 of the Housing Act of 1959 (12 U.S.C. 1701q)), evidence of such residential supervision as the Secretary determines is necessary to facilitate the adequate provision of such services; and

(III) the public or private sources of assistance that can reasonably be expected to fund or provide such services;

(iv) a certification from the public official responsible for submitting a housing strategy for the jurisdiction to be served in accordance with section 105 of the Cranston-Gonzalez National Affordable Housing Act (42 U.S.C. 12705) that the proposed project is consistent with the approved housing strategy; and

(v) such other information or certifications that the Secretary determines to be necessary or appropriate to achieve the purposes of this section.

(3) REJECTION- The Secretary shall not reject any application for assistance under this section on technical grounds without giving notice of that rejection and the basis therefore to the applicant.

(g) Selection Criteria- The Secretary shall establish selection criteria for assistance under this section, which shall include—

(1) criteria based upon—

(A) the ability of the applicant to develop and operate the proposed housing;

(B) the need for supportive housing for very low-income veteran families in the area to be served;

(C) the extent to which the proposed size and unit mix of the housing will enable the applicant to manage and operate the housing efficiently and ensure that the provision of supportive services will be accomplished in an economical fashion;

(D) the extent to which the proposed design of the housing will meet the physical needs of very low-income veteran families;

(E) the extent to which the applicant has demonstrated that the supportive services identified pursuant to subsection (f)(2)(B)(iii) will be provided on a consistent, long-term basis;

(F) the extent to which the proposed design of the housing will accommodate the provision of supportive services that are expected to be needed, either initially or over the useful life of the housing, by the very low-income veterans the housing is intended to serve; and

(G) such other factors as the Secretary determines to be appropriate to ensure that funds made available under this section are used effectively;

(2) a preference in such selection for applications proposing housing to be reserved for occupancy by very low-income veteran families who are homeless (as such term is defined in section 103 of the McKinney-Vento Homeless Assistance Act (42 U.S.C. 11302)); and

(3) criteria appropriate to consider the need for supportive housing for very low-income veteran families in nonmetropolitan areas and by Indian tribes.

(h) Provision of Supportive Services to Veteran Families-

(1) IN GENERAL- The Secretary of Veterans Affairs shall ensure that any housing assistance provided to veterans or veteran families includes a range of services tailored to the needs of the very low-income veteran families occupying such housing, which may include services for—

(A) outreach;

(B) health (including counseling, mental health, substance abuse, post-traumatic stress disorder, and traumatic brain injury) diagnosis and treatment;

(C) habilitation and rehabilitation;

(D) case management;

(E) daily living;

(F) personal financial planning;

(G) transportation;

(H) vocation;

(I) employment and training;

(J) education;

(K) assistance in obtaining veterans benefits and public benefits, including health and medical care provided by the Department of Veterans Affairs;

(L) assistance in obtaining income support;

(M) assistance in obtaining health insurance;

(N) fiduciary and representative payee;

(O) legal aid;

(P) child care;

(Q) housing counseling;

(R) service coordination; and

(S) other services necessary for maintaining independent living.

(2) LOCAL COORDINATION OF SERVICES-

(A) IN GENERAL- The Secretary shall ensure that owners of housing assisted under this section have the managerial capacity to—

(i) assess on an ongoing basis the service needs of residents;

(ii) coordinate the provision of supportive services and tailor such services to the individual needs of residents; and

(iii) seek on a continuous basis new sources of assistance to ensure the long-term provision of supportive services.

(B) CLASSIFICATION OF COSTS- Any cost associated with this subsection shall be an eligible cost under subsections (c)(3) and (i).

(i) Financial Assistance for Services-

(1) IN GENERAL- The Secretary of Veterans Affairs shall, to the extent amounts are available for assistance under this subsection, provide financial assistance for the provision of supportive services, and for coordinating the provision of such services, to very low-income veteran families occupying assisted housing. Such assistance shall be made through payments to owners of such housing for each resident of the housing based on the formula established under paragraph (2).

(2) FORMULA- The Secretary of Veterans Affairs shall establish a formula to determine the rate of the payments to be provided under this subsection. The formula shall determine a rate for each resident of the housing assisted under this section (which shall be adjusted not less than annually to take into consideration changes in the cost of living).

(3) AUTHORIZATION OF APPROPRIATIONS-

(A) IN GENERAL- There is authorized to be appropriated for the Department of Veterans Affairs to carry out this subsection amounts as follows:

(i) For fiscal year 2008, $25,000,000.

(ii) For each fiscal year after fiscal year 2008, such sums as may be necessary for such fiscal year.

(B) AVAILABILITY- Amounts authorized to be appropriated by subparagraph (A) shall remain available until expended.

(j) Development Cost Limitations-

(1) IN GENERAL- The Secretary shall periodically establish development cost limitations by market area for various types and sizes of supportive housing for very low-income veteran families by publishing a notice of the cost limitations in the Federal Register.

(2) CONSIDERATIONS- The cost limitations established under paragraph (1) shall reflect—

(A) the cost of construction, reconstruction, or moderate or substantial rehabilitation of supportive housing for very low-income veteran families that meets applicable State and local housing and building codes;

(B) the cost of movables necessary to the basic operation of the housing, as determined by the Secretary;

(C) the cost of special design features necessary to make the housing accessible to very low-income veteran families;

(D) the cost of congregate space necessary to accommodate the provision of supportive services to veteran families;

(E) if the housing is newly constructed, the cost of meeting the energy efficiency standards promulgated by the Secretary in accordance with section 109 of the Cranston-Gonzalez National Affordable Housing Act (42 U.S.C. 12709); and

(F) the cost of land, including necessary site improvement.

(3) USE OF DATA- In establishing development cost limitations for a given market area under this subsection, the Secretary shall use data that reflect currently prevailing costs of construction, reconstruction, or moderate or substantial rehabilitation, and land acquisition in the area.

(4) CONGREGATE SPACE- For purposes of paragraph (1), a congregate space shall include space for cafeterias or dining halls, community rooms or buildings, workshops, child care, adult day health facilities or other outpatient health facilities, or other essential service facilities.

(5) COMMERCIAL FACILITIES- Neither this section nor any other provision of law may be construed as prohibiting or preventing the location and operation, in a project assisted under this section, of commercial facilities for the benefit of residents of the project and the community in which the project is located, except that assistance made available under this section may not be used to subsidize any such commercial facility.

(6) ACQUISITION- In the case of existing housing and related facilities to be acquired, the cost limitations shall include—

(A) the cost of acquiring such housing;

(B) the cost of rehabilitation, alteration, conversion, or improvement, including the moderate or substantial rehabilitation thereof; and

(C) the cost of the land on which the housing and related facilities are located.

(7) ANNUAL ADJUSTMENTS- The Secretary shall adjust the cost limitation not less than annually to reflect changes in the general level of construction, reconstruction, and moderate and substantial rehabilitation costs.

(8) INCENTIVES FOR SAVINGS-

(A) SPECIAL HOUSING ACCOUNT-

(i) IN GENERAL- The Secretary shall use the development cost limitations established under paragraph (1) or (6) to calculate the amount of financing to be made available to individual owners.

(ii) ACTUAL DEVELOPMENTAL COSTS LESS THAN FINANCING- Owners which incur actual development costs that are less than the amount of financing shall be entitled to retain 50 percent of the savings in a special housing account.

(iii) BONUS FOR ENERGY EFFICIENCY- The percentage established under clause (ii) shall be increased to 75 percent for owners which add energy efficiency features which—

(I) exceed the energy efficiency standards promulgated by the Secretary in accordance with section 109 of the Cranston-Gonzalez National Affordable Housing Act (42 U.S.C. 12709);

(II) substantially reduce the life-cycle cost of the housing; and

(III) reduce gross rent requirements.

(B) USES- The special housing account established under subparagraph (A) may be used—

(i) to provide services to residents of the housing or funds set aside for replacement reserves; or

(ii) for such other purposes as determined by the Secretary.

(9) DESIGN FLEXIBILITY- The Secretary shall, to the extent practicable, give owners the flexibility to design housing appropriate to their location and proposed resident population within broadly defined parameters.

(10) USE OF FUNDS FROM OTHER SOURCES- An owner shall be permitted voluntarily to provide funds from sources other than this section for amenities and other features of appropriate design and construction suitable for supportive housing under this section if the cost of such amenities is—

(A) not financed with the advance; and

(B) is not taken into account in determining the amount of Federal assistance or of the rent contribution of tenants.

(k) Tenant Selection-

(1) IN GENERAL- An owner shall adopt written tenant selection procedures that are—

(A) satisfactory to the Secretary and which are—

(i) consistent with the purpose of improving housing opportunities for very low-income veteran families; and

(ii) reasonably related to program eligibility and an applicant's ability to perform the obligations of the lease; and

(B) compliant with subtitle C of title VI of the Housing and Community Development Act of 1992 (42 U.S.C.

SEC. 4. HOUSING CHOICE VOUCHERS FOR HOMELESS VETERANS.

Section 8(o)(19) of the United States Housing Act of 1937 (42 U.S.C. 1437f(o)) is amended to read as follows:

'(19) RENTAL VOUCHERS FOR HOMELESS VETERANS-

'(A) ADDITIONAL VOUCHERS- In addition to any amount made available for rental assistance under this subsection, the Secretary shall make available the amount specified in subparagraph (B), for use only for providing rental assistance for homeless veterans in conjunction with the Secretary of Veterans Affairs.

'(B) AMOUNT- The amount specified in this subparagraph is, for each fiscal year, the amount necessary to provide not fewer than 20,000 vouchers for rental assistance under this subsection.

'(C) FUNDING- The budget authority made available under any other provisions of law for rental assistance under this subsection for fiscal year 2008 and each fiscal year thereafter is authorized to be increased in each such fiscal year by such sums as may be necessary to provide the number of vouchers specified in subparagraph (B) for such fiscal year.'.

SEC. 5. INCLUSION OF VETERANS IN HOUSING PLANNING.

(a) Public Housing Agency Plans- Section 5A(d)(1) of the United States Housing Act of 1937 (42 U.S.C. 1437c-1(d)(1)) is amended by striking 'and disabled families' and inserting ', disabled families, and veterans (as such term is defined in section 101 of title 38, United States Code)'.

(b) Comprehensive Housing Affordability Strategies-

(1) IN GENERAL- Section 105 of the Cranston-Gonzalez National Affordable Housing Act (42 U.S.C. 12705) is amended—

(A) in subsection (b)(1), by inserting 'veterans (as such term is defined in section 101 of title 38, United States Code),' after 'acquired immunodeficiency syndrome,';

(B) in subsection (b)(20), by striking 'and service' and inserting 'veterans service, and other service'; and

(C) in subsection (e)(1), by inserting 'veterans (as such term is defined in section 101 of title 38, United States Code),' after 'homeless persons,'.

(2) CONSOLIDATED PLANS- The Secretary of Housing and Urban Development shall revise the regulations relating to submission of consolidated plans (part 91 of title 24, Code of Federal Regulations) in accordance with the amendments made by paragraph (1) of this subsection to require inclusion of appropriate information relating to veterans and veterans service agencies in all such plans.

SEC. 6. EXCLUSION OF VETERANS BENEFITS FROM ASSISTED HOUSING RENT CONSIDERATIONS.

(a) In General- Notwithstanding any other provision of law, for purposes of determining the amount of rent paid by a family for occupancy of a dwelling unit assisted under a federally assisted housing program under subsection (b) or in housing assisted under any other federally assisted housing program, the income and the adjusted income of the family shall not be considered to include any amounts received by any member of the family from the Secretary of Veterans Affairs as—

(1) compensation, as such term is defined in section 101(13) of title 38, United States Code;

(2) dependency and indemnity compensation, as such term is defined in section 101(14) of such title; and

(3) a pension, as such term is defined in section 101(15) of such title.

(b) Federally Assisted Housing Program- The federally assisted housing programs under this subsection are—

(1) the public housing program under the United States Housing Act of 1937 (42 U.S.C. 1437 et seq.);

(2) the tenant-based rental assistance program under section 8 of the United States Housing Act of 1937 (42 U.S.C. 1437f), including the program under subsection (o) (19) of such section for housing rental vouchers for low-income veteran families;

(3) the project-based rental assistance program under section 8 of the United States Housing Act of 1937 (42 U.S.C. 1437f);

(4) the program for housing opportunities for persons with AIDS under subtitle D of title VIII of the Cranston-Gonzalez National Affordable Housing Act (42 U.S.C. 12901 et seq.);

(5) the supportive housing for the elderly program under section 202 of the Housing Act of 1959 (12 U.S.C. 1701q);

(6) the supportive housing for persons with disabilities program under section 811 of the Cranston-Gonzalez National Affordable Housing Act (42 U.S.C. 8013);

(7) the supportive housing for the homeless program under subtitle C of title IV of the McKinney-Vento Homeless Assistance Act (42 U.S.C. 11381 et seq.);

(8) the program for moderate rehabilitation of single room occupancy dwellings for occupancy by the homeless under section 441 of the McKinney-Vento Homeless Assistance Act (42 U.S.C. 11401);

(9) the shelter plus care for the homeless program under subtitle F of title IV of the McKinney-Vento Homeless Assistance Act (42 U.S.C. 11403 et seq.);

(10) the supportive housing for very low-income veteran families program under section 3 of this Act;

(11) the rental assistance payments program under section 521(a)(2)(A) of the Housing Act of 1949 (42 U.S.C. 1490a(a)(2)(A);

(12) the rental assistance program under section 236 of the National Housing Act (12 U.S.C. 1715z-1);

(13) the rural housing programs under section 515 and 538 of the Housing Act of 1949 (42 U.S.C. 1485, 1490p-2);

(14) the HOME investment partnerships program under title II of the Cranston-Gonzalez National Affordable Housing Act (42 U.S.C. 12721 et seq.);

(15) the block grant programs for affordable housing for Native Americans and Native Hawaiians under titles I through IV and VIII of the Native American Housing Assistance and Self-Determination Act of 1996 (25 U.S.C. 4111 et seq., 4221 et seq.);

(16) the low-income housing tax credit program under section 42 of the Internal Revenue Code of 1986; and

(17) any other program for housing assistance administered by the Secretary of Housing and Urban Development or the Secretary of Agriculture under which eligibility for occupancy in the housing assisted or for housing assistance is based upon income.

SEC. 7. TECHNICAL ASSISTANCE GRANTS FOR HOUSING ASSISTANCE FOR VETERANS.

(a) In General- The Secretary of Housing and Urban Development shall, to the extent amounts are made available in appropriation Acts for grants under this section, make grants to eligible entities under subsection (b) to provide to nonprofit organizations technical assistance appropriate to assist such organizations in—

(1) sponsoring housing projects for veterans assisted under programs administered by the Department of Housing and Urban Development;

(2) fulfilling the planning and application processes and requirements necessary under such programs administered by the Department; and

(3) assisting veterans in obtaining housing or homeless assistance under programs administered by the Department.

(b) Eligible Entities- An eligible entity under this subsection is a nonprofit entity or organization having such expertise as the Secretary shall require in providing technical assistance to providers of services for veterans.

(c) Selection of Grant Recipients- The Secretary of Housing and Urban Development shall establish criteria for selecting applicants for grants under this section to receive such grants and shall select applicants based upon such criteria.

(d) Funding- Of any amounts made available in fiscal year 2008 or any fiscal year thereafter to the Department of Housing and Urban Development for salaries and expenses, $1,000,000 shall be available, and shall remain available until expended, for grants under this section.

SEC. 8. ANNUAL REPORT ON HOUSING ASSISTANCE TO VETERANS.

(a) In General- Not later than December 31 each year, the Secretary of Housing and Urban Development shall submit a report on the activities of the Department of Housing and Urban Development relating to veterans during such year to the following:

(1) The Committee on Banking, Housing, and Urban Affairs of the Senate.

(2) The Committee on Veterans' Affairs of the Senate.

(3) The Committee on Appropriations of the Senate.

(4) The Committee on Financial Services of the House of Representatives.

(5) The Committee on Veterans' Affairs of the House of Representatives.

(6) The Committee on Appropriations of the House of Representatives.

(7) The Secretary of Veterans Affairs.

(b) Contents- Each report required under subsection (a) shall include the following information with respect to the year for which the report is submitted:

(1) The number of very low-income veteran families provided assistance under the program of supportive housing for very low-income veteran families under section 3, the socioeconomic characteristics of such families, the types of assistance provided such families, and the number, types, and locations of owners of housing assisted under such section.

(2) The number of homeless veterans provided assistance under the program of housing choice vouchers for homeless veterans under section 8(o)(19) of the United States Housing Act of 1937 (42 U.S.C. 1437f(o)(19)) (as amended by section 4), the socioeconomic characteristics of such homeless veterans, and the number, types, and locations of entities contracted under such section to administer the vouchers.

(3) A summary description of the special considerations made for veterans under public housing agency plans submitted pursuant to section 5A of the United States Housing Act of 1937 (42 U.S.C. 1437c-1) and under comprehensive housing affordability strategies submitted pursuant to section 105 of the Cranston-Gonzalez National Affordable Housing Act (42 U.S.C. 12705).

(4) A description of the technical assistance provided to organizations pursuant to grants under section 7.

(5) A description of the activities of the Special Assistant for Veterans Affairs.

(6) A description of the efforts of the Department of Housing and Urban Development to coordinate the delivery of housing and services to veterans with other Federal departments and agencies, including the Department of Defense, Department of Justice, Department of Labor, Department of Health and Human Services, Department of Veterans Affairs, Interagency Council on Homelessness, and the Social Security Administration.

(7) The cost to the Department of Housing and Urban Development of administering the programs and activities relating to veterans.

(8) Any other information that the Secretary considers relevant in assessing the programs and activities of the Department of Housing and Urban Development relating to veterans .

(c) Assessment of Housing Needs of Very Low-Income Veteran Families-

(1) IN GENERAL- For the first report submitted pursuant to subsection (a) and every fifth report thereafter, the Secretary of Housing and Urban Development shall—

(A) conduct an assessment of the housing needs of very low-income veteran families (as such term is defined in section 3); and

(B) shall include in each such report findings regarding such assessment.

(2) CONTENT- Each assessment under this subsection shall include—

(A) conducting a survey of, and direct interviews with, a representative sample of very low-income veteran families (as such term is defined in section 3) to determine past and current—

(i) socioeconomic characteristics of such veteran families;

(ii) barriers to such veteran families obtaining safe, quality, and affordable housing;

(iii) levels of homelessness among such veteran families; and

(iv) levels and circumstances of, and barriers to, receipt by such veteran families of rental housing and homeownership assistance; and

(B) such other information that the Secretary determines, in consultation with the Secretary of Veterans Affairs and national nongovernmental organizations concerned with veterans, homelessness, and very low-income housing, may be useful to the assessment.

(3) CONDUCT- If the Secretary contracts with an entity other than the Department of Housing and Urban Development to conduct the assessment under this subsection, such entity shall be a nongovernmental organization determined by the Secretary to have appropriate expertise in quantitative and qualitative social science research.

(4) FUNDING- Of any amounts made available pursuant to section 501 of the Housing and Urban Development Act of 1970 (42 U.S.C. 1701z-1) for programs of research, studies, testing, or demonstration relating to the mission or programs of the Department of Housing and Urban Development for any fiscal year in which an assessment under this subsection is required pursuant to paragraph (1) of this subsection, $1,000,000 shall be available until expended for costs of the assessment under this subsection.

US SENATE BILL 1151

TITLE: A bill to provide incentives to the auto industry to accelerate efforts to develop more energy-efficient vehicles to lessen dependence on oil.

SPONSOR: Sen Obama, Barack [IL] (introduced 4/18/2007) Cosponsors (None)

RELATED BILLS: H.R.1920

Latest Major Action: 4/18/2007 Referred to Senate committee. Status: Read twice and referred to the Committee on Finance.

Summary As Of:

4/18/2007—Introduced.

Health Care for Hybrids Act - Requires the Secretaries of Energy, Health and Human Services, Transportation, and the Treasury to establish a task force to create a program to reimburse certain domestic automobile manufacturers for a portion (up to 10%) of the annual health care coverage costs for their retired employees. Requires such manufacturers to invest at least 50% of their health care cost savings in petroleum fuel reduction technologies, including alternative or flexible fuel vehicles and hybrids, and in the retraining of workers and retooling of manufacturing plants. Terminates such program on December 31, 2017.

Amends the Internal Revenue Code to: (1) define economic substance for purposes of evaluating tax shelter transactions; (2) impose penalties for understatements of tax liability resulting from transactions lacking in economic substance; and (3) deny a tax deduction for interest assessed on underpayments of tax resulting from transactions lacking in economic substance.

Major Actions:

¤NONE¤

All Actions:

4/18/2007:

Read twice and referred to the Committee on Finance.

Titles(s): (italics indicate a title for a portion of a bill)

¤NONE¤

Cosponsor(s):

¤NONE¤

Committee(s)

Committee/Subcommittee:

Activity:

Senate Finance

Referral, In Committee

Related Bill Details: (additional related bills may be indentified in Status)

Bill:

Relationship:

H.R.1920

Related bill identified by CRS

AMENDMENT(S)

¤NONE¤

IN THE SENATE OF THE UNITED STATES

April 18, 2007

Mr. OBAMA introduced the following bill; which was read twice and referred to the Committee on Finance

A BILL

To provide incentives to the auto industry to accelerate efforts to develop more energy-efficient vehicles to lessen dependence on oil.

Be it enacted by the Senate and House of Representatives of the United States of America in Congress assembled,

SECTION 1. SHORT TITLE; TABLE OF CONTENTS.

(a) Short Title- This Act may be cited as the 'Health Care for Hybrids Act'.

(b) Table of Contents- The table of contents for this Act is as follows:

SEC. 2. FINDINGS.

Congress makes the following findings:

(1) More than 50 percent of the oil consumed in the United States is imported.

(2) If present trends continue, foreign oil will represent 68 percent of the oil consumed in the United States by 2025.

(3) The United States has only 3 percent of the world's known oil reserves and the Nation's economic health is dependent on world oil prices.

(4) World oil prices are overwhelmingly dictated by other countries, which endangers the economic and national security of the United States.

(5) A major portion of the world's oil supply is controlled by unstable governments and countries that are known to finance, harbor, or otherwise support terrorists and terrorist activities.

(6) American automakers have lagged behind their foreign competitors in producing hybrid and other energy-efficient automobiles.

(7) Legacy health care costs associated with retiree workers are an increasing burden on the global competitiveness of American industries.

(8) Innovative uses of new technology in automobiles manufactured in the United States will—

(A) help retain American jobs;

(B) support health care obligations for retiring workers in the automotive sector;

(C) decrease our Nation's dependence on foreign oil; and

(D) address pressing environmental concerns.

TITLE I—RETIRED EMPLOYEE HEALTH BENEFITS REIMBURSEMENT PROGRAM

SEC. 101. COORDINATING TASK FORCE.

(a) Establishment- Not later than 6 months after the date of the enactment of this Act, the Secretary of Energy, the Secretary of Health and Human Services, the Secretary of Transportation, and the Secretary of the Treasury shall establish a task force (referred to in this Act as the 'task force') to administer the program established under section 102 (referred to in this Act as the 'program').

(b) Membership- The task force shall be composed representatives of the departments headed by the officials referred to in subsection (a), who shall be appointed by such officials in equal numbers.

SEC. 102. ESTABLISHMENT OF PROGRAM.

(a) In General- Not later than 1 year after the date of the enactment of this Act, the task force shall establish a program to reimburse eligible domestic automobile manufacturers for the costs incurred in providing health benefits to their retired employees. The task force shall determine compliance with the assurances under subsection (c)(4) through accepted measurements of fuel savings.

(b) Consultation- In establishing the program, the task force shall consult with representatives from—

(1) eligible domestic automobile manufacturers;

(2) unions representing employees of such manufacturers; and

(3) consumer and environmental groups.

(c) Eligibility Requirements- A domestic automobile manufacturer seeking reimbursement under the program shall—

(1) submit an application to the task force at such time, in such manner, and containing such information as the task force shall require;

(2) certify that such manufacturer is providing full health care coverage to all of its employees;

(3) provide assurances to the task force that the manufacturer will invest, in an amount equal to not less than 50 percent of the amount saved by the manufacturer through the reimbursement of its retiree health care costs under the program, in—

(A) the domestic manufacture and commercialization of petroleum fuel reduction technologies, including alternative or flexible fuel vehicles, hybrids, and other state-of-the-art fuel saving technologies;

(B) retraining workers and retooling assembly lines for the activities described in subparagraph (A);

(C) researching, developing, designing, and commercializing high-performance, fuel-efficient vehicles, and other activities related to diversifying the domestic production of automobiles; and

(D) assisting domestic automobile component suppliers to retool their domestic manufacturing plants to produce components for petroleum fuel reduction technologies, including alternative or flexible fuel vehicles and hybrid, advanced diesel, and other state-of-the-art fuel saving technologies; and

(4) provide assurances to the task force that average adjusted fuel economy savings achieved under paragraph (3) will not result in fuel economy decreases in other automobiles manufactured in the United States; and

(5) provide additional assurances and information as the task force may require, including information needed by the task force to audit the manufacturer's compliance with the requirements of the program.

(d) Limitation- Not more than 10 percent of the annual retiree health care costs of any domestic automobile manufacturer may be reimbursed under the program in any year.

(e) Termination of Program- The program shall terminate on December 31, 2017.

SEC. 103. REPORTING.

(a) Reimbursement Reports- Not later than 6 months after the date of the enactment of this Act, and every 6 months thereafter, the task force shall submit a report to Congress that—

(1) identifies the reimbursements paid under the program; and

(2) describes the changes in the manufacture and commercialization of fuel saving technologies implemented by automobile manufacturers as a result of such reimbursements.

(b) Consumer Incentives- Not later than 1 year after the date of the enactment of this Act, the task force shall submit a report to Congress that—

(1) indicates the effectiveness of financial incentives available to consumers for the purchase of hybrid vehicles in encouraging such purchases; and

(2) recommends whether such incentives should be expanded.

SEC. 104. AUTHORIZATION OF APPROPRIATIONS.

There are authorized to be appropriated such sums as may be necessary in each of fiscal years 2008 through 2018 to carry out this title.

TITLE II—TAX PROVISIONS

SEC. 201. CLARIFICATION OF ECONOMIC SUBSTANCE DOCTRINE.

(a) In General- Section 7701 of the Internal Revenue Code of 1986 is amended—

(1) by redesignating subsection (p) as subsection (q); and

(2) by inserting after subsection (o) the following:

'(p) Clarification of Economic Substance Doctrine-

'(1) GENERAL RULES-

'(A) IN GENERAL- In any case in which a court determines that the economic substance doctrine is relevant for purposes of this title to a transaction (or series of transactions), such transaction (or series of transactions) shall have economic substance only if the requirements of this paragraph are met.

'(B) DEFINITION OF ECONOMIC SUBSTANCE- For purposes of subparagraph (A):

'(i) IN GENERAL- A transaction has economic substance only if—

'(I) the transaction changes in a meaningful way (apart from Federal tax effects) the taxpayer's economic position, and

'(II) the taxpayer has a substantial nontax purpose for entering into such transaction and the transaction is a reasonable means of accomplishing such purpose.

In applying subclause (II), a purpose of achieving a financial accounting benefit shall not be taken into account in determining whether a transaction has a substantial nontax purpose if the origin of such financial accounting benefit is a reduction of income tax.

'(ii) SPECIAL RULE WHERE TAXPAYER RELIES ON PROFIT POTENTIAL- A transaction shall not be treated as having economic substance by reason of having a potential for profit unless—

'(I) the present value of the reasonably expected pre-tax profit from the transaction is substantial in relation to the present value of the expected net tax benefits that would be allowed if the transaction were respected, and

'(II) the reasonably expected pre-tax profit from the transaction exceeds a risk-free rate of return.

'(C) TREATMENT OF FEES AND FOREIGN TAXES- Fees and other transaction expenses and foreign taxes shall be taken into account as expenses in determining pre-tax profit under subparagraph (B)(ii).

'(2) SPECIAL RULES FOR TRANSACTION WITH TAX-INDIFFERENT PARTIES-

'(A) SPECIAL RULES FOR FINANCING TRANSACTIONS- The form of a transaction which is in substance the borrowing of money or the acquisition of financial capital directly or indirectly from a tax-indifferent party shall not be respected if the present value of the deductions to be claimed with respect to the transaction is substantially in excess of the present value of the anticipated economic returns of the person lending the money or providing the financial capital. A public offering shall be treated as a borrowing, or an acquisition of financial capital, from a tax-indifferent party if it is reasonably expected that at least 50 percent of the offering will be placed with tax-indifferent parties.

'(B) ARTIFICIAL INCOME SHIFTING AND BASIS ADJUSTMENTS- The form of a transaction with a tax-indifferent party shall not be respected if—

'(i) it results in an allocation of income or gain to the tax-indifferent party in excess of such party's economic income or gain, or

'(ii) it results in a basis adjustment or shifting of basis on account of overstating the income or gain of the tax-indifferent party.

'(3) DEFINITIONS AND SPECIAL RULES- For purposes of this subsection:

'(A) ECONOMIC SUBSTANCE DOCTRINE- The term 'economic substance doctrine' means the common law doctrine under which tax benefits under subtitle A with respect to a transaction are not allowable if the transaction does not have economic substance or lacks a business purpose.

'(B) TAX-INDIFFERENT PARTY- The term 'tax-indifferent party' means any person or entity not subject to tax imposed by subtitle A. A person shall be treated as a tax-indifferent party with respect to a transaction if the items taken into account with respect to the transaction have no substantial impact on such person's liability under subtitle A.

'(C) EXCEPTION FOR PERSONAL TRANSACTIONS OF INDIVIDUALS- In the case of an individual, this subsection shall apply only to transactions entered into in connection with a trade or business or an activity engaged in for the production of income.

'(D) TREATMENT OF LESSORS- In applying paragraph (1)(B)(ii) to the lessor of tangible property subject to a lease—

'(i) the expected net tax benefits with respect to the leased property shall not include the benefits of—

'(I) depreciation,

'(II) any tax credit, or

'(III) any other deduction as provided in guidance by the Secretary, and

'(ii) subclause (II) of paragraph (1)(B)(ii) shall be disregarded in determining whether any of such benefits are allowable.

'(4) OTHER COMMON LAW DOCTRINES NOT AFFECTED- Except as specifically provided in this subsection, the provisions of this subsection shall not be construed as altering or supplanting any other rule of law, and the requirements of this subsection shall be construed as being in addition to any such other rule of law.

'(5) REGULATIONS- The Secretary shall prescribe such regulations as may be necessary or appropriate to carry out the purposes of this subsection. Such regulations may include exemptions from the application of this subsection.'.

(b) Effective Date- The amendments made by this section shall apply to transactions entered into after the date of the enactment of this Act.

SEC. 202. PENALTY FOR UNDERSTATEMENTS ATTRIBUTABLE TO TRANSACTIONS LACKING ECONOMIC SUBSTANCE.

(a) In General- Subchapter A of chapter 68 of the Internal Revenue Code of 1986 is amended by inserting after section 6662A the following:

'SEC. 6662B. PENALTY FOR UNDERSTATEMENTS ATTRIBUTABLE TO TRANSACTIONS LACKING ECONOMIC SUBSTANCE.

'(a) Imposition of Penalty- If a taxpayer has an noneconomic substance transaction understatement for any taxable year, there shall be added to the tax an amount equal to 40 percent of the amount of such understatement.

'(b) Reduction of Penalty for Disclosed Transactions- Subsection (a) shall be applied by substituting '20 percent' for '40 percent' with respect to the portion of any noneconomic substance transaction understatement with respect to which the relevant facts affecting the tax treatment of the item are adequately disclosed in the return or a statement attached to the return.

'(c) Noneconomic Substance Transaction Understatement- For purposes of this section—

'(1) IN GENERAL- The term 'noneconomic substance transaction understatement' means any amount which would be an understatement under section 6662A(b)(1) if section 6662A were applied by taking into account items attributable to noneconomic substance transactions rather than items to which section 6662A would apply without regard to this paragraph.

'(2) NONECONOMIC SUBSTANCE TRANSACTION- The term 'noneconomic substance transaction' means any transaction if—

'(A) there is a lack of economic substance (within the meaning of section 7701(p)(1)) for the transaction giving rise to the claimed benefit or the transaction was not respected under section 7701(p)(2), or

'(B) the transaction fails to meet the requirements of any similar rule of law.

'(d) Rules Applicable to Compromise of Penalty-

'(1) IN GENERAL- If the 1st letter of proposed deficiency which allows the taxpayer an opportunity for administrative review in the Internal Revenue Service Office of Appeals has been sent with respect to a penalty to which this section applies, only the Commissioner of Internal Revenue may compromise all or any portion of such penalty.

'(2) APPLICABLE RULES- The rules of paragraphs (2) and (3) of section 6707A(d) shall apply for purposes of paragraph (1).

'(e) Coordination With Other Penalties- Except as otherwise provided in this part, the penalty imposed by this section shall be in addition to any other penalty imposed by this title.

'(f) Cross References-

'(1) For coordination of penalty with understatements under section 6662 and other special rules, see section 6662A(e).

'(2) For reporting of penalty imposed under this section to the Securities and Exchange Commission, see section 6707A(e).'.

(b) Coordination With Other Understatements and Penalties-

(1) The second sentence of section 6662(d)(2)(A) of the Internal Revenue Code of 1986 is amended by inserting 'and without regard to items with respect to which a penalty is imposed by section 6662B' before the period at the end.

(2) Subsection (e) of section 6662A of the Internal Revenue Code of 1986 is amended—

(A) in paragraph (1), by inserting 'and noneconomic substance transaction understatements' after 'reportable transaction understatements' both places it appears,

(B) in paragraph (2)(A), by inserting 'and a noneconomic substance transaction understatement' after 'reportable transaction understatement',

(C) in paragraph (2)(B), by inserting '6662B or' before '6663',

(D) in paragraph (2)(C)(i), by inserting 'or section 6662B' before the period at the end,

(E) in paragraph (2)(C)(ii), by inserting 'and section 6662B' after 'This section',

(F) in paragraph (3), by inserting 'or noneconomic substance transaction understatement' after 'reportable transaction understatement', and

(G) by adding at the end the following new paragraph:

'(3) NONECONOMIC SUBSTANCE TRANSACTION UNDERSTATEMENT- For purposes of this subsection, the term 'noneconomic substance transaction understatement' has the meaning given such term by section 6662B(c).'.

(3) Paragraph (2) of section 6707A(e) of the Internal Revenue Code of 1986 is amended—

(A) by striking 'or' at the end of subparagraph (B), and

(B) by striking subparagraph (C) and inserting the following new subparagraphs:

'(C) is required to pay a penalty under section 6662B with respect to any noneconomic substance transaction, or

'(D) is required to pay a penalty under section 6662(h) with respect to any transaction and would (but for section 6662A(e)(2)(C)) have been subject to penalty under section 6662A at a rate prescribed under section 6662A(c) or under section 6662B,'.

(c) Clerical Amendment- The table of sections for part II of subchapter A of chapter 68 of the Internal Revenue Code of 1986 is amended by inserting after the item relating to section 6662A the following:

'Sec. 6662B. Penalty for understatements attributable to transactions lacking economic substance, etc.'.

(d) Effective Date- The amendments made by this section shall apply to transactions entered into after the date of the enactment of this Act.

SEC. 203. DENIAL OF DEDUCTION FOR INTEREST ON UNDERPAYMENTS ATTRIBUTABLE TO NONECONOMIC SUBSTANCE TRANSACTIONS.

(a) In General- Section 163(m) of the Internal Revenue Code of 1986 (relating to interest on unpaid taxes attributable to nondisclosed reportable transactions) is amended—

(1) by striking 'attributable' and all that follows and inserting the following: 'attributable to—

'(1) the portion of any reportable transaction understatement (as defined in section 6662A(b)) with respect to which the requirement of section 6664(d)(2)(A) is not met, or

'(2) any noneconomic substance transaction understatement (as defined in section 6662B(c)).'; and

(2) by inserting 'and noneconomic substance transactions' after 'transactions'.

(b) Effective Date- The amendments made by this section shall apply to transactions after the date of the enactment of this Act in taxable years ending after such date.

US Senate Bill 1181

Title: A bill to amend the Securities Exchange Act of 1934 to provide shareholders with an advisory vote on executive compensation.

Sponsor: Sen Obama, Barack [IL] (introduced 4/20/2007) Cosponsors (6)

Related Bills: H.R.1257

Latest Major Action: 4/20/2007 Referred to Senate committee. Status: Read twice and referred to the Committee on Banking, Housing, and Urban Affairs.

Summary As Of:

4/20/2007—Introduced.

Shareholder Vote on Executive Compensation Act - Amends the Securities Exchange Act of 1934 to require a proxy, consent, or authorization for a shareholder meeting occurring on or after January 1, 2009, to permit a separate shareholder vote to approve executive compensation.

States that such shareholder vote shall not be binding on the board of directors, nor construed: (1) as overruling a board decision; (2) to create or imply additional fiduciary duty by such board; and (3) to restrict or limit shareholder ability to make proposals for inclusion in proxy materials related to executive compensation.

Requires proxy solicitation material for a shareholder meeting occurring on or after January 1, 2009, concerning disposition of substantially all of an issuer's assets, to disclose compensation agreements or understandings with the principal executive officers of either the issuer or acquiring issuer regarding any type of (golden parachute) compensation which: (1) relates to such disposition; and (2) has not been subject to a shareholder vote.

Provides that proxy solicitation material containing such executive compensation disclosures shall require a separate shareholder vote to approve such agreements or understandings.

States that such shareholder vote shall not be binding on the board of directors, nor construed: (1) as overruling a board decision; (2) to create or imply additional fiduciary duty by such board; and (3) to constrain shareholder ability to make proposals for inclusion in proxy materials related to executive compensation.

MAJOR ACTIONS:

¤NONE¤

ALL ACTIONS:

4/20/2007:

Read twice and referred to the Committee on Banking, Housing, and Urban Affairs.

TITLES(s): (italics indicate a title for a portion of a bill)

¤NONE¤

COSPONSORS(6), ALPHABETICAL [FOLLOWED BY COSPONSORS WITHDRAWN]: (Sort: by date)

Sen Brown, Sherrod [OH] - 4/30/2007

Sen Durbin, Richard [IL] - 4/25/2007

Sen Harkin, Tom [IA] - 4/25/2007

Sen Johnson, Tim [SD] - 6/4/2007

Sen Kerry, John F. [MA] - 4/26/2007

Sen Levin, Carl [MI] - 5/3/2007

COMMITTEE(S)

Committee/Subcommittee:

Activity:

Senate Banking, Housing, and Urban Affairs

Referral, In Committee

Related Bill Details: (additional related bills may be indentified in Status)

Bill:

Relationship:

H.R.1257

Related bill identified by CRS

Amendment(s)

¤NONE¤

In the Senate of the United States

April 20, 2007

Mr. OBAMA introduced the following bill; which was read twice and referred to the Committee on Banking, Housing, and Urban Affairs

A BILL

To amend the Securities Exchange Act of 1934 to provide shareholders with an advisory vote on executive compensation.

Be it enacted by the Senate and House of Representatives of the United States of America in Congress assembled,

SECTION 1. SHORT TITLE.

This Act may be cited as the 'Shareholder Vote on Executive Compensation Act'.

SEC. 2. SHAREHOLDER VOTE ON EXECUTIVE COMPENSATION DISCLOSURES.

(a) Amendment- Section 16 of the Securities Exchange Act of 1934 (15 U.S.C. 78n) is amended by adding at the end the following new subsection:

'(h) Annual Shareholder Approval of Executive Compensation-

'(1) IN GENERAL- Any proxy or consent or authorization for an annual or other meeting of the shareholders occurring on or after January 1, 2009, shall permit a separate shareholder vote to approve the compensation of executives as disclosed pursuant to the Commission's compensation disclosure rules (which disclosure shall include the compensation discussion and analysis, the compensation tables, and any related material). The shareholder vote shall not be binding on the board of directors and shall not be construed as overruling a decision by such board, nor to create or imply any additional fiduciary duty by such board, nor shall such vote be construed to restrict or limit the ability of shareholders to make proposals for inclusion in such proxy materials related to executive compensation.

'(2) SHAREHOLDER APPROVAL OF GOLDEN PARACHUTE COMPENSATION-

'(A) DISCLOSURE- In any proxy solicitation material for an annual or other meeting of the shareholders occurring on or after January 1, 2009, that concerns an acquisition, merger, consolidation, or proposed sale or other disposition of substantially all the assets of an issuer, the person making such solicitation shall disclose in the proxy solicitation material, in a clear and simple form in accordance with regulations of the Commission, any agreements or understandings that such person has with any principal executive officers of such issuer (or of the acquiring issuer, if such issuer is not the acquiring issuer) concerning any type of compensation (whether present, deferred, or contingent) that are based on or otherwise relate to the acquisition, merger, consolidation, sale, or other disposition, and that have not been subject to a shareholder vote under paragraph (1).

'(B) SHAREHOLDER APPROVAL- The proxy solicitation material containing the disclosure required by subparagraph (A) shall require a separate shareholder vote to approve such agreements or understandings. A vote by the shareholders shall not be binding on the board of directors and shall not be construed as overruling a decision by such board, nor to create or imply any additional fiduciary duty by such board, nor shall such vote be construed to restrict or limit the ability of shareholders to make proposals for inclusion in such proxy materials related to executive compensation.'.

(b) Deadline for Rulemaking- Not later than 1 year after the date of the enactment of this Act, the Securities and Exchange Commission shall issue any final rules and regulations required by the amendments made by subsection (a).

US SENATE BILL 1222

TITLE: A bill to stop mortgage transactions which operate to promote fraud, risk, abuse, and under-development, and for other purposes.

SPONSOR: Sen Obama, Barack [IL] (introduced 4/25/2007) Cosponsors (1)

LATEST MAJOR ACTION: 4/25/2007 Referred to Senate committee. Status: Read twice and referred to the Committee on Banking, Housing, and Urban Affairs.

SUMMARY AS OF:

4/25/2007—Introduced.

Stopping Mortgage Transactions which Operate to Promote Fraud, Risk, Abuse and Underdevelopment Act, or the STOP FRAUD Act - Amends federal criminal law to make it unlawful for any mortgage professional to: (1) defraud any natural person or financial institution regarding an offer of consumer credit secured by an interest either in real property or in personal property used as a principal dwelling; or (2) falsely obtain money or property from a natural person in connection with an extension of consumer credit secured by an interest in such property.

Subjects violations of this Act to civil and criminal penalties.

Directs the Attorney General to establish: (1) a system for authorized mortgage professionals to receive updates from federal law enforcement agencies on suspicious activity trends in the mortgage industry and mortgage fraud-related convictions; (2) a Debarred or Censured Mortgage Professional Database that may be accessed to determine the federal and state bar status of mortgage professionals; and (3) grants to assist law enforcement agencies establish and improve mortgage fraud task forces.

Grants whistleblower protection to personnel of a widely accepted private certification board.

Amends the Housing and Urban Development Act of 1968 to authorize the Secretary of Housing and Urban Development (HUD) to provide tenants, homeowners, and other consumers with mortgage fraud counseling.

Directs the Secretary to provide grants to state appraisal agencies to improve the monitoring and enforcement of housing appraisal regulations.

Sets forth additional rights of borrowers in foreclosure proceedings.

MAJOR ACTIONS:

¤NONE¤

ALL ACTIONS:

4/25/2007:

Sponsor introductory remarks on measure. (CR S5106)

4/25/2007:

Read twice and referred to the Committee on Banking, Housing, and Urban Affairs.

TITLES(s): (italics indicate a title for a portion of a bill)

¤NONE¤

COSPONSORS(1), ALPHABETICAL [followed by Cosponsors withdrawn]: (Sort: by date)

Sen Durbin, Richard [IL] - 4/25/2007

COMMITTEE(s)

Committee/Subcommittee:

Activity:

Senate Banking, Housing, and Urban Affairs

Referral, In Committee

RELATED BILL DETAILS:

¤NONE¤

AMENDMENT(s)

¤NONE¤

IN THE SENATE OF THE UNITED STATES

April 25, 2007

Mr. OBAMA (for himself and Mr. DURBIN) introduced the following bill; which was read twice and referred to the Committee on Banking, Housing, and Urban Affairs

A BILL

To stop mortgage transactions which operate to promote fraud, risk, abuse, and under-development, and for other purposes.

Be it enacted by the Senate and House of Representatives of the United States of America in Congress assembled,

SECTION 1. SHORT TITLE; TABLE OF CONTENTS.

(a) Short Title- This Act may be cited as the 'Stopping Mortgage Transactions which Operate to Promote Fraud, Risk, Abuse, and Underdevelopment Act' or the 'STOP FRAUD Act'.

(b) Table of Contents- The table of contents for this Act is as follows:

SEC. 2. MORTGAGE FRAUD.

(a) In General- Chapter 63 of title 18, United States Code, is amended by adding at the end the following:

'Sec. 1351. Mortgage fraud

'(a) In General- It shall be unlawful for any mortgage professional to knowingly execute, or attempt to execute, a scheme or artifice—

'(1) to defraud any natural person, financial institution, or purchaser of consumer credit or an interest in consumer credit in connection with the offer or extension of consumer credit (as such term is defined in subsections (e) and (h) under section 103 of the Truth in Lending Act (15 U.S.C. 1602(e) and (h))), which credit is, is to be, or is portrayed as being secured by an interest—

'(A) in real property; or

'(B) in personal property used or expected to be used as the principal dwelling (as such term is defined under section 103(v) of the Truth in Lending Act (15 U.S.C. 1602(v))) of the natural person to whom such consumer credit is offered or extended; or

'(2) to obtain, by means of false or fraudulent pretenses, representations, or promises, any money or property, including without limitation in the form of fees or charges, from a natural person in connection with an extension of consumer credit which is, is to be, or is portrayed as being secured by an interest—

'(A) in real property; or

'(B) in personal property used or expected to be used as the principal dwelling of such natural person;

'(b) Penalties-

'(1) CRIMINAL PENALTIES- Any mortgage professional who violates subsection (a) shall be fined not more than $5,000,000, or imprisoned not more than 35 years, or both.

'(2) CIVIL PENALTIES- Any mortgage professional who violates subsection (a) shall be liable for an amount equal to the sum of all finance charges and fees paid or payable by the natural person, financial institution, or purchaser who was defrauded unless the mortgage professional demonstrates that such violation is not material.

'(c) Private Right of Action by Persons Aggrieved-

'(1) IN GENERAL- Any person aggrieved by a violation of this section, or any regulation under this section may, but shall not be required to, file suit in any district court of the United States or any State court having jurisdiction of the parties to such suit—

'(A) without respect to the amount in controversy;

'(B) without regard to the citizenship of the parties; and

'(C) without regard to exhaustion of any administrative remedies.

'(2) REMEDIES- Any court in which a civil action has been brought under paragraph (1) may—

'(A) award damages and appropriate declaratory and injunctive relief for each violation of this section; and

'(B) provide such additional relief as the court deems appropriate, including the award of court costs, investigative costs, and reasonable attorneys' fees incurred by persons aggrieved.

'(d) Rule of Construction- Nothing in this section shall be construed to modify, lessen, or otherwise affect any other provision of this title relating to the rights afforded to financial institutions or purchasers of consumer credit or interests in consumer credit.

'(e) Definition- As used in this section, the term 'mortgage professional' includes real estate appraisers, real estate accountants, real estate attorneys, real estate brokers, mortgage brokers, mortgage underwriters, mortgage processors, mortgage settlement companies, mortgage title companies, mortgage loan originators, and any other provider of professional services engaged in the mortgage process.'.

(b) Table of Sections- The table of sections for chapter 63 of title 18, United States Code, is amended by inserting after the item relating to section 1350 the following:

'1351. Mortgage fraud.'.

(c) Conforming Amendment- Section 3293(2) of title 18, United States Code, is amended by striking 'or 1343' and inserting ', 1343, or 1351'.

SEC. 3. MANDATORY REPORTING REQUIREMENTS.

(a) Definition of Financial Institution- Section 5312(a)(2)(U) of title 31, United States Code, is amended by—

(1) inserting 'companies and other legal entities' after 'persons';

(2) inserting ', transactions,' after 'closings'; and

(3) inserting after 'settlements' the following: ', including the Federal National Mortgage Association, the Government National Mortgage Association, the Federal Home Loan Mortgage Corporation, mortgage appraisers, real estate accountants, real estate attorneys, real estate brokers, mortgage underwriters, mortgage processors, mortgage settlement and title companies, mortgage brokers, mortgage loan originators, and any other mortgage professional engaged in the mortgage industry'.

(b) Regulations-

(1) IN GENERAL- Not later than 1 year after the date of enactment of this Act, the Secretary of the Treasury shall issue regulations to implement the amendments made in subsection (a).

(2) CONTENT OF REGULATION- A regulation required under paragraph (1) shall—

(A) include a requirement that any suspicious activity by an individual or entity described in section 5312(a)(2)(U) of title 31, United States Code, be reported to the Secretary of the Treasury; and

(B) ensure compliance by an individual or entity described in such section with the requirement described under subparagraph (A), while simultaneously seeking to avoid any unnecessary duplication of paperwork or other administrative details.

(c) Authorization of Appropriations- There are authorized to be appropriated such sums as are necessary to implement the regulations issued under subsection (b).

SEC. 4. LAW ENFORCEMENT AND INDUSTRY COMMUNICATION.

(a) In General- Not later than 18 months after the date of enactment of this Act, the Attorney General, in consultation with the Secretary of the Treasury, shall establish a system by which mortgage brokers, lenders, title company employees, mortgage appraisers, securities and bond rating agencies, and other authorized mortgage professionals may register and receive updates from Federal law enforcement agencies on—

(1) suspicious activity trends in the mortgage industry; and

(2) mortgage fraud-related convictions.

(b) Authorization of Appropriations- There are authorized to be appropriated such sums as are necessary to establish and maintain the system required under subsection (a).

SEC. 5. DEBARRED OR CENSURED MORTGAGE PROFESSIONAL DATABASE.

(a) Establishment-

(1) IN GENERAL- Not later than 18 months after the date of enactment of this Act, the Attorney General shall establish a Debarred or Censured Mortgage Professional Database that may be accessed by authorized depository institutions, mortgage lenders, mortgage professionals, securities and bond rating agencies, and consumers to determine the Federal and State bar status of mortgage professionals regulated by any Federal or State agency.

(2) PRIVATE CERTIFICATION BOARDS- Any widely accepted private certification board shall have authority to access, maintain, and update the Debarred or Censured Mortgage Professional Database established in paragraph (1) for purposes of adding or removing the information of any mortgage professional contained in such Database.

(3) WIDELY ACCEPTED PRIVATE CERTIFICATION BOARD- Not later than 18 months after the date of enactment of this Act, the Attorney General, in consultation with the Secretary of the Treasury, shall—

(A) determine the definition of the term 'widely accepted private certification board'; and

(B) issue procedures and guidance on how officers, agents, and employees of such boards shall conduct the responsibilities described in paragraph (2).

(4) PUBLIC AVAILABILITY- The Attorney General shall make the Debarred or Censured Mortgage Professional Database established in paragraph (1) available to the public on the Internet, without fee or other access charge, in a searchable, sortable, and downloadable manner.

(b) Immunity From Civil Liability- Any officer, agent, or employee of a widely accepted private certification board, who in good faith follows the procedures and guidance set forth under subsection (a)(3)(B), shall not be liable in any court of any State or the United States to any mortgage professional or other person—

(1) for carrying out the responsibilities described in subsection (a)(2); or

(2) for nondisclosure to that mortgage professional or other person that such conduct occurred.

(c) Whistleblower Protection-

(1) IN GENERAL- No officer, agent, or employee of a widely accepted private certification board may be discharged, demoted, threatened, suspended, harassed, or in any other manner discriminated against in the terms and conditions of the employment of such officer, agent, or employee because of any lawful act done by such officer, agent, or employee to provide information, cause information to be provided, or otherwise assist in an investigation regarding any—

(A) possible violation of this section, including not following the procedures and guidance set forth under subsection (a)(3)(B); or

(B) other misconduct, by any other officer, agent, or employee of the board.

(2) CIVIL ACTION- An officer, agent, or employee injured by a violation of paragraph (1) may, in a civil action, obtain appropriate relief.

(d) Authorization of Appropriations- There are authorized to be appropriated such sums as are necessary to establish and maintain the database required under subsection (a).

SEC. 6. HOUSING COUNSELING.

Section 106 of the Housing and Urban Development Act of 1968 (12 U.S.C. 1701x), is amended by adding at the end the following:

'(g) Counseling for Mortgage Fraud-

'(1) IN GENERAL- The Secretary is authorized to provide, or contract with public or private organizations to provide, information, advice, counseling, and technical assistance to tenants, homeowners, and other consumers with respect—

'(A) to mortgage fraud, as such activity is described in section 1351 of title 18, United States Code; and

'(B) to any other activities or practices that the Secretary determines are likely to increase the risk of foreclosure by such individuals.

'(2) PREFERENCES- In distributing any funds authorized under paragraph (5), the Secretary shall give preference to—

'(A) organizations in those States with the highest rates of mortgage fraud, as such rates are determined by—

'(i) the Director of the Federal Bureau of Investigation; and

'(ii) mortgage industry statistics;

'(B) those nonprofit organizations—

'(i) approved by the Secretary under subsection (d); and

'(ii) that—

'(I) are experienced in the provision of prepurchase and foreclosure-prevention counseling; and

'(II) have a demonstrated record of success in the provision of such counseling services; and

'(C) organizations that provide—

'(i) in-person prepurchase and foreclosure-prevention counseling; and

'(ii) a brief assessment and review of the financial mortgage documents of a tenant, homeowner, or other consumer.

'(3) DUTIES OF THE SECRETARY- The Secretary shall—

'(A) monitor, record, track, and evaluate the performance of each public or private organization that is a recipient of a grant under subsection (a); and

'(B) make each evaluation under subparagraph (A) available to the public on the Internet, without fee or other access charge, in a searchable, sortable, and downloadable manner.

'(4) REPORT-

'(A) IN GENERAL- Each public or private organization that is a recipient of a grant under subsection (a) shall report to the Secretary, on a quarterly basis, on any instances or occurrences of fraud or deceptive practices by mortgage professionals uncovered in the course of providing the prepurchase and foreclosure-prevention counseling required under this section.

'(B) USE BY THE SECRETARY- Based upon the reports submitted under subparagraph (A), the Secretary shall—

'(i) identify and evaluate trends in the use and frequency of fraud or deceptive practices in the mortgage industry;

'(ii) identify new fraudulent schemes or deceptive practices, and forward to the appropriate Federal law enforcement agency information relating to such new schemes and practices; and

'(iii) establish, as needed, new requirements to train officers, agents, or employees of any public or private organization that is a recipient of a grant under subsection (a) to identify such schemes and practices, including by providing educational material to such officers, agents, or employees on such schemes and practices.

'(5) AUTHORIZATION OF APPROPRIATIONS- There are authorized to be appropriated $25,000,000, to implement the provisions of this subsection.'.

SEC. 7. STATE APPRAISAL DEMONSTRATION PROJECTS.

(a) In General- Not later than 18 months after the date of enactment of this Act, the Secretary of Housing and Urban Development shall provide grants to State appraisal agencies to improve the monitoring and enforcement of housing appraisal regulations in that State.

(b) Application- Each State appraisal agency seeking a grant under this section shall submit an application to the Secretary of Housing and Urban Development at such time, in such manner, and containing such information as the Secretary may require.

(c) Preference for States With Higher Incidents of Mortgage Fraud- In distributing any grant amounts authorized under this section, the Secretary of Housing and Urban Development shall give preference to those States with the highest rates of mortgage fraud, as such rates are determined by—

(1) the Director of the Federal Bureau of Investigation; and

(2) mortgage industry statistics.

(d) Authorization of Appropriations- There are authorized to be appropriated $10,000,000, to implement the provisions of this section.

SEC. 8. LAW ENFORCEMENT GRANTS TO STATE AND LOCAL LAW ENFORCEMENT AGENCIES.

(a) In General- Not later than 18 months after the date of enactment of this Act, the Attorney General shall provide grants to assist State and local law enforcement agencies in—

(1) establishing and improving mortgage fraud task forces; and

(2) improving communications regarding mortgage fraud cases between such agencies and other Federal, State and local law enforcement agencies.

(b) Application- Each State or local law enforcement agency seeking a grant under this section shall submit an application to the Attorney General at such time, in such manner, and containing such information as the Attorney General may require.

(c) Authorization of Appropriations- There are authorized to be appropriated $40,000,000, to implement the provisions of this section.

SEC. 9. ADDITIONAL DOJ FUNDING.

In addition to any other amounts otherwise authorized to be appropriated under this Act, there are authorized to be appropriated to the Attorney General $5,000,000, to increase mortgage fraud investigation efforts undertaken by the Department of Justice.

SEC. 10. ADDITIONAL RIGHTS OF BORROWERS.

(a) Borrowers Rights in Foreclosure Proceedings-

(1) IN GENERAL- Any creditor making a subprime mortgage related loan who has the legal right to foreclosure shall use the judicial foreclosure procedures, or if no such judicial proceeding exists the appropriate administrative proceeding, of the State where the property securing the loan is located if—

(A) the creditor is a party to a home loan contract described in paragraph (3); and

(B) the property to be secured is the principal residence (as determined by the Secretary of Housing and Urban Development) of the borrower.

(2) AFFIRMATIVE DEFENSE- In any foreclosure proceeding described in paragraph (1), the borrower may assert as an affirmative defense against any party to such contract, or any successor or assignee of such party—

(A) that such contract was the result of fraud or deceptive practices and as result of such fraud and deception that the terms of such contract are void; and

(B) any other claim or defense to acceleration and foreclosure, including any claim or defense based on a violation of this Act, though no such claim or defense shall be deemed a compulsory counterclaim.

(3) HOME LOAN CONTRACT- A home loan contract described in paragraph (1) is a contract that—

(A) does not include a fully-disclosed statement by the lender that the lending institution or the authorized representative or agent of such institution has evaluated and affirmed the ability of the individual to repay the loan based upon, at minimum, the maximum monthly payments that could be due during the first 7 years of the loan term, which shall be calculated with reference to the maximum interest rate allowable under the loan being offered based on a fully amortizing repayment schedule, taking into account negative amortization and escrows for taxes and insurance;

(B) does not contain a statement, the format of which shall be determined by the Secretary of Housing and Urban Development, with a plain language summary providing the borrower with a calculation of—

(i) the maximum monthly required minimum payment the borrower could face under the terms of the loan for each of the first 10 years of the loan in order to keep the loan in good standing, or if the borrower is receiving more than 1 loan, the same information for each loan separately and for the total of all of the loans together; and

(ii) how much it would cost the borrower to pay off the loan at the end of each of the first 10 years if the borrower makes the minimum required payments to keep the loan in good standing;

(C) was underwritten based only on the stated income of the individual, without third-party verification of all sources of income and assets of the individual, including by an examination of the individual's tax returns, payroll receipts, bank records, or other reliable documentation; or

(D) includes loan prepayment penalties that are applicable for prepayments made beyond 2 years after the loan origination date, beyond the initial interest rate adjustment period stated in such contract, or whichever is less.

(b) Coordination With Other Law- No provision of this section shall be construed as annulling, altering, affecting, or superseding any Federal law, or the laws of any State, relating to foreclosure proceedings in connection with home loans, except to the extent that those laws are inconsistent with the provisions of this section, and then only to the extent of the inconsistency.

(c) Applicability- This section shall apply to all home loan contracts entered into on, or after the date that is 90 days after the date of the enactment of this Act and to all controversies arising after such date.

(d) Definitions- As used in this section:

(1) HOME LOAN- The term 'home loan' means a loan secured by a mortgage or lien on residential property.

(2) RESIDENTIAL PROPERTY- The term 'residential property' means a 1-4 family, owner-occupied residence, including a 1-family unit in a condominium project, a membership interest and occupancy agreement in a cooperative housing project, and a manufactured home and the lot on which the home is situated.

(3) SUBPRIME MORTGAGE RELATED LOAN-

(A) IN GENERAL- The term 'subprime mortgage related loan' means with respect to a home loan, that the borrower under the loan, or the loan terms, exhibit characteristics that indicate that the loan is subject to a significantly higher risk of default than federally related mortgage loans made to borrowers at prime lending rates.

(B) REGULATIONS- The Secretary of Housing and Urban Development shall prescribe regulations to carry out this paragraph, which shall specify characteristics referred to in subparagraph (A) that indicate a higher risk of default and shall establish criteria based on such characteristics for determining whether a home loan is a subprime loan. Such characteristics shall include—

(i) higher loan fees or penalties;

(ii) higher interest rates;

(iii) higher debt-to-income ratios;

(iv) a history of loan delinquency;

(v) higher loan-to-value ratios;

(vi) lower credit scores or other credit ratings;

(vii) more recent declaration of bankruptcy;

(viii) lack of a credit history;

(ix) no-documentation or low-documentation loan underwriting; and

(x) any other factors that the Secretary considers appropriate.

SEC. 11. REPORT TO CONGRESS.

Not later than 120 days after the date of enactment of this Act, the Comptroller General of the United States shall survey, evaluate, and report to Congress on State mortgage lending practices and regulations related to—

(1) mortgage fraud and deception;

(2) predatory lending practices relating to mortgages; and

(3) foreclosure prevention and homeownership preservation programs offered by each State.

US SENATE BILL 1271

TITLE: A bill to provide for a comprehensive national research effort on the physical and mental health and other readjustment needs of the members of the Armed Forces and veterans who served in Operation Iraqi Freedom and Operation Enduring Freedom and their families.

SPONSOR: Sen Obama, Barack [IL] (introduced 5/2/2007) Cosponsors (4)

RELATED BILLS: H.R.3620

LATEST MAJOR ACTION: 5/2/2007 Referred to Senate committee. Status: Read twice and referred to the Committee on Armed Services.

SUMMARY AS OF:

5/2/2007—Introduced.

Homecoming Enhancement Research and Oversight (HERO) Act - Directs the Secretary of Defense to enter into an agreement with the National Academy of Sciences for a study of the physical and mental health and other readjustment needs of members and former members of the Armed Forces who deployed in Operations Iraqi Freedom or Enduring Freedom, and their families. Requires: (1) reports, from the Academy to the Secretaries of Defense and Veterans Affairs and from the Secretary to Congress, on such study; (2) the public availability of the reports; (3) such Secretaries to develop a joint plan to address report findings; and (4) the public availability of the Secretaries' response.

MAJOR ACTIONS:

¤NONE¤

ALL ACTIONS:

5/2/2007:

Read twice and referred to the Committee on Armed Services.

TITLES(s): (italics indicate a title for a portion of a bill)

¤NONE¤

COSPONSORS(4), ALPHABETICAL [FOLLOWED BY COSPONSORS WITHDRAWN]: (Sort: by date)

Sen Baucus, Max [MT] - 5/10/2007

Sen Casey, Robert P., Jr. [PA] - 6/12/2007

Sen Durbin, Richard [IL] - 5/10/2007

Sen McCaskill, Claire [MO] - 5/2/2007

COMMITTEE(S)

Committee/Subcommittee:

Activity:

Senate Armed Services

Referral, In Committee

RELATED BILL DETAILS: (additional related bills may be indentified in Status)

Bill:

Relationship:

H.R.3620

Related bill identified by CRS

AMENDMENT(S)

¤NONE¤

In the Senate of the United States

May 2, 2007

Mr. OBAMA (for himself and Mrs. MCCASKILL) introduced the following bill; which was read twice and referred to the Committee on Armed Services

A BILL

To provide for a comprehensive national research effort on the physical and mental health and other readjustment needs of the members of the Armed Forces and veterans who served in Operation Iraqi Freedom and Operation Enduring Freedom and their families.

Be it enacted by the Senate and House of Representatives of the United States of America in Congress assembled,

SECTION 1. SHORT TITLE.

This Act may be cited as the 'Homecoming Enhancement Research and Oversight (HERO) Act'.

SEC. 2. STUDY ON PHYSICAL AND MENTAL HEALTH AND OTHER READJUSTMENT NEEDS OF MEMBERS AND FORMER MEMBERS OF THE ARMED FORCES WHO DEPLOYED IN OPERATION IRAQI FREEDOM AND OPERATION ENDURING FREEDOM AND THEIR FAMILIES.

(a) Findings- Congress makes the following findings:

(1) The order on April 11, 2007 to extend the tour of duty for members of the Army on active duty in Operation Iraqi Freedom and Operation Enduring Freedom to 15 months is placing additional strains on the wellness of members of the Armed Forces and their families back home.

(2) 20,000 United States troops have been deployed at least 5 times since the war effort began. 70,000 have been deployed at 3 least times.

(3) Sixty percent of deployed members of the Armed Forces have family responsibilities.

(4) More than 500,000 children have one or more parents deployed in support of the Global War on Terror (GWOT) at any given time.

(5) It is estimated that more than 2,700 children in the United States have lost a parent in Operation Iraqi Freedom or Operation Enduring Freedom.

(6) Women now comprise 16 percent of the all voluntary military force, yet there is a lack of research on the psychological needs and readjustment concerns of female military personnel.

(7) Members of the Armed Forces who have screened positive for a mental health disorder were twice as likely as members who have screened negative for a mental health disorder to report concern about possible stigmatization and other barriers to accessing care. Among members of the Armed Forces who screened positive for a mental health disorder, only between 23 percent and 40 percent have sought care.

(8) As many as one quarter of all members of the Armed Forces returning from a combat zone have less visible psychological injuries.

(9) On average, more than 20 percent of wounded members of the Armed Forces have a Traumatic Brain Injury (TBI).

(10) More than a decade passed between the end of the conflict in Vietnam and the publication by the Federal Government of its landmark study on the readjustment needs of veterans of that conflict. The impacts of the wars in Iraq and Afghanistan on members of the Armed Forces, former members of the Armed Forces, and their families must be rigorously researched and addressed without a wait of 10 years.

(b) Study Required- The Secretary of Defense shall, in consultation with the Secretary of Veterans Affairs, enter into an agreement with the National Academy of Sciences for a study on the physical and mental health and other readjustment needs of members and former members of the Armed Forces who deployed in Operation Iraqi Freedom or Operation Enduring Freedom and their families as a result of such deployment.

(c) Phases- The study required under subsection (b) shall consist of two phases:

(1) A preliminary phase, to be completed not later than 180 days after the date of the enactment of this Act—

(A) to identify preliminary findings on the physical and mental health and other readjustment needs described in subsection (b) and on gaps in care for the members, former members, and families described in that subsection; and

(B) to determine the parameters of the second phase of the study under paragraph (2).

(2) A second phase, to be completed not later than three years after the date of the enactment of this Act, to carry out a comprehensive assessment, in accordance with the parameters identified under the preliminary report required by paragraph (1), of the physical and mental health and other readjustment needs of members and former members of the Armed Forces who deployed in Operation Iraqi Freedom or Operation Enduring Freedom and their families as a result of such deployment, including, at a minimum—

(A) an assessment of the psychological, social, and economic impacts of such deployment on such members and former members and their families;

(B) an assessment of the particular impacts of multiple deployments in Operation Iraqi Freedom or Operation Enduring Freedom on such members and former members and their families;

(C) an assessment of the full scope of the neurological, psychiatric, and psychological effects of Traumatic Brain Injury on members and former members of the Armed Forces, including the effects of such effects on the family members of such members and former members, and an assessment of the efficacy of current treatment approaches for Traumatic Brain Injury in the United States and the efficacy of screenings and treatment approaches for Traumatic Brain Injury within the Department of Defense and the Department of Veterans Affairs;

(D) an assessment of the effects of undiagnosed injuries such as Post-Traumatic Stress Disorder (PTSD) and Traumatic Brain Injury, and an estimate of the long-term costs associated with such injuries;

(E) an assessment of the particular needs and concerns of female members of the Armed Forces and female veterans;

(F) an assessment of the particular needs and concerns of minority members of the Armed Forces and minority veterans;

(G) an assessment of the particular educational and vocational needs of such members and former members and their families;

(H) the development, based on such assessments, of recommendations for programs, treatments, or policy remedies targeted at preventing, minimizing or addressing the impacts, gaps and needs identified; and

(I) the development, based on such assessments, of recommendations for additional research on such needs.

(d) Populations To Be Studied- The study required under subsection (b) shall consider the readjustment needs of each population of individuals as follows:

(1) Members of the regular components of the Armed Forces who are returning, or have returned, to the United States from deployment in Operation Iraqi Freedom or Operation Enduring Freedom.

(2) Members of the National Guard and Reserve who are returning, or have returned, to the United States from deployment in Operation Iraqi Freedom or Operation Enduring Freedom.

(3) Veterans of Operation Iraqi Freedom or Operation Enduring Freedom.

(4) Family members of the members and veterans described in paragraphs (1) through (3).

(e) Access to Information- The National Academy of Sciences shall have access to such personnel, information, records, and systems of the Department of Defense and the Department of Veterans Affairs as the National Academy of Sciences requires in order to carry out the study required under subsection (b).

(f) Privacy of Information- The National Academy of Sciences shall maintain any personally identifiable information accessed by the Academy in carrying out the study required under subsection (b) in accordance with all applicable laws, protections, and best practices regarding the privacy of such information, and may not permit access to such information by any persons or entities not engaged in work under the study.

(g) Reports-

(1) REPORTS BY NATIONAL ACADEMY OF SCIENCES- Upon the completion of each phase of the study required under subsection (b), the National Academy of Sciences shall submit to the Secretary of Defense and the Secretary of Veterans Affairs a report on such phase of the study.

(2) REPORTS BY SECRETARY OF DEFENSE- The Secretary of Defense shall submit to Congress a comprehensive report on each phase of the study required under

subsection (b) not later than 30 days after the date of the completion of such phase of the study. Each report shall set forth the report of the National Academy of Sciences on the phase of the study concerned under paragraph (1) and include such other information as the Secretary considers appropriate.

(3) PUBLIC AVAILABILITY OF REPORTS- The Secretary of Defense shall make available to the public each report submitted to Congress under paragraph (2), including by posting an electronic copy of such report on the Internet website of the Department of Defense that is available to the public.

(h) DoD and VA Response to NAS Reports-

(1) PRELIMINARY RESPONSE- Not later than 45 days after the receipt of a report under subsection (g)(1) on each phase of the study required under subsection (b), the Secretary of Defense and the Secretary of Veterans Affairs shall jointly develop a preliminary joint Department of Defense-Department of Veterans Affairs plan to address the findings and recommendations of the National Academy of Sciences contained in such report. The preliminary plan shall provide preliminary proposals on the matters set forth in paragraph (3).

(2) FINAL RESPONSE- Not later than 90 days after the receipt of a report under subsection (g)(1) on each phase of the study required under subsection (b), the Secretary of Defense and the Secretary of Veterans Affairs shall jointly develop a final joint Department of Defense-Department of Veterans Affairs plan to address the findings and recommendations of the National Academy of Sciences contained in such report. The final plan shall provide final proposals on the matters set forth in paragraph (3).

(3) COVERED MATTERS- The matters set forth in this paragraph with respect to a phase of the study required under subsection (b) are as follows:

(A) Modifications of policy or practice within the Department of Defense and the Department of Veterans Affairs that are necessary to address gaps in care or services as identified by the National Academy of Sciences under such phase of the study.

(B) Modifications of policy or practice within the Department of Defense and the Department of Veterans Affairs that are necessary to address recommendations made by the National Academy of Sciences under such phase of the study.

(C) An estimate of the costs of implementing the modifications set forth under subparagraphs (A) and (B), set forth by fiscal year for at least the first five fiscal years beginning after the date of the plan concerned.

(4) REPORTS ON RESPONSES- The Secretary of Defense and the Secretary of Veterans Affairs shall jointly submit to Congress a report setting forth each joint plan developed under paragraphs (1) and (2).

(5) PUBLIC AVAILABILITY OF RESPONSES- The Secretary of Defense and the Secretary of Veterans Affairs shall each make available to the public each report submitted to Congress under paragraph (4), including by posting an electronic copy of such report on the Internet website of the Department of Defense or the Department of Veterans Affairs, as applicable, that is available to the public.

(6) GAO AUDIT- Not later than 45 days after the submittal to Congress of the report under paragraph (4) on the final joint Department of Defense-Department of Veterans

Affairs plan under paragraph (2), the Comptroller General of the United States shall submit to Congress a report assessing the contents of such report under paragraph (4). The report of the Comptroller General under this paragraph shall include—

(A) an assessment of the adequacy and sufficiency of the final joint Department of Defense-Department of Veterans Affairs plan in addressing the findings and recommendations of the National Academy of Sciences as a result of the study required under subsection (b);

(B) an assessment of the feasibility and advisability of the modifications of policy and practice proposed in the final joint Department of Defense-Department of Veterans Affairs plan;

(C) an assessment of the sufficiency and accuracy of the cost estimates in the final joint Department of Defense-Department of Veterans Affairs plan; and

(D) the comments, if any, of the National Academy of Sciences on the final joint Department of Defense-Department of Veterans Affairs plan.

(i) Authorization of Appropriations- There is hereby authorized to be appropriated to the Department of Defense such sums as may be necessary to carry out this section.

US SENATE BILL 1306

TITLE: A bill to direct the Consumer Product Safety Commission to classify certain children's products containing lead to be banned hazardous substances.

SPONSOR: Sen Obama, Barack [IL] (introduced 5/3/2007) Cosponsors (9)

LATEST MAJOR ACTION: 5/3/2007 Referred to Senate committee. Status: Read twice and referred to the Committee on Commerce, Science, and Transportation.

SUMMARY AS OF:

5/3/2007—Introduced.

Lead Free Toys Act of 2007 - Directs the Consumer Product Safety Commission to prescribe regulations classifying any children's product containing lead to be a banned hazardous substance within the meaning of the Hazardous Substances Act.

Requires the Commission, if it determines that it is not feasible for certain electronic devices to comply with such regulations as of the effective date, to: (1) issue standards to reduce the exposure of and accessibility to lead in such electronic devices; and (2) establish a schedule by which such electronic devices must be in full compliance with the regulations.

MAJOR ACTIONS:

¤NONE¤

ALL ACTIONS:

5/3/2007:

Read twice and referred to the Committee on Commerce, Science, and Transportation.

TITLES(S): (italics indicate a title for a portion of a bill)

¤NONE¤

COSPONSORS(9), ALPHABETICAL [FOLLOWED BY COSPONSORS WITHDRAWN]: (Sort: by date)

Sen Brown, Sherrod [OH] - 9/5/2007

Sen Clinton, Hillary Rodham [NY] - 5/3/2007

Sen Durbin, Richard [IL] - 5/3/2007

Sen Kerry, John F. [MA] - 9/4/2007

Sen Klobuchar, Amy [MN] - 7/23/2007

Sen Sanders, Bernard [VT] - 9/4/2007

Sen Schumer, Charles E. [NY] - 9/4/2007

Sen Stabenow, Debbie [MI] - 9/4/2007

Sen Whitehouse, Sheldon [RI] - 9/5/2007

COMMITTEE(S)

Committee/Subcommittee:

Activity:

Senate Commerce, Science, and Transportation

Referral, In Committee

RELATED BILL DETAILS:

¤NONE¤

AMENDMENT(S)

ᵤNONEᵤ

IN THE SENATE OF THE UNITED STATES

May 3, 2007

Mr. OBAMA (for himself, Mr. DURBIN, and Mrs. CLINTON) introduced the following bill; which was read twice and referred to the Committee on Commerce, Science, and Transportation

A BILL

To direct the Consumer Product Safety Commission to classify certain children's products containing lead to be banned hazardous substances.

Be it enacted by the Senate and House of Representatives of the United States of America in Congress assembled,

SECTION 1. SHORT TITLE.

This Act may be cited as the 'Lead Free Toys Act of 2007'.

SEC. 2. BAN ON CHILDREN'S PRODUCTS CONTAINING LEAD.

(a) Banned Hazardous Substances- Not later than 180 days after the date of enactment of this Act, the Consumer Product Safety Commission (referred to in this Act as the 'Commission') shall prescribe regulations classifying any children's product containing lead to be a banned hazardous substance within the meaning of section 2(q)(1) of the Hazardous Substances Act (15 U.S.C. 1261(q)(1)).

(b) Definition of Children's Product Containing Lead- As used in subsection (a), the term 'children's product containing lead' means any consumer product marketed for use by children under age 6, or whose substantial use by children under age 6 is foreseeable, and containing more than trace amounts of lead, as determined by the Commission and prescribed in the regulations required by subsection (a).

(c) Certain Electronic Devices- If, in prescribing the regulations required by subsection (a), the Commission determines that it is not feasible for certain electronic devices to comply with such regulations at the time the regulations shall take effect, the Commission shall, by regulation—

(1) issue standards to reduce the exposure of and accessibility to lead in such electronic devices; and

(2) establish a schedule by which such electronic devices shall be in full compliance with the regulations prescribed under subsection (a).

US SENATE BILL 1324

TITLE: A bill to amend the Clean Air Act to reduce greenhouse gas emissions from transportation fuel sold in the United States.

SPONSOR: Sen Obama, Barack [IL] (introduced 5/7/2007) Cosponsors (2)

LATEST MAJOR ACTION: 5/7/2007 Referred to Senate committee. Status: Read twice and referred to the Committee on Environment and Public Works.

SUMMARY AS OF:

5/7/2007—Introduced.

National Low-Carbon Fuel Standard Act of 2007 - Amends the Clean Air Act to revise the renewable fuel standard for FY2009-FY2012. Directs the Administrator of the Environmental Protection Agency (EPA) to: (1) establish a fuel emission baseline; (2) identify qualifying low-carbon transportation fuels; (3) establish a low-carbon fuel certification and marketing process; and (4) require each obligated party to reduce the average lifecycle greenhouse gas (GHG) emissions per unit of energy of the aggregate quantity of fuels introduced into commerce to specified levels by not later than January 1, 2010, through the use of low-carbon fuels and improvements in the production of conventional fuels.

Requires the average lifecycle GHG emissions of the aggregate quantity for 2012 to be at least 3% below the 2007 average should emission limitation regulations not be promulgated.

Authorizes an obligated party to apply to the Administrator to receive a temporary suspension of the requirement to comply with such regulations if events outside of the control of the party could lead or have led to disruptions in the transportation fuel supply.

Permits obligated parties to receive credits for achieving greater reductions in lifecycle GHG emission of the fuel produced, distributed, or imported than are required.

Requires the Administrator to ensure that fuel sold or introduced into commerce in the United States (except in noncontiguous states or territories) contains, on an annual average basis, at least the specified volume of ultra-low carbon fuel for 2012-2025. Prohibits such regulations from restricting geographic areas in which low-carbon transportation fuel and ultra-low carbon fuel may be used or from imposing any per-gallon obligation for the use of those fuels. Sets forth a minimum applicable volume for 2026 and thereafter.

Requires the Administrator of the Energy Information Administration to provide to the EPA Administrator an estimate of the volumes of conventional fuels projected to be sold or introduced into commerce. Requires the EPA Administrator to determine the fuel obligations based on such an estimate.

Requires regulations concerning ultra-low carbon fuel to provide for the generation of specified credits by obligated parties.

Authorizes the EPA Administrator, on the receipt of a petition of one or more states, to waive ultra-low carbon regulations by reducing the national quantity of Category I or Category II ultra-low carbon fuel in the conventional transportation fuel pool if it is determined that: (1) implementation of the regulations would severely harm the economy or environment; or (2) there is an inadequate domestic supply of such fuel.

Considers 1 gallon of cellulosic biomass ethanol or waste derived ethanol to be the equivalent of 2.5 gallons of renewable fuel through 2017 (currently there is no time limit).

Requires the Administrator to establish: (1) a carbon intensity number and a green index number as part of the renewable identification number program; and (2) a set of standards to minimize the negative environmental impacts of an increase in the volume of fuels required by such Act and to ensure long term resource sustainability from the sourcing and production of low-carbon fuels.

MAJOR ACTIONS:

¤NONE¤

ALL ACTIONS:

5/7/2007:

Sponsor introductory remarks on measure. (CR S5660)

5/7/2007:

Read twice and referred to the Committee on Environment and Public Works.

TITLES(s): (italics indicate a title for a portion of a bill)

¤NONE¤

COSPONSORS(2), ALPHABETICAL [FOLLOWED BY COSPONSORS WITH-DRAWN]: (Sort: by date)

Sen Durbin, Richard [IL] - 5/10/2007

Sen Harkin, Tom [IA] - 5/7/2007

COMMITTEE(s)

Committee/Subcommittee:

Activity:

Senate Environment and Public Works

Referral, In Committee

RELATED BILL DETAILS:

¤NONE¤

AMENDMENT(s)

¤NONE¤

IN THE SENATE OF THE UNITED STATES

May 7, 2007

Mr. REID (for Mr. OBAMA (for himself and Mr. HARKIN)) introduced the following bill; which was read twice and referred to the Committee on Environment and Public Works

A BILL

To amend the Clean Air Act to reduce greenhouse gas emissions from transportation fuel sold in the United States.

Be it enacted by the Senate and House of Representatives of the United States of America in Congress assembled,

SECTION 1. SHORT TITLE.

This Act may be cited as the 'National Low-Carbon Fuel Standard Act of 2007'.

SEC. 2. FINDINGS.

Congress finds that—

(1) the dependence of the United States on imported oil imposes tremendous burdens on the economy, foreign policy, and military of the United States;

(2) according to the Energy Information Administration, 60 percent of the crude oil and petroleum products consumed in the United States are imported;

(3) at a cost of approximately $75 per barrel of oil, people in the United States remit more than $600,000 per minute to other countries for crude oil and petroleum imports;

(4) a significant percentage of those imports originate in countries controlled by regimes that are unstable or openly hostile to the interests of the United States;

(5) dependence on oil production from those countries contributes to the volatility of domestic and global markets and corresponding increase in oil prices paid by consumers in the United States (commonly known as a 'risk premium');

(6) the Energy Information Administration projects that the total petroleum demand in the United States will increase by 23 percent between 2006 and 2026, while domestic crude oil production is expected to decrease by 11 percent, resulting in an anticipated 28-percent increase in petroleum imports;

(7) absent significant action, the United States will become more vulnerable to oil price increases and more dependent on foreign oil;

(8) 2/3 of all domestic oil use occurs in the transportation sector, which is 97 percent reliant on petroleum-based fuels;

(9) passenger vehicles, including light trucks under 10,000 pounds gross vehicle weight, represent more than 60 percent of the oil used in the transportation sector;

(10) the oil used in the transportation sector accounts for approximately 1/3 of the emissions in the United States of the greenhouse gases that cause global warming;

(11) to avoid catastrophic global warming, the United States should take decisive action, in conjunction with other countries, to reduce greenhouse gas emissions by 60 to 80 percent from 1990 levels by 2050;

(12) transitioning the transportation sector in the United States to a more efficient use of low-carbon petroleum alternatives is essential both to increasing domestic energy security and reducing global warming pollution, but that transition must be accomplished while avoiding adverse impacts on the environment; and

(13) it is urgent, essential, and feasible to reduce emissions of greenhouse gases, enhance national security by reducing dependence on oil, and promote economic well-being without sacrificing land, water, and air quality by enacting energy policies that motivate environmental performance.

SEC. 3. RENEWABLE FUEL STANDARD.

The table contained in section 211(o)(2)(B)(i) of the Clean Air Act (42 U.S.C. 7545(o)(2)(B)(i)) is amended—

(1) in the row expressing applicable volume of renewable fuel (in billions of gallons) for calendar year 2009, by striking '6.1' and inserting '12.0';

(2) in the row expressing applicable volume of renewable fuel (in billions of gallons) for calendar year 2010, by striking '6.8' and inserting '13.0';

(3) in the row expressing applicable volume of renewable fuel (in billions of gallons) for calendar year 2011, by striking '7.4' and inserting '14.0'; and

(4) in the row expressing applicable volume of renewable fuel (in billions of gallons) for calendar year 2012, by striking '7.5' and inserting '15.0'.

SEC. 4. NATIONAL LOW-CARBON FUEL STANDARD.

(a) Definitions- Section 241 of the Clean Air Act (42 U.S.C. 7581) is amended—

(1) by striking 'For purposes of this part—' and inserting 'In this part:';

(2) by redesignating paragraphs (1), (2), (3), (4), (5), (6), and (7) as paragraphs (12), (2), (10), (1), (4), (5), and (3), respectively, and moving those paragraphs so as to appear in numerical order;

(3) by inserting after paragraph (5) (as redesignated by paragraph (2)) the following:

'(6) FUEL EMISSION BASELINE- The term 'fuel emission baseline' means the average lifecycle greenhouse gas emissions per unit of energy of the average of conventional transportation fuels in commerce in the United States during the period of calendar years 2005 through 2007.

'(7) GREENHOUSE GAS- The term 'greenhouse gas' means any of—

'(A) carbon dioxide;

'(B) methane;

'(C) nitrous oxide;

'(D) hydrofluorocarbons;

'(E) perfluorocarbons; and

'(F) sulfur hexafluoride.

'(8) LIFECYCLE GREENHOUSE GAS EMISSIONS- The term 'lifecycle greenhouse gas emissions' means, with respect to a fuel, the aggregate quantity of greenhouse gases emitted during production, feedstock extraction, distribution, and use of the fuel, as determined by the Administrator.

'(9) LOW-CARBON FUEL-

'(A) IN GENERAL- The term 'low-carbon fuel' means fuel produced, to the maximum extent practicable, in the United States—

'(i) that meets the requirements of an appropriate American Society for Testing and Materials standard; and

'(ii) the lifecycle greenhouse gas emissions of which are lower than the fuel emission baseline, as determined by the Administrator.

'(B) EXCLUSIONS- The term 'low-carbon fuel' does not include fuel produced from biomass derived from—

'(i) designated national interest land (such as land included in a national wildlife refuge, national park, national monument, national forest, or national grassland); or

'(ii) any—

'(I) old-growth forest;

'(II) roadless area within a national forest;

'(III) wilderness study area;

'(IV) protected native grassland; or

'(V) lawfully designated intact, rare, threatened, or endangered ecosystem.'; and

(4) by inserting after paragraph (10) (as redesignated by paragraph (2)) the following:

'(11) OBLIGATED PARTY-

'(A) IN GENERAL- The term 'obligated party' means an obligated party as described in section 80.1106 of title 40, Code of Federal Regulations (or a successor regulation).

'(B) RELATED TERM- The term 'any and all of the products', when used with respect to an obligated party, means diesel and aviation fuel to be included in the volume used to calculate the requirements applicable to the obligated party under section 250.'.

(b) National Low-Carbon Fuel Standard- Part C of title II of the Clean Air Act (42 U.S.C. 7581 et seq.) is amended—

(1) by redesignating section 250 (42 U.S.C. 7590) as section 251; and

(2) by inserting after section 249 (42 U.S.C. 7589) the following:

'SEC. 250. NATIONAL LOW-CARBON FUEL STANDARD.

'(a) In General- Not later than January 1, 2009, the Administrator shall, by regulation—

'(1) establish a fuel emission baseline based on the average lifecycle greenhouse gas emissions per unit of energy of the average of conventional transportation fuels in commerce in the United States during the period of calendar years 2005 through 2007;

'(2) identify qualifying low-carbon transportation fuels based on—

'(A) whether the lifecycle greenhouse gas emissions of a fuel are lower, per unit of energy delivered by use of a specific quantity of the fuel, than the fuel emission baseline, including the percentage greenhouse gas emission reduction provided by the fuel to the fuel emission baseline;

'(B) whether a fuel—

'(i) achieves a substantial reduction in petroleum content over the lifecycle of the fuel; and

'(ii) otherwise contributes to the energy security of the United States; and

'(C) with respect to calculation of the lifecycle greenhouse gas emissions of the fuels used in vehicles that run on electricity or a hydrogen fuel, the quantity of energy delivered by use of the fuel, which shall be determined by calculating the product obtained by multiplying—

'(i) a unit of energy delivered by use of the electricity or hydrogen fuel; and

'(ii) an adjustment factor determined by the Administrator to reflect the substantial lifecycle greenhouse gas benefits of using the electricity or hydrogen fuel, on a per-mile basis, resulting from reasonably anticipated energy efficiency of an average—

'(I) battery electric vehicle;

'(II) plug-in hybrid electric vehicle; or

'(III) hydrogen fuel cell vehicle; and

'(3) establish a low-carbon fuel certification and marketing process—

'(A) to certify fuels that qualify as low-carbon fuels under this section;

'(B) to make those certifications available to consumers; and

'(C) to label and market low-carbon fuels.

'(b) Environmental Sustainability Standards- Not later than January 1, 2012, the Administrator shall also identify qualifying low-carbon transportation fuels based on environmental sustainability standards established under section 211(t)(2)(B).

'(c) Requirements Applicable to Obligated Parties-

'(1) REQUIREMENTS-

'(A) CALENDAR YEARS 2010 THROUGH 2024- Not later than January 1, 2010, the Administrator shall, by regulation, require each obligated party to reduce, through the use of low-carbon fuels and improvements in the production of conventional fuels, the average lifecycle greenhouse gas emissions per unit of energy of the aggregate quantity of fuels introduced into commerce by the obligated party to a level that is, as determined by the Administrator, to the maximum extent practicable—

'(i) by calendar year 2011, substantially equivalent to the fuel emission baseline;

'(ii) by calendar year 2015, substantially equivalent to at least 5 percent below the fuel emission baseline; and

'(iii) by calendar year 2020, substantially equivalent to at least 10 percent below the fuel emission baseline.

'(B) CALENDAR YEAR 2025 AND THEREAFTER- For calendar year 2025, and by not later than each fifth calendar year thereafter, the Administrator shall, by regulation, require each obligated party to reduce the average lifecycle greenhouse gas emissions per unit of energy of the aggregate quantity of fuels introduced into commerce by the obligated party to a level that is, as determined by the Administrator, at least 13 percent below the fuel emission baseline (with respect to calendar year 2025), and at least 2 percent below the most recent percentage reduction (with respect to each fifth calendar year thereafter), unless the Administrator, in coordination with the Secretary of Agriculture and the Secretary of Energy, establishes an alternative required percentage reduction based on—

'(i) a review of the implementation of this paragraph during the period of calendar years 2010 through 2020;

'(ii) the expected annual rate of future production of low-carbon fuel, and Category I ultra-low carbon fuel and Category II ultra-low carbon fuel (as those terms are defined in subsection (p)); and

'(iii) the practicability of complying with environmental sustainability standards referred to in subsection (b).

'(2) FAILURE TO PROMULGATE REGULATIONS- If the Administrator does not promulgate regulations in accordance with this subsection, the average lifecycle greenhouse gas emissions of the aggregate quantity of fuel introduced by an obligated party for calendar year 2012 shall be at least 3 percent below the average lifecycle greenhouse gas emissions of gasoline in commerce in the United States during calendar year 2007.

'(3) TEMPORARY SUSPENSION- An obligated party may apply to the Administrator to receive a temporary suspension of the requirement to comply with this subsection if the obligated party demonstrates to the satisfaction of the Administrator that events outside of the control of the obligated party could lead or have led to supply disruptions in the transportation fuel supply of the United States.

'(4) ENFORCEMENT; PENALTIES- In carrying out this subsection, the Administrator—

'(A) shall enforce this subsection in accordance with the authority of the Administrator to enforce this Act; and

'(B) may commence a civil action and assess and collect penalties in accordance with the amounts and under the authority described in section 205.

'(d) Credits-

'(1) IN GENERAL- The regulations promulgated to carry out this section shall permit obligated parties to receive credits for achieving, during a calendar year, greater reductions in lifecycle greenhouse gas emissions of the fuel produced, distributed, or imported by the obligated party than are required under subsection (c).

'(2) METHOD OF CALCULATION- The number of credits received by an obligated party described in paragraph (1) for a calendar year shall be calculated by multiplying—

'(A) the aggregate quantity of fuel produced, distributed, or imported by the obligated party in the calendar year; and

'(B) the difference between—

'(i) the lifecycle greenhouse gas emissions of that quantity of fuel; and

'(ii) the maximum lifecycle greenhouse gas emissions of that quantity of fuel permitted for the calendar year under subsection (c).'.

SEC. 5. ULTRA-LOW CARBON FUEL STANDARD.

(a) In General- Section 211 of the Clean Air Act (42 U.S.C. 7545) is amended—

(1) by redesignating the first subsection (r) (relating to fuel and fuel additive importers and importation) as subsection (v) and moving that subsection so as to appear at the end of the section; and

(2) by inserting after subsection (o) the following:

'(p) Ultra-Low Carbon Fuel Standard-

'(1) DEFINITIONS- In this subsection and subsection (t):

'(A) CATEGORY I ULTRA-LOW CARBON FUELS-

'(i) IN GENERAL- The term 'Category I ultra-low carbon fuel' means fuel produced in the United States—

'(I) that meets the requirements of an appropriate American Society for Testing and Materials standard; and

'(II) the lifecycle greenhouse gas emissions of which are at least 50 percent lower than the average lifecycle greenhouse gas emissions of conventional transportation fuel, as determined by the Administrator.

'(ii) EXCLUSIONS- The term 'Category I ultra-low carbon fuel' does not include fuel produced from biomass derived from—

'(I) designated national interest land (such as land included in a national wildlife refuge, national park, national monument, national forest, or national grassland); or

'(II) any—

'(aa) old-growth forest;

'(bb) roadless area within a national forest;

'(cc) wilderness study area;

'(dd) protected native grassland; or

'(ee) lawfully-designated intact, rare, threatened, or endangered ecosystem.

'(B) CATEGORY II ULTRA-LOW CARBON FUEL-

'(i) IN GENERAL- The term 'Category II ultra-low carbon fuel' means any fuel produced in the United States—

'(I) that meets the requirements of an appropriate American Society for Testing and Materials standard; and

'(II) the average lifecycle greenhouse gas emissions of which are at least 75 percent lower than the average lifecycle greenhouse gas emissions of conventional transportation fuel, as determined by the Administrator.

'(ii) EXCLUSIONS- The term 'Category II ultra-low carbon fuel' does not include fuel produced from biomass derived from—

'(I) designated national interest land (such as land included in a national wildlife refuge, national park, national monument, national forest, or national grassland); or

'(II) any—

'(aa) old-growth forest;

'(bb) roadless area within a national forest;

'(cc) wilderness study area;

'(dd) protected native grassland; or

'(ee) lawfully designated intact, rare, threatened, or endangered ecosystem.

'(C) CONVENTIONAL TRANSPORTATION FUEL- The term 'conventional transportation fuel' means any fossil-fuel based transportation fuel used in the United States as of the date of enactment of this subsection.

'(D) LOW-CARBON FUEL- The term 'low-carbon fuel' has the meaning given the term in section 241.

'(2) ULTRA-LOW CARBON FUEL-

'(A) REGULATIONS-

'(i) IN GENERAL- Not later than 3 years after the date of enactment of this subsection, the Administrator shall promulgate regulations to ensure that fuel sold or introduced into commerce in the United States (except in noncontiguous States or territories), on an annual average basis, contains at least the applicable volume of ultra-low carbon fuel determined in accordance with subparagraph (B).

'(ii) PROVISIONS OF REGULATIONS- Regardless of the date of promulgation, the regulations promulgated under clause (i)—

'(I) shall contain compliance provisions applicable to obligated parties, as appropriate, to ensure that the requirements of this paragraph are met; but

'(II) shall not—

'(aa) restrict geographic areas in which low-carbon transportation fuel and ultra-low carbon fuel may be used; or

'(bb) impose any per-gallon obligation for the use of those fuels.

'(B) APPLICABLE VOLUME-

'(i) CALENDAR YEARS 2012 THROUGH 2025- For the purpose of subparagraph (A), the applicable volume of Category I ultra-low carbon fuel and Category II ultra-low carbon fuel for any of calendar years 2012 through 2025 shall be determined in accordance with the following table:

Calendar Year	Total applicable volume of Category I ultra-low carbon fuel (billions of gallons)	Total applicable volume of Category II ultra-low carbon fuel (billions of gallons)
2012	0.5	0.25
2014	1.5	0.75
2016	3.0	1.5
2018	5.0	2.5
2020	8.0	4.0
2022	11.0	6.0
2025	13.0	8.0

'(ii) CALENDAR YEAR 2026 AND THEREAFTER- Subject to clause (iii), the applicable volume for calendar year 2026 and each calendar year thereafter shall be determined by the Administrator, in coordination with the Secretary of Agriculture and the Secretary of Energy, based on a review of the implementation of the program under this subsection during the period of calendar years 2012 through 2025, including a review of—

'(I) the impact of the use of Category I ultra-low carbon fuel and Category II ultra-low carbon fuel on—

'(aa) environmental sustainability standards established under subsection (t)(2)(B);

'(bb) energy security; and

'(cc) job creation; and

'(II) the expected annual rate of future production of those fuels for use as blending components or replacements for a certain quantity of conventional fuel in the United States.

'(iii) MINIMUM APPLICABLE VOLUME- For the purpose of subparagraph (A), the applicable volume for calendar year 2026 and each calendar year thereafter shall be equal to the product obtained by multiplying—

'(I) the number of gallons of conventional transportation fuel that the Administrator estimates will be sold or introduced into commerce during the calendar year; and

'(II) the ratio that—

'(aa) for the applicable volume of Category I ultra-low carbon fuel, 13,000,000,000 gallons of that fuel bears to the total number of gallons of conventional transportation fuel sold or introduced into commerce in the United States in calendar year 2025; and

'(bb) for the applicable volume of Category II ultra-low carbon fuel, 8,000,000,000 gallons of that fuel bears to the total number of gallons of conventional transportation fuel sold or introduced into commerce in the United States in calendar year 2025.

'(3) APPLICABLE PERCENTAGES-

'(A) PROVISION OF ESTIMATE OF VOLUMES OF CONVENTIONAL FU-ELS SALES- Not later than October 31 of each of calendar years 2011 through 2025, the Administrator of the Energy Information Administration shall provide to the Administrator an estimate, with respect to the following calendar year, of the volumes of conventional fuels projected to be sold or introduced into commerce in the United States.

'(B) DETERMINATION OF APPLICABLE PERCENTAGES-

'(i) IN GENERAL- Not later than November 30 of each of calendar years 2012 through 2025, based on the estimate provided under subparagraph (A), the Administrator shall determine and publish in the Federal Register, with respect to the following calendar year, the fuel obligations that would meet the requirements of paragraph (2).

'(ii) REQUIRED ELEMENTS- The fuel obligations determined for a calendar year under clause (i) shall—

'(I) subject to subparagraph (C), be applicable to obligated parties, as appropriate; and

'(II) be expressed in terms of a volume percentage of conventional fuels sold or introduced into commerce in the United States.

'(C) ADJUSTMENTS- In determining the applicable percentage for a calendar year, the Administrator shall make adjustments to prevent the imposition of redundant obligations on any obligated party.

'(4) CREDIT PROGRAM-

'(A) IN GENERAL- The regulations promulgated pursuant to paragraph (2)(A) shall provide for the generation of an appropriate quantity of credits by obligated parties that includes a quantity of Category I ultra-low carbon fuel or Category II ultra-low carbon fuel that is greater than the applicable quantity required under paragraph (2).

'(B) USE OF CREDITS- A person that generates a credit under subparagraph (A) may use the credit, or transfer all or a portion of the credit to another person, for the purpose of complying with regulations promulgated pursuant to paragraph (2)(A).

'(C) DURATION OF CREDITS- A credit generated under this paragraph shall be valid—

'(i) during the calendar year in which the credit was generated; and

'(ii) for the 2-year period following that calendar year.

'(D) INABILITY TO GENERATE OR PURCHASE SUFFICIENT CREDITS- The regulations promulgated pursuant to paragraph (2)(A) shall include provisions allowing any person that is unable to generate or purchase sufficient credits under subparagraph (A) to meet the requirements of paragraph (2) by carrying forward a credit generated during a previous year on the condition that the person, during the calendar year following the year in which the ultra-low carbon fuel deficit is created—

'(i) achieves compliance with the fuel requirements under paragraph (2); and '(ii) generates or purchases additional credits under subparagraph (A) to offset the deficit of the previous year.

'(5) WAIVERS-

'(A) IN GENERAL- The Administrator, in consultation with the Secretary of Agriculture and the Secretary of Energy, may waive the requirements of paragraph (2), in whole or in part, on receipt of a petition of 1 or more States by reducing the national quantity of Category I ultra-low carbon fuel or Category II ultra-low carbon fuel in the conventional transportation fuel pool required under paragraph (2) based on a determination by the Administrator, after public notice and opportunity for comment, that—

'(i) implementation of the requirement would severely harm the economy or environment of a State, a region, or the United States; or

'(ii) there is an inadequate domestic supply of the applicable ultra-low carbon fuel.

'(B) PETITIONS FOR WAIVERS- Not later than 90 days after the date on which the Administrator receives a petition under subparagraph (A), the Administrator, in consultation with the Secretary of Agriculture and the Secretary of Energy, shall approve or disapprove the petition.

'(C) TERMINATION OF WAIVERS-

'(i) IN GENERAL- Except as provided in clause (ii), a waiver under subparagraph (A) shall terminate on the date that is 1 year after the date on which the waiver is provided.

'(ii) EXCEPTION- The Administrator, in consultation with the Secretary of Agriculture and the Secretary of Energy, may extend a waiver under subparagraph (A), as the Administrator determines to be appropriate.'.

(b) Credit for Cellulosic Ethanol- Section 211(o)(4) of the Clean Air Act (42 U.S.C. 7545(o)(4)) is amended by inserting 'through calendar year 2017,' before '1 gallon'.

(c) Performance Standards- Section 211 of the Clean Air Act (42 U.S.C. 7545) is amended by inserting after subsection (s) the following:

'(t) Performance Standards-

'(1) INTENSITY AND INDEX NUMBERS- Not later than 2 years after the date of enactment of this subsection, the Administrator shall establish, for fuels blended with low-carbon fuel, and Category I ultra-low carbon fuel and Category II ultra-low carbon fuel, as part of the renewable identification number program of the Environmental Protection Agency—

'(A) a carbon intensity number measured in the quantity of lifecycle greenhouse gas emissions per unit of energy provided by use of the fuel; and

'(B) a green index number representing the percentage reduction of greenhouse gas emissions achieved by the fuel as compared to the fuel emission baseline (as defined in section 241).

'(2) ENVIRONMENTAL SUSTAINABILITY STUDY-

'(A) IN GENERAL- Not later than 3 years after the date of enactment of this subsection, the Administrator, in conjunction with the Secretary of Agriculture and the Secretary of Energy, and based on recommendations issued by the National Academy of Sciences, the Food and Agricultural Policy Research Institute, and not more than 2 other appropriate independent research institutes, as determined by the Administrator, shall establish a methodology to assess and quantify environmental changes associated with an increase in the volume of fuels required by this section, as compared with the effects of an increase in conventional transportation fuels otherwise displaced by this section, as applicable, for the purpose of negating overall adverse environmental impacts, particularly with respect to the effects on or changes in—

'(i) land, air, and water quality, and quality of other resources, including changes resulting from production, handling, and transportation of fuel (and associated effects on public health and safety);

'(ii) land use patterns;

'(iii) the rate of deforestation, in the United States and globally;

'(iv) areas containing significant concentrations of biodiversity values (including endemism, endangered species, high species richness, and refugia), including habitats in which any alteration of the habitat would render the habitat unable to support most characteristic native species and ecological processes;

'(v) land enrolled in the conservation reserve program established under subchapter B of chapter 1 of subtitle D of title XII of the Food Security Act of 1985 (16 U.S.C. 3831 et seq.) or the wetlands reserve program established under subchapter C of chapter 1 of subtitle D of title XII of the Food Security Act of 1985 (16 U.S.C. 3837 et seq.);

'(vi) the long-term capacity of the United States to produce biomass feedstocks;

'(vii) the impact on areas at risk of wildfire, including the vicinity of buildings and other areas regularly occupied by people, or of infrastructure;

'(viii) the effects on materials produced, acquired, transported, or processed that would require an exemption from otherwise applicable Federal law (including regulations);

'(ix) the conversion of nonrenewable biomass into biofuel;

'(x) the conversion of biowaste and other wastes into fuels (as compared with use of those wastes for other beneficial purposes (such as recycling postconsumer waste paper), and any potential for the generation of toxic byproducts resulting from that conversion (such as painted, treated, or pressurized wood, or wood contaminated with plastic or metals);

'(xi) designated national interest land (including land that is within the National Wildlife Refuge System, the National Park System, a National Monument, the National Wilderness Preservation System, the National Landscape Conservation System, or the National Forest System, or that is otherwise under the administrative jurisdiction of the Secretary of the Interior or Secretary of Agriculture or protected by Federal law); and

'(xii) such other matters or activities as are identified by the Administrator.

'(B) ENVIRONMENTAL SUSTAINABILITY STANDARDS- Not later than January 1, 2012, the Administrator, in conjunction with the Secretary of Agriculture and the Secretary of Energy, shall, based on the methodology established under subparagraph (A), promulgate regulations to establish a set of standards to minimize, to the maximum extent practicable, the negative environmental impacts and ensure long term resource sustainability from the sourcing and production of low-carbon fuels.

'(u) State Authority- If the Administrator determines that a State law (including a regulation) provides for equivalent or greater greenhouse gas emission reductions than any provision in section 250 or subsection (p) or (t) of this section, the State law shall apply in the State in lieu of the provision.'.

(d) Penalties and Enforcement- Section 211(d) of the Clean Air Act (42 U.S.C. 7545(d)) is amended—

(1) in paragraph (1), by striking 'or (o)' each place it appears and inserting '(o), or (p)'; and

(2) in paragraph (2), by striking 'and (o)' each place it appears and inserting '(o), and (p)'.

(e) Technical Amendments- Section 211 of the Clean Air Act (42 U.S.C. 7545) is amended—

(1) in subsection (i)(4), by striking 'section 324' each place it appears and inserting 'section 325';

(2) in subsection (k)(10), by indenting subparagraphs (E) and (F) appropriately;

(3) in subsection (n), by striking 'section 219(2)' and inserting 'section 216(2)'; and

(4) in subsection (s)(1), by striking 'this subtitle' and inserting 'this part'.

US SENATE BILL 1389

TITLE: A bill to authorize the National Science Foundation to establish a Climate Change Education Program.

SPONSOR: Sen Obama, Barack [IL] (introduced 5/14/2007) Cosponsors (3)

RELATED BILLS: H.R.1728

LATEST MAJOR ACTION: 5/14/2007 Referred to Senate committee. Status: Read twice and referred to the Committee on Health, Education, Labor, and Pensions.

SUMMARY AS OF:

5/14/2007—Introduced.

Climate Change Education Act - Requires the Director of the National Science Foundation to establish a Climate Change Education Program to: (1) broaden the understanding of climate change, possible long and short-term consequences, and potential solutions; (2) apply the latest scientific and technological discoveries to provide learning opportunities to people; and (3) emphasize actionable information to help people understand and to pro-

mote implementation of new technologies, programs, and incentives related to energy conservation, renewable energy, and greenhouse gas reduction.

Requires such Program to include: (1) a national information campaign to disseminate information on and promote implementation of the new technologies, programs, and incentives; and (2) a competitive grant program to provide grants to states, municipalities, educational institutions, and other organizations to create materials relevant to climate change and climate science, develop climate science kindergarten through grade 12 curriculum and supplementary educational materials, or publish climate change and climate science information.

MAJOR ACTIONS:

¤NONE¤

ALL ACTIONS:

5/14/2007:

Sponsor introductory remarks on measure. (CR S6070-6071)

5/14/2007:

Read twice and referred to the Committee on Health, Education, Labor, and Pensions.

TITLES(s): (italics indicate a title for a portion of a bill)

¤NONE¤

COSPONSORS(3), ALPHABETICAL [FOLLOWED BY COSPONSORS WITH-DRAWN]: (Sort: by date)

Sen Bingaman, Jeff [NM] - 5/14/2007

Sen Kerry, John F. [MA] - 5/23/2007

Sen Snowe, Olympia J. [ME] - 5/14/2007

COMMITTEE(S)

Committee/Subcommittee:

Activity:

Senate Health, Education, Labor, and Pensions

Referral, In Committee

RELATED BILL DETAILS: (additional related bills may be indentified in Status)

Bill:

Relationship:

H.R.1728

Related bill identified by CRS

AMENDMENT(S)

¤NONE¤

IN THE SENATE OF THE UNITED STATES

May 14, 2007

Mr. OBAMA (for himself, Ms. SNOWE, and Mr. BINGAMAN) introduced the following bill; which was read twice and referred to the Committee on Health, Education, Labor, and Pensions

A BILL

To authorize the National Science Foundation to establish a Climate Change Education Program.

Be it enacted by the Senate and House of Representatives of the United States of America in Congress assembled,

SECTION 1. SHORT TITLE.

This Act may be cited as the 'Climate Change Education Act'.

SEC. 2. FINDINGS.

Congress finds that—

(1) greenhouse gases are accumulating in the atmosphere, causing global temperatures to rise at a rate that poses a significant threat to the economy and security of the United States, to public health and welfare, and to the global environment;

(2) there is scientific consensus that human activities are the major cause of atmospheric greenhouse gas accumulation;

(3) mandatory steps will be required to slow or stop the accumulation of atmospheric greenhouse gases;

(4) atmospheric greenhouse gases can be significantly reduced through conservation, by shifting to renewable energy sources such as solar, wind, tidal, and geothermal, and by increasing the efficiency of buildings, including domiciles, and transportation, and by advances in technology;

(5) providing clear information about global warming, in a variety of forms, can increase understanding and encourage individuals and communities to take action;

(6) implementation of measures that promote energy efficiency, conservation, and renewable energy will greatly reduce human impact on the environment; and

(7) informing people of new technologies and programs as they become available will ensure maximum understanding and maximum impact of those measures.

SEC. 3. CLIMATE CHANGE EDUCATION PROGRAM.

(a) Establishment- The Director of the National Science Foundation shall establish a Climate Change Education Program to—

(1) broaden the understanding of climate change, possible long and short-term consequences, and potential solutions;

(2) apply the latest scientific and technological discoveries to provide formal and informal learning opportunities to people of all ages, including those of diverse cultural and linguistic backgrounds; and

(3) emphasize actionable information to help people understand and to promote implementation of new technologies, programs, and incentives related to energy conservation, renewable energy, and greenhouse gas reduction.

(b) Program Elements- The Climate Change Education Program shall include—

(1) a national information campaign to disseminate information on and promote implementation of the new technologies, programs, and incentives described in subsection (a)(3); and

(2) a competitive grant program to provide grants to States, local municipalities, educational institutions, and other organizations to—

(A) create informal education materials, exhibits, and multimedia presentations relevant to climate change and climate science;

(B) develop climate science kindergarten through grade 12 curriculum and supplementary educational materials; or

(C) publish climate change and climate science information in print, electronic, and audio-visual forms.

(c) Report to Congress- Not later than 1 year after the date of enactment of this Act, and annually thereafter, the Director of the National Science Foundation shall transmit to Congress a report that evaluates the scientific merits, educational effectiveness, and broader impacts of activities under this section.

SEC. 4. AUTHORIZATION OF APPROPRIATIONS.

There are authorized to be appropriated to carry out this Act, such sums as may be necessary.

US Senate Bill 1430

Title: A bill to authorize State and local governments to direct divestiture from, and prevent investment in, companies with investments of $20,000,000 or more in Iran's energy sector, and for other purposes.

Sponsor: Sen Obama, Barack [IL] (introduced 5/17/2007) Cosponsors (26)

Related Bills: H.R.2347

Latest Major Action: 5/17/2007 Referred to Senate committee. Status: Read twice and referred to the Committee on Banking, Housing, and Urban Affairs.

Summary As Of:

5/17/2007—Introduced.

Iran Sanctions Enabling Act of 2007 - Directs the Secretary of the Treasury to: (1) publish biannually in the Federal Register a list of each person, whether within or outside of the United States, that has an investment of more than $20 million in the energy sector in Iran; and (2) maintain on the website of the Department of the Treasury the names of the persons on such list.

States it is the policy of the United States to support the decision of state and local governments and educational institutions to divest from, and to prohibit the investment of assets they control in, persons included on the most recent list.

Authorizes a state or local government to adopt and enforce measures to divest its assets from, or prohibit investment of assets in, persons included on the most recent list.

Amends the Investment Company Act of 1940 to shield any registered investment company from civil, criminal, or administrative action based upon its divesting from, or avoiding investing in, securities issued by companies included on such most recent list.

Amends the Employee Retirement Income Security Act of 1974 to shield from treatment as breaching a fiduciary duty any person divesting plan assets from, or avoiding investing plan assets in, persons included on such most recent list.

Expresses the sense of the Congress that the Federal Retirement Thrift Investment Board should: (1) initiate efforts to provide a terror-free international investment option among the funds of the Thrift Savings Fund; and (2) initiate similar efforts to provide a genocide-free international investment option.

MAJOR ACTIONS:

¤NONE¤

ALL ACTIONS:

5/17/2007:

Sponsor introductory remarks on measure. (CR S6309-6310)

5/17/2007:

Read twice and referred to the Committee on Banking, Housing, and Urban Affairs.

7/26/2007:

Sponsor introductory remarks on measure. (CR S10141-10142)

TITLES(s): (italics indicate a title for a portion of a bill)

¤NONE¤

COSPONSORS(26), ALPHABETICAL [followed by Cosponsors withdrawn]: (Sort: by date)

Sen Boxer, Barbara [CA] - 5/24/2007

Sen Brownback, Sam [KS] - 5/17/2007

Sen Casey, Robert P., Jr. [PA] - 6/26/2007

Sen Coburn, Tom [OK] - 6/26/2007

Sen Coleman, Norm [MN] - 12/7/2007

Sen Collins, Susan M. [ME] - 7/17/2007

Sen Dole, Elizabeth [NC] - 12/5/2007

Sen Feingold, Russell D. [WI] - 7/19/2007

Sen Johnson, Tim [SD] - 1/28/2008

Sen Kerry, John F. [MA] - 2/11/2008

Sen Klobuchar, Amy [MN] - 7/19/2007

Sen Lautenberg, Frank R. [NJ] - 6/25/2007

Sen Lieberman, Joseph I. [CT] - 5/24/2007

Sen Lott, Trent [MS] - 9/18/2007

Sen Martinez, Mel [FL] - 2/7/2008

Sen Menendez, Robert [NJ] - 9/11/2007

Sen Mikulski, Barbara A. [MD] - 5/24/2007

Sen Murray, Patty [WA] - 7/17/2007

Sen Nelson, Bill [FL] - 6/6/2007

Sen Pryor, Mark L. [AR] - 2/14/2008

Sen Roberts, Pat [KS] - 12/5/2007

Sen Salazar, Ken [CO] - 9/10/2007

Sen Smith, Gordon H. [OR] - 7/19/2007

Sen Thune, John [SD] - 10/17/2007

Sen Vitter, David [LA] - 9/19/2007

Sen Wyden, Ron [OR] - 6/5/2007

COMMITTEE(S)

Committee/Subcommittee:

Activity:

Senate Banking, Housing, and Urban Affairs

Referral, In Committee

RELATED BILL DETAILS: (additional related bills may be indentified in Status)

Bill:

Relationship:

H.R.2347

Related bill identified by CRS

AMENDMENT(S)

¤NONE¤

IN THE SENATE OF THE UNITED STATES

May 17, 2007

Mr. OBAMA (for himself and Mr. BROWNBACK) introduced the following bill; which was read twice and referred to the Committee on Banking, Housing, and Urban Affairs

A BILL

To authorize State and local governments to direct divestiture from, and prevent investment in, companies with investments of $20,000,000 or more in Iran's energy sector, and for other purposes.

Be it enacted by the Senate and House of Representatives of the United States of America in Congress assembled,

SECTION 1. SHORT TITLE.

This Act may be cited as the 'Iran Sanctions Enabling Act'.

SEC. 2. FINDINGS.

Congress finds as follows:

(1) The Convention on the Prevention and Punishment of the Crime of Genocide, done at Paris December 9, 1948 (commonly referred to as the 'Genocide Convention') defines genocide as, among other things, the act of killing members of a national, ethnic, racial, or religious group with the intent to destroy, in whole or in part, the targeted group. In addition, the Genocide Convention also prohibits conspiracy to commit genocide, as well as '[d]irect and public incitement to commit genocide'.

(2) 133 member states of the United Nations have ratified the Genocide Convention and thereby pledged to prosecute individuals who violate the Genocide Convention's prohibition on incitement to commit genocide, as well as those individuals who commit genocide directly.

(3) On October 27, 2005, at the World Without Zionism Conference in Tehran, Iran, the President of Iran, Mahmoud Ahmadinejad, called for Israel to be 'wiped off the map,' described Israel as 'a disgraceful blot [on] the face of the Islamic world,' and declared that '[a]nybody who recognizes Israel will burn in the fire of the Islamic nation's fury.' President Ahmadinejad has subsequently made similar types of comments.

(4) On December 23, 2006, the United Nations Security Council unanimously approved Resolution 1737, which bans the supply of nuclear technology and equipment

to Iran and freezes the assets of certain organizations and individuals involved in Iran's nuclear program, until Iran suspends its enrichment of uranium, as verified by the International Atomic Energy Agency.

(5) Following Iran's failure to comply with Resolution 1737, on March 24, 2007, the United Nations Security Council unanimously approved Resolution 1747, to tighten sanctions on Iran, imposing a ban on arms sales and expanding the freeze on assets, in response to the country's uranium-enrichment activities.

(6) There are now signs of domestic discontent within Iran, and targeted financial and economic measures could produce a change in Iranian policy. According to the Economist Intelligence Unit, the nuclear crisis 'is imposing a heavy opportunity cost on Iran's economic development, slowing down investment in the oil, gas, and petro-chemical sectors, as well as in critical infrastructure projects, including electricity'.

(7) Targeted financial measures represent one of the strongest non-military tools available to convince the Government of Iran that it can no longer afford to engage in dangerous, destabilizing activities such as its nuclear weapons program and its support for terrorism.

(8) Foreign persons that have invested in Iran's energy sector, despite Iran's support of international terrorism and its nuclear program, have provided additional financial means for Iran's activities in these areas, and many United States persons have un-knowingly invested in those same foreign persons.

(9) There is an increasing interest by States, local governments, educational institu-tions, and private institutions to seek to disassociate themselves from companies that directly or indirectly support the Government of Iran's efforts to achieve a nuclear weapons capability.

(10) Policy makers and fund managers may find moral, prudential, or reputational reasons to divest assets from persons that accept the business risk of operating in countries that are subject to international economic sanctions or that have business relationships with countries, governments, or entities with which any United States person would be prohibited from dealing because of economic sanctions imposed by the United States.

SEC. 3. TRANSPARENCY IN UNITED STATES CAPITAL MARKETS.

(a) List of Persons Investing in Iran Energy Sector-

(1) PUBLICATION OF LIST- Not later than 180 days after the date of the enact-ment of this Act, and every 180 days thereafter, the Secretary of the Treasury, in consultation with the Secretary of Energy, the Secretary of State, the Securities and Exchange Commission, and the heads of other appropriate Federal departments and agencies, shall publish in the Federal Register a list of persons, whether within or outside of the United States, that, as of the date of the publication, have made an in-vestment of more than $20,000,000 in the energy sector of Iran. The list shall include a description of the investment made by each such person, including the dollar value, intended purpose, and status of the investment, as of the date of the publication of the list.

(2) PRIOR NOTICE TO PERSONS- Not later than 30 days before the list is published under paragraph (1), the Secretary of the Treasury shall notify each person that the Secretary intends to include on the list.

(3) DELAY IN INCLUDING PERSONS ON THE LIST- After notifying a person under paragraph (2) that the Secretary intends to include such person on the list, the Secretary may delay including such person on the list for not more than 60 days if the Secretary determines and certifies to Congress that such person has taken specific and effective actions to divest or terminate the investment in the energy sector of Iran that resulted in the notification under paragraph (2).

(4) REMOVAL OF PERSONS FROM THE LIST- The Secretary of the Treasury may remove a person from the list under paragraph (1) before the next publication of the list if the Secretary, in consultation with, as appropriate, the Secretary of Energy, the Secretary of State, the Securities and Exchange Commission, and the heads of other Federal departments and agencies, determines that the person has divested or terminated the investment in the energy sector of Iran that resulted in the Secretary including such person on the list.

(b) Publication on Website- The Secretary of the Treasury shall maintain on the website of the Department of the Treasury the names of the persons on the list published under subsection (a)(1), updating the list as necessary to take into account any person removed from the list under subsection (a)(4).

(c) Definition- In this section, the term 'investment' has the meaning given that term in section 14(9) of the Iran Sanctions Act (50 U.S.C. 1701 note).

SEC. 4. AUTHORITY OF STATE AND LOCAL GOVERNMENTS TO DIVEST ASSETS FROM CERTAIN COMPANIES INVESTED IN IRAN'S ENERGY SECTOR.

(a) Authority to Divest-

(1) IN GENERAL- Notwithstanding any other provision of law, a State or local government may adopt and enforce measures to divest the assets of the State or local government from, or prohibit investment of the assets of the State or local government in, persons that are included on the most recent list published under section 3(a)(1), as modified under section 3(a)(4).

(2) APPLICABILITY- This subsection applies to measures adopted by a State or local government before, on, or after the date of the enactment of this Act.

(3) DEFINITIONS- In this subsection:

(A) INVESTMENT OF THE ASSETS OF THE STATE OR LOCAL GOVERNMENT- The term 'investment of the assets of the State or local government' includes—

(i) a commitment or contribution of assets; and

(ii) a loan or other extension of credit of assets.

(B) ASSETS- The term 'assets' refers to public monies and includes any pension, retirement, annuity, or endowment fund, or similar instrument, that is controlled by a State or local government.

(b) Preemption- A measure of a State or local government that is authorized by subsection (a) is not preempted by any Federal law or regulation except to the extent that a person is unable to comply with both the measure and the Federal law or regulation.

SEC. 5. SAFE HARBOR FOR CHANGES OF INVESTMENT POLICIES BY MUTUAL FUNDS.

Section 13 of the Investment Company Act of 1940 (15 U.S.C. 80a-13) is amended by adding at the end the following new subsection:

'(c) Safe Harbor for Changes in Investment Policies- Notwithstanding any other provision of Federal or State law, no person may bring any civil, criminal, or administrative action against any registered investment company or person providing services to such registered investment company (including its investment adviser), or any employee, officer, or director thereof, based upon the investment company divesting from, or avoiding investing in, securities issued by companies that are included on the most recent list published under section 3(a)(1) of the Iran Sanctions Enabling Act, as modified under section 3(a)(4) of that Act. For purposes of this subsection the term 'person' shall include the Federal government and any State or political subdivision of a State.'.

SEC. 6. SAFE HARBOR FOR CHANGES OF INVESTMENT POLICIES BY EMPLOYEE BENEFIT PLANS.

Section 502 of the Employee Retirement Income Security Act of 1974 (29 U.S.C. 1132) is amended by adding at the end the following new subsection:

'(n) Divestment of Assets in Fiduciaries Investing in Iran- No person shall be treated as breaching any of the responsibilities, obligations, or duties imposed upon fiduciaries by this title, and no action may be brought under this section against any person, for divesting plan assets from, or avoiding investing plan assets in, persons that are included on the most recent list published under section 3(a)(1) of the Iran Sanctions Enabling Act, as modified under section 3(a)(4) of such Act.'.

SEC. 7. SENSE OF CONGRESS REGARDING THRIFT SAVINGS PLAN.

It is the sense of the Congress that—

(1) the Federal Retirement Thrift Investment Board should initiate efforts to provide a terror-free international investment option among the funds of the Thrift Savings Fund that would invest in stocks in which the International Stock Index Investment Fund may invest under section 8438(b)(4) of title 5, United States Code, other than the stock of companies that do business in any country the government of which the Secretary of State has determined is a government that has repeatedly provided support for acts of international terrorism, for purposes of section 40 of the Arms Export Control Act (22 U.S.C. 2780), section 620A of the Foreign Assistance Act of 1961 (22 U.S.C. 2371), section 6(j) of the Export Administration Act of 1979 (50 U.S.C. App. 2405(j)), as continued in effect pursuant to the International Emergency Economic Powers Act (50 U.S.C. 1701 et seq.), or any other provision of law relating to governments that provide support for acts of international terrorism; and

(2) the Federal Retirement Thrift Investment Board should initiate efforts similar to those described in paragraph (1) to provide a genocide-free international investment option.

SEC. 8. DEFINITIONS.

In this Act:

(1) IRAN- The term 'Iran' includes any agency or instrumentality of the Government of Iran.

(2) ENERGY SECTOR- The term 'energy sector' refers to activities to develop petroleum or natural gas resources.

(3) PERSON- The term 'person' means a natural person as well as a corporation, business association, partnership, society, trust, any other nongovernmental entity, organization, or group, and any governmental entity or instrumentality of a government.

(4) STATE- The term 'State' includes the District of Columbia, the Commonwealth of Puerto Rico, the Virgin Islands, Guam, American Samoa, and the Commonwealth of the Northern Mariana Islands.

(5) STATE OR LOCAL GOVERNMENT- The term 'State or local government' includes—

(A) any State and any agency or instrumentality thereof;

(B) any local government within a State, and any agency or instrumentality thereof; and

(C) any public institution of higher education, as defined in section 102 of the Higher Education Act of 1965 (20 U.S.C. 1002).

SEC. 9. SUNSET.

The provisions of this Act shall terminate 30 days after the date on which the President has certified to Congress that—

(1) the Government of Iran has ceased providing support for acts of international terrorism and no longer satisfies the requirements for designation as a state sponsor of terrorism for purposes of section 40 of the Arms Export Control Act (22 U.S.C. 2780), section 620A of the Foreign Assistance Act of 1961 (22 U.S.C. 2371), section 6(j) of the Export Administration Act of 1979 (50 U.S.C. App. 2405(j)), as continued in effect pursuant to the International Emergency Economic Powers Act (50 U.S.C. 1701 et seq.), or any other provision of law relating to governments that provide support for acts of international terrorism;

(2) the Government of Iran has ceased the pursuit, acquisition, and development of nuclear, biological, and chemical weapons and ballistic missiles and ballistic missile launch technology; and

(3) the Government of Iran has retracted the statements of the President of Iran, Mahmoud Ahmadinejad, calling for the destruction of Israel.

US SENATE BILL 1513

TITLE: A bill to amend the Higher Education Act of 1965 to authorize grant programs to enhance the access of low-income African-American students to higher education.

Sponsor: Sen Obama, Barack [IL] (introduced 5/24/2007) Cosponsors (None)

Related Bills: H.R.4216

Latest Major Action: 5/24/2007 Referred to Senate committee. Status: Read twice and referred to the Committee on Health, Education, Labor, and Pensions.

Summary As Of:

5/24/2007—Introduced.

Predominantly Black Institution Act of 2007 - Amends the Higher Education Act of 1965 to provide grants to Predominantly Black Institutions to: (1) enhance their capacity to serve more low and middle-income African-American students; (2) expand higher education opportunities for students eligible for student assistance under title IV of the Act by encouraging such students to prepare for college and persist in secondary and postsecondary education; and (3) strengthen their financial ability to serve the academic needs of such students.

Defines such institutions as accredited institutions serving at least 1,000 undergraduate students at least: (1) 50% of whom are pursuing a bachelor's or associate's degree; (2) 40% of whom are African-Americans; and (3) 50% of whom are low-income or first-generation college students. Requires the spending per full-time undergraduate student of such institutions to be low in comparison to that of institutions offering similar instruction.

Allows grant recipients to use up to 20% of their grant on an endowment fund, provided they raise nonfederal matching funds at least equal to the amount of the grant used for such endowment. Allots funding among institutions on the basis of their share of Pell Grant recipients, graduates, and graduates pursuing a higher degree.

Establishes a minimum allotment for each institution of $250,000, which is to be ratably reduced if appropriations are insufficient to pay such amount.

Major Actions:

¤NONE¤

All Actions:

5/24/2007:

Sponsor introductory remarks on measure. (CR S6875)

5/24/2007:

Read twice and referred to the Committee on Health, Education, Labor, and Pensions.

Titles(s): (italics indicate a title for a portion of a bill)

¤NONE¤

COSPONSOR(S):

¤NONE¤

COMMITTEE(S)

Committee/Subcommittee:

Activity:

Senate Health, Education, Labor, and Pensions

Referral, In Committee

RELATED BILL DETAILS: (additional related bills may be indentified in Status)

Bill:

Relationship:

H.R.4216

Related bill identified by CRS

AMENDMENT(S)

¤NONE¤

IN THE SENATE OF THE UNITED STATES

May 24, 2007

Mr. OBAMA introduced the following bill; which was read twice and referred to the Committee on Health, Education, Labor, and Pensions

A BILL

To amend the Higher Education Act of 1965 to authorize grant programs to enhance the access of low-income African-American students to higher education.

Be it enacted by the Senate and House of Representatives of the United States of America in Congress assembled,

SECTION 1. SHORT TITLE.

This Act may be cited as the 'Predominantly Black Institution Act of 2007'.

SEC. 2. PREDOMINANTLY BLACK INSTITUTIONS.

(a) Amendment- Part A of title III of the Higher Education Act of 1965 (20 U.S.C. 1057 et seq.) is amended by inserting after section 317 the following:

'SEC. 318. PREDOMINANTLY BLACK INSTITUTIONS.

'(a) Findings and Purpose-

'(1) FINDINGS- Congress finds that—

'(A) although African-Americans have made significant progress in closing the gap between African-American and White enrollment in higher education—

'(i) African-Americans continue to trail Whites in the percentage of the college-age cohort who enroll and graduate from college;

'(ii) among recent secondary school graduates, the college participation rate of Whites was 46 percent from 2000 through 2002, while such rate for African-Americans was only 39 percent; and

'(iii) the gap between White and African-American bachelor's degree attainment rates also remains high, continuing to exceed 10 percent;

'(B) a growing number of African-American students are participating in higher education and are enrolled at an increasing number of urban and rural Predominantly Black Institutions that have included in their mission the provision of academic training and education for both traditional and nontraditional minority students;

'(C) the overwhelming majority of students attending Predominantly Black Institutions come from low- and middle-income families and qualify for participation in the Federal student assistance programs or other need-based Federal programs as indicated by recent data from the National Postsecondary Student Aid Study which demonstrates that 47 percent of African-American undergraduates are Federal Pell Grant recipients, compared to 21 percent of non-Hispanic Whites;

'(D) many of the students who enroll in Predominantly Black Institutions are also first generation college students who often lack the appropriate academic preparation for success in college and whose parents lack the requisite knowledge and information regarding financing a college education;

'(E) there is a particular national need to aid institutions of higher education that have become Predominantly Black Institutions by virtue of the fact that the Predominantly Black Institutions have expanded opportunities for African-American and other minority students;

'(F) Predominantly Black Institutions fulfill a unique mission within American higher education, far beyond that which was initially envisioned;

'(G) Predominantly Black Institutions serve the cultural and social advancement of low-income, African-American and other minority students and are a significant access point for these students to higher education and the opportunities offered by American society;

'(H) the concentration of the students described in subparagraph (G) in a limited number of 2-year and 4-year Predominantly Black Institutions and the desire of these students to secure a degree to prepare these students for a successful career places special burdens on those institutions who attract, retain, and graduate these students; and

'(I) financial assistance to establish or strengthen the academic resources, physical plants, financial management, and endowments of the Predominantly Black Institutions are appropriate methods to enhance the educational quality of the Predominantly Black Institutions, to facilitate decreased long-term reliance on governmental financial support, and to encourage reliance on endowments and private sources.

'(2) PURPOSE- It is the purpose of this section to assist Predominantly Black Institutions in expanding educational opportunity through a program of Federal assistance.

'(b) Definitions- In this section:

'(1) EDUCATIONAL AND GENERAL EXPENDITURES- The term 'educational and general expenditures' has the meaning given the term in section 312.

'(2) ELIGIBLE INSTITUTION- The term 'eligible institution' means an institution of higher education that—

'(A) has an enrollment of needy undergraduate students;

'(B) has an average educational and general expenditure which is low, per full-time equivalent undergraduate student in comparison with the average educational and general expenditure per full-time equivalent undergraduate student of institutions that offer similar instruction, except that the Secretary may apply the waiver requirements described in section 392(b) to this subparagraph in the same manner as the Secretary applies the waiver requirements to section 312(b)(1)(B);

'(C) has an enrollment of undergraduate students that is not less than 40 percent African-American students;

'(D) is legally authorized to provide, and provides within the State, an educational program for which the institution of higher education awards a baccalaureate degree, or in the case of a junior or community college, an associate's degree; and

'(E) is accredited by a nationally recognized accrediting agency or association determined by the Secretary to be a reliable authority as to the quality of training offered, or is, according to such an agency or association, making reasonable progress toward accreditation.

'(3) ENDOWMENT FUND- The term 'endowment fund' has the meaning given the term in section 312.

'(4) ENROLLMENT OF NEEDY STUDENTS- The term 'enrollment of needy students' means the enrollment at an eligible institution with respect to which not less than 50 percent of the undergraduate students enrolled in an academic program leading to a degree—

'(A) in the second fiscal year preceding the fiscal year for which the determination is made, were Federal Pell Grant recipients for such year;

'(B) come from families that receive benefits under a means-tested Federal benefit program;

'(C) attended a public or nonprofit private secondary school—

'(i) that is in the school district of a local educational agency that was eligible for assistance under part A of title I of the Elementary and Secondary Education Act of 1965 for any year during which the student attended such secondary school; and

'(ii) which for the purpose of this paragraph and for that year was determined by the Secretary (pursuant to regulations and after consultation with the State educational agency of the State in which the school is located) to be a school in which the enrollment of children counted under section 1113(a)(5) of such Act exceeds 30 percent of the total enrollment of such school; or

'(D) are first generation college students and a majority of such first generation college students are low-income individuals.

'(5) FIRST GENERATION COLLEGE STUDENT- The term 'first generation college student' has the meaning given the term in section 402A(g).

'(6) INSTITUTION OF HIGHER EDUCATION- The term 'institution of higher education' has the meaning given the term in section 101(a).

'(7) LOW-INCOME INDIVIDUAL- The term 'low-income individual' has the meaning given such term in section 402A(g).

'(8) MEANS-TESTED FEDERAL BENEFIT PROGRAM- The term 'means-tested Federal benefit program' means a program of the Federal Government, other than a program under title IV, in which eligibility for the program's benefits, or the amount of such benefits, are determined on the basis of income or resources of the individual or family seeking the benefit.

'(9) PREDOMINANTLY BLACK INSTITUTION- The term 'Predominantly Black Institution' means an institution of higher education—

'(A) that is an eligible institution with not less than 1,000 undergraduate students;

'(B) at which not less than 50 percent of the undergraduate students enrolled at the eligible institution are low-income individuals or first generation college students; and

'(C) at which not less than 50 percent of the undergraduate students are enrolled in an educational program leading to a bachelor's or associate's degree that the eligible institution is licensed to award by the State in which the eligible institution is located.

'(10) STATE- The term 'State' means each of the 50 States and the District of Columbia.

'(c) Grant Authority-

'(1) IN GENERAL- The Secretary is authorized to award grants, from allotments under subsection (e), to Predominantly Black Institutions to enable the Predominantly Black Institutions to carry out the authorized activities described in subsection (d).

'(2) PRIORITY- In awarding grants under this section the Secretary shall give priority to Predominantly Black Institutions with large numbers or percentages of students described in subsections (b)(2)(A) or (b)(2)(C). The level of priority given to Predominantly Black Institutions with large numbers or percentages of students described in subsection (b)(2)(A) shall be twice the level of priority given to Predominantly Black Institutions with large numbers or percentages of students described in subsection (b)(2)(C).

'(d) Authorized Activities-

'(1) REQUIRED ACTIVITIES- Grant funds provided under this section shall be used—

'(A) to assist the Predominantly Black Institution to plan, develop, undertake, and implement programs to enhance the institution's capacity to serve more low- and middle-income African-American students;

'(B) to expand higher education opportunities for students eligible to participate in programs under title IV by encouraging college preparation and student persistence in secondary school and postsecondary education; and

'(C) to strengthen the financial ability of the Predominantly Black Institution to serve the academic needs of the students described in subparagraphs (A) and (B).

'(2) ADDITIONAL ACTIVITIES- Grant funds provided under this section shall be used for 1 or more of the following activities:

'(A) The activities described in paragraphs (1) through (11) of section 311(c).

'(B) Academic instruction in disciplines in which African-Americans are underrepresented.

'(C) Establishing or enhancing a program of teacher education designed to qualify students to teach in a public elementary school or secondary school in the State that shall include, as part of such program, preparation for teacher certification or licensure.

'(D) Establishing community outreach programs that will encourage elementary school and secondary school students to develop the academic skills and the interest to pursue postsecondary education.

'(E) Establishing or increasing an endowment fund in accordance with paragraph (3).

'(F) Other activities proposed in the application submitted pursuant to subsection (f) that—

'(i) contribute to carrying out the purpose of this section; and

'(ii) are approved by the Secretary as part of the review and approval of an application submitted under subsection (f).

'(3) ENDOWMENT FUND-

'(A) IN GENERAL- A Predominantly Black Institution may use not more than 20 percent of the grant funds provided under this section to establish or increase an endowment fund at the institution.

'(B) MATCHING REQUIREMENT- In order to be eligible to use grant funds in accordance with subparagraph (A), a Predominantly Black Institution shall provide matching funds from non-Federal sources, in an amount equal to or greater than the Federal funds used in accordance with subparagraph (A), for the establishment or increase of the endowment fund.

'(C) COMPARABILITY- The provisions of part C of title III, regarding the establishment or increase of an endowment fund, that the Secretary determines are not inconsistent with this subsection, shall apply to funds used under subparagraph (A).

'(4) LIMITATION- Not more than 50 percent of the grant funds provided to a Predominantly Black Institution under this section may be available for the purpose of constructing or maintaining a classroom, library, laboratory, or other instructional facility.

'(e) Allotments to Predominantly Black Institutions-

'(1) FEDERAL PELL GRANT BASIS- From the amounts appropriated to carry out this section for any fiscal year, the Secretary shall allot to each Predominantly Black Institution having an application approved under subsection (f) a sum that bears the same ratio to one-half of that amount as the number of Federal Pell Grant recipients in attendance at such institution at the end of the academic year preceding the beginning of that fiscal year, bears to the total number of Federal Pell Grant recipients at all such institutions at the end of such academic year.

'(2) GRADUATES BASIS- From the amounts appropriated to carry out this section for any fiscal year, the Secretary shall allot to each Predominantly Black Institution having an application approved under subsection (f) a sum that bears the same ratio to one-fourth of that amount as the number of graduates for such academic year at such institution, bears to the total number of graduates for such academic year at all such institutions.

'(3) GRADUATES SEEKING A HIGHER DEGREE BASIS- From the amounts appropriated to carry out this section for any fiscal year, the Secretary shall allot to each Predominantly Black Institution having an application approved under subsection (f) a sum that bears the same ratio to one-fourth of that amount as the percentage of graduates from such institution who are admitted to and in attendance at, not later than 2 years after graduation with an associate's degree or a baccalaureate degree, a baccalaureate degree-granting institution or a graduate or professional school in a degree program in disciplines in which African-American students are underrepresented, bears to the percentage of such graduates for all such institutions.

'(4) MINIMUM ALLOTMENT-

'(A) IN GENERAL- Notwithstanding paragraphs (1), (2), and (3), the amount allotted to each Predominantly Black Institution under this section shall not be less than $250,000.

'(B) INSUFFICIENT AMOUNT- If the amount appropriated pursuant to section 399(a)(1)(D) for a fiscal year is not sufficient to pay the minimum allotment provided under subparagraph (A) for the fiscal year, then the amount of such minimum allotment shall be ratably reduced. If additional sums become available for such fiscal year, such reduced allotment shall be increased on the same basis as the allotment was reduced until the amount allotted equals the minimum allotment required under subparagraph (A).

'(5) REALLOTMENT- The amount of a Predominantly Black Institution's allotment under paragraph (1), (2), (3), or (4) for any fiscal year that the Secretary determines will not be required for such institution for the period such allotment is available, shall be available for reallotment to other Predominantly Black Institutions in proportion to the original allotment to such other institutions under this section for such fiscal year. The Secretary shall reallot such amounts from time to time, on such date and during such period as the Secretary determines appropriate.

'(f) Applications- Each Predominantly Black Institution desiring a grant under this section shall submit an application to the Secretary at such time, in such manner, and containing or accompanied by such information as the Secretary may reasonably require.

'(g) Prohibition- No Predominantly Black Institution that applies for and receives a grant under this section may apply for or receive funds under any other program under part A or part B of title III.

'(h) Duration and Carryover- Any grant funds paid to a Predominantly Black Institution under this section that are not expended or used for the purposes for which the funds were paid within 10 years following the date on which the grant was awarded, shall be repaid to the Treasury.

'(i) Applicability of Part F- Part F, other than section 399, shall not apply to this section.'.

(b) Authorization of Appropriations- Section 399(a)(1) of the Higher Education Act of 1965 (20 U.S.C. 1068h(a)(1)) is amended by adding at the end the following new subparagraph:

'(D) There are authorized to be appropriated to carry out section 318 such sums as may be necessary for fiscal year 2008 and each of the 5 succeeding fiscal years.'.

US SENATE BILL 1574

TITLE: A bill to establish Teaching Residency Programs for preparation and induction of teachers.

SPONSOR: Sen Obama, Barack [IL] (introduced 6/7/2007) Cosponsors (None)

LATEST MAJOR ACTION: 6/7/2007 Referred to Senate committee. Status: Read twice and referred to the Committee on Health, Education, Labor, and Pensions.

SUMMARY AS OF:

6/7/2007—Introduced.

Teaching Residency Act - Amends the Elementary and Secondary Education Act of 1965 to direct the Secretary of Education to make competitive matching grants to partnerships of high-need local educational agencies (LEAs), nonprofit community agencies, and institutions of higher education to support one-year teaching residency programs under which recent college graduates or professionals outside the field of education engage in rigorous master's level coursework while undertaking a guided teaching apprenticeship alongside a trained and experienced mentor teacher.

Requires program participants to earn a master's degree and attain full state teaching certification or licensure prior to completing the program and accept placement for three years thereafter in a high-need school served by the high-need LEA.

MAJOR ACTIONS:

¤NONE¤

All Actions:

6/7/2007:

Sponsor introductory remarks on measure. (CR S7349-7350)

6/7/2007:

Read twice and referred to the Committee on Health, Education, Labor, and Pensions.

Titles(s): (italics indicate a title for a portion of a bill)

¤NONE¤

Cosponsor(s):

¤NONE¤

Committee(s)

Committee/Subcommittee:

Activity:

Senate Health, Education, Labor, and Pensions

Referral, In Committee

Related Bill Details:

¤NONE¤

Amendment(s)

¤NONE¤

In the Senate of the United States

June 7, 2007

Mr. OBAMA introduced the following bill; which was read twice and referred to the Committee on Health, Education, Labor, and Pensions

A BILL

To establish Teaching Residency Programs for preparation and induction of teachers.

Be it enacted by the Senate and House of Representatives of the United States of America in Congress assembled,

SECTION 1. SHORT TITLE.

This Act may be cited as the 'Teaching Residency Act'.

SEC. 2. FINDINGS.

Congress finds the following:

(1) There are large and unrelenting gaps in student achievement among various student subgroups, with low-income and minority children performing at levels measurably

317

lower than their more affluent peers. In urban elementary schools, African-American and Latino students are several times less likely than their white peers to be reading at even a basic level, and children living in poverty are several times less likely than their more affluent peers to be proficient in reading or mathematics. Students in poor rural communities are also harmed. In some States, only 60 percent of white students graduate from secondary school.

(2) Three out of every 10 9th-grade students will not graduate from high school on schedule, and about half of all African-American and Hispanic 9th graders will not earn a diploma in 4 years. Of those who do graduate and continue on to college, over a quarter must enroll in remedial courses on material they should have learned in high school.

(3) It is children of color and children of poverty who suffer most from a failure to provide them with adequate resources and expert teachers. For example, students of color and low-income students are more likely to be assigned teachers who are teaching outside their field of expertise, and twice as likely as white and affluent students to be assigned to inexperienced teachers.

(4) Having an effective teacher throughout elementary school can substantially overcome the disadvantage of a low socioeconomic background, and the influence of teachers on student achievement is greater than other variables.

(5) Inexperienced teachers are less effective than teachers with several years of experience. Successful teacher preparation programs, providing ongoing support, can make novice teachers effective more rapidly. The majority of new teachers lack such support, and so leave the profession before becoming effective.

(6) Urban and high poverty schools often lose 1/5 of their teaching staff each year. More than 40 percent of teachers have 3 or fewer years experience in their current school. This constant turnover of inexperienced, underprepared teachers, especially in high-poverty schools, thwarts efforts at school improvement. Teachers leave the profession much sooner if they have inadequate preparation and ineffective mentoring support in their first years of teaching. The national costs of teacher attrition are estimated at more than $2,000,000,000 annually.

(7) Teacher candidates must see expert practices modeled and must then practice them with ongoing mentoring support. Teacher preparation often fails to provide the opportunity to learn under the direct supervision of expert teachers working in schools that effectively serve high-need students. Student teaching is too often conducted in classrooms that do not model effective practice, or in classrooms that do not serve high-need students, and the lessons learned do not generalize to effective teaching in high-need schools.

(8) It is critical to develop programs that increase the probability recruits will succeed and stay in the high-need classrooms where they are needed. Because many teacher candidates choose to teach where they grew up or went to college, it is important to have strong programs in hard-to-staff urban and rural locations.

(9) Teaching Residency Programs effectively build teacher supply, since they recruit and prepare candidates in the districts that sponsor them. Teaching residency programs have demonstrated the capacity to recruit, prepare, retain, and provide effective support for teachers in high-need schools.

SEC. 3. GRANT PROGRAM FOR TEACHING RESIDENCY PROGRAMS.

Title II of the Higher Education Act of 1965 (20 U.S.C. 1021 et seq.) is amended by adding at the end the following:

'PART C—TEACHING RESIDENCY PROGRAMS

'SEC. 231. GRANT PROGRAM FOR TEACHING RESIDENCY PROGRAMS.

'(a) Definitions- In this section:

'(1) HIGH-NEED LOCAL EDUCATIONAL AGENCY- The term 'high-need local educational agency' means a local educational agency—

'(A) that is among the highest 50 percent of local educational agencies in the State in terms of percentage of students from families with incomes below the poverty line (as defined in section 201);

'(B) that is among the lowest 50 percent of local educational agencies in the State on assessments required under part A of title I of the Elementary and Secondary Education Act of 1965, or, where feasible, the lowest 50 percent of local educational agencies in the State in terms of measures of teaching effectiveness; and

'(C) for which there is a high percentage of classes taught by teachers not teaching in the academic subjects or grade levels that the teachers were prepared to teach.

'(2) HIGH-NEED SCHOOL- The term 'high-need school' means a school that—

'(A) is among the highest 50 percent of schools in the local educational agency that serves the school in terms of percentage of students from families with incomes below the poverty line (as defined in section 201);

'(B) is among the lowest 50 percent of schools in the local educational agency that serves the school on assessments required under part A of title I of the Elementary and Secondary Education Act of 1965, or, where feasible, the lowest 50 percent of schools in the State in terms of measures of teaching effectiveness; and

'(C) is not undergoing the process of corrective action, as described in section 1116 of the Elementary and Secondary Education Act of 1965.

'(3) INSTITUTION OF HIGHER EDUCATION- The term 'institution of higher education' has the meaning given the term in section 101(a).

'(4) TEACHING RESIDENCY PROGRAM- The term 'teaching residency program' means a school-based teacher preparation program in which a prospective teacher—

'(A) for 1 academic year, teaches alongside a mentor teacher, who is the teacher of record;

'(B) receives concurrent instruction, which may be taught by district or residency program faculty, in the teaching of the content area in which the teacher will become certified or licensed to teach;

'(C) acquires knowledge of planning, content, pedagogy, student learning, and assessment, management of the classroom environment, and professional responsibilities, including interaction with families and colleagues;

'(D) earns a master's degree and attains full State certification or licensure to teach prior to completion of the program; and

'(E) receives ongoing mentoring support in a structured induction program for not less than the first 2 years as teacher of record.

'(b) Authorization- The Secretary shall establish a program to award grants, on a competitive basis, to 20 high-need local educational agencies, or a consortium of such local educational agencies, in partnership with nonprofit community agencies and an institution of higher education, to enable such partnerships to carry out the following:

'(1) Support teaching residency programs to prepare teachers in high-needs subject areas as determined by local educational agency needs.

'(2) Modify staffing procedures, in consultation and cooperation with local teacher organizations, to provide greater flexibility for agency and school leaders to establish effective school-level staffing to facilitate placement of graduates of the teaching residency programs in cohorts that facilitate professional collaboration, both among graduates of the teaching residency program, and between such graduates and mentor teachers in the receiving school. Staffing procedures shall include consideration of equitable distribution of effective teachers to ensure that poor and minority students are not disproportionately taught by teachers who are—

'(A) poorly prepared in the subject being taught; and

'(B) less likely to excel in other measures of teacher effectiveness.

'(3) Ensure that residents receive both effective mentoring during preparation and effective induction once they become the teacher of record.

'(c) Application- A high-need local educational agency that desires to receive a grant under this section shall submit an application to the Secretary at such time, in such manner, and accompanied by such information as the Secretary shall require.

'(d) Teaching Residency Programs-

'(1) IN GENERAL-

'(A) ESTABLISHMENT- A high-need local educational agency that receives a grant under this section shall use the grant funds to establish a Teaching Residency Program, based upon models of successful teaching residencies, as a mechanism to prepare teachers for success in such local educational agency.

'(B) DESIGN- Each Teaching Residency Program shall be designed to meet the following characteristics of successful programs:

'(i) Teaching residencies integrate pedagogy and classroom practice. Residents engage in rigorous master's level coursework while undertaking a guided teaching apprenticeship.

'(ii) Residents learn alongside a trained and experienced mentor. Mentor teachers shall complement the residency program so that classroom clinical practice is tightly aligned with coursework. Mentor teachers shall have extra responsibilities as teacher leaders of the Teaching Residency Program, as mentors for residents, and as teacher coaches during the induction of novice teachers. These responsibilities shall include establishing, within the program, a learning community in which all individuals are expected to continually improve their capacity to advance student learning. Mentor teachers may have relief from teaching duties as a result of such additional responsibilities. The Teaching Residency Program shall establish clear criteria for selection of mentor teachers based on measures of teacher effectiveness and the appropriate subject area knowledge. Evaluation of teacher effectiveness shall be based on observations of such domains of teaching as the following:

'(I) Planning and preparation, including demonstrated knowledge of content, pedagogy, and assessment, including the use of formative assessment to improve student learning.

'(II) Appropriate instruction that engages students with different learning styles.

'(III) Collaboration with colleagues to improve instruction.

'(IV) Appropriate and fair analysis of gains in student learning. When feasible, this may include valid and reliable objective measure of the influence of teachers on the rate of student academic progress.

'(iii) Teaching Residency Programs group teacher candidates in cohorts to facilitate professional collaboration among residents.

'(iv) Teaching Residency Programs admissions goals and priorities are developed in concert with the hiring objectives of the local educational agency, which commits to hire graduates from the residency program. Residents learn to teach in the same district in which they will work, learning the instructional initiatives and curriculum of the district.

'(v) Teaching Residency Programs support residents once they are hired as teachers of record. Residencies continue to provide mentoring, professional development, and networking opportunities to support residents through their first years of teaching.

'(2) ELIGIBLE INDIVIDUALS- An individual may be eligible for a grant to attend a Teaching Residency Program if the individual is a recent college graduate or mid-career professional from outside the field of education, possessing strong content knowledge or a record of achievement.

'(3) APPLICATION- An individual who is eligible under paragraph (2) and who desires a grant under this subsection shall submit an application to the Teaching Residency Program.

'(4) SELECTION CRITERIA- The Teaching Residency Program shall establish criteria for selection of individuals to receive grants under this subsection, based on the following characteristics:

'(A) Demonstrated comprehensive subject knowledge or record of accomplishment in the field or subject area to be taught.

'(B) Strong verbal and written communication skills, which may be demonstrated by performance on appropriate tests.

'(C) Other attributes linked to effective teaching, which may be determined by interviews or performance assessments, as determined by the Teaching Residency Program.

'(5) RECEIPT OF GRANT- An individual who receives a grant under this subsection shall enroll in the program of the Teaching Residency Program, which shall include the following:

'(A) A 1-year teaching residency program in a school served by the local educational agency, under the supervision of a mentor teacher serving as the teacher of record, with demonstrated teaching effectiveness, who will instruct the resident in planning and preparation, instruction of students, management of the classroom environment, and other professional responsibilities.

'(B) A living stipend or salary for the period of residency.

'(C) Concurrent instruction from a partner college, State-approved organization, or school of education at an institution of higher education in pedagogy classes to augment the expertise of district or residency program faculty, and to the extent necessary to receive full certification as a teacher.

'(D) Ongoing mentoring and coaching during the first 2 or more years of induction into classroom teaching.

'(6) PLACEMENT IN HIGH-NEED SCHOOL-

'(A) IN GENERAL- An eligible individual who receives a grant under this subsection shall teach in a high-need school served by the local educational agency for a period of 3 years after completing the 1-year teaching residency program.

'(B) REPAYMENT- If an eligible individual does not complete the teaching requirement described in subparagraph (A), such individual shall repay to the local educational agency a pro rata portion of the grant amount for the amount of teaching time the individual did not complete.

'(e) Teaching Residency Program Evaluation- Of the amounts appropriated to carry out this section, the Secretary shall reserve 5 percent for an evaluation of the effectiveness of the program established under this section, in relation to the effectiveness of other programs that prepare teachers for employment with high-need schools and high-need local educational agencies, including, where feasible, value-added measures of learning gains of students taught by graduates of each Teaching Residency Program, to be conducted by the Institute of Education Sciences, the National Science Foundation, or the National Academy of Sciences, at the direction of the Secretary. Not later than 5 years after the date of enactment of the Teaching Residency Act, the Secretary shall make the results of such evaluation public.

'(f) Matching Funds- A high-need local educational agency that receives a grant under this section shall provide matching funds in an amount equal to 100 percent of grant funds provided to the agency under this section to carry out the activities supported by the grant, which may be provided by community partners, institutions of higher education, or others.

'(g) Authorization of Appropriations-

'(1) IN GENERAL- There is authorized to be appropriated to carry out this section $50,000,000 for each of fiscal years 2008 through 2012.

'(2) REDIRECTION OF APPROPRIATIONS- For each of fiscal years 2008 through 2012, the Secretary shall redirect amounts appropriated to carry out this title, other than this section, that the Secretary determines to be ineffective, to carry out this section.'.

US Senate Bill 1713

Title: A bill to provide for the issuance of a commemorative postage stamp in honor of Rosa Parks.

Sponsor: Sen Obama, Barack [IL] (introduced 6/27/2007) Cosponsors (27)

Related Bills: H.R.18

Latest Major Action: 7/13/2007 Referred to Senate subcommittee. Status: Committee on Homeland Security and Governmental Affairs referred to Subcommittee on Federal Financial Management, Government Information, Federal Services, and International Security.

Summary As Of:

6/27/2007—Introduced.

Requires the Postmaster General to issue a commemorative postage stamp in honor of Rosa Parks.

Major Actions:

¤NONE¤

All Actions:

6/27/2007:

Read twice and referred to the Committee on Homeland Security and Governmental Affairs.

7/13/2007:

Committee on Homeland Security and Governmental Affairs referred to Subcommittee on Federal Financial Management, Government Information, Federal Services, and International Security.

Titles(s): (italics indicate a title for a portion of a bill)

¤NONE¤

COSPONSORS(27), ALPHABETICAL [followed by Cosponsors withdrawn]: (Sort: by date)

Sen Alexander, Lamar [TN] - 6/27/2007

Sen Bayh, Evan [IN] - 6/27/2007

Sen Biden, Joseph R., Jr. [DE] - 6/27/2007

Sen Bingaman, Jeff [NM] - 6/27/2007

Sen Boxer, Barbara [CA] - 6/27/2007

Sen Brown, Sherrod [OH] - 6/27/2007

Sen Cantwell, Maria [WA] - 6/27/2007

Sen Cardin, Benjamin L. [MD] - 6/27/2007

Sen Clinton, Hillary Rodham [NY] - 6/28/2007

Sen Coburn, Tom [OK] - 6/28/2007

Sen Coleman, Norm [MN] - 6/27/2007

Sen Dodd, Christopher J. [CT] - 6/28/2007

Sen Durbin, Richard [IL] - 6/27/2007

Sen Feinstein, Dianne [CA] - 6/28/2007

Sen Harkin, Tom [IA] - 6/27/2007

Sen Kennedy, Edward M. [MA] - 6/27/2007

Sen Kerry, John F. [MA] - 6/27/2007

Sen Landrieu, Mary L. [LA] - 6/27/2007

Sen Levin, Carl [MI] - 6/27/2007

Sen Lieberman, Joseph I. [CT] - 6/28/2007

Sen Lugar, Richard G. [IN] - 6/27/2007

Sen Mikulski, Barbara A. [MD] - 6/27/2007

Sen Reid, Harry [NV] - 6/27/2007

Sen Schumer, Charles E. [NY] - 6/27/2007

Sen Stabenow, Debbie [MI] - 6/27/2007

Sen Voinovich, George V. [OH] - 6/27/2007

Sen Wyden, Ron [OR] - 6/28/2007

COMMITTEE(S)

Committee/Subcommittee:

Activity:

Senate Homeland Security and Governmental Affairs

Referral, In Committee

Subcommittee on Federal Financial Management, Government Information, Federal Services, and International Security

Referral

RELATED BILL DETAILS: (additional related bills may be indentified in Status)

Bill:

Relationship:

H.R.18

Related bill identified by CRS

Amendment(s)

¤NONE¤

In the Senate of the United States

June 27, 2007

Mr. OBAMA (for himself, Mr. DURBIN, Mr. ALEXANDER, Mr. BAYH, Mr. COLEMAN, Mr. BIDEN, Mr. LUGAR, Mr. BINGAMAN, Mr. VOINOVICH, Mrs. BOXER, Mr. BROWN, Ms. CANTWELL, Mr. CARDIN, Mr. HARKIN, Mr. KENNEDY, Mr. KERRY, Ms. LANDRIEU, Mr. LEVIN, Ms. MIKULSKI, Mr. SCHUMER, Ms. STABENOW, and Mr. REID) introduced the following bill; which was read twice and referred to the Committee on Homeland Security and Governmental Affairs

A BILL

To provide for the issuance of a commemorative postage stamp in honor of Rosa Parks.

Be it enacted by the Senate and House of Representatives of the United States of America in Congress assembled,

SECTION 1. ROSA PARKS COMMEMORATIVE POSTAGE STAMP.

(a) In General- The Postmaster General shall issue a commemorative postage stamp in honor of Rosa Parks.

(b) Denomination and Design- The commemorative postage stamp issued under this Act shall—

(1) be issued in the denomination used for 1st class mail up to 1 ounce in weight; and

(2) bear such designs as the Postmaster General shall determine.

(c) Issuance Period- The commemorative postage stamp issued under this Act shall—

(1) be placed on sale as soon as practicable after the date of the enactment of this Act; and

(2) be sold for such period thereafter as the Postmaster General shall determine.

US SENATE BILL 1790

TITLE: A bill to make grants to carry out activities to prevent the incidence of unintended pregnancies and sexually transmitted infections among teens in racial or ethnic minority or immigrant communities, and for other purposes.

SPONSOR: Sen Obama, Barack [IL] (introduced 7/16/2007) Cosponsors (2)

RELATED BILLS: H.R.468

LATEST MAJOR ACTION: 7/16/2007 Referred to Senate committee. Status: Read twice and referred to the Committee on Health, Education, Labor, and Pensions.

SUMMARY AS OF:

7/16/2007—Introduced.

Communities of Color Teen Pregnancy Prevention Act of 2007 - Requires the Secretary of Health and Human Services to make grants for projects to prevent teen pregnancies in racial, ethnic minority, or immigrant communities with a substantial incidence or prevalence of cases of teen pregnancy compared to the average number in communities in the state.

Allows the Secretary to make grants to: (1) carry out activities to prevent unintended pregnancy and sexually transmitted infections among teens; (2) provide necessary social and cultural support services regarding teen pregnancy; (3) provide health and educational services related to the prevention of unintended pregnancy and sexually transmitted infections among teens; (4) promote better health and educational outcomes among pregnant teens; and (5) provide relevant training for individuals who plan to work in school-based support programs.

Requires the Secretary to make grants to: (1) provide public education and increase awareness with respect to the issue of reducing the rates of unintended pregnancy and sexually transmitted infections among teens and related social and emotional issues; and (2) establish and operate a National Clearinghouse for Teen Pregnancy Prevention.

Requires the Secretary, acting through the Director of the Centers for Disease Control and Prevention (CDC), to make grants for research on the prevention of unintended pregnancy and sexually transmitted infections among teens in such communities.

Allows a grant to be made under this Act only if the applicant agrees that: (1) all information provided pursuant to the Act will be age-appropriate, factually and medically accurate and complete, and scientifically based; and (2) information, activities, and services under the grant will be provided in the language and cultural context that is most appropriate for individual groups.

MAJOR ACTIONS:

¤NONE¤

ALL ACTIONS:

7/16/2007:

Read twice and referred to the Committee on Health, Education, Labor, and Pensions.

TITLES(s): (italics indicate a title for a portion of a bill)

¤NONE¤

COSPONSORS(2), ALPHABETICAL [FOLLOWED BY COSPONSORS WITHDRAWN]: (Sort: by date)

Sen Boxer, Barbara [CA] - 7/26/2007

Sen Durbin, Richard [IL] - 7/30/2007

COMMITTEE(S)

Committee/Subcommittee:

Activity:

Senate Health, Education, Labor, and Pensions

Referral, In Committee

RELATED BILL DETAILS: (additional related bills may be indentified in Status)

Bill:

Relationship:

H.R.468

Related bill identified by CRS

AMENDMENT(S)

¤NONE¤

IN THE SENATE OF THE UNITED STATES

July 16, 2007

Mr. OBAMA introduced the following bill; which was read twice and referred to the Committee on Health, Education, Labor, and Pensions

A BILL

To make grants to carry out activities to prevent the incidence of unintended pregnancies and sexually transmitted infections among teens in racial or ethnic minority or immigrant communities, and for other purposes.

Be it enacted by the Senate and House of Representatives of the United States of America in Congress assembled,

SECTION 1. SHORT TITLE.

This Act may be cited as the 'Communities of Color Teen Pregnancy Prevention Act of 2007'.

SEC. 2. FINDINGS.

Congress makes the following findings:

(1) Each year, nearly 750,000 American teens ages 15 through 19 become pregnant.

(2) In 2002, the pregnancy rate for African American and Latino teens ages 15 through 19 was double the rate for white teens (134.2 and 131.5 compared to 65.0).

(3) An estimated 4,883 youth ages 13 through 24 were diagnosed with HIV or AIDS in 2004, representing approximately 13 percent of all individuals given a diagnosis during that year.

(4) African American youth comprised the largest single group of young people affected by HIV, accounting for 55 percent of all HIV infections among youth ages 13 through 24 in 2004.

(5) Although African American teens (ages 13 through 19) represent only 16 percent of United States teens, they accounted for 69 percent of new AIDS cases reported among teens in 2005.

(6) In 2005, Latino teens, ages 13 through 19, accounted for 17 percent of AIDS cases among teens, the same as their proportion of the United States teenage population that year. Latinos ages 20 through 24 accounted for 22 percent of new AIDS reported among young adults, but represented 18 percent of United States young adults.

(7) Recent estimates suggest that while 15- to 24-year olds represent 25 percent of the ever sexually active population, they acquire nearly one-half of all new sexually transmitted infections.

(8) In 2005, the gonorrhea rate among African American teens ages 15 through 19 was 17 times higher than among white teens of the same age. The rates of primary and secondary syphilis were 19 times higher among black teens ages 15 through 19 than among their white peers.

(9) In 2005, nearly three-fourths of all reported cases of gonorrhea occurred among African American teens, for whom the gonorrhea rate was 2,106 per 100,000 population.

SEC. 3. COMMUNITY-BASED AND SCHOOL-BASED INTERVENTION PROGRAMS.

(a) Community-Based Intervention Programs-

(1) IN GENERAL- The Secretary of Health and Human Services (referred to in this Act as the 'Secretary') shall make grants to public and nonprofit private entities for the purpose of carrying out projects to prevent teen pregnancies in racial or ethnic minority or immigrant communities with a substantial incidence or prevalence of cases of teen pregnancy as compared to the average number of such cases in communities in the State involved (referred to in this Act as 'eligible communities').

(2) REQUIREMENTS REGARDING PURPOSE OF GRANTS- A grant may be made under paragraph (1) only if, with respect to the expenditure of the grant to carry out the purpose described in such paragraph, the applicant involved agrees to use one or more of the following strategies:

(A) Promote effective communication among families about preventing teen pregnancy, particularly communication among parents or guardians and their children.

(B) Educate community members about the consequences of teen pregnancy.

(C) Encourage young people to postpone sexual activity and prepare for a healthy, successful adulthood, including by teaching them skills to avoid making or receiving unwanted verbal, physical, and sexual advances.

(D) Provide information about the health benefits and side effects of all contraceptives and barrier methods as a means to prevent pregnancy and reduce the risk of contracting sexually transmitted infections, including HIV/AIDS.

(E) Provide educational information, including medically accurate information about the health benefits and side effects of all contraceptives and barrier methods, for young people in such communities who are already sexually active or are at risk of becoming sexually active and inform young people in such communities about the responsibilities and consequences of being a parent, and how early pregnancy and parenthood can interfere with educational and other goals.

(3) UTILIZING EFFECTIVE STRATEGIES- A grant may be made under paragraph (1) only if the applicant involved agrees that, in carrying out the purpose described in such paragraph, the applicant will, whenever possible, use strategies that have been demonstrated to be effective (on the basis of rigorous scientific research), or that incorporate characteristics of effective programs.

(b) School-Based Projects-

(1) IN GENERAL- The Secretary may make grants to public and nonprofit private entities for the purpose of establishing and operating for eligible communities, in association with public secondary schools for such communities, projects for one or more of the following:

(A) To carry out activities, including counseling, to prevent unintended pregnancy and sexually transmitted infections, including HIV/AIDS, among teens.

(B) To provide necessary social and cultural support services regarding teen pregnancy.

(C) To provide health and educational services related to the prevention of unintended pregnancy and sexually transmitted infections, including HIV/AIDS, among teens.

(D) To promote better health and educational outcomes among pregnant teens.

(E) To provide training for individuals who plan to work in school-based support programs regarding the prevention of unintended pregnancy and sexually transmitted infections, including HIV/AIDS, among teens.

(2) PRIORITY- In making grants under paragraph (1), the Secretary shall give priority to providing for projects under such paragraph in eligible communities.

(3) REQUIRED COALITION- A grant may be made under paragraph (1) only if the applicant involved has formed an appropriate coalition of entities for purposes of carrying out a project under such paragraph, including—

(A) one or more public secondary schools for the eligible community involved; and

(B) entities to provide the services of the project.

(4) TRAINING- A grant under paragraph (1) may be expended to train individuals to provide the services described in subparagraphs (A) and (B) of such paragraph for the project involved.

(c) Reporting and Evaluation-

(1) REPORT- A grant may be made under subsection (a) or (b) only if the applicant involved agrees to submit to the Secretary, in accordance with the criteria of the Secretary, a report that provides information on the project under such subsection, including project outcomes and increased education and awareness about the prevention of unintended pregnancy and sexually transmitted infections, including HIV/AIDS, among teens. The Secretary shall make such reports available to the public.

(2) EVALUATIONS- Not later than 12 months after the date of the enactment of this Act, the Secretary shall, directly or through contract, provide for evaluations of at least 10 percent or not less than 6 projects carried out with grants under each of subsections (a) and (b). Each such evaluation shall describe—

(A) the activities carried out with the grant; and

(B) the extent to which the activities were effective in changing attitudes and behavior to achieve the project strategies consistent with—

(i) subsection (a)(2) for grants under subsection (a); or

(ii) subsection (b)(1) for grants under subsection (b).

(d) Authorization of Appropriations-

(1) COMMUNITY-BASED INTERVENTION PROGRAMS- For the purpose of carrying out subsection (a), there is authorized to be appropriated $40,000,000 for each of the fiscal years 2008 through 2012.

(2) SCHOOL-BASED PROJECTS- For the purpose of carrying out subsection (b), there is authorized to be appropriated $10,000,000 for each of the fiscal years 2008 through 2012.

(3) EVALUATIONS- Of the total amount appropriated to carry out this section for a fiscal year, the Secretary shall reserve 10 percent of such amount to carry out subsection (c)(2).

SEC. 4. MULTIMEDIA CAMPAIGNS.

(a) In General- The Secretary shall make grants to public and nonprofit private entities for the purpose of carrying out multimedia campaigns to provide public education and increase awareness with respect to the issue of reducing the rates of unintended pregnancy and sexually transmitted infections, including HIV/AIDS, among teens, and related social, physical, and emotional issues.

(b) Priority- In making grants under subsection (a), the Secretary shall give priority to campaigns described in such subsection that are directed toward eligible
communities.

(c) Requirements- A grant may be made under subsection (a) only if the applicant
involved agrees that the multimedia campaign under such subsection will—

(1) provide information on the prevention of unintended pregnancy and sexually
transmitted infections, including HIV/AIDS, among teens;

(2) provide information that identifies organizations in the communities involved
that—

(A) provide health and educational services related to the prevention of unintended
pregnancy and sexually transmitted infections, including HIV/AIDS, for teens; and

(B) provide necessary social and cultural support services; and

(3) coincide with efforts of the National Clearinghouse for Teen Pregnancy Prevention that are made under section 5(b)(1).

(d) Authorization of Appropriations- For the purpose of carrying out this section,
there is authorized to be appropriated $6,000,000 for each of the fiscal years 2008
through 2012.

SEC. 5. NATIONAL CLEARINGHOUSE.

(a) In General- The Secretary shall make grants to a nonprofit private entity to establish and operate a National Clearinghouse for Teen Pregnancy Prevention (referred to
in this section as the 'Clearinghouse') for the purposes described in subsection (b).

(b) Purposes of Clearinghouse- The purposes referred to in subsection (a) regarding
the Clearinghouse are as follows:

(1) To provide information and technical assistance to States, Indian tribes, local communities, and other public or private entities to develop content and messages for teens
and adults that address and seek to reduce the rate of unintended pregnancy and sexually transmitted infections, including HIV/AIDS, among teens.

(2) To support parents in their essential role in preventing unintended pregnancy and
sexually transmitted infections, including HIV/AIDS, among teens by equipping
parents with information and resources to promote and strengthen communication
with their children about sex, values, and positive relationships, including healthy
relationships.

(c) Requirements for Grantee- A grant may be made under subsection (a) only if the
applicant involved is an organization that meets the following conditions:

(1) The organization is a nationally recognized, nonpartisan organization that has at
least 10 years of experience focusing on preventing teen pregnancy and working with
diverse groups to reduce the rate of teen pregnancy.

(2) The organization has a demonstrated ability to work with and provide assistance to
a broad range of individuals and entities, including teens; parents; the entertainment
and news media; State, tribal, and local organizations; networks of teen pregnancy

prevention practitioners; reproductive health providers; businesses; faith and community leaders; and researchers.

(3) The organization has experience in the use of culturally competent and linguistically appropriate methods to address teen pregnancy in eligible communities.

(4) The organization conducts or supports research and has experience with scientific analyses and evaluations.

(5) The organization has comprehensive knowledge and data about strategies for the prevention of teen pregnancy.

(6) The organization has experience in carrying out functions similar to the functions described in subsection (b).

(d) Authorization of Appropriations- For the purpose of carrying out this section, there is authorized to be appropriated $1,500,000 for each of the fiscal years 2008 through 2012.

SEC. 6. RESEARCH.

(a) In General- The Secretary, acting through the Director of the Centers for Disease Control and Prevention, shall make grants to public or nonprofit private entities to conduct, support, and coordinate research on the prevention of unintended pregnancy and sexually transmitted infections, including HIV/AIDS, among teens in eligible communities, including research on the factors contributing to the disproportionate rates of teen pregnancy and sexually transmitted infections in such communities and research-based strategies for addressing such disparities.

(b) Research- In carrying out subsection (a), the Secretary shall support research that—

(1) investigates the incidence and prevalence of teen pregnancy and sexually transmitted infections, including HIV/AIDS, among teens in communities described in such subsection;

(2) examines—

(A) the relationships between teen pregnancy and one or more of—

(i) the mental and physical health and well-being of teens in the communities;

(ii) teen access to a full range of family planning services;

(iii) the scholastic achievement of such teens;

(iv) family structure and communication; and

(v) other factors contributing to disproportionate rates of teen pregnancy and sexually transmitted infections among teens in such communities;

(B) the variance in the rates of teen pregnancy and by—

(i) location (such as inner cities, inner suburbs, outer suburbs, and rural areas);

(ii) population subgroup (such as Hispanic, Asian-Pacific Islander, African-American, and Native American);

(iii) level of acculturation; and

(iv) socioeconomic status (such as income, educational attainment of the parents of the teen, and school attendance of the teen);

(C) the importance of the physical and social environment as a factor in placing communities at risk of increased rates of pregnancy and sexually transmitted infections; and

(D) the importance of aspirations and motivations as factors affecting young people's risk of teen pregnancy;

(3) is used to propose or identify additional strategies that will address the disproportionate rates of teen pregnancy and sexually transmitted infections in such communities; and

(4) wherever possible, includes efforts to link the measures to relevant databases, including health databases.

(c) Priority- In making grants under subsection (a), the Secretary shall give priority to research that incorporates—

(1) interdisciplinary approaches; or

(2) a strong emphasis on community-based participatory research.

(d) Authorization of Appropriations- For the purpose of carrying out this section, there is authorized to be appropriated $7,500,000 for each of the fiscal years 2008 through 2012.

SEC. 7. GENERAL REQUIREMENTS.

(a) Medically Accurate Information- A grant may be made under this Act only if the applicant involved agrees that all information provided pursuant to the grant will be age-appropriate, factually and medically accurate and complete, and scientifically based.

(b) Cultural Context of Services- A grant may be made under this Act only if the applicant involved agrees that information, activities, and services under the grant that are directed toward a particular population group will be provided in the language and cultural context that is most appropriate for individuals in such group.

(c) Application for Grant- A grant may be made under this Act only if an application for the grant is submitted to the Secretary and the application is in such form, is made in such manner, and contains such agreements, assurances, and information as the Secretary determines to be necessary to carry out the program involved.

SEC. 8. DEFINITIONS.

For purposes of this Act:

(1) The term 'eligible community' has the meaning indicated for such term in section 3(a)(1).

(2) The term 'HIV/AIDS' means the human immunodeficiency virus, and includes the acquired immune deficiency syndrome.

(3) The term 'medically accurate' with respect to information, means information that is supported by research, recognized as accurate and objective by leading medical,

psychological, psychiatric, and public health organizations and agencies, and where relevant, published in peer review journals.

(4) The term 'racial or ethnic minority or immigrant communities' means communities with a substantial number of residents who are members of racial or ethnic minority groups or who are immigrants.

(5) The term 'Secretary' has the meaning indicated for such term in section 3(a)(1).

US SENATE BILL 1811

TITLE: A bill to amend the Toxic Substances Control Act to assess and reduce the levels of lead found in child-occupied facilities in the United States, and for other purposes.

SPONSOR: Sen Obama, Barack [IL] (introduced 7/18/2007) Cosponsors (2)

RELATED BILLS: H.R.3085

LATEST MAJOR ACTION: 7/18/2007 Referred to Senate committee. Status: Read twice and referred to the Committee on Environment and Public Works.

SUMMARY AS OF:

7/18/2007—Introduced.

Lead Poisoning Reduction Act of 2007 - Amends the Toxic Substances Control Act to establish a Select Group on Lead Exposure. Requires the Group to: (1) conduct a study of state, tribal, and local programs to protect children from exposure to lead at child-occupied facilities constructed before January 1, 1978; (2) develop baseline standards such programs must meet to receive a grant under this Act; and (3) develop a model program to protect children from exposure to lead at such facilities that can be adopted by state, local, and tribal governments.

Requires the model program to meet or exceed standards that require facilities to be notified as soon as practicable after a child is diagnosed with lead poisoning and to be tested for the presence of lead upon receiving such notification.

Directs the Administrator to: (1) establish a program to provide grants to assist such facilities in carrying out activities to protect children from lead exposure; (2) promulgate regulations requiring such facilities to test applicable exposure pathways for lead, prohibiting states and Indian tribes from issuing a license to such facilities until the testing is complete and the exposure to lead is eliminated, and requiring all child-occupied facilities to eliminate the risk of exposure to lead through applicable exposure pathways; and (3) apply regulations governing lead-based paint activities to contractors and workers engaged in the renovation, remodeling, or painting of such facilitates and to establish a program to provide information and training about those activities to them.

Major Actions:

¤NONE¤

All Actions:

7/17/2007:

Sponsor introductory remarks on measure. (CR 7/18/2007 S9498-9499)

7/18/2007:

Read twice and referred to the Committee on Environment and Public Works.

Titles(s): (italics indicate a title for a portion of a bill)

¤NONE¤

Cosponsors(2), Alphabetical [followed by Cosponsors withdrawn]: (Sort: by date)

Sen Clinton, Hillary Rodham [NY] - 7/18/2007

Sen Schumer, Charles E. [NY] - 7/18/2007

Committee(s)

Committee/Subcommittee:

Activity:

Senate Environment and Public Works

Referral, In Committee

Related Bill Details: (additional related bills may be indentified in Status)

Bill:

Relationship:

H.R.3085

Related bill identified by CRS

Amendment(s)

¤NONE¤

In the Senate of the United States

July 18 (legislative day, July 17), 2007

Mr. OBAMA (for himself, Mr. SCHUMER, and Mrs. CLINTON) introduced the following bill; which was read twice and referred to the Committee on Environment and Public Works

A BILL

To amend the Toxic Substances Control Act to assess and reduce the levels of lead found in child-occupied facilities in the United States, and for other purposes.

Be it enacted by the Senate and House of Representatives of the United States of America in Congress assembled,

SECTION 1. SHORT TITLE.

This Act may be cited as the 'Lead Poisoning Reduction Act of 2007'.

SEC. 2. FINDINGS.

Congress finds that—

(1) the number of children suffering from lead poisoning remains unacceptably high;

(2) children younger than 6 years of age are much more likely to suffer the devastating effects of lead poisoning;

(3) the health of children may be impacted at lower levels of lead exposure than previously thought;

(4) lead poisoning can lead to organ damage, as well as serious developmental, learning, and behavioral problems in children;

(5) owners and managers of childcare and pre-school facilities constructed before 1978 need guidance with respect to protecting children of the United States from exposure to lead; and

(6) the Administrator of the Environmental Protection Agency has the authority, but, as of the date of enactment of this Act, has elected not, to promulgate regulations pursuant to section 402 of the Toxic Substances Control Act (15 U.S.C. 2682) to reduce lead exposure in child-occupied facilities.

SEC. 3. LEAD ASSESSMENT IN CHILD-OCCUPIED FACILITIES.

Section 402 of the Toxic Substances Control Act (15 U.S.C. 2682) is amended by adding at the end the following:

'(d) Child-Occupied Facilities-

'(1) DEFINITIONS- In this subsection:

'(A) CHILD-OCCUPIED FACILITY-

'(i) IN GENERAL- The term 'child-occupied facility' means a facility described in clause (ii) that was constructed before January 1, 1978, and that is visited regularly by a child of not more than 6 years old for at least 2 days within any week for not less than—

'(I) 3 hours each visit;

'(II) 6 hours each week; and

'(III) 60 hours each calendar year.

'(ii) DESCRIPTION OF FACILITY- A facility referred to in clause (i) is—

'(I) a childcare center;

'(II) a pre-school or kindergarten classroom; or

'(III) except as provided in clause (iii), any other facility (including a facility used for a Head Start program or a similar program) at which a childcare provider receives compensation or a subsidy for services provided.

'(iii) EXCLUSION- The term 'child-occupied facility' does not include a home-based childcare facility.

'(B) EXPOSURE PATHWAY- The term 'exposure pathway' includes, with respect to lead—

'(i) lead-based paint and lead-based paint hazards; and

'(ii) lead contained in—

'(I) drinking water plumbing and fixtures;

'(II) furniture, fixtures, and playground equipment; and

'(III) products used by or for children.

'(C) HOME-BASED CHILDCARE FACILITY- The term 'home-based childcare facility' means an owner-occupied or rental housing unit—

'(i) at which 1 or more individuals reside; and

'(ii) that meets the requirements under clauses (i) and (ii) of subparagraph (A) for a child-occupied facility.

'(D) SELECT GROUP- The term 'Select Group' means the Select Group on Lead Exposure established by paragraph (2)(A).

'(2) SELECT GROUP ON LEAD EXPOSURE-

'(A) ESTABLISHMENT- There is established a Select Group on Lead Exposure, to be composed of—

'(i) the Secretary of Education (or a designee);

'(ii) the Director of the Centers for Disease Control and Prevention (or a designee);

'(iii) the Director of the National Institute of Environmental Health Science (or a designee);

'(iv) the Assistant Secretary of the Administration for Children and Families (or a designee);

'(v) the Director of the National Institute of Child Health and Human Development (or a designee); and

'(vi) the head of any other Federal agency (or a designee), as the Administrator determines to be appropriate.

'(B) DUTIES- The Select Group shall advise the Administrator on actions necessary to carry out this subsection and related activities.

'(C) COMPENSATION OF MEMBERS- A member of the Select Group shall serve without compensation.

'(D) TRAVEL EXPENSES- A member of the Select Group shall be allowed travel expenses, including per diem in lieu of subsistence, at rates authorized for an employee of an agency under subchapter I of chapter 57 of title 5, United States Code, while away from the home or regular place of business of the member in the performance of the duties of the Select Group.

'(3) BASELINE STANDARDS AND MODEL PROGRAM-

'(A) STUDY- Not later than 180 days after the date of enactment of this subsection, the Select Group shall conduct a study of State, tribal, and local programs the purpose of which is to protect children from exposure to lead at child-occupied facilities.

'(B) STANDARDS AND PROGRAM-

'(i) DEVELOPMENT- Not later than 1 year after the date of enactment of this subsection, the Select Group shall develop—

'(I) baseline standards with which a State, tribal, or local program described in subparagraph (A) shall comply to be eligible to receive a grant under paragraph (4); and

'(II) a model program to protect children from exposure to lead at child-occupied facilities that can be adopted for use by State, tribal, and local governments.

'(ii) FACTORS FOR CONSIDERATION- In developing the baseline standards and model program under clause (i), the Select Group shall take into consideration—

'(I) the results of the study under subparagraph (A);

'(II) regulations promulgated pursuant to subsection (a) (including the process of promulgating the regulations); and

'(III) guidance for childcare providers produced by agencies and other groups, including—

'(aa) any member of the Select Group;

'(bb) the American Academy of Pediatrics;

'(cc) the American Public Health Association; and

'(dd) the National Center for Healthy Housing.

'(iii) REQUIREMENTS-

'(I) BASELINE STANDARDS- The baseline standards developed under clause (i)(I) shall include guidelines for—

'(aa) assessing child-occupied facilities for the identification and remediation of exposure pathways; and

'(bb) informing children and families that visit child-occupied facilities of the exposure pathways and related hazards.

'(II) MODEL PROGRAM- The model program developed under clause (i)(II) shall meet or exceed such applicable standards (including the baseline standards under clause (i)(I)) as the Administrator may establish with respect to grant programs carried out by the Administrator, including standards requiring that—

'(aa) each appropriate child-occupied facility shall be provided a notice as soon as practicable after a child served by the child-occupied facility is diagnosed with lead poisoning, subject to such guidelines as the Select Group determines to be necessary to ensure the protection of privileged medical information; and

'(bb) on receiving a notification under item (aa), a child-occupied facility that has not been tested for the presence of lead in exposure pathways shall be so tested.

'(4) GRANT PROGRAM-

'(A) DEFINITION OF ELIGIBLE FACILITY-

'(i) IN GENERAL- In this paragraph, the term 'eligible facility' means a child-occupied facility that participates in a State, tribal, or local program—

'(I) the purpose of which is to protect children from exposure to lead at child-occupied facilities; and

'(II) that—

'(aa) is based on the model program developed under paragraph (3)(B)(i)(II); or

'(bb) otherwise meets the baseline standards developed under paragraph (3)(B)(i)(I).

'(ii) EXCLUSION- The term 'eligible facility' does not include a home-based childcare facility.

'(B) ESTABLISHMENT- Not later than 1 year after, but in no case before, the date of development of baseline standards and the model program under paragraph (3), the Administrator, in consultation with the Select Group, shall establish a program under which the Administrator shall provide grants to eligible facilities to assist the eligible facilities in carrying out activities to protect children from exposure to lead at eligible facilities.

'(C) APPLICATION- To be eligible to receive a grant under this paragraph, an eligible facility shall submit to the Administrator an application at such time, in such manner, and containing such information as the Administrator, in consultation with the Select Group, may require.

'(D) COST SHARING-

'(i) IN GENERAL- The non-Federal share of the cost of an activity funded by a grant under this paragraph shall be 20 percent.

'(ii) PROVISION- The non-Federal share under clause (i)—

'(I) may be provided using State, tribal, and local government funds and private funds; and

'(II) shall not be provided using funds appropriated pursuant to any Federal program.

'(E) AUTHORIZATION OF APPROPRIATIONS- There is authorized to be appropriated to carry out this paragraph $42,600,000 for the period of fiscal years 2008 through 2012.

'(5) REGULATIONS-

'(A) TESTING- Not later than 18 months after the date of enactment of this subsection, the Administrator shall promulgate regulations requiring that—

'(i) child-occupied facilities placed into service after that date shall test each applicable exposure pathway for the presence of lead; and

'(ii) no State or Indian tribe shall issue to a child-occupied facility described in clause (i) a license until—

'(I) the testing required under clause (i) is completed; and

'(II) the exposure to lead, if any, in each applicable exposure pathway is eliminated.

'(B) ELIMINATION OF RISK-

'(i) IN GENERAL- Not later than 3 years after the date of enactment of this subsection, the Administrator shall promulgate proposed regulations requiring all child-occupied facilities to eliminate the risk of exposure to lead through applicable exposure pathways.

'(ii) FINALIZATION AND EFFECTIVE DATE- The proposed regulations under clause (i)—

'(I) shall be finalized by the Administrator not later than 4 years after the date of enactment of this subsection; and

'(II) shall take effect not later than 5 years after the date of enactment of this subsection.

'(6) CONTRACTORS ENGAGED IN RENOVATION, REMODELING, AND PAINTING OF CHILD-OCCUPIED FACILITIES- Not later than 18 months after the date of enactment of this subsection, the Administrator, in consultation with the Select Group, shall—

'(A) apply regulations promulgated pursuant to subsection (c)(3) to contractors and other workers engaged in the renovation, remodeling, or painting of child-occupied facilities; and

'(B) establish a program to provide information, training, and materials concerning those activities to the contractors and workers.

'(7) REPORT TO CONGRESS- Not later than 3 years after the date of enactment of this subsection, the Administrator, in consultation with the Select Group, shall submit to Congress a report containing—

'(A) a list of States and Indian tribes carrying out programs to protect children from exposure to lead at child-occupied facilities that meet the baseline standards developed under paragraph (3)(B)(i)(I) (including by adopting the model program developed under paragraph (3)(B)(i)(II));

'(B) the number of child-occupied facilities that received grants under paragraph (4) during the preceding 3-year period; and

'(C) recommendations for additional Federal funds and resources, if any, required to ensure the protection of children from exposure to lead at child-occupied facilities.'.

US Senate Bill 1817

Title: A bill to ensure proper administration of the discharge of members of the Armed Forces for personality disorder, and for other purposes.

Sponsor: Sen Obama, Barack [IL] (introduced 7/19/2007) Cosponsors (11)

Related Bills: H.R.3167

Latest Major Action: 7/19/2007 Referred to Senate committee. Status: Read twice and referred to the Committee on Armed Services.

Summary As Of:

7/19/2007—Introduced.

Prohibits the Secretary of a military department from discharging due to a personality disorder a member of the Armed Forces who has served on active duty in a combat zone until the later of the date of: (1) completion by the Secretary of Defense (Secretary) of a review of Department of Defense (DOD) policies and procedures for diagnosing such a disorder; (2) issuance by the Secretary of policies and procedures to ensure the appropriate use of such a discharge; (3) establishment by the Secretary of an independent review board for personality disorder discharges; (4) submittal by the Secretary of a report to Congress on progress in implementing the requirements under (1) through (3), above; or (5) the date that is 45 days after the date of the submission of the report referred to in (4), which period shall permit Congress to consider the report.

Provides an exception to such requirement in the case of a member who, during recruitment for or enlistment in the Armed Forces, provided false or misleading information, or omitted providing information about past criminal behavior, that is material to a discharge for personality disorder.

Major Actions:

¤NONE¤

All Actions:

7/19/2007:

Read twice and referred to the Committee on Armed Services.

Titles(s): (italics indicate a title for a portion of a bill)

¤NONE¤

Cosponsors(11), Alphabetical [followed by Cosponsors withdrawn]: (Sort: by date)

Sen Biden, Joseph R., Jr. [DE] - 7/26/2007

Sen Bond, Christopher S. [MO] - 7/19/2007

Sen Boxer, Barbara [CA] - 7/19/2007

Sen Durbin, Richard [IL] - 7/19/2007

Sen Johnson, Tim [SD] - 7/19/2007

Sen Kerry, John F. [MA] - 7/31/2007

Sen Lieberman, Joseph I. [CT] - 7/19/2007

Sen McCaskill, Claire [MO] - 7/19/2007

Sen Murray, Patty [WA] - 7/19/2007

Sen Sanders, Bernard [VT] - 7/26/2007

Sen Whitehouse, Sheldon [RI] - 7/19/2007

COMMITTEE(S)

Committee/Subcommittee:

Activity:

Senate Armed Services

Referral, In Committee

RELATED BILL DETAILS: (additional related bills may be indentified in Status)

Bill:

Relationship:

H.R.3167

Related bill identified by CRS

AMENDMENT(S)

¤NONE¤

IN THE SENATE OF THE UNITED STATES

July 19, 2007

Mr. OBAMA (for himself, Mr. BOND, Mrs. MCCASKILL, Mrs. BOXER, Mrs. MURRAY, Mr. LIEBERMAN, Mr. DURBIN, Mr. JOHNSON, and Mr. WHITEHOUSE) introduced the following bill; which was read twice and referred to the Committee on Armed Services

A BILL

To ensure proper administration of the discharge of members of the Armed Forces for personality disorder, and for other purposes.

Be it enacted by the Senate and House of Representatives of the United States of America in Congress assembled,

SECTION 1. DISCHARGE OF MEMBERS OF THE ARMED FORCES FOR PERSONALITY DISORDER.

(a) Temporary Moratorium on Discharges- Effective as of the date of the enactment of this Act, the Secretary of a military department may not, except as provided in subsection (b), discharge from the Armed Forces for personality disorder any member of the Armed Forces (including a member of the National Guard or Reserve) who has served on active duty in a combat zone until the later of the dates as follows:

(1) The date of the completion by the Secretary of Defense of a review of the policies and procedures of the Department of Defense for diagnosing a personality disorder in members of the Armed Forces.

(2) The date of the issuance by the Secretary of Defense of policies and procedures to ensure the appropriate use of discharge of members of the Armed Forces for personality disorder, which discharges shall be based on standard clinical diagnostic practices, including the practices outlined in the most recent edition of the Diagnostic Statistical Manual for Mental Disorders.

(3) The date of the establishment by the Secretary of Defense of an independent review board for discharges of members of the Armed Forces for personality discharge, including for members so discharged on or after September 12, 2001, and before the date of the enactment of this Act.

(4) The date of the submittal by the Secretary of Defense of a report to Congress on the progress in implementing the requirements of paragraphs (1) through (3).

(5) The date that is 45 days after the date of the submittal of the report referred to in paragraph (4), which period shall permit Congress to consider the report.

(b) Exception- The limitation in subsection (a) shall not apply with respect to any member of the Armed Forces who provided false or misleading information, or omitted providing information about past criminal behavior, that is material to a discharge for personality disorder during recruitment for or enlistment in the Armed Forces.

US Senate Bill 1818

TITLE: A bill to amend the Toxic Substances Control Act to phase out the use of mercury in the manufacture of chlorine and caustic soda, and for other purposes.

SPONSOR: Sen Obama, Barack [IL] (introduced 7/19/2007) Cosponsors (4)

LATEST MAJOR ACTION: 7/19/2007 Referred to Senate committee. Status: Read twice and referred to the Committee on Environment and Public Works.

SUMMARY AS OF:

7/19/2007—Introduced.

Missing Mercury in Manufacturing Monitoring and Mitigation Act - Declares that the United States should develop policies and programs that will reduce: (1) mercury use and emissions; (2) mercury releases from the reservoir of mercury currently in use or circulation; and (3) exposures to mercury, particularly exposures of women of childbearing age and young children.

Amends the Toxic Substances Control Act to prohibit the manufacture of chlorine or caustic soda using mercury cells, effective January 1, 2012. Requires the owner or operator of each chlor-alkali facility to submit to the Environmental Protection Agency (EPA) Administrator and the state in which the facility is located an annual report for 2008-2012 concerning mercury waste, emissions, and content in products.

Requires EPA to conduct a comprehensive mercury inventory covering the life and closure of chlor-alkali facilities that cease operations on or after July 1, 2008.

Establishes the Mercury Storage Advisory Committee, which shall report to Congress on: (1) requirements necessary to prevent the release of, or worker exposure to, elemental mercury; and (2) annual costs of, federal facilities needed for, barriers to, and an optimal plan for, mercury storage.

Requires: (1) EPA to establish regulations to facilitate the transfer and storage of mercury located at closed facilities; and (2) beginning on July 1, 2008, the transfer of elemental mercury located at a closed facility that has ceased operations to a storage facility established by EPA in accordance with such regulations.

Requires EPA, in coordination with the Administrator of the Agency for Toxic Substances and Disease Registry Administrator, by July 1, 2009, to conduct a health assessment of employees at chlor-alkali facilities that continue to operate as of July 1, 2008.

MAJOR ACTIONS:

¤NONE¤

ALL ACTIONS:

7/19/2007:

Sponsor introductory remarks on measure. (CR S9615)

7/19/2007:

Read twice and referred to the Committee on Environment and Public Works.

TITLES(s): (italics indicate a title for a portion of a bill)

¤NONE¤

COSPONSORS(4), ALPHABETICAL [FOLLOWED BY COSPONSORS WITHDRAWN]: (Sort: by date)

Sen Biden, Joseph R., Jr. [DE] - 10/24/2007

Sen Cardin, Benjamin L. [MD] - 2/6/2008

Sen Feingold, Russell D. [WI] - 9/19/2007

Sen Menendez, Robert [NJ] - 9/11/2007

COMMITTEE(S)

Committee/Subcommittee:

Activity:

Senate Environment and Public Works

Referral, In Committee

RELATED BILL DETAILS:

¤NONE¤

AMENDMENT(S)

¤NONE¤

IN THE SENATE OF THE UNITED STATES

July 19, 2007

Mr. OBAMA introduced the following bill; which was read twice and referred to the Committee on Environment and Public Works

A BILL

To amend the Toxic Substances Control Act to phase out the use of mercury in the manufacture of chlorine and caustic soda, and for other purposes.

Be it enacted by the Senate and House of Representatives of the United States of America in Congress assembled,

SECTION 1. SHORT TITLE.

This Act may be cited as the 'Missing Mercury in Manufacturing Monitoring and Mitigation Act'.

SEC. 2. FINDINGS.

Congress finds that—

(1) mercury and mercury compounds are highly toxic to humans, ecosystems, and wildlife;

(2) as many as 10 percent of women in the United States of childbearing age have mercury in their bloodstreams at a level that could pose risks to their unborn babies, and as many as 630,000 children born annually in the United States are at risk of neurological problems relating to mercury exposure in utero;

(3) the most significant source of mercury exposure to people in the United States is ingestion of mercury-contaminated fish;

(4) the long-term solution to mercury pollution is to minimize global mercury use and releases of mercury to eventually achieve reduced contamination levels in the environment, rather than reducing fish consumption, since uncontaminated fish represents a critical and healthy source of nutrition for people worldwide;

(5) an estimated additional 24,000 to 30,000 tons of mercury are used at mercury cell chlor-alkali plants worldwide;

(6) mercury pollution is a transboundary pollutant that—

(A) is deposited locally, regionally, and globally; and

(B) affects bodies of water near industrial areas, such as the Great Lakes, as well as bodies of water in remote areas, such as the Arctic Circle;

(7) of the approximately 30 plants in the United States that produce chlorine, only 8 use the obsolete 'mercury cell' chlor-alkali process, and 5 have not yet committed to phasing out mercury use;

(8)(A) only about 10 percent of the total quantity of chlorine and caustic soda produced in the United States comes from the chlor-alkali plants described in paragraph (7) that use the mercury cell chlor-alkali process;

(B) cost-effective alternatives are available and in use in the remaining 90 percent of chlorine and caustic soda production; and

(C) other countries, including Japan, have already banned the mercury cell chlor-alkali process;

(9) the chlor-alkali industry acknowledges that—

(A) mercury can contaminate products manufactured at mercury cell facilities; and

(B) the use of some of those products results in the direct and indirect release of mercury;

(10) despite those quantities of mercury known to have been used or to be in use, neither the chlor-alkali industry nor the Environmental Protection Agency is able—

(A) to adequately account for the disposition of the mercury used at those facilities; or

(B) to accurately estimate current mercury emissions; and

(11) it is critically important that the United States work aggressively toward the minimization of supply, demand, and releases of mercury, both domestically and internationally.

SEC. 3. STATEMENT OF POLICY.

Congress declares that the United States should develop policies and programs that will—

(1) reduce mercury use and emissions within the United States;

(2) reduce mercury releases from the reservoir of mercury currently in use or circulation within the United States; and

(3) reduce exposures to mercury, particularly exposures of women of childbearing age and young children.

SEC. 4. USE OF MERCURY IN CHLORINE AND CAUSTIC SODA MANUFACTURING.

(a) In General- Title I of the Toxic Substances Control Act (15 U.S.C. 2601 et seq.) is amended by inserting after section 6 the following:

'SEC. 6A. USE OF MERCURY IN CHLORINE AND CAUSTIC SODA MANUFACTURING.

'(a) Definitions- In this section:

'(1) CHLOR-ALKALI FACILITY- The term 'chlor-alkali facility' means a facility used for the manufacture of chlorine or caustic soda using a mercury cell process.

'(2) HAZARDOUS WASTE; SOLID WASTE- The terms 'hazardous waste' and 'solid waste' have the meanings given those terms in section 1004 of the Solid Waste Disposal Act (42 U.S.C. 6903).

'(b) Prohibition- Effective beginning January 1, 2012, the manufacture of chlorine or caustic soda using mercury cells is prohibited in the United States.

'(c) Reporting-

'(1) IN GENERAL- Not later than April 1, 2008, and annually thereafter through April 1, 2012, the owner or operator of each chlor-alkali facility shall submit to the Administrator and the State in which the chlor-alkali facility is located a report that identifies—

'(A) each type and quantity of mercury-containing hazardous waste and nonhazardous solid waste generated by the chlor-alkali facility during the preceding calendar year;

'(B) the mercury content of the wastes;

'(C) the manner in which each waste was managed, including the location of each offsite location to which the waste was transported for subsequent handling or management;

'(D) the volume of mercury released, intentionally or unintentionally, into the air or water by the chlor-alkali facility, including mercury released from emissions or vaporization;

'(E) the volume of mercury estimated to have accumulated in pipes and plant equipment of the chlor-alkali facility, including a description of—

'(i) the applicable volume for each type of equipment; and

'(ii) methods of accumulation; and

'(F) the quantity and forms of mercury found in all products produced for sale by the chlor-alkali facility.

'(2) AVOIDANCE OF DUPLICATION- To avoid duplication, the Administrator may permit the owner or operator of a facility described in paragraph (1) to combine and submit the report required under this subsection with any report required to be submitted by the owner or operator under subtitle C of the Solid Waste Disposal Act (42 U.S.C. 6921 et seq.).

'(d) Inventory-

'(1) IN GENERAL- For each chlor-alkali facility that ceases operations on or after July 1, 2008, not later than 1 year after the date of cessation of operations, the Administrator, in consultation with the State in which the facility is located, shall conduct a comprehensive mercury inventory covering the life and closure of the chlor-alkali facility, taking into account—

'(A) the total quantity of mercury purchased to start and operate the chlor-alkali facility;

'(B) the total quantity of mercury remaining in mercury cells and other equipment at the time of closure of the chlor-alkali facility;

'(C) the estimated quantity of mercury in hazardous waste, nonhazardous solid waste, and products generated at the chlor-alkali facility during the operational life of the chlor-alkali facility; and

'(D) the estimated aggregate mercury releases from the chlor-alkali facility into air and other environmental media.

'(2) RECORDS AND INFORMATION- In carrying out paragraph (1), the Administrator shall obtain mercury purchase records and such other information from each chlor-alkali facility as are necessary to determine, as accurately as practicable from available information, the magnitude and nature of mercury releases from the chlor-alkali facility into air and other environmental media.

'(e) Mercury Storage Advisory Committee-

'(1) ESTABLISHMENT- There is established an advisory committee, to be known as the 'Mercury Storage Advisory Committee' (referred to in this subsection as the 'Committee').

'(2) MEMBERSHIP-

'(A) IN GENERAL- The Committee shall be composed of 9 members, of whom—

'(i) 2 members shall be jointly appointed by the Speaker of the House of Representatives and the majority leader of the Senate—

'(I) 1 of whom shall be designated to serve as Chairperson of the Committee; and

'(II) 1 of whom shall be designated to serve as Vice-Chairperson of the Committee;

'(ii) 1 member shall be the Administrator;

'(iii) 1 member shall be the Secretary of Defense;

'(iv) 1 member shall be a representative of State environmental agencies;

'(v) 1 member shall be a representative of State attorneys general;

'(vi) 1 member shall be a representative of the chlorine industry;

'(vii) 1 member shall be a representative of the mercury waste treatment industry; and

'(viii) 1 member shall be a representative of a nonprofit environmental organization.

'(B) APPOINTMENTS- Not later than 45 days after the date of enactment of this section, the Administrator, in consultation with the appropriate congressional committees, shall appoint the members of the Committee described in clauses (iv) through (viii) of subparagraph (A).

'(3) INITIAL MEETING- Not later than 30 days after the date on which all members of the Committee have been appointed, the Committee shall hold the initial meeting of the Committee.

'(4) MEETINGS- The Committee shall meet at the call of the Chairperson.

'(5) QUORUM- A majority of the members of the Committee shall constitute a quorum.

'(6) REPORT- Not later than 1 year after the date of enactment of this section, the Committee shall submit to Congress a report describing the findings and recommendations of the Committee, if any, relating to—

'(A) the environmental, health, and safety requirements necessary to prevent—

'(i) the release of elemental mercury into the environment; and

'(ii) worker exposure from the storage of elemental mercury;

'(B) the estimated annual cost of storing elemental mercury on a per-pound or per-ton basis;

'(C) for the 40-year period beginning on the date of submission of the report, the optimal size, number, and other characteristics of Federal facilities required to store elemental mercury under current and anticipated jurisdictions of each Federal agency;

'(D) the estimated quantity of—

'(i) elemental mercury that will result from the discontinuance of mercury cells at chlor-alkali facilities in the United States required under this section; and

'(ii) any other supplies that may require storage to carry out this section;

'(E) for the 40-year period beginning on the date of submission of the report, the estimated quantity of elemental mercury generated from the recycling of unwanted products and other wastes that will require storage to comply with any export prohibitions of elemental mercury;

'(F) any legal, technical, economic, or other barrier that may prevent the private sector from storing elemental mercury produced by the private sector during the 40-year period beginning on the date of submission of the report, including a description of measures to address the barriers;

'(G) the advantages and disadvantages of consolidating the storage of mercury produced by public and private sources under the management of the public or private sector;

'(H) the optimal plan of the Committee for storing excess mercury produced by public and private sources; and

'(I) additional research, if any, required to determine a long-term disposal option for the storage of excess mercury.

'(7) COMPENSATION OF MEMBERS-

'(A) IN GENERAL-

'(i) NON-FEDERAL EMPLOYEES- A member of the Committee who is not an officer or employee of the Federal Government shall be compensated at a rate equal to the daily equivalent of the annual rate of basic pay prescribed for level V of the Executive Schedule under section 5316 of title 5, United States Code, for each day (including travel time) during which the member is engaged in the performance of the duties of the Committee.

'(ii) FEDERAL EMPLOYEES- A member of the Committee who is an officer or employee of the Federal Government shall serve without compensation in addition to the compensation received for the services of the member as an officer or employee of the Federal Government.

'(B) TRAVEL EXPENSES- A member of the Committee shall be allowed travel expenses, including per diem in lieu of subsistence, at rates authorized for an employee of an agency under subchapter I of chapter 57 of title 5, United States Code, while away from the home or regular place of business of the member in the performance of the duties of the Committee.

'(8) STAFF AND FUNDING- The Administrator shall provide to the Committee such funding and additional personnel as are necessary to enable the Committee to perform the duties of the Committee.

'(9) TERMINATION- The Committee shall terminate 180 days after the date on which the Committee submits the report of the Committee under paragraph (6).

'(f) Transfer to Storage-

'(1) REGULATIONS- Not later than July 1, 2008, the Administrator shall promulgate regulations establishing the terms and conditions necessary to facilitate the transfer and storage of mercury located at closed or closing chlor-alkali facilities, including the allocation of costs and potential liabilities of that transfer and storage.

'(2) DEADLINE FOR TRANSFER- Beginning on July 1, 2008, elemental mercury located at a closed or closing chlor-alkali facility that has ceased operations shall be transferred to a storage facility established by the Administrator in accordance with the regulations promulgated under paragraph (1).

'(g) Health Assessment- Not later than July 1, 2009, for each chlor-alkali facility that continues to operate as of July 1, 2008, the Administrator, in coordination with the Administrator of the Agency for Toxic Substances and Disease Registry, shall conduct a health assessment of employees at the chlor-alkali facility.

'(h) Regulations- In addition to regulations described in subsection (f)(1), the Administrator may promulgate such regulations, including the establishment of a reporting form for use in accordance with subsection (c), as are necessary to carry out this section.'.

(b) Conforming Amendment- The table of contents of the Toxic Substances Control Act (15 U.S.C. 2601 note) is amended by inserting after the item relating to section 6 the following:

'Sec. 6A. Use of mercury in chlorine and caustic soda manufacturing.'.

US SENATE BILL 1824

TITLE: A bill to amend title XVIII of the Social Security Act to establish a Hospital Quality Report Card Initiative under the Medicare program to assess and report on health care quality in hospitals.

SPONSOR: Sen Obama, Barack [IL] (introduced 7/19/2007) Cosponsors (None)

LATEST MAJOR ACTION: 7/19/2007 Referred to Senate committee. Status: Read twice and referred to the Committee on Finance.

SUMMARY AS OF:

7/19/2007—Introduced.

Hospital Quality Report Card Act of 2007 - Amends title XVIII (Medicare) of the Social Security Act to direct the Secretary of Health and Human Services, acting through the Administrator of the Centers for Medicare & Medicaid Services, to establish a Hospital Quality Report Card Initiative under the Medicare program to report on health care quality in subsection (d) hospitals.

Directs the Administrator to establish the Hospital Quality Advisory Committee to advise on the submission, collection, and reporting of quality measures data.

MAJOR ACTIONS:

¤NONE¤

ALL ACTIONS:

7/19/2007:

Sponsor introductory remarks on measure. (CR S9617)

7/19/2007:

Read twice and referred to the Committee on Finance.

TITLES(s): (italics indicate a title for a portion of a bill)

¤NONE¤

COSPONSOR(s):

¤NONE¤

COMMITTEE(s)

Committee/Subcommittee:

Activity:

Senate Finance

Referral, In Committee

Related Bill Details:

¤NONE¤

Amendment(s)

¤NONE¤

In the Senate of the United States

July 19, 2007

Mr. OBAMA introduced the following bill; which was read twice and referred to the Committee on Finance

A BILL

To amend title XVIII of the Social Security Act to establish a Hospital Quality Report Card Initiative under the Medicare program to assess and report on health care quality in hospitals.

Be it enacted by the Senate and House of Representatives of the United States of America in Congress assembled,

SECTION 1. SHORT TITLE.

This Act may be cited as the 'Hospital Quality Report Card Act of 2007'.

SEC. 2. PURPOSE.

The purpose of this Act is to expand hospital quality reporting by establishing the Hospital Quality Report Card Initiative under the Medicare program to ensure that hospital quality measures data are readily available and accessible in order to—

(1) assist patients and consumers in making decisions about where to get health care;

(2) assist purchasers and insurers in making decisions that determine where employees, subscribers, members, or participants are able to go for their health care; and

(3) assist health care providers in identifying opportunities for quality improvement and cost containment.

SEC. 3. HOSPITAL QUALITY REPORT CARD INITIATIVE.

(a) In General- Title XVIII of the Social Security Act (42 U.S.C. 1395 et seq.) is amended by adding at the end the following new section:

'HOSPITAL QUALITY REPORT CARD INITIATIVE

'Sec. 1898. (a) In General- Not later than 18 months after the date of the enactment of the Hospital Quality Report Card Act of 2007, the Secretary, acting through the Administrator of the Centers for Medicare & Medicaid Services (in this section referred to as the 'Administrator') and in consultation with the Director of the Agency for Healthcare Research and Quality, shall, directly or through contracts with States or appropriate entities (such as utilization and quality control peer review organizations under part B of title XI, commonly known as Quality Improvement Organizations), establish and implement a Hospital Quality Report Card Initiative (in this section referred to as the 'Initiative') to report on health care quality in subsection (d) hospitals.

'(b) Subsection (d) Hospital- For purposes of this section, the term 'subsection (d) hospital' has the meaning given such term in section 1886(d)(1)(B).

'(c) Requirements of Initiative-

'(1) QUALITY MEASUREMENT REPORTS FOR HOSPITALS-

'(A) QUALITY MEASURES- Not less than 2 times each year, the Secretary shall publish reports on hospital quality. Such reports shall include quality measures data submitted under section 1886(b)(3)(B)(viii), and other data as feasible, that allow for an assessment of health care—

'(i) effectiveness;

'(ii) safety;

'(iii) timeliness;

'(iv) efficiency;

'(v) patient-centeredness; and

'(vi) equity.

'(B) REPORT CARD FEATURES- In collecting and reporting data as provided for under subparagraph (A), the Secretary shall include hospital information, as possible, relating to—

'(i) staffing levels of nurses and other health professionals, as appropriate;

'(ii) rates of hospital acquired infections;

'(iii) the volume of various procedures performed;

'(iv) the availability of interpreter services on-site;

'(v) the accreditation of hospitals, as well as sanctions and other violations found by accreditation or State licensing boards;

'(vi) the quality of care for various patient populations, including pediatric populations and racial and ethnic minority populations;

'(vii) the availability and accessibility of emergency rooms, including measures of crowding such as diversion status, patient boarding in the emergency room, and un-treated patients due to extended wait time;

'(viii) the availability of intensive care units, obstetrical units, and burn units;

'(ix) the quality of care in various hospital settings, including inpatient, outpatient, emergency, maternity, and intensive care unit settings;

'(x) the use of health information technology, telemedicine, and electronic medical records;

'(xi) ongoing patient safety initiatives; and

'(xii) other measures determined appropriate by the Secretary.

'(C) TAILORING OF HOSPITAL QUALITY REPORTS- The Director of the Agency for Healthcare Research and Quality may modify and publish hospital reports to include quality measures for diseases and health conditions of particular relevance to certain regions, States, or local areas.

'(D) RISK ADJUSTMENT-

'(i) IN GENERAL- In reporting data as provided for under subparagraph (A), the Secretary may risk adjust quality measures to account for differences relating to—

'(I) the characteristics of the reporting hospital, such as licensed bed size, geography, teaching hospital status, and profit status; and

'(II) patient characteristics, such as health status, severity of illness, insurance status, and socioeconomic status.

'(ii) AVAILABILITY OF UNADJUSTED DATA- If the Secretary reports data under subparagraph (A) using risk-adjusted quality measures, the Secretary shall establish procedures for making the unadjusted data available to the public in a manner determined appropriate by the Secretary.

'(E) COSTS AND CHARGES- The Secretary shall—

'(i) compile data relating to the average hospital cost and charges for ICD-9 conditions for which quality measures data are collected; and

'(ii) report such information in a manner that allows cost and charge comparisons between or among subsection (d) hospitals.

'(F) VERIFICATION- Under the Initiative, the Secretary may verify data reported under this paragraph to ensure accuracy and validity.

'(G) DISCLOSURE- The Secretary shall disclose the entire methodology for the reporting of data under this paragraph to all relevant organizations and all subsection (d) hospitals that are the subject of any such information that is to be made available to the public prior to the public disclosure of such information.

'(H) PUBLIC INPUT- The Secretary shall provide an opportunity for public review and comment with respect to the quality measures to be reported for subsection (d) hospitals under this section for at least 60 days prior to the finalization by the Secretary of the quality measures to be used for such hospitals.

'(I) AVAILABILITY OF REPORTS AND FINDINGS-

'(i) ELECTRONIC AVAILABILITY- The Secretary shall ensure that reports are made available under this section in an electronic format, in an understandable manner with respect to various populations (including those with low functional health literacy), and in a manner that allows health care quality comparisons to be made between local hospitals.

'(ii) FINDINGS- The Secretary shall establish procedures for making report findings available to the public, upon request, in a nonelectronic format, such as through the toll-free telephone number 1-800-MEDICARE.

'(J) IDENTIFICATION OF METHODOLOGY- The analytic methodologies and limitations on data sources utilized by the Secretary to develop and disseminate the comparative data under this section shall be identified and acknowledged as part of the dissemination of such data, and include the appropriate and inappropriate uses of such data.

'(K) ADVERSE SELECTION OF PATIENTS- On at least an annual basis, the Secretary shall compare quality measures data submitted by each subsection (d) hospital under section 1886(b)(3)(B)(viii) with data submitted in the prior year or years by the same hospital in order to identify and report actions that would lead to false or artificial improvements in the hospital's quality measurements, including—

'(i) adverse selection against patients with severe illness or other factors that predispose patients to poor health outcomes; and

'(ii) provision of health care that does not meet established recommendations or accepted standards for care.

'(2) DATA SAFEGUARDS-

'(A) UNAUTHORIZED USE AND DISCLOSURE- The Secretary shall develop and implement effective safeguards to protect against the unauthorized use or disclosure of hospital data that is reported under this section.

'(B) INACCURATE INFORMATION- The Secretary shall develop and implement effective safeguards to protect against the dissemination of inconsistent, incomplete, invalid, inaccurate, or subjective hospital data.

'(C) IDENTIFIABLE DATA- The Secretary shall ensure that identifiable patient data shall not be released to the public.

'(d) Grants and Technical Assistance- The Secretary may award grants to national or State organizations, partnerships, utilization and quality control peer review organizations under part B of title XI, or other entities that may assist with hospital quality improvement.

'(e) Hospital Quality Advisory Committee-

'(1) ESTABLISHMENT- The Administrator, in consultation with the Director of the Agency for Healthcare Research and Quality, shall establish the Hospital Quality Advisory Committee (in this subsection referred to as the 'Advisory Committee') to provide advice to the Administrator on the submission, collection, and reporting of quality measures data. The Administrator shall serve as the chairperson of the Advisory Committee.

'(2) MEMBERSHIP- The Advisory Committee shall include representatives of the following (except with respect to subparagraphs (A) through (D), to be appointed by the Administrator):

'(A) The Agency for Healthcare Research and Quality.

'(B) The Health Resources and Services Administration.

'(C) The Department of Veterans Affairs.

'(D) The Centers for Disease Control and Prevention.

'(E) National membership organizations that focus on health care quality improvement.

'(F) Public and private hospitals.

'(G) Physicians, nurses, and other health professionals.

'(H) Patients and patient advocates.

'(I) Health insurance purchasers and other payers.

'(J) Health researchers, policymakers, and other experts in the field of health care quality.

'(K) Health care accreditation entities.

'(L) Representatives of utilization and quality control peer review organizations under part B of title XI.

'(M) Other agencies and groups as determined appropriate by the Administrator.

'(3) DUTIES- The Advisory Committee shall review and provide guidance and recommendations to the Administrator on—

'(A) the establishment of the Initiative;

'(B) integration and coordination of Federal quality measures data submission requirements, to avoid needless duplication and inefficiency;

'(C) legal and regulatory barriers that may hinder quality measures data collection and reporting; and

'(D) necessary technical and financial assistance to encourage quality measures data collection and reporting.

'(4) STAFF AND RESOURCES- The Administrator shall provide the Advisory Committee with appropriate staff and resources for the functioning of the Advisory Committee.

'(5) DURATION- The Advisory Committee shall terminate at the discretion of the Administrator, but in no event later than 5 years after the date of enactment of this section.

'(f) Authorization of Appropriations- There are authorized to be appropriated to carry out this section such sums as may be necessary for each of fiscal years 2008 through 2017.'.

(b) Conforming Amendment- Section 1886(b)(3)(B)(viii)(VII) of the Social Security Act (42 U.S.C. 1395ww(b)(3)(B)(viii)(VII)), as added by section 5001 of the Deficit Reduction Act of 2005, is amended to read as follows:

'(VII) The Secretary shall use the data submitted under this clause for the Hospital Quality Report Card Initiative under section 1898.'.

SEC. 4. EVALUATION OF THE HOSPITAL QUALITY REPORT CARD INITIATIVE.

(a) In General- The Director of the Agency for Healthcare Research and Quality, directly or through contract, shall evaluate and periodically report to Congress on the effectiveness of the Hospital Quality Report Card Initiative established under section 1898 of the Social Security Act, as added by section 3, including the effectiveness of the Initiative in meeting the purpose described in section 2. The Director shall make such reports available to the public.

(b) Research- The Director of the Agency for Healthcare Research and Quality, in consultation with the Administrator of the Centers for Medicare & Medicaid Services, shall use the outcomes from the evaluation conducted pursuant to subsection (a) to increase the usefulness of the Hospital Quality Report Card Initiative, particularly for patients, as necessary.

US Senate Bill 1873

Title: A bill to amend the Public Health Service Act to establish demonstration programs on regionalized systems for emergency care, to support emergency medicine research, and for other purposes.

Sponsor: Sen Obama, Barack [IL] (introduced 7/25/2007) Cosponsors (None)

Related Bills: H.R.3173

Latest Major Action: 7/25/2007 Referred to Senate committee. Status: Read twice and referred to the Committee on Health, Education, Labor, and Pensions.

Summary As Of:

7/25/2007—Introduced.

Improving Emergency Medical Care and Response Act of 2007 - Amends the Public Health Service Act to require the Secretary of Health and Human Services, acting though the Assistant Secretary for Preparedness and Response, to award contracts or competitive grants to support demonstration programs that design, implement, and evaluate innovative models of regionalized, comprehensive, and accountable emergency care systems. Requires the Secretary to give priority to entities that serve a population in a medically underserved area.

Directs the Secretary to: (1) support federal programs involved in improving the emergency care system to expand and accelerate research in emergency medical care systems and emergency medicine; and (2) support research to determine the estimated economic impact of, and savings that result from, the implementation of coordinated emergency care systems.

Major Actions:

¤NONE¤

All Actions:

7/25/2007:

Read twice and referred to the Committee on Health, Education, Labor, and Pensions.

7/26/2007:

Sponsor introductory remarks on measure. (CR S10143)

TITLES(s): (italics indicate a title for a portion of a bill)

¤NONE¤

COSPONSOR(s):

¤NONE¤

COMMITTEE(s)

Committee/Subcommittee:

Activity:

Senate Health, Education, Labor, and Pensions

Referral, In Committee

RELATED BILL DETAILS: (additional related bills may be indentified in Status)

Bill:

Relationship:

H.R.3173

Related bill identified by CRS

AMENDMENT(s)

¤NONE¤

IN THE SENATE OF THE UNITED STATES

July 25, 2007

Mr. OBAMA introduced the following bill; which was read twice and referred to the Committee on Health, Education, Labor, and Pensions

A BILL

To amend the Public Health Service Act to establish demonstration programs on regionalized systems for emergency care, to support emergency medicine research, and for other purposes.

Be it enacted by the Senate and House of Representatives of the United States of America in Congress assembled,

SECTION 1. SHORT TITLE.

This Act may be cited as the 'Improving Emergency Medical Care and Response Act of 2007'.

SEC. 2. FINDINGS AND PURPOSES.

(a) Findings- Congress makes the following findings:

(1) Emergency medical services play a critically important role in health care, public health, and public safety by frequently providing immediate lifesustaining care and making decisions with limited time and information.

(2) Between 1993 and 2003, the population of the United States grew by 12 percent and hospital admissions increased by 13 percent, yet emergency department visits rose by more than 25 percent during this same period of time, from 90,300,000 visits in 1993 to 113,900,000 visits in 2003.

(3) The demand for emergency care in the United States continues to grow at a rapid pace.

(4) In 2003, hospital emergency departments received nearly 114,000,000 visits, which is more than 1 visit for every 3 people in the United States, however, between 1993 and 2003, the number of emergency departments declined by 425.

(5) Many emergency medical services are highly fragmented, overburdened, poorly equipped, and insufficiently prepared for day-to-day operations and response to major disasters.

(6) There are more than 6,000 Public Safety Answering Points that receive 9-1-1 calls.

(7) These Public Safety Answering Points are often operated by police departments, fire departments, city or county governments, or other local entities, which makes attempts to coordinate efforts between locations very difficult.

(8) Regionalized, accountable systems of emergency care show substantial promise in improving the day-to-day system-wide coordination essential to assure that Public Safety Answering Points, emergency medical services organizations, public safety agencies, public health agencies, medical facilities, and others coordinate their activities to ensure that patients receive the appropriate care at the scene, are transported to the most appropriate facility in the shortest time, and receive excellent care at the destination medical facility.

(9) Regionalized, accountable systems of emergency care also show promise in management of the special problems of disaster preparation and response, including management of patient surge, tracking of patients, and coordination and allocation of medical resources.

(10) While there are potentially substantial benefits to be derived from regionalized, accountable emergency care systems, little is known about the most effective and efficient methods of regional emergency care system development.

(b) Purposes- The purposes of this Act are to design, implement, and evaluate regionalized, comprehensive, and accountable systems of emergency care that—

(1) support and improve the day-to-day operations and coordination of a regional emergency medical care system;

(2) increase disaster preparedness and medical surge capacity;

(3) include different models of regionalized emergency care systems, including models for urban and rural communities;

(4) can be implemented by private or public entities; and

(5) meet quality and accountability standards for the operation of emergency care systems and the impact of such systems on patient outcomes.

SEC. 3. DESIGN AND IMPLEMENTATION OF REGIONALIZED SYSTEMS FOR EMERGENCY CARE.

Part B of title III of the Public Health Service Act (42 U.S.C. 243 et seq.) is amended by inserting after section 314 the following:

'SEC. 315. REGIONALIZED COMMUNICATION SYSTEMS FOR EMERGENCY CARE RESPONSE.

'(a) In General- The Secretary, acting through the Assistant Secretary for Preparedness and Response, shall award not fewer than 4 multiyear contracts or competitive grants to eligible entities to support demonstration programs that design, implement, and evaluate innovative models of regionalized, comprehensive, and accountable emergency care systems.

'(b) Eligible Entity; Region-

'(1) ELIGIBLE ENTITY- In this section, the term 'eligible entity' means a State or a partnership of 1 or more States and 1 or more local governments.

'(2) REGION- In this section, the term 'region' means an area within a State, an area that lies within multiple States, or a similar area (such as a multicounty area), as determined by the Secretary.

'(c) Demonstration Program- The Secretary shall award a contract or grant under subsection (a) to an eligible entity that proposes a demonstration program to design, implement, and evaluate an emergency medical system that—

'(1) coordinates with public safety services, public health services, emergency medical services, medical facilities, and other entities within a region;

'(2) coordinates an approach to emergency medical system access throughout the region, including 9-1-1 Public Safety Answering Points and emergency medical dispatch;

'(3) includes a mechanism, such as a regional medical direction or transport communications system, that operates throughout the region to ensure that the correct patient is taken to the medically appropriate facility (whether an initial facility or a higher-level facility) in a timely fashion;

'(4) allows for the tracking of prehospital and hospital resources, including inpatient bed capacity, emergency department capacity, on-call specialist coverage, ambulance diversion status, and the coordination of such tracking with regional communications and hospital destination decisions; and

'(5) includes a consistent region-wide prehospital, hospital, and interfacility data management system that—

'(A) complies with the National EMS Information System, the National Trauma Data Bank, and others;

'(B) reports data to appropriate Federal and State databanks and registries; and

'(C) contains information sufficient to evaluate key elements of prehospital care, hospital destination decisions, including initial hospital and interfacility decisions, and relevant outcomes of hospital care.

'(d) Application-

'(1) IN GENERAL- An eligible entity that seeks a contract or grant described in subsection (a) shall submit to the Secretary an application at such time and in such manner as the Secretary may require.

'(2) APPLICATION INFORMATION- Each application shall include—

'(A) an assurance from the eligible entity that the proposed system—

'(i) has been coordinated with the applicable State Office of Emergency Medical Services (or equivalent State office);

'(ii) is compatible with the applicable State emergency medical services system;

'(iii) includes consistent indirect and direct medical oversight of prehospital, hospital, and interfacility transport throughout the region;

'(iv) coordinates prehospital treatment and triage, hospital destination, and interfacility transport throughout the region;

'(v) includes a categorization or designation system for special medical facilities throughout the region that is—

'(I) consistent with State laws and regulations; and

'(II) integrated with the protocols for transport and destination throughout the region; and

'(vi) includes a regional medical direction system, a patient tracking system, and a resource allocation system that—

'(I) support day-to-day emergency care system operation;

'(II) can manage surge capacity during a major event or disaster; and

'(III) are integrated with other components of the national and State emergency preparedness system; and

'(B) such other information as the Secretary may require.

'(e) Priority- The Secretary shall give priority for the award of the contracts or grants described subsection (a) to any eligible entity that serves a population in a medically underserved area (as defined in section 330(b)(3)).

'(f) Report- Not later than 90 days after the completion of a demonstration program under subsection (a), the recipient of such contract or grant described in shall submit to the Secretary a report containing the results of an evaluation of the program, including an identification of—

'(1) the impact of the regional, accountable emergency care system on patient outcomes for various critical care categories, such as trauma, stroke, cardiac emergencies, and pediatric emergencies;

'(2) the system characteristics that contribute to the effectiveness and efficiency of the program (or lack thereof);

'(3) methods of assuring the long-term financial sustainability of the emergency care system;

'(4) the State and local legislation necessary to implement and to maintain the system; and

'(5) the barriers to developing regionalized, accountable emergency care systems, as well as the methods to overcome such barriers.

'(g) Dissemination of Findings- The Secretary shall, as appropriate, disseminate to the public and to the appropriate Committees of the Congress, the information contained in a report made under subsection (f).

'(h) Authorization of Appropriations- There are authorized to be appropriated to carry out this section $12,000,000 for each of fiscal years 2008 through 2013.'.

SEC. 4. SUPPORT FOR EMERGENCY MEDICINE RESEARCH.

Part H of title IV of the Public Health Service Act (42 U.S.C. 289 et seq.) is amended by inserting after the section 498C the following:

'SEC. 498D. SUPPORT FOR EMERGENCY MEDICINE RESEARCH.

'(a) Emergency Medical Research- The Secretary shall support Federal programs administered by the National Institutes of Health, the Agency for Healthcare Research and Quality, the Health Resources and Services Administration, the Centers for Disease Control and Prevention, and other agencies involved in improving the emergency care system to expand and accelerate research in emergency medical care systems and emergency medicine, including—

'(1) the basic science of emergency medicine;

'(2) the model of service delivery and the components of such models that contribute to enhanced patient outcomes;

'(3) the translation of basic scientific research into improved practice; and

'(4) the development of timely and efficient delivery of health services.

'(b) Impact Research- The Secretary shall support research to determine the estimated economic impact of, and savings that result from, the implementation of coordinated emergency care systems.

'(c) Authorization of Appropriations- There are authorized to be appropriated to carry out this section such sums as may be necessary for each of fiscal years 2008 through 2013.'.

US SENATE BILL 1885

TITLE: A bill to provide certain employment protections for family members who are caring for members of the Armed Forces recovering from illnesses and injuries incurred on active duty.

Sponsor: Sen Obama, Barack [IL] (introduced 7/26/2007) Cosponsors (10)

Related Bills: H.R.3993

Latest Major Action: 7/26/2007 Referred to Senate committee. Status: Read twice and referred to the Committee on Health, Education, Labor, and Pensions.

Summary As Of:

7/26/2007—Introduced.

Military Family Job Protection Act - Prohibits a covered family member who is caring for a servicemember who is undergoing medical treatment for an injury, illness, or disease incurred or aggravated while on active military duty from being denied retention in employment, promotion, or any employment benefit by an employer on the basis of the family member's absence from such employment for a period of not more than 52 weeks.

Includes as a covered family member one who, while caring for the recovering servicemember, is: (1) on invitational orders; (2) a non-medical attendee; or (3) receiving per diem payments from the Department of Defense (DOD).

Major Actions:

¤NONE¤

All Actions:

7/26/2007:

Read twice and referred to the Committee on Health, Education, Labor, and Pensions.

Titles(s): (italics indicate a title for a portion of a bill)

¤NONE¤

Cosponsors(10), Alphabetical [followed by Cosponsors withdrawn]: (Sort: by date)

Sen Baucus, Max [MT] - 7/26/2007

Sen Biden, Joseph R., Jr. [DE] - 7/26/2007

Sen Brown, Sherrod [OH] - 7/31/2007

Sen Conrad, Kent [ND] - 9/17/2007

Sen Durbin, Richard [IL] - 7/26/2007

Sen Harkin, Tom [IA] - 7/26/2007

Sen Kennedy, Edward M. [MA] - 7/26/2007

Sen Kerry, John F. [MA] - 7/26/2007

Sen Landrieu, Mary L. [LA] - 7/31/2007

 Claire [MO] - 7/26/2007

COMMITTEE(S)

Committee/Subcommittee:

Activity:

Senate Health, Education, Labor, and Pensions

Referral, In Committee

RELATED BILL DETAILS: (additional related bills may be indentified in Status)

Bill:

Relationship:

H.R.3993

Identical bill identified by CRS

AMENDMENT(S)

¤NONE¤

Sen McCaskill,

IN THE SENATE OF THE UNITED STATES

July 26, 2007

Mr. REID (for Mr. OBAMA (for himself, Mrs. MCCASKILL, Mr. HARKIN, Mr. KERRY, Mr. BAUCUS, Mr. BIDEN, Mr. DURBIN, and Mr. KENNEDY)) introduced the following bill; which was read twice and referred to the Committee on Health, Education, Labor, and Pensions

A BILL

To provide certain employment protections for family members who are caring for members of the Armed Forces recovering from illnesses and injuries incurred on active duty.

Be it enacted by the Senate and House of Representatives of the United States of America in Congress assembled,

SECTION 1. SHORT TITLE.

This Act may be cited as the 'Military Family Job Protection Act'.

SEC. 2. PROHIBITION ON DISCRIMINATION IN EMPLOYMENT AGAINST CERTAIN FAMILY MEMBERS CARING FOR RECOVERING MEMBERS OF THE ARMED FORCES.

(a) Prohibition- A family member of a recovering servicemember described in subsection (b) shall not be denied retention in employment, promotion, or any benefit of employment by an employer on the basis of the family member's absence from employment as described in that subsection, for a period of not more than 52 workweeks.

(b) Covered Family Members- A family member described in this subsection is a family member of a recovering servicemember who is—

(1) on invitational orders while caring for the recovering servicemember;

(2) a non-medical attendee caring for the recovering servicemember; or

(3) receiving per diem payments from the Department of Defense while caring for the recovering servicemember.

(c) Treatment of Actions- An employer shall be considered to have engaged in an action prohibited by subsection (a) with respect to a person described in that subsection if the absence from employment of the person as described in that subsection is a motivating factor in the employer's action, unless the employer can prove that the action would have been taken in the absence of the absence of employment of the person.

(d) Definitions- In this section:

(1) BENEFIT OF EMPLOYMENT- The term 'benefit of employment' has the meaning given such term in section 4303 of title 38, United States Code.

(2) CARING FOR- The term 'caring for', used with respect to a recovering servicemember, means providing personal, medical, or convalescent care to the recovering servicemember, under circumstances that substantially interfere with an employee's ability to work.

(3) EMPLOYER- The term 'employer' has the meaning given such term in section 4303 of title 38, United States Code, except that the term does not include any person who is not considered to be an employer under title I of the Family and Medical Leave Act of 1993 (29 U.S.C. 2611 et seq.) because the person does not meet the requirements of section 101(4)(A)(i) of such Act (29 U.S.C. 2611(4)(A)(i)).

(4) FAMILY MEMBER- The term 'family member', with respect to a recovering servicemember, has the meaning given that term in section 411h(b) of title 37, United States Code.

(5) RECOVERING SERVICEMEMBER- The term 'recovering servicemember' means a member of the Armed Forces, including a member of the National Guard or a Reserve, who is undergoing medical treatment, recuperation, or therapy, or is otherwise in medical hold or medical holdover status, for an injury, illness, or disease incurred or aggravated while on active duty in the Armed Forces.

US Senate Bill 1977

Title: A bill to provide for sustained United States leadership in a cooperative global effort to prevent nuclear terrorism, reduce global nuclear arsenals, stop the spread of nuclear weapons and related material and technology, and support the responsible and peaceful use of nuclear technology.

Sponsor: Sen Obama, Barack [IL] (introduced 8/2/2007) Cosponsors (2)

Latest Major Action: 8/2/2007 Referred to Senate committee. Status: Read twice and referred to the Committee on Foreign Relations.

SUMMARY AS OF:

8/2/2007—Introduced.

Nuclear Weapons Threat Reduction Act of 2007 - Authorizes the President, upon a specified congressional certification by the Secretary of State, to make voluntary contributions for creation of a low enriched uranium reserve administered by the International Atomic Energy Agency (IAEA) that would help guarantee the availability of fuel for commercial nuclear reactors and dissuade countries from building their own uranium enrichment capability.

Authorizes appropriations for voluntary contributions to the IAEA.

Directs the National Academy of Sciences to report to Congress on a verification regime for a fissile material cutoff treaty.

Directs the President to report to Congress respecting: (1) a plan to ensure the security of all nuclear weapons and weapons usable material at vulnerable sites worldwide and for working with other countries to ensure such materials' security; and (2) U.S. strategy and policies regarding the 2010 Nuclear Non-Proliferation Treaty Review Conference.

Authorizes appropriations to establish a national technical forensics program to develop technologies and procedures for determining the origin of nuclear materials, whether seized intact or collected after the detonation of a nuclear bomb.

Establishes the Commission on United States Objectives and Strategy for Nuclear Nonproliferation and Peaceful Use of Nuclear Technology.

MAJOR ACTIONS:

¤NONE¤

ALL ACTIONS:

8/2/2007:

Sponsor introductory remarks on measure. (CR S10811-10812)

8/2/2007:

Read twice and referred to the Committee on Foreign Relations.

TITLES(s): (italics indicate a title for a portion of a bill)

¤NONE¤

COSPONSORS(2), ALPHABETICAL [FOLLOWED BY COSPONSORS WITHDRAWN]: (Sort: by date)

Sen Durbin, Richard [IL] - 9/11/2007

Sen Hagel, Chuck [NE] - 8/2/2007

COMMITTEE(s)

Committee/Subcommittee:

Activity:

Senate Foreign Relations

Referral, In Committee

Related Bill Details:

¤NONE¤

Amendment(s)

¤NONE¤

In the Senate of the United States

August 2, 2007

Mr. OBAMA (for himself and Mr. HAGEL) introduced the following bill; which was read twice and referred to the Committee on Foreign Relations

A BILL

To provide for sustained United States leadership in a cooperative global effort to prevent nuclear terrorism, reduce global nuclear arsenals, stop the spread of nuclear weapons and related material and technology, and support the responsible and peaceful use of nuclear technology.

Be it enacted by the Senate and House of Representatives of the United States of America in Congress assembled,

SECTION 1. SHORT TITLE.

This Act may be cited as the 'Nuclear Weapons Threat Reduction Act of 2007'.

SEC. 2. FINDINGS.

Congress makes the following findings:

(1) Sustained global leadership by the United States will remain essential in a cooperative global effort to prevent nuclear terrorism, reduce global nuclear arsenals, stop the spread of nuclear weapons and related material and technology, and support the responsible and peaceful use of nuclear technology.

(2) The National Commission on Terrorist Attacks Upon the United States (commonly referred to as the '9/11 Commission') concluded that 'a trained nuclear engineer with an amount of highly enriched uranium or plutonium about the size of a grapefruit or an orange, together with commercially available material, could fashion a nuclear device that would fit in a van like the one Ramzi Yousef parked in the garage of the World Trade Center in 1993. Such a bomb would level Lower Manhattan.'

(3) The International Atomic Energy Agency (IAEA) confirmed 16 incidents between 1993 and 2005 that involved trafficking in relatively small quantities of highly enriched uranium and plutonium.

(4) United States cooperative threat reduction programs have made significant progress in securing, monitoring, and reducing nuclear stockpiles, but there are still sig-

nificant quantities of weapons-usable nuclear material that remain vulnerable to theft or diversion.

(5) There are an estimated 60 tons of highly enriched uranium, enough to make over 1,000 nuclear bombs, that are located at facilities associated with civilian industries spread among over 40 countries around the world, and physical security standards governing such materials vary, creating vulnerabilities to theft or diversion.

(6) Securing nuclear weapons and weapons-usable material at their source is the most direct and reliable way to disrupt efforts by terrorist organizations to acquire such material. Interdiction and other measures based on international cooperation and collaboration must also be sustained.

(7) The dangers posed by the spread of nuclear weapons-related technology and the need to strengthen the global nonproliferation regime are highlighted by—

(A) the announcement by the Government of North Korea in 2003 that it was withdrawing from the Treaty on the Non-Proliferation of Nuclear Weapons, done at Washington, London, and Moscow July 1, 1968, and entered into force March 5, 1970 (commonly referred to as the 'Nuclear Non-Proliferation Treaty'), and the nuclear test explosion carried out by that government in 2006; and

(B) the violations by the Government of Iran of its safeguards commitments and the refusal of that government to comply with United Nations Security Council resolutions demanding a suspension of its uranium enrichment program and other sensitive nuclear activities.

(8) The Nuclear Non-Proliferation Treaty permits countries to acquire a capability to produce fissile material for civilian purposes that brings them to the brink of a capability to produce weapons-usable nuclear material without necessarily violating the agreement, giving them the ability to then leave without penalty unless the United Nations Security Council or other countries take meaningful action.

(9) The threat of nuclear weapons to the United States and the rest of the world cannot be reduced without stronger international cooperation to achieve universal compliance with tighter nuclear nonproliferation rules and standards as part of a comprehensive and balanced nonproliferation strategy that recognizes legitimate, peaceful nuclear uses.

(10) To bolster international support for nuclear nonproliferation and reduce the saliency of nuclear weapons, nuclear weapons states should reaffirm their commitment to Article VI of the Nuclear Non-Proliferation Treaty, and all states, particularly nuclear weapons states, should actively reaffirm their commitment to Article IV of the Nuclear Non-Proliferation Treaty and tangibly support the responsible and peaceful use of nuclear technology.

(11) The Cold War rivalry that led to the stockpiling of tens of thousands of nuclear weapons ended more than 15 years ago, but the nuclear weapons doctrines of the United States and the Russian Federation have changed very little and large arsenals of strategic and tactical nuclear weapons remain in each country.

SEC. 3. SENSE OF CONGRESS.

It is the sense of Congress that the United States should have a balanced and comprehensive strategy to strengthen global nuclear nonproliferation, prevent nuclear terrorism, and uphold all of the commitments of the Nuclear Non-Proliferation Treaty, including by—

(1) slowing and eventually halting the spread of sensitive nuclear technologies to enrich uranium or separate plutonium;

(2) establishing multilayered, multilateral nuclear fuel supply assurances, including an international nuclear fuel bank, consistent with United States nonproliferation objectives to dissuade countries from building their own uranium enrichment capability;

(3) strengthening the inspection and nuclear safety capabilities and authority of the IAEA and reaffirming support for appropriate measures to strengthen the Nuclear Non-Proliferation Treaty;

(4) taking steps to ensure that all countries adopt the Additional Protocol of the IAEA, which grants the IAEA expanded rights of access to information and nuclear-related sites;

(5) reaffirming the commitment of the United States to fulfill its obligations under the Nuclear Non-Proliferation Treaty, and encouraging other nuclear weapon states to reaffirm their commitments to fulfill obligations under the Treaty, including by taking steps to achieve deeper, verifiable reductions in global nuclear arsenals and their means of delivery;

(6) initiating talks with the Government of the Russian Federation to reduce the number of nonstrategic nuclear weapons and further reduce the number of strategic nuclear weapons in the respective nuclear stockpiles of the United States and the Russian Federation in a transparent and verifiable fashion and in a manner consistent with the security of the United States;

(7) taking measures to reduce the risk of an accidental, unauthorized, or mistaken launch of nuclear weapons, including by considering changes in the alert status in United States and Russian forces and rapidly completing the Joint Data Exchange Center, which would improve communications and transparency between the United States and the Russian Federation;

(8) continuing the United States moratorium on nuclear test explosions, initiating a bipartisan process to achieve ratification of the Comprehensive Test Ban Treaty, working to secure ratification by other key countries, and fully supporting United States commitments to fund the international monitoring system to help detect and deter possible nuclear explosions by other countries;

(9) pursuing and concluding an agreement to verifiably halt the production of fissile materials for nuclear weapons;

(10) strengthening Nuclear Suppliers Group export control guidelines, national border and transhipment controls, and intelligence and law enforcement efforts to investigate and block the transfer of sensitive nuclear materials and technologies in order to prevent future black-market nuclear networks like the A.Q. Khan network;

(11) strengthening the Proliferation Security Initiative (PSI) through appropriate measures;

(12) fully implementing the Lugar-Obama initiative (sections 10, 11, and 12 of the State Department Authorities Act of 2006 (Public Law 109-472; 22 U.S.C. 2349bb-5, 22 U.S.C. 2349bb-6, and 22 U.S.C. 2751 note), which strengthens the ability of foreign countries friendly to the United States to detect and interdict weapons of mass destruction and related material;

(13) achieving increased and sustained financial and other support from Russia, the European Union and its member states, China, Japan, and other countries for stronger, standardized, and worldwide physical security for nuclear weapons and material as well as for other global nuclear nonproliferation efforts;

(14) accelerating United States programs to secure, consolidate, and reduce global stocks of nuclear weapons and weapons-usable material and ensuring that the highest priority is placed on the security for those stockpiles that pose the greatest risk; and

(15) taking steps to delegitimize and eventually eliminate the use of highly enriched uranium in civilian commerce.

SEC. 4. ESTABLISHMENT OF AN INTERNATIONAL NUCLEAR FUEL BANK.

(a) Authority- The President is authorized to make voluntary contributions to support the creation of a low enriched uranium reserve administered by the IAEA that would help guarantee the availability of fuel for commercial nuclear reactors and dissuade countries from building their own uranium enrichment capability.

(b) Authorization of Appropriations- There is authorized to be appropriated to the President $50,000,000 for voluntary contributions to support the establishment of an international nuclear fuel bank.

(c) Certification- Voluntary contributions under subsection (b) may be provided only if the Secretary of State certifies to the Committee on Foreign Affairs of the House of Representatives and the Committee on Foreign Relations of the Senate that the IAEA has received a pledge or pledges in a total amount of not less than $50,000,000 from a country or group of countries other than the United States.

(d) Report-

(1) IN GENERAL- Not later than 1 year after the date of the enactment of this Act, and annually thereafter, the President shall submit to Congress a report on efforts by the United States Government to facilitate and support the establishment of a low-enriched uranium reserve administered by the IAEA.

(2) CONTENT- The report required under paragraph (1) shall include detailed descriptions of—

(A) the international diplomatic efforts to create global support for a fuel bank;

(B) financial support for a fuel bank from other countries;

(C) any obstacles impeding the establishment of the reserve;

(D) efforts by the United States Government to remove or resolve such obstacles; and

(E) the structure, mandate, scope, location, duration, decisionmaking authority, rules and guidelines, and physical security measures of a fuel bank.

SEC. 5. STRENGTHENING THE CAPABILITIES OF THE IAEA.

(a) Finding- Congress finds that the International Atomic Energy Agency plays a critical role in safeguarding the nuclear programs of countries around the world and in promulgating security guidance for nuclear materials.

(b) Authorization of Appropriations- There are authorized to be appropriated for the President for fiscal years 2008 through 2012, in addition to other amounts available for such purposes, for voluntary contributions to the IAEA—

(1) $10,000,000 for each such fiscal year for the Department of Safeguards of the IAEA to improve, strengthen, and expand as necessary, the ability of the IAEA to conduct effective monitoring and inspections to ensure compliance with safeguards and to monitor transfers of dual-use nuclear items and technologies that could be used to subvert those safeguards; and

(2) $5,000,000 for the Department of Nuclear Safety and Security of the IAEA to strengthen the efforts of the Department to develop guidelines for securing nuclear materials and to assist national authorities with implementation of these guidelines.

(c) Certification Requirement- Voluntary contributions under subsection (b) may be provided in fiscal years 2010, 2011, and 2012 only if the Secretary of State certifies to the Committee on Foreign Relations of the Senate and the Committee on Foreign Affairs of the House of Representatives that countries other than the United States are providing, or have agreed to provide, significant additional funds to the International Atomic Energy Agency's Department of Safeguards, Department of Nuclear Safety and Security, or both.

SEC. 6. FISSILE MATERIAL CUTOFF TREATY.

(a) Statement of Policy- It is in the interest of the United States to achieve a comprehensive, verifiable, and effective treaty to end the production of fissile materials for nuclear weapons worldwide, and to actively encourage countries that are producing fissile material for nuclear weapons to suspend such activities.

(b) Report- Not later than 1 year after the date of the enactment of this Act, the National Academy of Sciences shall submit to Congress a comprehensive report on the nature of a verification regime that would be necessary for an effectively verifiable fissile material cutoff treaty.

SEC. 7. COMPREHENSIVE NUCLEAR THREAT REDUCTION AND SECURITY PLAN.

(a) Statement of Policy- It shall be the policy of the United States to work cooperatively with other countries and the IAEA to develop, promulgate, and implement a comprehensive set of standards and best practices to fulfill the requirement of United Nations Security Council Resolution 1540 (2004) to provide 'appropriate effective' physical protection and accounting for all stockpiles of nuclear weapons and weapons-usable material.

(b) Sense of Congress- It is the sense of Congress that—

(1) the United States should work with other countries and the IAEA to reach a common understanding of the essential elements of an effective physical protection system for nuclear weapons-usable materials stockpiles, including best practices and security measures that will ensure that such systems will be effective in defeating the threats that terrorists and criminals have demonstrated they can pose; and

(2) the United States should encourage and materially assist other countries to the extent needed to put such effective nuclear security systems in place as rapidly as possible.

(c) Plan Required- Not later than 180 days after the date of the enactment of this Act, the President shall submit to Congress a comprehensive nuclear threat reduction and security plan, in classified and unclassified forms, for ensuring that all nuclear weapons and weapons usable material at vulnerable sites worldwide are secure by 2012 and for working with other countries to ensure adequate accounting and security for such materials on an ongoing basis thereafter.

(d) Content- For each element of the accounting and security effort, the plan submitted under subsection (c) shall—

(1) clearly designate agency and departmental responsibility and accountability;

(2) specify program goals, with metrics for measuring progress, estimated schedules, and specified milestones to be achieved;

(3) provide estimates of the program budget requirements and resources to meet the goals for each year;

(4) provide the strategy for diplomacy and related tools and authority to accomplish the program element;

(5) provide a strategy for expanding the resources, financing, and other support and assistance provided by other countries, particularly Russia, the European Union and its member states, China, and Japan, for the purposes of securing nuclear weapons and weapons-usable material worldwide;

(6) outline the progress in and impediments to securing agreement from all countries that possess nuclear weapons or weapons-usable material on a set of global nuclear security standards, consistent with their obligation to comply with United Nations Security Council Resolution 1540;

(7) describe the steps required to overcome impediments that have been identified; and

(8) describe global efforts to promulgate best practices for securing nuclear materials and outline options to support the establishment of an international voluntary organization to promote best practices for nuclear material security among nuclear facility operators worldwide.

(e) Annual Report- Not later than September 30, 2008, and annually thereafter, the President shall submit to Congress an integrated annual report, in classified and unclassified form, that describes the progress made by the Department of Defense, the Department of Energy, and the Department of State in implementing the comprehensive threat reduction plan submitted under subsection (c), including an assessment of progress relative to the milestones set forth in the plan.

(f) Authorization of Appropriations for Global Threat Reduction Initiative- There is authorized to be appropriated to the Secretary of Energy $20,000,000 for fiscal years 2008 through 2010 for the Global Threat Reduction Initiative (GTRI), in addition to other amounts made available for such purposes, to expand the scope of facilities covered under the initiative, encourage countries and sites to relinquish vulnerable nuclear material, accelerate security upgrades at research reactors, and encourage the conversion of civilian reactors from the use of highly enriched uranium fuel to low enriched uranium fuel.

SEC. 8. ATTRIBUTION CAPABILITY TO DETER NUCLEAR TERRORISM.

(a) Statement of Policy- It shall be the policy of the United States to cooperate with the IAEA, Russia, and other countries that possess nuclear weapons-usable material to develop greater technical expertise and data necessary to identify the source of any nuclear weapons-usable material that might be transferred illegally or that might be used in a terrorist attack in order to help dissuade countries from participating in nuclear proliferation.

(b) Authorization of Appropriations- There are authorized to be appropriated to the Secretary of Energy $15,000,000 for fiscal year 2008 and $10,000,000 for fiscal years 2009 through 2012, in addition to other amounts available for such purposes, to establish a national technical forensics program to develop the best practicable technologies and procedures for determining the origin of nuclear materials, whether seized while still intact or collected after the detonation of a nuclear bomb.

SEC. 9. REVIEW CONFERENCE OF THE NUCLEAR NONPROLIFERATION TREATY.

(a) Statement of Policy- It shall be the policy of the United States—

(1) to strongly support the objectives of the Nuclear Non-Proliferation Treaty;

(2) to strongly support all appropriate measures to strengthen the Treaty and to attain its objectives; and

(3) to pursue a comprehensive and balanced approach to strengthen the global nuclear nonproliferation system in advance of and during the 2010 Nuclear Non-Proliferation Treaty Review Conference to realize a more robust and effective global nuclear nonproliferation system for the 21st century.

(b) Reports-

(1) REPORT ON COMPREHENSIVE OBJECTIVES, STRATEGY, AND POLICIES-

(A) IN GENERAL- Not later than October 31, 2009, the President shall submit to Congress a report, in classified and unclassified forms, that details the comprehensive objectives, strategy, and policies of the United States regarding the 2010 Nuclear Non-Proliferation Treaty Review Conference.

(B) CONTENT- The report required under subparagraph (A) shall describe—

(i) overall changes or revisions to the international nuclear nonproliferation frame-work, including the Nuclear Non-Proliferation Treaty, that may be needed to realize a more robust and effective global nuclear nonproliferation system;

(ii) the spread of sensitive nuclear technologies, in particular uranium enrichment and nuclear fuel reprocessing;

(iii) country-specific nuclear proliferation concerns;

(iv) efforts to uphold Article IV commitments on peaceful nuclear use, including the establishment of a nuclear fuel bank;

(v) accelerated implementation of obligations and commitments under the Nuclear Non-Proliferation Treaty for the purpose of reducing the world's stockpiles of nuclear weapons and weapons-grade fissile material;

(vi) nuclear and other nonproliferation initiatives such as the Proliferation Security Initiative;

(vii) the United States assessment of the objectives and strategies of other states with regard to the 2010 Nuclear Non-Proliferation Treaty Review Conference, including the Nuclear Weapons States, members of the Nuclear Suppliers Group, and leading member states associated with the Non-Aligned Movement; and

(viii) the United States diplomatic strategy leading up to the Conference to build and strengthen the international consensus regarding United States objectives.

(2) REPORT ON OUTCOMES ON CONFERENCE-

(A) IN GENERAL- Not later than 60 days after the conclusion of the 2010 Nuclear Non-Proliferation Treaty Review Conference, the President shall submit to Congress a report, in classified and unclassified forms, regarding the outcomes of the Conference.

(B) CONTENT- The report required under subparagraph (A) shall provide an assessment of the overall outcome of the Conference as well as United States consultations and negotiations and outcomes regarding the items listed in paragraph (1)(B).

SEC. 10. COMMISSION ON NUCLEAR NONPROLIFERATION AND PEACEFUL USE OF NUCLEAR TECHNOLOGY.

(a) Establishment- There is hereby established a commission to be known as the Commission on United States Objectives and Strategy for Nuclear Nonproliferation and Peaceful Use of Nuclear Technology (in this section referred to as the 'Commission').

(b) Membership-

(1) IN GENERAL- The Commission shall be comprised of 15 members appointed by the President. In selecting individuals for appointment, the President shall consult with—

(A) the Majority Leader of the Senate regarding the appointment of 4 of the members of the Commission;

(B) the Speaker of the House of Representatives regarding the appointment of 4 of the members of the Commission;

(C) the minority leader of the Senate regarding the appointment of 2 of the members of the Commission; and

(D) the minority leader of the House of Representatives regarding the appointment of 2 of the members of the Commission.

(2) CHAIRMAN- The Majority Leader of the Senate, in consultation with the Speaker of the House of Representatives and the respective minority leaders of the Senate and the House of Representatives, shall designate 1 of the Commission members to serve as chairman of the Commission.

(3) QUALIFICATIONS- Members of the Commission shall be appointed from among private United States citizens with knowledge and expertise in the political, security, military, and energy aspects of nuclear proliferation, disarmament, and peaceful use.

(4) SECURITY CLEARANCES- All Commission members shall hold appropriate security clearances.

(5) DEADLINE FOR APPOINTMENTS- All appointments to the Commission shall be made not later than 45 days after the date of the enactment of this Act.

(6) TERM- Members shall be appointed for the life of the Commission. Any vacancies shall be filled in the same manner as the original appointment.

(c) Duties- The duties of the Commission shall include—

(1) assessing and providing recommendations for United States objectives, strategy, and policies regarding the nature, scope, and magnitude of the threat posed by the spread of nuclear weapons and nuclear weapons-related technology, including the threat of nuclear terrorism; and

(2) reporting on—

(A) the status of efforts by nuclear weapons states to reduce global nuclear arsenals;

(B) the development by nuclear weapons states of next generation nuclear weapons and nuclear warheads;

(C) the need and requirements of peaceful nuclear use, including nuclear energy; and

(D) the role and capabilities of existing multilateral and international entities related to nuclear issues.

(d) Initial Meeting- The Commission shall convene its first meeting not later than 30 days after the date as of which all Commission members have been appointed.

(e) Procedures- Procedures for the operation of the Commission shall be established upon the approval of 10 of the 15 members of the Commission.

(f) Cooperation From Other Federal Agencies- The Commission shall receive the full and timely cooperation of the Secretary of State, the Secretary of Defense, the Director of National Intelligence, and the heads of other relevant Federal agencies, including analyses, briefings, and other information necessary for the fulfillment of the Commission's responsibilities.

(g) Report- Not later than 270 days after the date if its first meeting, the Commission shall submit to Congress the assessment and report described under subsection (c).

(h) Authorization of Appropriations- There is authorized to be appropriated $5,000,000 for the President to establish the Commission.

US SENATE BILL 1989

TITLE: A bill to provide a mechanism for the determination on the merits of the claims of claimants who met the class criteria in a civil action relating to racial discrimination by the Department of Agriculture but who were denied that determination.

SPONSOR: Sen Obama, Barack [IL] (introduced 8/3/2007) Cosponsors (None)

RELATED BILLS: H.R.3073

LATEST MAJOR ACTION: 8/3/2007 Referred to Senate committee. Status: Read twice and referred to the Committee on the Judiciary.

SUMMARY AS OF:

8/3/2007—Introduced.

Pigford Claims Remedy Act of 2007 - Declares that any Pigford claimant (relating to a racial discrimination action against the Department of Agriculture) who has not previously obtained a determination on the merits of a Pigford claim may, in a civil action, obtain that determination.

Asserts that it is Congress's intent that this Act be liberally construed so as to effectuate its remedial purpose of giving a full determination on the merits for each denied Pigford claim.

Directs the Secretary of Agriculture to provide a claimant with a report on farm credit loans made within the claimant's county or adjacent county during a specified period which shall contain information on all accepted applicants (but without any personally identifiable information), including: (1) the applicant's race; (2) the application and loan decision dates; and (3) the location of the office making the loan decision.

Sets forth provisions respecting: (1) expedited claim resolution; and (2) foreclosure limitation.

Defines: (1) "Pigford claimant" as an individual who previously submitted a late-filing request under the consent decree in the case of Pigford v. Glickman (1999); and (2) "Pigford claim" as a discrimination complaint as defined and documented by such consent decree.

MAJOR ACTIONS:

¤NONE¤

ALL ACTIONS:

8/3/2007:

Read twice and referred to the Committee on the Judiciary.

Titles(s): (italics indicate a title for a portion of a bill)

¤NONE¤

Cosponsor(s):

¤NONE¤

Committee(s)

Committee/Subcommittee:

Activity:

Senate Judiciary

Referral, In Committee

Related Bill Details: (additional related bills may be indentified in Status)

Bill:

Relationship:

H.R.3073

Identical bill identified by CRS

Amendment(s)

¤NONE¤

In the Senate of the United States

August 3, 2007

Mr. OBAMA introduced the following bill; which was read twice and referred to the Committee on the Judiciary

Λ BILL

To provide a mechanism for the determination on the merits of the claims of claimants who met the class criteria in a civil action relating to racial discrimination by the Department of Agriculture but who were denied that determination.

Be it enacted by the Senate and House of Representatives of the United States of America in Congress assembled,

SECTION 1. SHORT TITLE.

This Act may be cited as the 'Pigford Claims Remedy Act of 2007'.

SEC. 2. DETERMINATION ON MERITS OF PIGFORD CLAIMS.

(a) In General- Any Pigford claimant who has not previously obtained a determination on the merits of a Pigford claim may, in a civil action, obtain that determination.

(b) Intent of Congress as to Remedial Nature of Section- It is the intent of Congress that this section be liberally construed so as to effectuate its remedial purpose of giving a full determination on the merits for each Pigford claim denied that determination.

(c) Loan Data-

(1) REPORT TO PERSON SUBMITTING PETITION- Not later than 60 days after the Secretary of Agriculture receives notice of a complaint filed by a claimant under subsection (a), the Secretary shall provide to the claimant a report on farm credit loans made within the claimant's county or adjacent county by the Department during the period beginning on January 1 of the year preceding the year or years covered by the complaint and ending on December 31 of year following such year or years. Such report shall contain information on all persons whose application for a loan was accepted, including—

(A) the race of the applicant;

(B) the date of application;

(C) the date of the loan decision;

(D) the location of the office making the loan decision; and

(E) all data relevant to the process of deciding on the loan.

(2) NO PERSONALLY IDENTIFIABLE INFORMATION- The reports provided pursuant to paragraph (1) shall not contain any information that would identify any person that applied for a loan from the Department of Agriculture.

(d) Expedited Resolutions Authorized- Any person filing a complaint under this Act for discrimination in the application for, or making or servicing of, a farm loan, at his or her discretion, may seek liquidated damages of $50,000, discharge of the debt that was incurred under, or affected by, the discrimination that is the subject of the person's complaint, and a tax payment in the amount equal to 25 percent of the liquidated damages and loan principal discharged, in which case—

(1) if only such damages, debt discharge, and tax payment are sought, the complainant shall be able to prove his or her case by substantial evidence; and

(2) the court shall decide the case based on a review of documents submitted by the complainant and defendant relevant to the issues of liability and damages.

(e) Limitation on Foreclosures- Notwithstanding any other provision of law, the Secretary of Agriculture may not begin acceleration on or foreclosure of a loan if the borrower is a Pigford claimant and, in an appropriate administrative proceeding, makes a prima facie case that the foreclosure is related to a Pigford claim.

(f) Definitions- In this Act—

(1) the term 'Pigford claimant' means an individual who previously submitted a late-filing request under section 5(g) of the consent decree in the case of Pigford v. Glickman, approved by the United States District Court for the District of Columbia on April 14, 1999; and

(2) the term 'Pigford claim' means a discrimination complaint, as defined by section 1(h) of that consent decree and documented under section 5(b) of that consent decree.

US SENATE BILL 2030

TITLE: A bill to amend the Federal Election Campaign Act of 1971 to require reporting relating to bundled contributions made by persons other than registered lobbyists.

SPONSOR: Sen Obama, Barack [IL] (introduced 9/6/2007) Cosponsors (1)

LATEST MAJOR ACTION: 9/6/2007 Referred to Senate committee. Status: Read twice and referred to the Committee on Rules and Administration.

SUMMARY AS OF:

9/6/2007—Introduced.

Amends the Federal Election Campaign Act of 1971, as amended by the Honest Leadership and Open Government Act of 2007, to revise requirements for disclosure of bundled contributions, particularly by an authorized committee of a candidate for the office of President or for nomination to such office (presidential candidate committee).

Applies such reporting requirements to bundled contributions by persons other than registered lobbyists. Requires reporting of lobbyist contributions on a separate schedule.

Sets the covered period for such reports as the two-year period preceding a presidential election, as well as any applicable reporting period during which any person provided two or more bundled contributions in an aggregate amount greater than the specified applicable amount.

Increases the applicable threshold triggering such reporting requirement from $15,000 (currently applicable to any authorized committee of a candidate, a leadership PAC, or a political party committee) to $50,000 in the case of a presidential candidate committee.

Excludes from the calculation of a bundled contribution any contribution by the candidate or the candidate's spouse.

MAJOR ACTIONS:

¤NONE¤

ALL ACTIONS:

9/6/2007:

Read twice and referred to the Committee on Rules and Administration.

TITLES(s): (italics indicate a title for a portion of a bill)

¤NONE¤

COSPONSORS(1), ALPHABETICAL [followed by Cosponsors withdrawn]: (Sort: by date)

Sen Feingold, Russell D. [WI] - 9/6/2007

COMMITTEE(S)

Committee/Subcommittee:

Activity:

Senate Rules and Administration

Referral, In Committee

RELATED BILL DETAILS:

¤NONE¤

AMENDMENT(S)

¤NONE¤

IN THE SENATE OF THE UNITED STATES

September 6, 2007

Mr. REID (for Mr. OBAMA (for himself and Mr. FEINGOLD)) introduced the following bill; which was read twice and referred to the Committee on Rules and Administration

A BILL

To amend the Federal Election Campaign Act of 1971 to require reporting relating to bundled contributions made by persons other than registered lobbyists.

Be it enacted by the Senate and House of Representatives of the United States of America in Congress assembled,

SECTION 1. REPORTING OF BUNDLED CONTRIBUTIONS BY PERSONS OTHER THAN REGISTERED LOBBYISTS.

(a) In General- Subsection (i) of section 304 of the Federal Election Campaign Act of 1971 (2 U.S.C. 434(i)), as added by the Honest Leadership and Open Government Act of 2007, is amended—

(1) in paragraph (1), by striking 'reasonably known by the committee to be a person described in paragraph (7)';

(2) in paragraph (2), by striking 'means, with respect to a committee' and all that follows through 'threshold.' and inserting the following: 'means—

'(A) with respect to a committee which is an authorized committee of a candidate for the office of President or for nomination to such office—

'(i) the 2-year period preceding the date of the election for the office of the President; and

'(ii) any reporting period applicable to the committee under this section during which any person provided 2 or more bundled contributions to the committee in an aggregate amount greater than the applicable threshold; and

'(B) with respect to any other committee—

'(i) the period beginning January 1 and ending June 30 of each year;

'(ii) the period beginning July 1 and ending December 31 of each year; and

'(iii) any reporting period applicable to the committee under this section during which any person provided 2 or more bundled contributions to the committee in an aggregate amount greater than the applicable threshold.';

(3) in paragraph (3)—

(A) by striking subparagraph (A) and inserting the following:

'(A) IN GENERAL- In this subsection, the 'applicable threshold' is—

'(i) $50,000 in the case of a committee which is an authorized committee of a candidate for the office of President or for nomination to such office; and

'(ii) $15,000 in the case of any other committee.

In determining whether the amount of bundled contributions provided to a committee by a person exceeds the applicable threshold, there shall be excluded any contribution made to the committee by the person or the person's spouse.'; and

(B) in subparagraph (B), by striking 'the amount' each place it appears and inserting 'each amount';

(4) in paragraph (5), by striking 'described in paragraph (7)' each place it appears in subparagraphs (C) and (D);

(5) by striking paragraph (7) and inserting the following:

'(7) SEPARATE REPORTING FOR CERTAIN PERSONS- Each committee required to include a schedule under paragraph (1) shall also include a separate schedule setting forth the name, address, and employer of each person listed on the schedule required under paragraph (1) who, at the time a contribution is forwarded to a committee as described in paragraph (8)(A)(i) or is received by a committee as described in paragraph (8)(A)(ii), is—

'(A) a current registrant under section 4(a) of the Lobbying Disclosure Act of 1995;

'(B) an individual who is listed on a current registration filed under section 4(b)(6) of such Act or a current report under section 5(b)(2)(C) of such Act; or

'(C) a political committee established or controlled by such a registrant or individual.

The schedule required under the preceding sentence shall also include the aggregate amount of bundled contributions provided by each such person during the covered period.'; and

(6) in paragraph (8)(A)—

(A) by striking 'and a person described in paragraph (7)'; and

(B) by adding at the end the following flush sentence:

'The term 'bundled contribution' shall not include any contribution forwarded by or credited to (through records, designations, or other means of recognizing a certain amount of money has been raised) a person who is a regularly paid employee of the committee.'.

(b) Effective Date- The amendments made by this section shall take effect as if included in section 204 of the Honest Leadership and Open Government Act of 2007.

US SENATE BILL 2044

TITLE: A bill to provide procedures for the proper classification of employees and independent contractors, and for other purposes.

SPONSOR: Sen Obama, Barack [IL] (introduced 9/12/2007) Cosponsors (6)

LATEST MAJOR ACTION: 9/12/2007 Referred to Senate committee. Status: Read twice and referred to the Committee on Finance.

SUMMARY AS OF:

9/12/2007—Introduced.

Independent Contractor Proper Classification Act of 2007 - Amends the Revenue Act of 1978 to: (1) require employers to treat workers misclassified as independent contractors as employees for employment tax purposes upon a determination of misclassification by the Secretary of the Treasury; (2) repeal the ban on Treasury regulations or revenue rulings on employee/independent contractor classifications; and (3) eliminate the defense of industry practice as a justification for misclassifying workers as independent contractors.

Requires the Secretary to establish a procedure for workers to petition for a determination of their status as employees or independent contractors. Prohibits employers from retaliating against workers filing a petition. Requires the Secretary to take certain actions upon determining that an employee has been misclassified as an independent contractor, including informing the Department of Labor of such misclassification.

Requires the Secretaries of the Treasury and Labor to issue annual reports and exchange information on worker misclassification cases. Directs the Secretary of Labor to: (1) identify and track complaints involving worker misclassification for purposes of enforcing wage and hour laws; and (2) investigate industries identified by the Internal Revenue Service (IRS) as misclassifying workers.

Directs the Secretary of Labor to include on workplace posters required by the Fair Labor Standards Act a notice informing workers of their right to seek a status determination (i.e., whether they are employees or independent contractors) from the IRS.

Requires employers to: (1) notify their independent contractors of their federal tax obligations, the labor and employment protections inapplicable to independent contractors, and their right to seek a status determination from the IRS; and (2) maintain for three years a list of their independent contractors, including names and tax identification numbers.

MAJOR ACTIONS:

¤NONE¤

ALL ACTIONS:

9/12/2007:

Read twice and referred to the Committee on Finance.

TITLES(s): (italics indicate a title for a portion of a bill)

¤NONE¤

COSPONSORS(6), ALPHABETICAL [FOLLOWED BY COSPONSORS WITHDRAWN]: (Sort: by date)

Sen Boxer, Barbara [CA] - 9/19/2007

Sen Clinton, Hillary Rodham [NY] - 9/24/2007

Sen Durbin, Richard [IL] - 9/12/2007

Sen Kennedy, Edward M. [MA] - 9/12/2007

Sen Mikulski, Barbara A. [MD] - 9/24/2007

Sen Murray, Patty [WA] - 9/12/2007

COMMITTEE(S)

Committee/Subcommittee:

Activity:

Senate Finance

Referral, In Committee

RELATED BILL DETAILS:

¤NONE¤

AMENDMENT(S)

¤NONE¤

IN THE SENATE OF THE UNITED STATES

September 12, 2007

Mr. OBAMA (for himself, Mr. DURBIN, Mr. KENNEDY, and Mrs. MURRAY) introduced the following bill; which was read twice and referred to the Committee on Finance

A BILL

To provide procedures for the proper classification of employees and independent contractors, and for other purposes.

Be it enacted by the Senate and House of Representatives of the United States of America in Congress assembled,

SECTION 1. SHORT TITLE.

This Act may be cited as the 'Independent Contractor Proper Classification Act of 2007'.

SEC. 2. REFORMATION OF SAFE HARBOR TO CLOSE ITS USE AS A TAX LOOPHOLE.

(a) Allowance of Prospective Reclassifications-

(1) IN GENERAL- Section 530(a) of the Revenue Act of 1978, as amended by section 269(c)(1) of the Tax Equity and Fiscal Responsibility Act of 1982, is amended by adding at the end the following new paragraph:

'(5) ALLOWANCE OF RECLASSIFICATIONS- Paragraph (1) shall not apply with respect to the treatment by a taxpayer of any individual for employment tax purposes for any period beginning after a determination by the Secretary of the Treasury that the individual should be treated as an employee of the taxpayer.'.

(2) EFFECTIVE DATE- The amendment made by this subsection shall apply to determinations made after the date of the enactment of this Act.

(b) Elimination of Ban on IRS Issuing Regulations or Revenue Rulings on Employee/ independent Contractor Status-

(1) IN GENERAL- Section 530 of the Revenue Act of 1978, as amended by section 269(c)(2) of the Tax Equity and Fiscal Responsibility Act of 1982, section 1706(a) of the Tax Reform Act of 1986, section 1122(a) of the Small Business Job Protection Act of 1996, and section 864(a) of the Pension Protection Act of 2006, is amended by striking subsection (b) and by redesignating subsections (c), (d), (e), and (f) as subsections (b), (c), (d), and (e), respectively.

(2) EFFECTIVE DATE- The amendments made by this subsection shall take effect on the date of the enactment of this Act.

(c) Elimination of Ability of Employers To Rely on Industry Practice as a Basis for Claiming Safe Harbor-

(1) IN GENERAL- Section 530(a)(2) of the Revenue Act of 1978 is amended—

(A) by striking the semicolon at the end of subparagraph (A) and inserting '; or',

(B) by striking the semicolon at the end of subparagraph (B) and inserting a period, and

(C) by striking subparagraph (C).

(2) CONFORMING AMENDMENTS-

(A) Section 530(d)(2) of the Revenue Act of 1978, as redesignated by subsection (b)(1), is amended—

(i) by striking the comma at the end of subparagraph (A) and inserting a period,

(ii) by striking subparagraphs (B) and (C), and

(iii) by striking 'subsection (a)(2)' in the matter preceding subparagraph (A) and all that follows through 'a taxpayer' and inserting 'subsection (a)(2), a taxpayer'.

(B) Section 530(d)(4)(B) of such Act (as so redesignated) is amended by striking 'subparagraph (A), (B), or (C)' and inserting 'subparagraph (A) or (B)'.

(3) EFFECTIVE DATE- The amendments made by this subsection shall apply to periods beginning after the date which is 60 days after the date of the enactment of this Act.

SEC. 3. REVIEW OF CLASSIFICATION STATUS.

(a) In General- Section 530 of the Revenue Act of 1978, as amended by section 2(b)(1), is amended by adding at the end the following new subsections:

'(f) Petitions for Review of Status-

'(1) IN GENERAL- Under procedures established by the Secretary of the Treasury not later than 90 days after the date of the enactment of this subsection, any individual who performs services for a taxpayer may petition (either personally or through a designated representative or attorney) for a determination of the individual's status for employment tax purposes.

'(2) ADMINISTRATIVE PROCEDURES- The procedures established under paragraph (1) shall provide for—

'(A) a determination of status not later than 90 days after the filing of the petition with respect to employment in any industry (such as the construction industry) in which employment is transient, casual, or seasonal,

'(B) an administrative appeal of any determination that an individual is not an employee of the taxpayer,

'(C) the award of expenses, including expert witness fees and reasonable attorneys' fees for the individual against the taxpayer in any case in which the individual achieves reclassification, and

'(D) the assessment of such expenses against the taxpayer by the Secretary of the Treasury on behalf of such individual.

'(3) PROHIBITION AGAINST RETALIATION-

'(A) IN GENERAL- No taxpayer may discharge an individual, refuse to contract with an individual, or otherwise discriminate against an individual with respect to compensation, terms, conditions, or privileges of the services provided by the individual because the individual (or any designated representative or attorney on behalf of such individual) filed a petition under paragraph (1).

'(B) ENFORCEMENT ACTION- An individual who alleges discharge or other discrimination by any taxpayer in violation of subparagraph (A) may seek relief under the procedures and remedies established under section 42121 of title 49, United States Code.

'(C) RIGHTS RETAINED BY INDIVIDUAL- Nothing in this paragraph shall be deemed to diminish the rights, privileges, or remedies of any individual under any Federal or State law, or under any collective bargaining agreement.

'(g) Results of Misclassification Determinations- In any case in which the Secretary of the Treasury determines that a taxpayer has misclassified an individual as not an employee for employment tax purposes, the Secretary of the Treasury shall—

'(1) if necessary, perform an employment tax audit of such taxpayer,

'(2) inform the Department of Labor about such misclassification,

'(3) notify the individual of any eligibility for the refund of self-employment taxes under chapter 2 of the Internal Revenue Code of 1986, and

'(4) apply the provisions of section 3509 of the Internal Revenue Code of 1986 and direct the taxpayer to take affirmative action to abate the violation.'.

(b) Effective Date- The amendment made by this section shall take effect on the date of the enactment of this Act.

SEC. 4. COORDINATION, ENFORCEMENT, AND COMPLIANCE.

(a) Annual Reports- The Secretary of the Treasury and the Secretary of Labor shall each issue annual reports on worker misclassification, including—

(1) information on the number and type of enforcement actions against, and audits of, employers who have misclassified workers,

(2) relief obtained as a result of such actions against, and audits of, employers who have misclassified workers,

(3) an overall estimate of the number of employers misclassifying workers, the number of workers affected, and the industries involved,

(4) the impact of such misclassification on the Federal tax system, and

(5) the aggregate number of worker misclassification cases with respect to which each Secretary has provided information to the other Secretary and the outcome of actions taken, if any, by each Secretary in each worker misclassification case with respect to which the Secretary has received such information.

As part of the annual report, the Secretary of the Treasury shall include information on the outcomes of the petitions filed under section 530(f) of the Revenue Act of 1978 and the Secretary of Labor shall include information on the outcomes of the complaints and actions described in subsection (b)(1)(A) and the investigations required in subsection (b)(1)(B).

(b) Enforcement Activities-

(1) DEPARTMENT OF LABOR-

(A) WAGE AND HOUR ENFORCEMENT- The Secretary of Labor shall identify and track complaints and enforcement actions involving misclassification of independent contractors for the purposes of the laws enforced by the Wage and Hour Division of the Department of Labor.

(B) INVESTIGATIONS OF INDUSTRIES WITH WORKER MISCLASSI-FICATIONS- The Secretary of Labor shall conduct investigations of industries in which worker misclassification is present as determined by information (other than return information (as defined in section 6103(b)(2)) received from the Secretary of the Treasury and any other relevant information, including reports from other Federal agencies and State workforce, labor, and revenue agencies.

(2) AUTHORIZATION OF APPROPRIATIONS- There is authorized such sums as are necessary for the Department of the Treasury and the Department of Labor to carry out the purposes of the provisions of, and amendments made by, this Act.

(3) INFORMATION SHARING- The Secretary of the Treasury and the Secretary of Labor shall exchange information on worker misclassification cases and shall provide such information with relevant State agencies. Upon receipt of such information, the Secretary of the Treasury and the Secretary of Labor shall determine whether further investigation is warranted in each case.

SEC. 5. NOTICE TO EMPLOYEES AND INDEPENDENT CONTRACTORS AND MAINTENANCE OF INFORMATION REGARDING INDEPENDENT CONTRACTORS.

(a) Notice of Right To Challenge Classification- The Secretary of Labor shall provide for the placement of information on any poster required under the Fair Labor Standards Act informing workers of their right to seek a status determination from the Internal Revenue Service.

(b) Employer Notices to Independent Contractors- Each employer shall notify any individual who is hired by the employer as an independent contractor within the scope of the employer's trade or business, at the time of hire, of the Federal tax obligations of an independent contractor, the labor and employment law protections that do not apply to independent contractors, and the right of such independent contractor to seek a status determination from the Internal Revenue Service. The Secretary of the Treasury and the Secretary of Labor shall develop model materials for providing such notice.

(c) Maintenance of Information Regarding Independent Contractors- Each employer shall maintain for 3 years a list of the independent contractors retained by the employer, including name, address, Social Security number and Federal tax identification number, and shall make the records available for inspection during investigations.

US Senate Bill 2066

Title: A bill to establish nutrition and physical education standards for schools.

Sponsor: Sen Obama, Barack [IL] (introduced 9/18/2007) Cosponsors (None)

Latest Major Action: 9/18/2007 Referred to Senate committee. Status: Read twice and referred to the Committee on Agriculture, Nutrition, and Forestry.

Summary As Of:

9/18/2007—Introduced.

Back to School: Improving Standards for Nutrition and Physical Education in Schools Act of 2007 - Directs the Secretary of Agriculture to revise

the standards that set a minimal nutritional value for competitive foods and beverages (sold outside of the federally-funded school lunch and breakfast programs) so that they are consistent with those described in a report of the Institute of Medicine (Institute) of the National Academy of Sciences (NAS), dated April 25, 2007.

Applies such standards to all competitive foods and beverages sold on school campuses during the school day.

Requires the Secretary of Health and Human Services (Secretary) to arrange for the Institute to develop recommendations, every five years, for updating such standards so they reflect the current Dietary Guidelines for Americans and scientific knowledge. Requires the Secretary of Agriculture, after receiving the Institute's recommendations, to revise such standards.

Directs the Secretary to establish the Nutrition Standards in Schools Task Force to assist in establishing a user friendly system for identifying foods and beverages that meet nutrition standards.

Directs the Secretary of Agriculture to award grants to states, high-need local educational agencies (LEAs), and Indian tribes to provide food service and school personnel with the training needed to implement nutrition standards.

Requires federally-funded LEAs to implement policies requiring student participation in physical education programs that meet standards for physical activity issued by the Secretary, based on recommendations from the National Association for Sport and Physical Education.

Directs the Secretary to award competitive grants to states, high-need LEAs, and Indian tribes to provide teachers with the training and support needed to implement such physical education programs.

Requires the Carol M. White Physical Education program to meet the Secretary's standards for physical activity.

MAJOR ACTIONS:

¤NONE¤

ALL ACTIONS:

9/18/2007:

Read twice and referred to the Committee on Agriculture, Nutrition, and Forestry.

TITLES(s): (italics indicate a title for a portion of a bill)

¤NONE¤

COSPONSOR(s):

¤NONE¤

COMMITTEE(s)

Committee/Subcommittee:

Activity:

Senate Agriculture, Nutrition, and Forestry

Referral, In Committee

Related Bill Details:

¤NONE¤

Amendment(s)

¤NONE¤

In the Senate of the United States

September 18, 2007

Mr. OBAMA introduced the following bill; which was read twice and referred to the Committee on Agriculture, Nutrition, and Forestry

A BILL

To establish nutrition and physical education standards for schools.

Be it enacted by the Senate and House of Representatives of the United States of America in Congress assembled,

SECTION 1. SHORT TITLE.

This Act may be cited as the 'Back to School: Improving Standards for Nutrition and Physical Education in Schools Act of 2007'.

SEC. 2. FINDINGS.

(1) National data show that 1 out of every 3 children and youth, or about 25,000,000 children and youth, in the United States are overweight or obese. There is clear evidence that this epidemic of excess weight and obesity is due to excessive dietary intake and sedentary activity.

(2) The foods served in the school lunch program established under the Richard B. Russell National School Lunch Act and the school breakfast program established by section 4 of the Child Nutrition Act of 1966 are required to meet Federal nutrition guidelines and comply with the Dietary Guidelines for Americans. Competitive foods and beverages, purchased by children and youth outside of the federally reimbursed school lunch and breakfast programs, are only required to meet limited nutrition standards pertaining to 'foods of minimal nutritional value'.

(3) The Secretary of Agriculture defined the term 'foods of minimal nutritional value' for competitive foods and beverages in 1979. This definition is not consistent with current scientific evidence regarding nutrition.

(4) In response to a request by Congress, the Institute of Medicine of the National Academy of Sciences developed science-based nutrition standards for competitive foods and beverages offered during the school day, based on the Dietary Guidelines for Americans.

(5) Because all foods and beverages available on a school campus provide significant calories, they should be required to meet those science-based nutrition standards.

(6) Currently, government, scientific, and public health agencies recommend guidelines suggesting that school-age children and youth engage in at least 60 minutes of moderate to vigorous physical activity, that is developmentally appropriate and that involves a variety of activities, on most of the 7 days of the week. However, more than 1/3 of children and youth do not meet the recommended guidelines for physical activity. The percentages of children that meet the recommended guidelines are 5 to 10 percentage points lower among ethnic minorities than among whites.

(7) The Centers for Disease Control and Prevention reported that only 8 percent of elementary schools, 6.4 percent of middle and junior high schools, and 5.8 percent of senior high schools offered daily physical education during the school year. Daily student participation in high school physical education classes dropped from 42 percent in 1991 to 28 percent in 2003.

(8)(A) Key methods of improving the physical activity of children and youth are—

(i) ensuring that classes meet national standards for physical education that have been embraced by States and local educational agencies; and

(ii) ensuring that teachers are adequately trained to implement those standards.

(B) The National Association for Sport and Physical Education and the Centers for Disease Control and Prevention support the use of the National Standards for Physical Education as a framework that can be used to design, implement, and evaluate quality physical education curricula.

(9) Physical education classes for children and youth are not consistently required to meet those national standards. Forty-three States allow classroom teachers, without any training in physical education, to teach physical education.

(10) Children should participate in physical education classes based on standards grounded in science, to ensure quality programs. Adequate and well-trained teachers are needed to ensure the implementation of those quality programs.

SEC. 3. ESTABLISHING AND IMPLEMENTING NUTRITION STANDARDS FOR SCHOOL FOODS.

(a) Definition of Nutrition Standards- In this section:

(1) ESTABLISHED NUTRITION STANDARDS- The term 'established nutrition standards' means the nutrition standards for competitive foods and beverages in schools described in the report of the Institute of Medicine entitled 'Nutrition Standards for Foods in Schools: Leading the Way toward Healthier Youth' and dated April 25, 2007.

(2) NUTRITION STANDARDS- The term 'nutrition standards' means the nutrition standards for competitive foods and beverages in schools.

(3) SCHOOL- The term 'school' means a school that participates in the reimbursable school meal programs under—

(A) the Richard B. Russell National School Lunch Act (42 U.S.C. 1751 et seq.); or

(B) the Child Nutrition Act of 1966 (42 U.S.C. 1771 et seq.).

(4) UPDATED NUTRITION STANDARDS- The term 'updated nutrition standards' means the nutrition standards used as the basis for regulations promulgated under subsection (b)(4).

(b) Foods of Minimal Nutritional Value-

(1) PROPOSED REGULATIONS BASED ON ESTABLISHED NUTRITION STANDARDS-

(A) IN GENERAL- Not later than 180 days after the date of enactment of this Act, the Secretary of Agriculture shall promulgate proposed regulations to revise the definition of 'foods of minimal nutritional value' that is used to carry out this Act, the Richard B. Russell National School Lunch Act, and the Child Nutrition Act of 1966, to be consistent with the established nutrition standards, in accordance with recommendations contained in the report described in subsection (a).

(B) APPLICATION- The revised definition of 'foods of minimal nutritional value' shall apply to all foods and beverages sold—

(i) independent of the reimbursable school meal programs carried out under the Richard B. Russell National School Lunch Act (42 U.S.C. 1751 et seq.) and the Child Nutrition Act of 1966 (42 U.S.C. 1771 et seq.);

(ii) on the school campus; and

(iii) at any time during the school day.

(2) IMPLEMENTATION OF REGULATIONS BASED ON ESTABLISHED NUTRITION STANDARDS-

(A) EFFECTIVE DATE-

(i) IN GENERAL- Except as provided in clause (ii), the final regulations to revise the definition as described in paragraph (1) shall take effect at the beginning of the school year following the date on which the regulations are finalized.

(ii) EXCEPTION- If the regulations are finalized on a date that is not more than 60 days before the beginning of the school year, the regulations shall take effect at the beginning of the following school year.

(B) FAILURE TO PROMULGATE- If the Secretary of Agriculture has not promulgated final regulations as of the date that is 1 year after the date of enactment of this Act, the proposed regulations shall be considered to be final regulations.

(3) RECOMMENDATIONS FOR REVISED NUTRITION STANDARDS-

(A) STUDY- Not later than 2 years after the date of enactment of this Act, and not less than every 5 years thereafter, the Secretary of Health and Human Services in collaboration with the Secretary of Agriculture shall enter into an arrangement with the Institute of Medicine under which the Institute shall conduct a study to develop recommendations regarding necessary updates for nutrition standards to ensure that—

(i) the most current scientific knowledge (as of the date of the study) is included in information used to establish the nutrition standards; and

(ii) the nutrition standards are consistent with the current Dietary Guidelines for Americans (as of the date of the study), with specifications for different age groups and other segments of the population as recommended by the Institute of Medicine.

(B) REPORT- The Institute of Medicine shall prepare and submit a report containing the recommendations described in subparagraph (A), under each arrangement described in subsection (a), to the Secretary of Health and Human Services, the Secretary of Agriculture, appropriate committees of Congress, and the general public.

(4) REGULATIONS BASED ON UPDATED NUTRITION STANDARDS- Not later than 3 months after receiving a report under paragraph (3), the Secretary of Agriculture shall promulgate regulations to revise the definition described in paragraph (1)(A), taking into consideration the recommendations for nutrition standards contained in the report. The revised definition shall apply to all foods and beverages described in paragraph (1)(B).

(5) USE- The Secretary of Health and Human Services and the Secretary of Agriculture shall take into consideration the established nutrition standards or updated nutrition standards, as appropriate, during the proposal and issuance of any regulation for any Federal program that provides or subsidizes foods or beverages.

(c) Task Force To Establish a User Friendly Identification System for Foods and Beverages That Meet Nutrition Standards-

(1) IN GENERAL- Not later than 12 months after the date of enactment of this Act, the Secretary of Health and Human Services (referred to in this subsection as the 'Secretary'), after consultation with the Secretary of Agriculture, shall establish the Nutrition Standards in Schools Task Force (referred to in this subsection as the 'Task Force') to assist in establishing a user friendly identification system for identifying foods and beverages that meet the established nutrition standards or updated nutrition standards, as appropriate.

(2) MEMBERSHIP-

(A) COMPOSITION- The Task Force shall be composed of—

(i) a representative of the Department of Health and Human Services;

(ii) a representative of the Department of Agriculture;

(iii) a representative of the Department of Education;

(iv) a representative of the food and beverage industry, appointed by the Secretary;

(v) a representative of public school administrators and food service operators, appointed by the Secretary;

(vi) a representative of parent organizations, appointed by the Secretary;

(vii) a representative of public health and nutrition advocacy organizations, appointed by the Secretary; and

(viii) other members as determined appropriate by the Secretary.

(B) PERIOD OF APPOINTMENT; VACANCIES- Members shall be appointed for the life of the Task Force. Any vacancy in the Task Force shall not affect its powers, but shall be filled in the same manner as the original appointment.

(C) CHAIRPERSON- The Secretary or the Secretary's designee shall serve as the chairperson of the Task Force.

(3) DUTIES- The Task Force shall—

(A) make recommendations to the Secretary concerning guidelines for the user friendly identification system described in paragraph (1);

(B) after the Secretary issues guidelines for such a system, coordinate and facilitate the development of the system;

(C) report the guidelines for such a system to representatives from—

(i) education and child development groups;

(ii) parents and parent organizations;

(iii) school boards and local education agencies;

(iv) State agencies;

(v) Federal agencies;

(vi) public health organizations;

(vii) nutrition advocacy organizations; and

(viii) food and beverage producers and vendors;

(D) recommend to the Secretary an evaluation plan for monitoring the implementation of the system.

(4) PERSONNEL-

(A) TRAVEL EXPENSES- The members of the Task Force shall not receive compensation for the performance of services for the Task Force, but shall be allowed travel expenses, including per diem in lieu of subsistence, at rates authorized for employees of agencies under subchapter I of chapter 57 of title 5, United States Code, while away from their homes or regular places of business in the performance of services for the Task Force. Notwithstanding section 1342 of title 31, United States Code, the Secretary may accept the voluntary and uncompensated services of members of the Task Force.

(B) DETAIL OF GOVERNMENT EMPLOYEES- Any Federal Government employee may be detailed to the Task Force without reimbursement, and such detail shall be without interruption or loss of civil service status or privilege.

(5) PERMANENT COMMITTEE- Section 14 of the Federal Advisory Committee Act (5 U.S.C. App.) shall not apply to the Task Force.

(d) Training School Food Service Personnel To Implement Nutrition Standards-

(1) GRANTS- The Secretary of Agriculture (referred to in this subsection as the 'Secretary') shall make grants to eligible entities to train food service and other appropriate school personnel to provide the personnel with the knowledge and skills necessary to implement the established nutrition standards or updated nutrition standards, as appropriate.

(2) ELIGIBILITY- To be eligible to receive a grant under this subsection, an entity shall—

(A) be a State educational agency, high-need local educational agency, or Indian tribe; and

(B) submit an application to the Secretary at such time, in such manner, and containing such information as the Secretary may require.

(3) PRIORITY- In making grants under this subsection, the Secretary shall give priority to eligible entities that serve underserved populations, including racial and ethnic minority populations and low-income populations.

(4) USE OF FUNDS- An entity that receives a grant under this subsection shall use the amounts received through the grant to train personnel described in paragraph (1) to implement the nutrition standards described in paragraph (1) in schools.

(5) TECHNICAL ASSISTANCE- The Director of the Centers for Disease Control and Prevention shall provide each entity that receives a grant under this subsection with technical support—

(A) to facilitate the implementation of the nutrition standards described in paragraph (1); and

(B) to the maximum extent practicable, to ensure healthy eating behaviors among children.

(6) EVALUATION- Not later than 2 years after the date on which a grant is awarded to an eligible entity under this subsection, the entity shall submit to the Director of the Centers for Disease Control and Prevention a report that describes and contains an evaluation of the activities carried out with funds received through the grant.

(7) DEFINITIONS- In this subsection:

(A) INDIAN TRIBE- The term 'Indian tribe' has the meaning given the term in section 2 of the Tribally Controlled College or University Assistance Act of 1978 (25 U.S.C. 1801).

(B) LOCAL EDUCATIONAL AGENCY; STATE EDUCATIONAL AGENCY- The terms 'local educational agency' and 'State educational agency' have the meanings given the terms in section 9101 of the Elementary and Secondary Education Act of 1965 (20 U.S.C. 7801).

(8) AUTHORIZATION OF APPROPRIATIONS- There are authorized to be appropriated such sums as are necessary to carry out this subsection.

SEC. 4. ESTABLISHING AND IMPLEMENTING PHYSICAL EDUCATION STANDARDS IN SCHOOLS.

(a) Definitions- In this section, the terms 'Indian tribe', 'local educational agency', and 'State educational agency' have the meanings given the terms in section 3(d)(7).

(b) Physical Education Standards in Schools- The Secretary of Health and Human Services, acting through the Director of the Centers for Disease Control and Prevention (referred to in this section as the 'Secretary'), in collaboration with the Secretary of Education, shall ensure that local educational agencies that receive Federal funds establish and implement policies to ensure that students participate in physical education programs that meet standards for physical activity issued by the Secretary, based on standards recommended by the National Association for Sport and Physical Education.

(c) Grants for Training-

(1) GRANTS- The Secretary shall award grants on a competitive basis to eligible entities to support activities that provide teacher training, and provide the support needed, to implement physical education programs that meet the standards described in subsection (b).

(2) ELIGIBILITY- To be eligible to receive a grant under this subsection, an entity shall be a State educational agency, high-need local educational agency, or Indian tribe.

(3) APPLICATIONS- To be eligible to receive a grant under this subsection, an entity shall submit an application to the Secretary at such time, in such manner, and containing such agreements, assurances, and other information as the Secretary may require.

(4) PRIORITY- In awarding grants under this subsection, the Secretary shall give priority to eligible entities submitting applications proposing to provide training and support for programs for students from populations at high risk for sedentary activity, including racial and ethnic minority populations and low-income populations.

(5) USE OF FUNDS- An entity that receives a grant under this subsection shall use the amounts received through the grant to provide the training and support described in paragraph (1).

(6) EVALUATION- Not later than 3 years after the date on which a grant is awarded to an eligible entity under this subsection, the entity shall submit to the Secretary a report that describes the activities carried out with funds received through the grant and the effectiveness of such activities in ensuring students meet the standards described in subsection (b).

(d) Carol M. White Physical Education Program-

(1) REQUIRED STANDARDS- Section 5503 of the Elementary and Secondary Education Act of 1965 (20 U.S.C. 7216b) is amended—

(A) in subsection (a), by striking 'grants' and inserting 'grants and contracts'; and

(B) in subsection (b)—

(i) by redesignating paragraphs (1) through (6) as subparagraphs (A) through (F); and

(ii) by striking 'subpart may provide' and inserting 'subpart—

'(1) shall, not later than 2 years after the date of enactment of the Back to School: Improving Standards for Nutrition and Physical Education in Schools Act of 2007, meet standards for physical activity, as issued by the Secretary of Health and Human Services, based on standards recommended by the National Association for Sport and Physical Education; and

'(2) may provide'.

(2) EVALUATION- Section 5505 of such Act (20 U.S.C. 7261d) is amended—

(A) in subsection (b), by striking 'grant' and inserting 'grant or contract'; and

(B) by adding at the end the following:

'(c) Evaluation- Not later than 2 years after the date on which a grant or contract is awarded to an eligible entity under this subpart, the entity shall submit to the Secretary a report that describes the activities carried out with the funds received through the grant or contract and the effectiveness of such activities in meeting the standards described in section 5503(b)(1).'.

(3) PRIORITY- Section 5506(b) of such Act (20 U.S.C. 7261e(b)) is amended—

(A) in the subsection header, by striking 'Proportionality- ' and inserting 'Awards- ' ;

(B) by inserting before 'To the extent' the following:

'(1) PROPORTIONALITY- ';

(C) by striking 'grants' and inserting 'grants and contracts'; and

(D) by adding at the end the following:

'(2) PRIORITY- In awarding grants and contracts under this subpart, the Secretary shall give priority to eligible entities submitting applications proposing to carry out programs for students from populations at high risk for sedentary activity, including racial and ethnic minority populations and low-income populations.'.

US SENATE BILL 2111

TITLE: A bill to amend the Elementary and Secondary Education Act of 1965 to allow State educational agencies, local educational agencies, and schools to increase implementation of early intervention services, particularly school-wide positive behavior supports.

SPONSOR: Sen Obama, Barack [IL] (introduced 9/27/2007) Cosponsors (3)

RELATED BILLS: H.R.3407

LATEST MAJOR ACTION: 9/27/2007 Referred to Senate committee. Status: Read twice and referred to the Committee on Health, Education, Labor, and Pensions.

SUMMARY AS OF:

9/27/2007—Introduced.

Positive Behavior for Effective Schools Act - Amends the Elementary and Secondary Education Act of 1965 (ESEA) to allow states to allocate school improvement funds under title I of the ESEA for coordinated, early intervention services for all students. Includes among such services, schoolwide positive behavior support, defined as a systematic approach to embed proven practices for early intervention services in order to achieve important

social outcomes and increase student learning, while preventing problem behaviors.

Requires improvements in schoolwide learning climates, including school-wide positive behavior supports, to be a target of: (1) technical assistance provided by states to local educational agencies (LEAs) and schools, and by LEAs to schools identified as needing improvement; (2) schoolwide programs that allow LEAs to consolidate educational funds to upgrade the entire educational program of schools that serve a high proportion of low-income families; (3) professional development funding; (4) funding under the Safe and Drug-Free Schools and Communities program; and (5) elementary and secondary school counseling programs.

Amends the Department of Education Organization Act to establish, within the Department of Education, an Office of Specialized Instructional Support Services to oversee, implement, and ensure adequate evaluation of, the provision of specialized instructional support services in schools by school counselors, social workers, psychologists, and other qualified professionals.

MAJOR ACTIONS:

¤NONE¤

ALL ACTIONS:

9/27/2007:

Sponsor introductory remarks on measure. (CR S12291)

9/27/2007:

Read twice and referred to the Committee on Health, Education, Labor, and Pensions.

TITLES(S): (italics indicate a title for a portion of a bill)

¤NONE¤

COSPONSORS(3), ALPHABETICAL [FOLLOWED BY COSPONSORS WITH-DRAWN]: (Sort: by date)

Sen Durbin, Richard [IL] - 9/27/2007

Sen Sanders, Bernard [VT] - 9/27/2007

Sen Schumer, Charles E. [NY] - 11/16/2007

COMMITTEE(S)

Committee/Subcommittee:

Activity:

Senate Health, Education, Labor, and Pensions

Referral, In Committee

RELATED BILL DETAILS: (additional related bills may be indentified in Status)

Bill:

Relationship:

H.R.3407

Related bill identified by CRS

AMENDMENT(S)

¤NONE¤

IN THE SENATE OF THE UNITED STATES

September 27, 2007

Mr. OBAMA (for himself, Mr. DURBIN, and Mr. SANDERS) introduced the following bill; which was read twice and referred to the Committee on Health, Education, Labor, and Pensions

A BILL

To amend the Elementary and Secondary Education Act of 1965 to allow State educational agencies, local educational agencies, and schools to increase implementation of early intervention services, particularly school-wide positive behavior supports.

Be it enacted by the Senate and House of Representatives of the United States of America in Congress assembled,

SECTION 1. SHORT TITLE.

This Act may be cited as the 'Positive Behavior for Effective Schools Act'.

SEC. 2. FINDINGS AND PURPOSES.

(a) Findings- Congress makes the following findings:

(1) Educators, parents, and the general public cite a lack of discipline as a leading challenge facing many public schools.

(2) Negative and reactive school management practices, such as metal detectors or surveillance cameras, and zero tolerance or other get-tough approaches to school discipline, are ineffective and often counterproductive.

(3) Learning is linked to student behavior. Successful schools implement high academic and behavior standards, where improvements in student behavior and school climate are correlated with improved academic outcomes.

(4) Effective implementation of positive behavior supports is linked to greater academic achievement, significantly fewer disciplinary problems, lower suspension and expulsion rates, and increased time for instruction.

(5) Evidence-based and scientifically valid practices for improving behavior and creating a school climate more conducive to learning have not been widely adopted, accurately implemented, or sustained.

(6) Early intervening services are an effective strategy for instructional support. Following implementation of positive behavior support, out-of-school suspensions at an elementary school in Illinois decreased 85 percent, from 243 to 37 or fewer in 2 subsequent years, with a resultant gain of 386 days of instructional time. The percentage of students meeting or exceeding proficiency on State standards increased measurably.

(7) Problem behaviors can be minimized with effective positive behavior support, including active supervision, positive feedback, and social skills instruction, which reduce the need for more intensive and more costly interventions. Upon implementing such supports, an elementary school in Maryland witnessed a decrease in office discipline referrals for major rule violations by 42 percent, recouping 119 days of instructional time for students, and 40 days of administrator time, within 1 school year.

(8) Schools that implement school-wide positive behavior supports are perceived by teachers to be safer teaching environments. In South Carolina, a school using a system of positive behavior supports found that teacher transfer requests declined by 100 percent and teacher absence days decreased by 36 percent.

(9) When approaches such as positive behavior support are paired with effective interventions and services for students with significant needs, all students, including those with the most challenging behaviors, can succeed.

(b) Purposes- The purposes of this Act are to expand the use of positive behavior supports and other early intervening services in schools in order to systematically create a school climate that is highly conducive to learning, to reduce discipline referrals, and to improve student academic outcomes.

SEC. 3. DEFINITION OF POSITIVE BEHAVIOR SUPPORT.

In this Act, the term 'positive behavior support' means a systematic approach to embed proven practices for early intervening services, including a range of systemic and individualized strategies to reinforce desired behaviors and eliminate reinforcement for problem behaviors, in order to achieve important social outcomes and increase student learning, while preventing problem behaviors.

SEC. 4. SCHOOLWIDE POSITIVE BEHAVIOR SUPPORT.

(a) Flexibility To Use Title I Funds To Implement School-Wide Positive Behavior Support-

(1) IN GENERAL- Section 1003(b) of the Elementary and Secondary Education Act of 1965 (20 U.S.C. 6303(b)) is amended—

(A) by redesignating paragraphs (1) and (2) as subparagraphs (A) and (B), respectively;

(B) by inserting '(1)' before 'Of the amount'; and

(C) by adding at the end the following:

'(2) Of the amount reserved under subsection (a) for any fiscal year, the State educational agency may allocate funds to develop and implement coordinated, early intervening services (including school-wide positive behavior supports) for all students, including those who have not been identified as needing special education but who need additional academic and behavioral support to succeed in a general education environment. Funds so allocated shall be—

'(A) aligned with funds authorized under section 613(f) of the Individuals with Disabilities Education Act; and

'(B) used to supplement, and not supplant, funds made available under such Act for such activities and services.'.

(2) TECHNICAL ASSISTANCE- The Elementary and Secondary Education Act of 1965 (20 U.S.C. 6301 et seq.) is amended—

(A) in section 1116(b)(4)(B)—

(i) by redesignating clauses (iii) and (iv) as clauses (iv) and (v), respectively; and

(ii) by inserting after clause (ii) the following:

'(iii) shall include assistance in implementation of school-wide positive behavior supports and other approaches with evidence of effectiveness for improving the learning environment in the school;';

(B) in section 1117(a)(3), by inserting 'any technical assistance center on schoolwide positive behavior supports funded under section 665(b) of the Individuals with Disabilities Education Act,' after '2002),'; and

(C) in section 1117(a)(5)(B)—

(i) by redesignating clauses (iii) and (iv) as clauses (iv) and (v), respectively; and

(ii) by inserting after clause (ii) the following:

'(iii) review the number of discipline referrals in the school and the overall school climate and engagement of families, and use that information to assist the school to implement school-wide positive behavior supports or other early intervening services, or both;'.

(b) LEA Flexibility To Improve School Climate- Section 1114(b)(1)(B)(iii)(I) of the Elementary and Secondary Education Act of 1965 (20 U.S.C. 6314(b)(1)(B)(iii)(I)) is amended—

(1) by redesignating items (bb) and (cc) as items (cc) and (dd), respectively; and

(2) by inserting after item (aa) the following:

'(bb) improving the learning environment in the school, including the implementation of school-wide positive behavioral supports, in order to improve academic outcomes for students;'.

SEC. 5. TEACHER AND PRINCIPAL PREPARATION TO IMPROVE SCHOOL CLIMATE.

Section 2122(c)(2) of the Elementary and Secondary Education Act of 1965 (20 U.S.C. 6622(c)(2)) is amended—

(1) by striking 'subject matter knowledge and teaching skills' and inserting 'subject matter knowledge, teaching skills, and an understanding of social or emotional, or

both, learning in children and approaches that improve the school climate for learning (such as positive behavior support)'; and

(2) by inserting 'to improve the teachers' schools' climate for learning' after 'instructional leadership skills to help teachers'.

SEC. 6. SAFE AND DRUG FREE SCHOOLS AND COMMUNITIES.

Section 4002 of the Elementary and Secondary Education Act of 1965 (20 U.S.C. 7102) is amended—

(1) by redesignating paragraphs (1) through (4) as paragraphs (2) through (5), respectively; and

(2) by striking all that precedes paragraph (2) and inserting the following: 'The purpose of this part is to support programs that improve the whole school climate in order to foster learning, including programs that prevent discipline problems, that prevent violence in and around schools, that prevent the illegal use of alcohol, tobacco, and drugs, that involve parents and communities in the school programs and activities, and that are coordinated with related Federal, State, school, and community efforts and resources to foster a safe and drug-free learning environment that supports student academic achievement, through the provision of Federal assistance to—

'(1) States for grants to local educational agencies and consortia of such agencies to establish, operate, and improve local programs relating to improving the school-wide climate (including implementation of positive behavior supports and other programs);'.

SEC. 7. EARLY INTERVENING SERVICES UNDER SCHOOL COUNSELORS PROGRAM.

Section 5421(b)(2) of the Elementary and Secondary Education Act of 1965 (20 U.S.C. 7245(b)(2)) is amended—

(1) by redesignating subparagraphs (C) through (H) as subparagraphs (D) through (I), respectively; and

(2) by inserting after subparagraph (B) the following:

'(C) describe how the local educational agency will address the need for early intervening services that improve the school climate for learning, such as through schoolwide positive behavior supports;'.

SEC. 8. OFFICE OF SPECIALIZED INSTRUCTIONAL SUPPORT SERVICES.

The Department of Education Organization Act (20 U.S.C. 3401 et seq.) is amended by adding at the end of title II the following:

'SEC. 221. OFFICE OF SPECIALIZED INSTRUCTIONAL SUPPORT SERVICES.

'(a) In General- There shall be, within the Office of the Deputy Secretary in the Department of Education, an Office of Specialized Instructional Support Services (referred to in this section as the 'Office').

'(b) Purpose- The purpose of the Office shall be to administer, coordinate, implement, and ensure adequate evaluation of the effectiveness of programs and activities concerned with providing specialized instructional support services in schools, delivered by trained, qualified specialized instructional support personnel.

'(c) Director- The Office established under subsection (a) shall be headed by a Director who shall be selected by the Secretary and report directly to the Deputy Secretary of Education.

'(d) Activities- In carrying out subsection (b), the Director shall support activities to—

'(1) improve specialized instructional support services in schools in order to improve academic achievement and educational results for students;

'(2) identify scientifically valid practices in specialized instructional support services that support learning and improve academic achievement and educational results for students;

'(3) provide continuous training and professional development opportunities for specialized instructional support personnel and other school personnel in the use of effective techniques to address academic, behavioral, and functional needs;

'(4) provide technical assistance to local educational agencies and State educational agencies in the provision of effective, scientifically valid, specialized instructional support services;

'(5) coordinate specialized instructional support services programs and services in schools between the Department of Education and other Federal agencies, as appropriate; and

'(6) ensure evaluation of the effectiveness of the activities described in this subsection, as directed by the Secretary and Deputy Secretary.

'(e) Specialized Instructional Support Personnel; Specialized Instructional Support Services- In this section:

'(1) SPECIALIZED INSTRUCTIONAL SUPPORT PERSONNEL- The term 'specialized instructional support personnel' means school counselors, school social workers, school psychologists, and other qualified professional personnel involved in providing assessment, diagnosis, counseling, educational, therapeutic, and other necessary corrective or supportive services (including related services, as such term is defined in section 602 of the Individuals with Disabilities Education Act) as part of a comprehensive program to meet student needs.

'(2) SPECIALIZED INSTRUCTIONAL SUPPORT SERVICES- The term 'specialized instructional support services' means the services provided by specialized instructional support personnel, including any other corrective or supportive services to meet student needs.'.

SEC. 9. DEFINITION IN ELEMENTARY AND SECONDARY EDUCATION ACT OF 1965.

Section 9101 of the Elementary and Secondary Education Act of 1965 (20 U.S.C. 7801) is amended—

(1) by redesignating paragraphs (33) through (43) as paragraphs (34) through (44); and

(2) by inserting after paragraph (32) the following:

'(33) POSITIVE BEHAVIOR SUPPORT- The term 'positive behavior support' means a systematic approach to embed proven practices for early intervening services, including a range of systemic and individualized strategies to reinforce desired behaviors and eliminate reinforcement for problem behaviors, in order to achieve important social outcomes and increase student learning, while preventing problem behaviors.'.

US Senate Bill 2132

Title: A bill to prohibit the introduction or delivery for introduction into interstate commerce of children's products that contain lead, and for other purposes.

Sponsor: Sen Obama, Barack [IL] (introduced 10/3/2007) Cosponsors (6)

Related Bills: H.R.3743

Latest Major Action: 10/3/2007 Referred to Senate committee. Status: Read twice and referred to the Committee on Commerce, Science, and Transportation.

Summary As Of:

10/3/2007—Introduced.

Bans as a hazardous substance within the meaning of the Federal Hazardous Substances Act any children's product containing more than the specified amounts of lead. Defines the term "children's product" to mean any consumer product marketed for use by children under age six, or whose substantial use by children under age six is foreseeable.

Sets forth standards for the amount of lead that may be in such products over time. Authorizes the Consumer Product Safety Commission (CPSC) to revise the standards to any lower amount of lead that CPSC determines is feasible to achieve. Requires CPSC to review and revise the standards to require the lowest amount of lead that is feasible to achieve five years after this Act's enactment.

Requires children's products that are electronic devices to be equipped with a child-resistant cover or casing that limits exposure of and accessibility to the parts of the product containing lead if the CPSC determines it is not feasible for such products to attain lead standards. Requires such an alternative standard to be considered to be a consumer product safety rule under the Consumer Product Safety Act. Authorizes CPSC to establish a schedule by which such electronic devices shall be in full compliance.

Major Actions:

¤NONE¤

All Actions:

10/3/2007:

Read twice and referred to the Committee on Commerce, Science, and Transportation.

10/4/2007:

Star Print ordered on on the bill.

TITLES(s): (italics indicate a title for a portion of a bill)

¤NONE¤

COSPONSORS(6), ALPHABETICAL [FOLLOWED BY COSPONSORS WITH-DRAWN]: (Sort: by date)

Sen Brown, Sherrod [OH] - 10/30/2007

Sen Clinton, Hillary Rodham [NY] - 10/3/2007

Sen Durbin, Richard [IL] - 10/3/2007

Sen Kerry, John F. [MA] - 10/3/2007

Sen Schumer, Charles E. [NY] - 10/3/2007

Sen Whitehouse, Sheldon [RI] - 10/3/2007

COMMITTEE(s)

Committee/Subcommittee:

Activity:

Senate Commerce, Science, and Transportation

Referral, In Committee

RELATED BILL DETAILS: (additional related bills may be indentified in Status)

Bill:

Relationship:

H.R.3743

Related bill identified by CRS

AMENDMENT(s)

¤NONE¤

IN THE SENATE OF THE UNITED STATES

October 3, 2007

Mr. REID (for Mr. OBAMA (for himself, Mr. SCHUMER, Mr. WHITEHOUSE, Mr. KERRY, Mrs. CLINTON, and Mr. DURBIN)) introduced the following bill; which was read twice and referred to the Committee on Commerce, Science, and Transportation

A BILL

To prohibit the introduction or delivery for introduction into interstate commerce of children's products that contain lead, and for other purposes.

Be it enacted by the Senate and House of Representatives of the United States of America in Congress assembled,

SECTION 1. BAN ON CHILDREN'S PRODUCTS THAT CONTAIN LEAD.

(a) In General- Beginning on the date that is 30 days after the date of the enactment of this Act, any children's product that contains more than the amount of lead set forth in subsection (b) shall be treated as a banned hazardous substance under the Federal Hazardous Substances Act (15 U.S.C. 1261 et seq.) and the prohibitions contained in section 4 of such Act shall apply.

(b) Standard for Amount of Lead- The amount of lead set forth in this subsection is—

(1) 600 parts per million lead for any part of a product, effective 30 days after the date of the enactment of this Act;

(2) 250 parts per million lead for any part of a product, effective 1 year after the date of the enactment of this Act; and

(3) 100 parts per million lead for any part of a product, effective 2 years after the date of the enactment of this Act.

(c) Commission Authority To Revise the Standard-

(1) MORE STRINGENT STANDARD- The Consumer Product Safety Commission may revise the standard set forth in subsection (b) to any amount of lead that is lower than the level set forth in such subsection if the Commission determines such lower amount is feasible to achieve.

(2) MANDATORY REVIEW- After the date that is 5 years after the date of the enactment of this Act, the Consumer Product Safety Commission shall, based on the best available scientific and technical information, review and revise the standard then effective to require the lowest amount of lead that the Commission determines is feasible to achieve.

(d) Certain Electronic Devices-

(1) ALTERNATE STANDARD- If the Consumer Product Safety Commission determines that it is not feasible for certain children's products that are electronic devices to attain the standard set forth in subsection (b) or (c), such products shall be equipped with a child-resistant cover or casing that limits exposure of, and accessibility to, the parts of the product containing such amounts of lead.

(2) TREATMENT AS CONSUMER PRODUCT SAFETY RULE- The requirement of paragraph (1) shall be considered to be a consumer product safety rule issued by the Consumer Product Safety Commission under section 9 of the Consumer Product Safety Act (15 U.S.C. 2058). The Commission may establish a schedule by which such electronic devices shall be in full compliance with the requirement of paragraph (1).

(e) Definition of Children's Product- In this section, the term 'children's product' means any consumer product marketed for use by children under age 6, or whose substantial use by children under age 6 is foreseeable.

(f) No Preemption of More Protective State Laws- Nothing in this Act preempts any law or ordinance of a State or political subdivision of a State containing a standard for lead in children's products that provides equal or greater protection to consumers.

US SENATE BILL 2147

TITLE: A bill to require accountability for contractors and contract personnel under Federal contracts, and for other purposes.

SPONSOR: Sen Obama, Barack [IL] (introduced 10/4/2007) Cosponsors (7)

RELATED BILLS: H.R.2740

LATEST MAJOR ACTION: 10/4/2007 Referred to Senate committee. Status: Read twice and referred to the Committee on the Judiciary.

SUMMARY AS OF:

10/4/2007—Introduced.

Security Contractor Accountability Act of 2007 - Provides that persons who, while employed under a federal agency contract in or in close proximity to an area where the Armed Forces are conducting a contingency operation, engage in conduct that would constitute an offense punishable by imprisonment for more than one year if engaged in within U.S. jurisdiction shall be punished as provided for that offense.

Requires the Inspector General of the Department of Justice (DOJ) to report to Congress on the status of the Department's investigations of violations alleged to have been committed by contract personnel and findings and recommendations about the Department's capacity and effectiveness in prosecuting misconduct by contract personnel.

Requires the Director of the Federal Bureau of Investigation (FBI) to ensure, through the creation of Theater Investigative Units, that there are adequate personnel to investigate allegations of criminal violations by contract personnel.

MAJOR ACTIONS:

¤NONE¤

ALL ACTIONS:

10/4/2007:

Sponsor introductory remarks on measure. (CR S12991)

10/4/2007:

Read twice and referred to the Committee on the Judiciary.

TITLES(s): (italics indicate a title for a portion of a bill)

¤NONE¤

Cosponsors(7), Alphabetical [followed by Cosponsors withdrawn]: (Sort: by date)

Sen Akaka, Daniel K. [HI] - 10/15/2007

Sen Boxer, Barbara [CA] - 11/1/2007

Sen Byrd, Robert C. [WV] - 10/4/2007

Sen Durbin, Richard [IL] - 10/4/2007

Sen Kerry, John F. [MA] - 10/4/2007

Sen Sanders, Bernard [VT] - 12/3/2007

Sen Whitehouse, Sheldon [RI] - 10/4/2007

Committee(s)

Committee/Subcommittee:

Activity:

Senate Judiciary

Referral, In Committee

Related Bill Details: (additional related bills may be indentified in Status)

Bill:

Relationship:

H.R.2740

Related bill identified by CRS

Amendment(s)

¤NONE¤

In the Senate of the United States

October 4, 2007

Mr. REID (for Mr. OBAMA (for himself, Mr. DURBIN, Mr. WHITEHOUSE, Mr. BYRD, and Mr. KERRY)) introduced the following bill; which was read twice and referred to the Committee on the Judiciary

A BILL

To require accountability for contractors and contract personnel under Federal contracts, and for other purposes.

Be it enacted by the Senate and House of Representatives of the United States of America in Congress assembled,

SECTION 1. SHORT TITLE.

This Act may be cited as the 'Security Contractor Accountability Act of 2007'.

SEC. 2. LEGAL STATUS OF CONTRACT PERSONNEL.

(a) Clarification of the Military Extraterritorial Jurisdiction Act-

(1) INCLUSION OF CONTRACTORS- Subsection (a) of section 3261 of title 18, United States Code, is amended—

(A) by striking 'or' at the end of paragraph (1);

(B) by striking the comma at the end of paragraph (2) and inserting '; or'; and

(C) by inserting after paragraph (2) the following:

'(3) while employed under a contract (or subcontract at any tier) awarded by any department or agency of the United States, where the work under such contract is carried out in an area, or in close proximity to an area (as designated by the Department of Defense), where the Armed Forces is conducting a contingency operation,'.

(2) DEFINITION- Section 3267 of title 18, United States Code, is amended by adding at the end the following:

'(5) The term 'contingency operation' has the meaning given such term in section 101(a)(13) of title 10.'.

(b) Department of Justice Inspector General Report-

(1) REPORT REQUIRED- Not later than 180 days after the date of the enactment of this Act, the Inspector General of the Department of Justice shall submit to Congress a report in accordance with this subsection.

(2) CONTENT OF REPORT- The report under paragraph (1) shall include—

(A) a description of the status of Department of Justice investigations of alleged violations of section 3261 of title 18, United States Code, to have been committed by contract personnel, which shall include—

(i) the number of complaints received by the Department of Justice;

(ii) the number of investigations into complaints opened by the Department of Justice;

(iii) the number of criminal cases opened by the Department of Justice; and

(iv) the number and result of criminal cases closed by the Department of Justice; and

(B) findings and recommendations about the number of criminal cases prosecuted by the Department of Justice involving violations of section 3261 of title 18, United States Code.

(3) FORMAT OF REPORT- The report under paragraph (1) shall be submitted in unclassified format, but may contain a classified annex as appropriate.

SEC. 3. FEDERAL BUREAU OF INVESTIGATION INVESTIGATIVE UNIT FOR CONTINGENCY OPERATIONS.

(a) Establishment of Theater Investigative Unit- The Director of the Federal Bureau of Investigation shall ensure that there are adequate personnel through the creation of Theater Investigative Units to investigate allegations of criminal violations of section 3261 of title 18, United States Code, by contract personnel.

(b) Responsibilities of Theater Investigative Unit- The Theater Investigative Unit established for a theater of operations shall—

(1) investigate reports that raise reasonable suspicion of criminal misconduct by contract personnel;

(2) investigate reports of fatalities resulting from the use of force by contract personnel; and

(3) upon conclusion of an investigation of alleged criminal misconduct, refer the case to the Attorney General of the United States for further action, as appropriate in the discretion of the Attorney General.

(c) Responsibilities of Federal Bureau of Investigation-

(1) RESOURCES- The Director of the Federal Bureau of Investigation shall ensure that each Theater Investigative Unit has adequate resources and personnel to carry out its responsibilities.

(2) NOTIFICATION- The Director of the Federal Bureau of Investigation shall notify Congress whenever a Theater Investigative Unit is established or terminated in accordance with this section.

(d) Responsibilities of Other Federal Agencies- An agency operating in an area, or in close proximity to an area (as designated by the Department of Defense), where the Armed Forces is conducting a contingency operation shall cooperate with and support the activities of the Theater Investigative Unit. Any investigation carried out by the Inspector General of an agency shall be coordinated with the activities of the Theater Investigative Unit as appropriate.

SEC. 4. DEFINITIONS.

In this Act:

(1) COVERED CONTRACT- The term 'covered contract' means an agreement—

(A) that is—

(i) a prime contract awarded by an agency;

(ii) a subcontract at any tier under any prime contract awarded by an agency; or

(iii) a task order issued under a task or delivery order contract entered into by an agency; and

(B) according to which the work under such contract, subcontract, or task order is carried out in a region outside the United States in which the Armed Forces are conducting a contingency operation.

(2) AGENCY- The term 'agency' has the meaning given the term 'Executive agency' in section 105 of title 5, United States Code.

(3) CONTINGENCY OPERATION- The term 'contingency operation' has the meaning given the term section 101(13) of title 10, United States Code.

(4) CONTRACTOR- The term 'contractor' means an entity performing a covered contract.

(5) CONTRACT PERSONNEL- The term 'contract personnel' means persons assigned by a contractor (including subcontractors at any tier) to perform work under a covered contract.

SEC. 5. EFFECTIVE DATE.

(a) Applicability- The provisions of this Act shall apply to all covered contracts and all covered contract personnel in which the work under the contract is carried out in an area, or in close proximity to an area (as designated by the Department of Defense), where the Armed Forces is conducting a contingency operation on or after the date of the enactment of this Act.

(b) Immediate Effectiveness- The provisions of this Act shall enter into effect immediately upon the enactment of this Act.

(c) Implementation- With respect to covered contracts and covered contract personnel discussed in subsection (a)(1), the Director of the Federal Bureau of Investigation, and the head of any other agency to which this Act applies, shall have 90 days after the date of the enactment of this Act to ensure compliance with the provisions of this Act.

US Senate Bill 2202

TITLE: A bill to amend the Clean Air Act to increase the renewable content of gasoline, and for other purposes.

SPONSOR: Sen Obama, Barack [IL] (introduced 10/18/2007) Cosponsors (2)

LATEST MAJOR ACTION: 10/18/2007 Referred to Senate committee. Status: Read twice and referred to the Committee on Environment and Public Works.

SUMMARY AS OF:

10/18/2007—Introduced.

Renewable Fuel Standard Extension Act of 2007 - Amends the Clean Air Act to redefine the term "cellulosic biomass ethanol" to mean ethanol derived from any cellulose, hemicellulose, or lignin that is derived from renewable biomass. Redefines the term "renewable fuel" to include motor vehicle fuel that is derived from renewable biomass other than ethanol derived from corn starch.

Increases the volume of renewable fuel that gasoline is required to contain for 2008-2012. Sets forth the applicable volume of renewable fuel for 2013-2016.

Revises the calculation used to determine the applicable volume of renewable fuel for 2017 and beyond by using the ratio of 18 billion gallons (currently, 7.5 billion gallons) of renewable fuels to the number of gallons of gasoline sold or introduced into commerce in 2012.

MAJOR ACTIONS:

¤NONE¤

All Actions:

10/18/2007:

Read twice and referred to the Committee on Environment and Public Works.

Titles(s): (italics indicate a title for a portion of a bill)

¤NONE¤

Cosponsors(2), Alphabetical [followed by Cosponsors withdrawn]: (Sort: by date)

Sen Durbin, Richard [IL] - 10/22/2007

Sen Harkin, Tom [IA] - 10/18/2007

Committee(s)

Committee/Subcommittee:

Activity:

Senate Environment and Public Works

Referral, In Committee

Related Bill Details:

¤NONE¤

Amendment(s)

¤NONE¤

IN THE SENATE OF THE UNITED STATES

October 18, 2007

Mr. REID (for Mr. OBAMA (for himself and Mr. HARKIN)) introduced the following bill; which was read twice and referred to the Committee on Environment and Public Works

A BILL

To amend the Clean Air Act to increase the renewable content of gasoline, and for other purposes.

Be it enacted by the Senate and House of Representatives of the United States of America in Congress assembled,

SECTION 1. SHORT TITLE.

This Act may be cited as the 'Renewable Fuel Standard Extension Act of 2007'.

SEC. 2. RENEWABLE CONTENT OF GASOLINE.

(a) Findings- Congress finds that—

(1) the renewable fuel standard established under section 211(o) of the Clean Air Act (42 U.S.C. 7545(o)) is one of the most significant steps taken by Congress to increase

domestic biofuels production and decrease the dangerous dependence of the United States on foreign oil;

(2) in the 12 years after 1992, domestic ethanol production increased by 2,000,000,000 gallons;

(3) in only 2 years following the establishment of the renewable fuel standard, ethanol production has increased by 5,000,000,000 gallons;

(4) the renewable fuel standard has spurred investment and resulted in ethanol production that surpassed Federal targets 5 years ahead of schedule;

(5) the failure of the petroleum industry to install pumps so that ethanol is available to motorists and the failure of the automotive industry to manufacture ethanol-capable vehicles, as compared to rising ethanol production volumes, has prevented fuel ethanol from reaching consumers;

(6) the resulting excess of ethanol in the marketplace has depressed ethanol prices and jeopardized the financial stability of the domestic renewable fuel infrastructure, particularly smaller, local, and farmer-owned ethanol plants;

(7) jeopardizing the existing ethanol infrastructure will put at risk 20 years of progress on a national biofuel industry and destroy the bridge to next-generation biofuel made from cellulosic feedstocks; and

(8) it is imperative for Congress to increase the renewable fuel standard now to ensure the path towards cellulosic fuel production is not jeopardized in the short term.

(b) Definitions- Section 211(o)(1) of the Clean Air Act (42 U.S.C. 7545(o)(1)) is amended—

(1) by redesignating subparagraphs (B), (C), and (D) as subparagraphs (F), (D), and (E), respectively, and moving those subparagraphs so as to appear in alphabetical order;

(2) by striking subparagraph (A) and inserting the following:

'(A) ADVANCED BIOFUEL-

'(i) IN GENERAL- The term 'advanced biofuel' means fuel derived from renewable biomass other than ethanol derived from corn starch.

'(ii) INCLUSIONS- The term 'advanced biofuel' includes—

'(I) ethanol derived from cellulose, hemicellulose, or lignin;

'(II) ethanol derived from sugar or starch, other than ethanol derived from corn starch;

'(III) ethanol derived from waste material, including crop residue, other vegetative waste material, animal waste, and food waste and yard waste;

'(IV) diesel-equivalent fuel derived from renewable biomass, including vegetable oil and animal fat;

'(V) biogas (including landfill gas and sewage waste treatment gas) produced through the conversion of organic matter from renewable biomass;

'(VI) butanol or other alcohols produced through the conversion of organic matter from renewable biomass; and

'(VII) other fuel derived from cellulosic biomass.

'(B) CELLULOSIC BIOMASS ETHANOL- The term 'cellulosic biomass ethanol' means ethanol derived from any cellulose, hemicellulose, or lignin that is derived from renewable biomass.

'(C) RENEWABLE BIOMASS- The term 'renewable biomass' means—

'(i) nonmerchantable materials or precommercial thinnings that—

'(I) are byproducts of preventive treatments, such as trees, wood, brush, thinnings, chips, and slash, that are removed—

'(aa) to reduce hazardous fuels;

'(bb) to reduce or contain disease or insect infestation; or

'(cc) to restore forest health;

'(II) would not otherwise be used for higher-value products; and

'(III) are harvested from National Forest System land or public land (as defined in section 103 of the Federal Land Policy and Management Act of 1976 (43 U.S.C. 1702)), where permitted by law and in accordance with—

'(aa) applicable land management plans; and

'(bb) the requirements for old-growth maintenance, restoration, and management direction of paragraphs (2), (3), and (4) of subsection (e) and the requirements for large-tree retention of subsection (f) of section 102 of the Healthy Forests Restoration Act of 2003 (16 U.S.C. 6512); or

'(ii) any organic matter that is available on a renewable or recurring basis from non-Federal land or from land belonging to an Indian tribe, or an Indian individual, that is held in trust by the United States or subject to a restriction against alienation imposed by the United States, including—

'(I) renewable plant material, including—

'(aa) feed grains;

'(bb) other agricultural commodities;

'(cc) other plants and trees; and

'(dd) algae; and

'(II) waste material, including—

'(aa) crop residue;

'(bb) other vegetative waste material (including wood waste and wood residues);

'(cc) animal waste and byproducts (including fats, oils, greases, and manure); and

'(dd) food waste and yard waste.'; and

(3) in clause (ii) of subparagraph (D) (as redesignated by paragraph (1))—

(A) in subclause (I), by striking 'and' at the end;

(B) in subclause (II), by striking the period at the end and inserting '; and'; and

(C) by adding at the end the following:

'(III) advanced biofuel.'.

(c) Renewable Content of Gasoline- Section 211(o) of the Clean Air Act (42 U.S.C. 7545(o)) is amended—

(1) in paragraph (2)(B)—

(A) by striking clause (i) and inserting the following:

'(i) CALENDAR YEARS 2008 THROUGH 2016-

'(I) RENEWABLE FUEL- For the purpose of subparagraph (A), the applicable volume for any of calendar years 2008 through 2016 shall be determined in accordance with the following table:

Applicable volume of renewable fuel

'Calendar year: (in billions of gallons):

2008	—	8.5
2009	—	10.5
2010	—	12.0
2011	—	12.6
2012	—	13.2
2013	—	13.8
2014	—	14.4
2015	—	15.0
2016	—	18.0

'(II) ADVANCED BIOFUEL- For the purpose of subparagraph (A), of the volume of renewable fuel required under subclause (I), the applicable volume for calendar year 2016 for advanced biofuel shall be determined in accordance with the following table:

Applicable volume of advanced biofuel

'Calendar year: (in billions of gallons):

2016	—	3.0';

(B) in clause (ii)—

(i) in the clause heading, by striking '2013' and inserting '2017';

(ii) by striking '2013' and inserting '2017'; and

(iii) by striking '2012' and inserting '2016';

(C) in clause (iii), by striking '2013' and inserting '2017'; and

(D) in clause (iv)—

(i) by striking '2013' and inserting '2017'; and

(ii) in subclause (II)(aa), by striking '7,500,000,000' and inserting '18,000,000';

(2) in paragraph (3)—

(A) in subparagraph (A), by striking '2011' and inserting '2015'; and

(B) in subparagraph (B)(i), by striking '2012' and inserting '2016'; and

(3) in paragraph (6)(A), by striking '2012' and inserting '2016'.

US SENATE BILL 2224

TITLE: A bill to require a licensee to notify the Nuclear Regulatory Commission, and the State and county in which a facility is located, whenever there is an unplanned release of radioactive substances.

SPONSOR: Sen Obama, Barack [IL] (introduced 10/24/2007) Cosponsors (1)

LATEST MAJOR ACTION: 10/24/2007 Referred to Senate committee. Status: Read twice and referred to the Committee on Environment and Public Works.

SUMMARY:

¤NONE¤

MAJOR ACTIONS:

¤NONE¤

ALL ACTIONS:

10/24/2007:

Read twice and referred to the Committee on Environment and Public Works.

TITLES(s): (italics indicate a title for a portion of a bill)

¤NONE¤

COSPONSORS(1), ALPHABETICAL [followed by Cosponsors withdrawn]: (Sort: by date)

Sen Durbin, Richard [IL] - 10/24/2007

COMMITTEE(s)

Committee/Subcommittee:

Activity:

Senate Environment and Public Works

Referral, In Committee

RELATED BILL DETAILS:

¤NONE¤

AMENDMENT(S)

¤NONE¤

IN THE SENATE OF THE UNITED STATES

October 24, 2007

Mr. OBAMA (for himself and Mr. DURBIN) introduced the following bill; which was read twice and referred to the Committee on Environment and Public Works

A BILL

To require a licensee to notify the Nuclear Regulatory Commission, and the State and county in which a facility is located, whenever there is an unplanned release of radioactive substances.

Be it enacted by the Senate and House of Representatives of the United States of America in Congress assembled,

SECTION 1. SHORT TITLE.

This Act may be cited as the 'Nuclear Release Notice Act of 2007'.

SEC. 2. NUCLEAR RELEASE NOTICE REQUIREMENT.

Section 103 of the Atomic Energy Act of 1954 (42 U.S.C. 2133) is amended by inserting after subsection d. the following:

'e. Notice of Unplanned Release of Radioactive Substances-

'(1) REGULATIONS-

'(A) IN GENERAL- Not later than 2 years after the date of enactment of the Nuclear Release Notice Act of 2007, the Commission shall promulgate regulations that require civilian nuclear power facilities licensed under this section or section 104b. to provide notice of any release to the environment of quantities of fission products or other radioactive substances.

'(B) CONSIDERATIONS- In developing the regulations under subparagraph (A), the Commission shall consider requiring licensees of civilian nuclear power facilities to provide notice of the release—

'(i) not later than 24 hours after the release;

'(ii) to the Commission and the governments of the State and county in which the civilian nuclear power facility is located, if the unplanned release—

'(I)(aa) exceeds allowable limits for normal operation established by the Commission; and

'(bb) is not subject to more stringent reporting requirements established in existing regulations of the Commission; or

'(II)(aa) enters into the environment; and

'(bb) may cause drinking water sources to exceed a maximum contaminant level established by the Environmental Protection Agency for fission products or other radioactive substances under the Safe Drinking Water Act (42 U.S.C. 300f et seq.); and

'(iii) to the governments of the State and county in which the civilian nuclear power facility is located if the unplanned release reaches the environment by a path otherwise not allowed or recognized by the operating license of the civilian nuclear power facility and falls within the allowable limits specified in clause (ii), including—

'(I) considering any recommendations issued by the Liquid Radioactive Release Lessons-Learned Task Force;

'(II) the frequency and form of the notice; and

'(III) the threshold, volume, and radiation content that trigger the notice.

'(2) EFFECT- Nothing in this subsection provides to any State or county that receives a notice under this subsection regulatory jurisdiction over a licensee of a civilian nuclear power facility.'.

US Senate Bill 2227

Title: A bill to provide grants to States to ensure that all students in the middle grades are taught an academically rigorous curriculum with effective supports so that students complete the middle grades prepared for success in high school and postsecondary endeavors, to improve State and district policies and programs relating to the academic achievement of students in the middle grades, to develop and implement effective middle school models for struggling students, and for other purposes.

Sponsor: Sen Obama, Barack [IL] (introduced 10/24/2007) Cosponsors (2)

Related Bills: H.R.3406

Latest Major Action: 10/24/2007 Referred to Senate committee. Status: Read twice and referred to the Committee on Health, Education, Labor, and Pensions.

Summary As Of:

10/24/2007—Introduced.

Success in the Middle Act of 2007 - Directs the Secretary of Education to make matching grants to states, based on their proportion of poor children aged 5 to 17, to: (1) implement state middle school needs analyses and, on the basis of such analyses, improvement plans that describe what students must master to successfully complete the middle grades and succeed in academically rigorous high school coursework; and (2) award competitive matching subgrants to local educational agencies (LEAs) to implement a comprehensive middle school improvement plan for each eligible school. Favors LEAs with high proportions of poor children and eligible schools.

Defines "eligible schools" as those where: (1) a majority of middle grade students matriculate to high schools with graduation rates below 60%; (2) more than 25% of the students who finish grade six, or the school's earliest middle grade level, exhibit key risk factors for failure; and (3) a majority of middle grade students are not rated proficient on required state assessments in mathematics, reading, or language arts.

Permits states to make subgrants to LEAs that did not receive a competitive subgrant to assist them in applying for competitive subgrants and developing comprehensive middle school improvement plans.

Provides the Secretary with funding to: (1) contract for studies that identify promising practices for, and review existing research to identify factors that might lead to, the improvement of middle school education; (2) create a national clearinghouse in best middle grade educational practices and a national database identifying factors that facilitate or impede middle grade student achievement; (3) require certain educational field research designed to enhance the performance of middle grade schools and students; (4) create a research and development center that addresses topics pertinent to middle grade schools; and (5) provide grants to entities that partner with states and LEAs to develop, adapt, or replicate effective models for turning around low-performing middle grade schools.

MAJOR ACTIONS:

¤NONE¤

ALL ACTIONS:

10/24/2007:

Read twice and referred to the Committee on Health, Education, Labor, and Pensions.

TITLES(s): (italics indicate a title for a portion of a bill)

¤NONE¤

COSPONSORS(2), ALPHABETICAL [FOLLOWED BY COSPONSORS WITH-DRAWN]: (Sort: by date)

Sen Reed, Jack [RI] - 10/24/2007

Sen Whitehouse, Sheldon [RI] - 10/26/2007

COMMITTEE(S)

Committee/Subcommittee:

Activity:

Senate Health, Education, Labor, and Pensions

Referral, In Committee

Related Bill Details: (additional related bills may be indentified in Status)

Bill:

Relationship:

H.R.3406

Related bill identified by CRS

Amendment(s)

¤NONE¤

In the Senate of the United States

October 24, 2007

Mr. OBAMA (for himself and Mr. REED) introduced the following bill; which was read twice and referred to the Committee on Health, Education, Labor, and Pensions

A BILL

To provide grants to States to ensure that all students in the middle grades are taught an academically rigorous curriculum with effective supports so that students complete the middle grades prepared for success in high school and postsecondary endeavors, to improve State and district policies and programs relating to the academic achievement of students in the middle grades, to develop and implement effective middle school models for struggling students, and for other purposes.

Be it enacted by the Senate and House of Representatives of the United States of America in Congress assembled,

SECTION 1. SHORT TITLE.

This Act may be cited as the 'Success in the Middle Act of 2007'.

SEC. 2. FINDINGS.

In this Act:

(1) Assessments indicate that the interval between the 4th and 8th grades is a period where academic achievement for United States students falls dramatically, with the most severe losses in academic achievement among minority and low-income students. International comparisons indicate that students in the United States do not start out behind students of other nations in mathematics and science, but that they fall behind by the end of the middle grades.

(2) Only 1/3 of the students in 8th grade, and only 5 percent of English language learners, can read with proficiency, according to the 2007 National Assessment on Educational Progress (NAEP). The percentage of 8th grade students proficient at reading has decreased since 1998, and the NAEP average reading score for 8th graders has remained static. In contrast, NAEP reading scores and achievement levels for 4th graders have increased significantly.

(3) In mathematics, again less than 1/3 of students in 8th grade show skills at the NAEP proficient level, and nearly 30 percent score below the basic level. The percentage of 8th grade students scoring above the basic level was 8 points higher in 2007 than in 2000, but for 4th graders, the percentage increased 17 points, more than double the increase for middle school students. In 8th grade, the gaps between the average mathematics scores of white and black students and between white and Hispanic students were as wide in 2007 as in 1990.

(4) Lack of basic skills at the end of middle school has serious implications for students. Students who enter high school 2 or more years behind grade level in mathematics and literacy have only a 50 percent chance of progressing on time to the 10th grade; those not progressing are at grave risk of dropping out of high school.

(5) Middle school students are hopeful about their future, with 93 percent believing that they will complete high school and 92 percent anticipating that they will attend college. Yet about 1/3 of students who enter high school do not graduate with their peers, and another 1/3 graduate but do not have the knowledge and skills to succeed in college. In fact, results from ACT's EXPLORE assessment reflect that only 11 percent of 8th grade students are on track to succeed in first-year college English, algebra, biology and social science courses.

(6) Sixth-grade students who do not attend school regularly, who are subjected to frequent disciplinary actions, or who fail mathematics or English have no more than a 10 percent chance of graduating high school on time and a 20 percent chance of graduating 1 year late. Significant numbers of 6th grade students exhibit attendance or behavior problems, or need additional supports in reading or mathematics; without effective interventions and proper supports, these students are at risk of subsequent failure in high school, or of dropping out.

(7) Student transitions from elementary school to middle school and from middle school to high school are often complicated by poor curriculum alignment, inadequate counseling services to help them make decisions about high school classes that will prepare them for college, and unsatisfactory sharing of student performance and academic achievement data between schools.

(8) Middle schools are more likely than elementary schools or high schools to be identified for improvement. Although middle schools represented only 15 percent of the schools that received funds under part A of title I of the Elementary and Secondary Education Act of 1965 (20 U.S.C. 6311 et seq.), they accounted for 32 percent of those schools in corrective action or restructuring during 2005-2006. In the 2004-2005 academic year, 36 percent of middle schools that received funds under part A of title I of the Elementary and Secondary Education Act of 1965 (20 U.S.C. 6311 et seq.), were deemed in need of improvement, compared with 10 percent of elementary schools.

(9) Federal funding has long focused on early elementary grades and on higher education. Students in the middle grades represent 23 percent of the Nation's student population and 58 percent of the Nation's annual test-takers under the Elementary and Secondary Education Act of 1965 (20 U.S.C. 6301 et seq.). Yet, of the funds appropriated in fiscal year 2005 for part A of title I of the Elementary and Secondary Education Act of 1965 (20 U.S.C. 6311 et seq.), only 10 percent were allocated to middle schools by the States.

(10) Middle school improvement strategies should be tailored based on a variety of performance indicators and data, so that educators can create and implement successful school improvement strategies to address the needs of the individual schools, and so that schools can provide effective instruction and adequate assistance to meet the needs of at-risk students.

(11) To stem a dropout rate twice that of students without disabilities, students with disabilities in the critical middle grades must receive appropriate academic accommodations and access to assistive technology, high-risk behaviors such as absenteeism and course failure must be monitored, and problem-solving skills with broad application must be taught.

(12) Local educational agencies and State educational agencies often do not have the capacity to provide support for school improvement strategies. Successful models do exist for turning around low-performing middle schools, and Federal support should be provided to increase the capacity to apply promising practices based on evidence from successful schools.

SEC. 3. DEFINITIONS.

In this Act:

(1) MIDDLE SCHOOL- The term 'middle school' means a nonprofit public school, including a public charter middle school, that provides education in any 2 or more successive grades beginning with grade 5 and ending with grade 8, as determined under State law.

(2) MIDDLE GRADE- The term 'middle grade' means grade 5, 6, 7, or 8.

(3) SCIENTIFICALLY VALID- The term 'scientifically valid' means the rationale, design, and interpretation are soundly developed in accordance with accepted principles of scientific research.

(4) SECRETARY- The term 'Secretary' means the Secretary of Education.

(5) STATE- The term 'State' means each of the 50 States, the District of Columbia, and the Commonwealth of Puerto Rico.

TITLE I—MIDDLE SCHOOL IMPROVEMENT

SEC. 101. PURPOSES.

The purposes of this title are to—

(1) improve middle school student academic achievement to prepare students for rigorous high school course work, and eventually for postsecondary education, independent living, and employment;

(2) align curriculum and student supports between elementary school and middle school and between middle school and high school;

(3) provide resources to State educational agencies and local educational agencies to collaboratively develop school improvement plans in order to deliver support and technical assistance to schools serving students in the middle grades; and

(4) increase the capacity of States and local educational agencies to develop effective, sustainable, and replicable school improvement programs and models and evidence-

based or, when available, scientifically valid student interventions for implementation by schools serving students in the middle grades.

SEC. 102. FORMULA GRANTS TO STATE EDUCATIONAL AGENCIES FOR MIDDLE SCHOOL IMPROVEMENT.

(a) In General- From amounts appropriated under section 107, the Secretary shall make grants under this title for a fiscal year to each State educational agency for which the Secretary has approved an application under subsection (h) in an amount equal to the allotment determined for such agency under subsection (c) for such fiscal year.

(b) Reservations- From the total amount made available to carry out this title for a fiscal year, the Secretary—

(1) shall reserve not more than 1 percent for the Secretary of the Interior (on behalf of the Bureau of Indian Affairs) and the outlying areas for activities carried out in accordance with this section;

(2) shall reserve 1 percent to evaluate the effectiveness of this title in achieving the purposes of this title and ensuring that results are peer-reviewed and widely disseminated, which may include hiring an outside evaluator; and

(3) shall reserve 5 percent for technical assistance and dissemination of best practices in middle grades education to States and local educational agencies.

(c) Amount of State Allotments-

(1) IN GENERAL- Of the total amount made available to carry out this title for a fiscal year and not reserved under subsection (b), the Secretary shall allot such amount among the States in proportion to the number of children, aged 5 to 17, who reside within the State and are from families with incomes below the poverty line for the most recent fiscal year for which satisfactory data are available, compared to the number of such individuals who reside in all such States for that fiscal year, determined in accordance with section 1124(c)(1)(A) of the Elementary and Secondary Education Act of 1965(20 U.S.C. 6333(c)(1)(A)).

(2) MINIMUM ALLOTMENTS- No State educational agency shall receive an allotment under this subsection for a fiscal year that is less than 1/2 of 1 percent of the amount made available to carry out this title for such fiscal year.

(d) Matching Requirement-

(1) IN GENERAL- To be eligible to receive a grant under this title, a State educational agency shall provide non-Federal matching funds equal to not less than 25 percent of the amount of the grant.

(2) IN-KIND CONTRIBUTIONS- In-kind contributions, fairly assessed, may be used to meet the requirement of paragraph (1) but only to the extent of 10 percent of the amount of the grant.

(e) Special Rule- For any fiscal year for which the funds appropriated to carry out this title are less that $500,000,000, the Secretary is authorized to award grants to State educational agencies, on a competitive basis, rather than as allotments described in this section, to enable such agencies to award subgrants, on a competitive basis, to carry out the activities authorized under section 104.

(f) Reallotment-

(1) FAILURE TO APPLY; APPLICATION NOT APPROVED- If any State does not apply for an allotment under this title for a fiscal year, or if the application from the State educational agency is not approved, the Secretary shall reallot the amount of the State's allotment to the remaining States in accordance with this section.

(2) UNUSED FUNDS- The Secretary may reallot any amount of an allotment to a State if the Secretary determines that the State will be unable to use such amount within 2 years of such allotment. Such reallotments shall be made on the same basis as allotments are made under subsection (c).

(g) Application- In order to receive a grant under this title, a State educational agency shall submit an application to the Secretary at such time, in such manner, and accompanied by such information as the Secretary may reasonably require, including a State middle school improvement plan described in section 103(a)(4).

(h) Peer Review and Selection- The Secretary—

(1) shall establish a peer-review process to assist in the review and approval of proposed State applications;

(2) shall appoint individuals to participate in the peer-review process who are educators and experts in identifying, evaluating, and implementing effective education programs and practices, including areas of teaching and learning, educational standards and assessments, school improvement, and academic and behavioral supports for middle school students, including recognized exemplary middle level teachers and principals who have been recognized at the State or national level for exemplary work or contributions to the field;

(3) shall ensure that States are given the opportunity to receive timely feedback, and to interact with peer-review panels, in person or via electronic communication, on issues that need clarification during the peer-review process;

(4) shall approve a State application submitted under this title not later than 120 days after the date of submission of the application unless the Secretary determines that the application does not meet the requirements of this title;

(5) may not decline to approve a State's application before—

(A) offering the State an opportunity to revise the State's application;

(B) providing the State with technical assistance in order to submit a successful application; and

(C) providing a hearing to the State; and

(6) shall direct the Inspector General of the Department to review final determinations reached by the Secretary to approve or deny State applications, and to analyze the consistency of the process used by peer review panels in reviewing and recommending to the Secretary approval or denial of such State applications, and report the findings of this review and

SEC. 103. STATE PLAN; AUTHORIZED ACTIVITIES.

(a) Mandatory Activities-

(1) IN GENERAL- A State educational agency that receives a grant under this title shall use the grant funds—

(A) to prepare and implement the needs analysis and middle school improvement plan described in paragraphs (3) and (4) of such agency;

(B) to make subgrants to local educational agencies under section 104; and

(C) to assist local educational agencies when determined necessary, or at the request of a local educational agency, in designing an improvement plan and carrying out the activities under section 104.

(2) FUNDS FOR SUBGRANTS- A State educational agency that receives a grant under this title shall use not less than 80 percent of the grant funds to make subgrants to local educational agencies under section 104.

(3) MIDDLE SCHOOL NEEDS ANALYSIS-

(A) IN GENERAL- A State educational agency that receives a grant under this title shall enter into a contract, or similar formal agreement, to work with entities such as national and regional comprehensive centers (as described in section 203 of the Educational Technical Assistance Act of 2002), institutions of higher education, or nonprofit organizations, to prepare a plan that analyzes how to strengthen the programs, practices, and policies of the State in supporting middle school education, including the factors, such as local implementation, that influence variation in the effectiveness of such programs, practices, and policies.

(B) PREPARATION OF PLAN- In preparing the plan under subparagraph (A), the State educational agency shall examine policies and practices of the State, and of local educational agencies within the State, affecting—

(i) middle school curriculum instruction and assessment;

(ii) education accountability and data systems;

(iii) teacher quality and equitable distribution; and

(iv) interventions that support learning in school.

(4) MIDDLE SCHOOL IMPROVEMENT PLAN-

(A) IN GENERAL- A State educational agency that receives a grant under this title shall develop a middle school improvement plan that shall be a statewide plan to improve student academic achievement, based on the needs analysis described in paragraph (3), that describes what students are required to know and do to successfully—

(i) complete the middle grades; and

(ii) make the transition to succeed in an academically rigorous high school coursework, that prepares students for college, independent living, and employment.

(B) PLAN COMPONENTS- A middle school improvement plan described in subparagraph (A) shall also describe how the State educational agency will do each of the following:

(i) Ensure that the curricula and assessments for middle grades education are aligned with high school curricula and assessments and prepare students to take challenging high school courses and successfully engage in postsecondary education, ensuring coordination, where applicable, with grants for P-16 alignment as provided in section 6401 of the America COMPETES Act (Public Law 110-69).

(ii) Provide professional development to school leaders, teachers, and other school personnel in addressing the needs of diverse learners, including students with disabilities and English language learners, in using challenging and relevant research-based best practices and curricula, and in using data to inform instruction.

(iii) Identify and disseminate information on effective schools and instructional strategies for middle grade learners based on high-quality research.

(iv) Include specific provisions for students most at-risk of failure, including English language learners and students with disabilities.

(v) Develop and implement early identification data systems (as defined in section 104(k)) to alert schools when students begin to exhibit outcomes or behaviors that indicate the student is at increased risk for low academic achievement or is unlikely to progress to high school graduation, to and develop and implement a system of evidence based interventions that schools can use to effectively intervene.

(vi) Define a set of comprehensive school performance indicators that shall be used, in addition to the indicators used to determine adequate yearly progress, to evaluate school performance, and guide the school improvement process, such as—

(I) student attendance and absenteeism;

(II) earned on-time promotion rates from grade to grade;

(III) percent of students failing a mathematics, reading or language arts, or science course, or failing 2 or more of any course;

(IV) teacher quality and attendance measures;

(V) in-school and out-of-school suspension or other measurable evidence of at-risk behavior; and

(VI) additional indicators proposed by the State educational agency, and approved by the Secretary pursuant to the peer-review process described in section 102(h).

(vii) Ensure that such plan is coordinated with State activities to turn around other schools in need of improvement, including State activities to improve high schools and elementary schools.

(b) Permissible Activities-

(1) IN GENERAL- A State educational agency that receives a grant under this title may use the grant funds to make competitive grants to eligible entities to carry out the following activities:

(A) Develop and encourage collaborations among researchers at institutions of higher education, State educational agencies, educational service agencies (as defined in section 9101 of the Elementary and Secondary Education Act of 1965 (20 U.S.C. 7801), local educational agencies, and nonprofit organizations to expand the use of effective practices in the middle grades and to improve middle grade education.

(B) Support local educational agencies in implementing effective middle grade practices, models and programs that are evidence-based or, when available, scientifically valid and that lead to improved student academic achievement.

(C) Support collaborative communities of middle school teachers, administrators, and researchers in creating and sustaining informational databases to disseminate results from rigorous research on effective practices and programs for middle grade education.

(D) Increase student support services, such as school counseling on the transition to high school.

(2) ELIGIBLE ENTITY- In this subsection, the term 'eligible entity' means any partnership that includes not less than 1 local educational agency and may include an institution of higher education, an educational service agency, and any non-profit organization with demonstrated expertise in high quality middle grade interventions.

SEC. 104. COMPETITIVE SUBGRANTS TO LOCAL EDUCATIONAL AGENCIES TO IMPROVE LOW-PERFORMING MIDDLE GRADES.

(a) In General- A State educational agency that receives a grant under this title shall make competitive subgrants to eligible local educational agencies.

(b) Priorities- In making subgrants under this section, a State educational agency shall give priority to eligible local educational agencies based on—

(1) the local educational agency's respective populations of children described in section 102(c)(1); and

(2) the local educational agency's respective populations of children attending eligible schools.

(c) Matching Requirement-

(1) IN GENERAL- To be eligible to receive a subgrant under this section, an eligible local educational agency shall provide non-Federal matching funds equal to not less than 15 percent of the amount of the subgrant.

(2) IN-KIND CONTRIBUTIONS- In-kind contributions, fairly assessed, may be used to meet the requirement of paragraph (1) but only to the extent of 10 percent of the amount of the subgrant.

(d) Application- An eligible local educational agency that desires to receive a subgrant under this title shall submit an application to the State educational agency at such time, in such manner, and accompanied by such information as the State educational agency may reasonably require, including—

(1) a comprehensive schoolwide improvement plan described in subsection (e);

(2) a description of how activities described in such plan will be coordinated with activities specified in plans for schoolwide programs under section 1114 of the Elementary and Secondary Education Act of 1965 (20 U.S.C. 6314) and school improvement plans required under section 1116 of such Act (20 U.S.C. 6316); and

(3) a description of how activities described in such plan will be complementary to, and coordinated with, school improvement activities for elementary schools and high schools in need of improvement that serve the same students within the local educational agency.

(e) Comprehensive Schoolwide Improvement Plan- An eligible local educational agency that desires to receive a subgrant under this title shall develop a comprehensive schoolwide improvement plan that shall include the information described in subsection (d)(2) and describe how the agency will—

(1) identify eligible schools;

(2) ensure that funds go to the highest priority eligible schools first;

(3) use funds to improve the academic achievement of all students, including English language learners and students with disabilities, in eligible schools and middle grades;

(4) implement an early identification data system and use this data to guide decisions on implementing appropriate interventions;

(5) increase academic rigor and foster student engagement to ensure students are entering high school prepared for success in a rigorous college-ready curriculum, including a description of how such readiness will be measured;

(6) implement a systemic transition plan for all students and encourage collaboration between elementary, middle, and high schools; and

(7) provide evidence of an ongoing commitment to sustain the plan for a period of not less than 4 years.

(f) Review and Selection of Subgrants- In making subgrants under this section, the State educational agency shall—

(1) establish a peer-review process to assist in the review and approval of eligible local educational agency applications; and

(2) appoint individuals to participate in the peer-review process who are educators and experts in identifying, evaluating, and implementing effective education programs and practices, including areas of teaching and learning, educational standards and assessments, school improvement, and academic and behavioral supports for middle school students, including recognized exemplary middle level teachers and principals who have been recognized at the State or national level for exemplary work or contributions to the field.

(g) Revision of Subgrants- If a State educational agency, using the peer-review process described in subsection (f), determines that an eligible local educational agency's application does not meet the requirements of this title, the State educational agency shall notify the local educational agency of such determination and the reasons for such determination, and offer—

(1) the local educational agency an opportunity to revise and resubmit the application; and

(2) technical assistance to the local educational agency to revise the application.

(h) Mandatory Uses of Funds- An eligible local educational agency that receives a subgrant under this section shall carry out the following in each eligible school served by the agency:

(1) Align curricula among elementary grades, middle grades, and high schools to improve transitions from elementary school to middle school and from middle school to high school within the local educational agency, and across all grade levels within middle schools to improve grade to grade transitions.

(2) Implement evidence-based or, when available, scientifically valid instructional strategies, programs, and learning environments that meet the needs of all students and ensure that school leaders and teachers receive professional development on the use of these strategies.

(3) Ensure that school leaders, teachers, pupil service personnel, and other school staff understand the developmental stages of adolescents in the middle grades and how to deal with those stages appropriately in an educational setting.

(4) Implement organizational practices and school schedules that allow for effective leadership, collaborative staff participation, effective teacher teaming, and parent and community involvement.

(5) Create a more personalized and engaging learning environment for middle grade students by developing a personal academic plan for each student and assigning not less than 1 adult to help monitor student progress.

(6) Provide all students with information and assistance about the requirements for high school graduation, college admission, and career success.

(7) Utilize data from an early identification data system and guidance resources to identify struggling students and assist the students as the students transition from elementary school to middle school and from middle school to high school.

(8) Implement academic supports and effective and coordinated additional assistance programs to ensure that students have a strong foundation in reading, writing, mathematics, and science skills.

(9) Implement evidence-based or, when available, scientifically valid schoolwide programs and targeted supports to promote positive academic outcomes, such as increased attendance rates and the promotion of physical, personal, and social development.

(10) Develop and use an effective formative assessment to inform instruction.

(i) Permissible Uses of Funds- An eligible local educational agency that receives a subgrant under this section may use the subgrant funds to carry out the following:

(1) Implement extended learning opportunities in core academic areas including more instructional time in literacy, mathematics, science, history, and civics in addition to opportunities for language instruction and understanding other cultures and the arts.

(2) Provide evidence-based professional development activities with specific benchmarks to enable teachers and other school staff to appropriately monitor academic and behavioral progress, modify curricula, and implement accommodations and assistive technology services for students with disabilities, consistent with individualized edu-

cation programs under section 614(d) of the Individuals with Disabilities Education Act (20 U.S.C. 1414(d)).

(3) Employ and use instructional coaches, including literacy, mathematics, and English language learner coaches.

(4) Provide professional development for content-area teachers on working effectively with English language learners and students with disabilities, as well as professional development for English as a second language educators, bilingual educators, and special education personnel.

(5) Encourage and facilitate the sharing of data among elementary schools, middle schools, and high schools as well as postsecondary institutions.

(6) Create collaborative study groups composed of principals or teachers, or both, among middle schools within the eligible local educational agency, or between the eligible local educational agency and another local educational agency, with a focus on developing and sharing methods to increase student learning and academic achievement.

(j) Planning Subgrants-

(1) IN GENERAL- In addition to the subgrants to which the preceding provisions of this section apply, a State educational agency may (without regard to such preceding provisions) make planning subgrants, and provide technical assistance, to eligible local educational agencies that have not received a subgrant under subsection (a) to assist the local educational agencies in meeting the requirements of subsections (d) and (e).

(2) AMOUNT AND DURATION- Subgrants under this subsection may not exceed $50,000 nor 1 year in duration.

(k) Definitions- In this section:

(1) EARLY IDENTIFICATION DATA SYSTEM- The term 'early identification data system' means an electronic system—

(A) that is maintained by the State educational agency for use by local educational agencies and schools containing not less than 1 middle grade;

(B) that stores individual middle grade student level data (including data necessary to make the determinations under paragraph (3)(B)) tied to a unique student identifier on school outcomes that has been shown to be highly predictive of whether or not a student is on track to graduate from high school with a regular diploma, such as—

(i) student attendance and absenteeism;

(ii) earned on-time promotion rates from grade to grade;

(iii) a failing grade in a mathematics, reading or language arts course;

(iv) in-school and out-of-school suspension or other measurable evidence of at-risk behavior; and

(v) additional indicators proposed by the State educational agency and approved by the Secretary;

(C) the data in which is easily accessible to teachers and administrators; and

(D) that is updated on a regular basis to measure student progress over time.

(2) ELIGIBLE LOCAL EDUCATIONAL AGENCY- The term 'eligible local educational agency' means a local educational agency that serves not less than 1 eligible school.

(3) ELIGIBLE SCHOOL- The term 'eligible school' means a school containing not less than 1 middle grade and—

(A) more than 50 percent of the middle grade students go on to attend a high school with a graduation rate of less than 60 percent;

(B) more than 25 percent of the students who finish grade 6, or the earliest middle grade level in the school, exhibit 1 or more of the key risk factors and early risk identification signs, including—

(i) student attendance below 90 percent;

(ii) a failing grade in a mathematics, reading or language arts course;

(iii) 2 failing grades in any courses; and

(iv) out-of-school suspension or other evidence of at-risk behavior; or

(C) more than 50 percent of the middle grade students do not perform at a proficient level on State assessments required under section 1111(b)(3) of the Elementary and Secondary Education Act of 1965 (20 U.S.C. 6311(b)(3)) in mathematics or reading or language arts.

SEC. 105. DURATION OF GRANTS; SUPPLEMENT NOT SUPPLANT.

(a) Duration of Grants-

(1) IN GENERAL- Except as provided in paragraph (2), grants and subgrants under this title may not exceed 3 years in duration.

(2) RENEWALS-

(A) IN GENERAL- Grants and subgrants under this title may be renewed in 2-year increments.

(B) CONDITIONS- In order to be eligible to have a grant or subgrant renewed under this paragraph, the grant or subgrant recipient shall demonstrate, to the satisfaction of the granting entity, that—

(i) the recipient has complied with the terms of the grant or subgrant, including by undertaking all required activities; and

(ii) during the period of the grant or subgrant, there has been significant progress in student academic achievement, as measured by the annual measurable objectives established pursuant to section 1111(b)(2)(C)(v) of the Elementary and Secondary Education Act (20 U.S.C. 6311(b)(2)(C)(v)) and other key risk factors such as attendance and on-time promotion.

(b) Federal Funds to Supplement, Not Supplant, Non-Federal Funds-

(1) IN GENERAL- A State educational agency or local educational agency shall use Federal funds received under this title only to supplement the funds that would, in

the absence of such Federal funds, be made available from non-Federal sources for the education of pupils participating in programs assisted under this title, and not to supplant such funds.

(2) SPECIAL RULE- Nothing in this title shall be construed to authorize an officer, employee, or contractor of the Federal Government to mandate, direct, limit, or control a State, local educational agency, or school's specific instructional content, academic achievement standards and assessments, curriculum, or program of instruction.

SEC. 106. EVALUATION AND REPORTING.

(a) Evaluation- Not later than 180 days after the date of enactment of this Act, and annually thereafter for the period of the grant, each State receiving a grant under this title shall—

(1) conduct an evaluation of the State's progress regarding the impact of the changes made to the policies and practices of the State in accordance with this title, including—

(A) a description of the specific changes made, or in the process of being made, to policies and practices as a result of the grant;

(B) a discussion of any barriers hindering the identified changes in policies and practices, and implementations strategies to overcome such barriers;

(C) evidence of the impact of changes to policies and practices on behavior and actions at the local educational agency and school level; and

(D) evidence of the impact of the changes to State and local policies and practices on improving measurable learning gains by middle school students;

(2) use the results of the evaluation conducted under paragraph (1) to adjust the policies and practices of the State as necessary to achieve the purposes of this title; and

(3) submit the results of the evaluation to the Secretary.

(b) Availability- The Secretary shall make the results of each State's evaluation under subsection (a) available to other States and local educational agencies.

(c) Local Educational Agency Reporting- On an annual basis, each eligible local educational agency receiving a subgrant under this title shall report to the State educational agency and to the public on—

(1) the school performance indicators (as described in section 103(a)(4)(B)(vi)) for each eligible school (as defined in section 104(k)) served by the local educational agency, in the aggregate and disaggregated by the subgroups described in section 1111(b)(2)(C) (v)(II) of the Elementary and Secondary Education Act of 1965 (20 U.S.C. 6311(b) (2)(C)(v)(II)); and

(2) the use of funds by the local educational agency and each such school.

(d) State Educational Agency Reporting- On an annual basis, each State educational agency receiving grant funds under this title shall report to the Secretary and to the public on—

(1) the school performance indicators (as described in section 103(a)(4)(B)(vi)) in the aggregate and disaggregated by the subgroups described in section 1111(b)(2)(C)(v)

(II) of the Elementary and Secondary Education Act of 1965 (20 U.S.C. 6311(b)(2) (C)(v)(II)); and

(2) the use of the funds by each local educational agency and each school served with such funds.

(e) Report to Congress- Every 2 years, the Secretary shall report to the public and to Congress—

(1) a summary of the State reports under subsection (d); and

(2) the use of funds by each State under this title.

SEC. 107. AUTHORIZATION OF APPROPRIATIONS.

There are authorized to be appropriated to carry out this title $1,000,000,000 for fiscal year 2008 and such sums as may be necessary for each of the 5 succeeding fiscal years.

TITLE II—RESEARCH RECOMMENDATIONS

SEC. 201. PURPOSE.

The purpose of this title is to facilitate the generation, dissemination, and application of research needed to identify and implement effective practices that lead to continual student learning and high academic achievement at the middle level.

SEC. 202. RESEARCH RECOMMENDATIONS.

(a) Study on Promising Practices-

(1) IN GENERAL- Not later than 60 days after the date of enactment of this Act, the Secretary shall enter into a contract with the Center for Education of the National Academies to identify promising practices for the improvement of middle school education.

(2) CONTENT OF STUDY- The study described in paragraph (1) shall identify promising practices currently being implemented for the improvement of middle school education. The study shall be conducted in an open and transparent way that provides interim information to the public about criteria being used to identify—

(A) promising practices;

(B) the practices that are being considered; and

(C) the kind of evidence needed to document effectiveness.

(3) REPORT- The contract entered into pursuant to this subsection shall require that the Center for Education of the National Academies submit to the Secretary, the Committee on Health, Education, Labor, and Pensions of the Senate, and the Committee on Education and Labor of the House of Representatives a final report regarding the study conducted under this subsection not later than 1 year after the date of the commencement of the contract.

(4) PUBLICATION- The Secretary shall make public and post on the website of the Department of Education the findings of the study conducted under this subsection.

(b) Synthesis Study of Effective Teaching and Learning in Middle School-

(1) IN GENERAL- Not later than 60 days after the date of enactment of this Act, the Secretary shall enter into a contract with the Center for Education of the National Academies to review existing research on middle school education, and on factors that might lead to increased effectiveness and enhanced innovation in middle school education.

(2) CONTENT OF STUDY- The study described in paragraph (1) shall review research on education programs, practices, and policies, as well as research on the cognitive, social, and emotional development of children in the middle grades age range, in order to provide an enriched understanding of the factors that might lead to the development of innovative and effective middle school programs, practices, and policies. The study shall focus on—

(A) the areas of curriculum, instruction, and assessment (including additional supports for students who are below grade level in reading, writing, mathematics, and science, and the identification of students with disabilities) to better prepare all students for subsequent success in high school, college, and cognitively challenging employment;

(B) the quality of, and supports for, the teacher workforce;

(C) aspects of student behavioral and social development, and of social interactions within schools that affect the learning of academic content;

(D) the ways in which schools and local educational agencies are organized and operated that may be linked to student outcomes; and

(E) identification of areas where further research and evaluation may be needed on these topics to further the development of effective middle school practices.

(3) REPORT- The contract entered into pursuant to this subsection shall require that the Center for Education of the National Academies submit to the Secretary, the Committee on Health, Education, Labor, and Pensions of the Senate, and the Committee on Education and Labor of the House of Representatives a final report regarding the study conducted under this subsection not later than 2 years after the date of commencement of the contract.

(4) PUBLICATION- The Secretary shall make public and post on the website of the Department of Education the findings of the study conducted under this subsection.

(c) Other Activities- The Secretary shall carry out each of the following:

(1) Create a national clearinghouse, in coordination with entities such as What Works and the Doing What Works Clearinghouses, for research in best practices in the middle grades and in the approaches that successfully take those best practices to scale in schools and local educational agencies.

(2) Create a national middle grades database accessible to educational researchers, practitioners, and policymakers that identifies school, classroom, and system-level factors that facilitate or impede student academic achievement in the middle grades.

(3) Require the Institute for Education Sciences to develop a strand of field-initiated and scientifically valid research designed to enhance performance of middle grade schools and students who are most at risk of educational failure, which may be coordinated with the Regional Education Laboratories, institutions of higher education, agencies recognized for their research work that has been published in peer-reviewed

journals, and organizations that have regional education laboratories funded through the Institute for Education Sciences. Such research shall target specific issues such as—

(A) effective practices for instruction and assessment in mathematics, science, technology, and literacy;

(B) academic interventions for adolescent English language learners;

(C) school improvement programs and strategies for closing the academic achievement gap;

(D) evidence-based or, when available, scientifically valid professional development planning targeted to improve pedagogy and student academic achievement;

(E) the effects of increased learning or extended school time in the middle grades; and

(F) the effects of decreased class size or increased instructional and support staff.

(4) Strengthen the work of the existing National Research and Development Centers by adding an Educational Research and Development Center dedicated to addressing—

(A) curricular, instructional, and assessment issues pertinent to the middle grades (such as mathematics, science, technological fluency, the needs of English language learners, and students with disabilities);

(B) comprehensive school-wide reforms for low-performing middle grade schools; and

(C) other topics pertinent to middle schools.

(5) Provide grants to nonprofit organizations, for-profit organizations, institutions of higher education, and others to partner with State educational agencies and local educational agencies to develop, adapt, or replicate effective models for turning around low-performing middle schools.

SEC. 203. AUTHORIZATION OF APPROPRIATIONS; RESERVATIONS.

(a) Authorization- There are authorized to be appropriated to carry out this title $100,000,000 for fiscal year 2008 and such sums as may be necessary for each of the 5 succeeding fiscal years.

(b) Reservations- From the total amount made available to carry out this title, the Secretary shall reserve—

(1) 2.5 percent for the studies described in subsections (a) and (b) of section 202;

(2) 5 percent for the clearinghouse described in section 202(c)(1);

(3) 5 percent for the database described in section 202(c)(2);

(4) 42.5 percent for the activities described in section 202(c)(3);

(5) 15 percent for the activities described in section 202(c)(4); and

(6) 30 percent for the activities described in section 202(c)(5).

US Senate Bill 2330

Title: A bill to authorize a pilot program within the Departments of Veterans Affairs and Housing and Urban Development with the goal of preventing at-risk veterans and veteran families from falling into homelessness, and for other purposes.

Sponsor: Sen Obama, Barack [IL] (introduced 11/8/2007) Cosponsors (1)

Latest Major Action: 11/8/2007 Referred to Senate committee. Status: Read twice and referred to the Committee on Banking, Housing, and Urban Affairs.

SUMMARY:

¤NONE¤

Major Actions:

¤NONE¤

All Actions:

11/8/2007:

Read twice and referred to the Committee on Banking, Housing, and Urban Affairs.

Titles(s): (italics indicate a title for a portion of a bill)

¤NONE¤

COSPONSORS(1), ALPHABETICAL [followed by Cosponsors withdrawn]: (Sort: by date)

Sen Menendez, Robert [NJ] - 11/8/2007

Committee(s)

Committee/Subcommittee:

Activity:

Senate Banking, Housing, and Urban Affairs

Referral, In Committee

Related Bill Details:

¤NONE¤

Amendment(s)

¤NONE¤

IN THE SENATE OF THE UNITED STATES

November 8, 2007

Mr. REID (for Mr. OBAMA (for himself and Mr. MENENDEZ)) introduced the following bill; which was read twice and referred to the Committee on Banking, Housing, and Urban Affairs

A BILL

To authorize a pilot program within the Departments of Veterans Affairs and Housing and Urban Development with the goal of preventing at-risk veterans and veteran families from falling into homelessness, and for other purposes.

Be it enacted by the Senate and House of Representatives of the United States of America in Congress assembled,

SECTION 1. SHORT TITLE.

This Act may be cited as the 'Veterans Homelessness Prevention Act'.

SEC. 2. PILOT PROGRAM TO PROVIDE SUPPORTIVE HOUSING FOR VERY LOW-INCOME VETERAN FAMILIES.

(a) Purpose- The purposes of this section are—

(1) to expand the supply of permanent housing for very low-income veteran families; and

(2) to provide supportive services through such housing to support the needs of such veteran families.

(b) Establishment of Pilot Program-

(1) IN GENERAL- The Secretary of Housing and Urban Development shall establish a pilot program to provide assistance to private nonprofit organizations and consumer cooperatives to expand the supply of supportive housing for very low-income veteran families

(2) AUTHORITY TO PROVIDE ASSISTANCE- The Secretary shall, to the extent amounts are made available for assistance under this section and the Secretary receives approvable applications for such assistance, provide assistance to private nonprofit organizations and consumer cooperatives to carry out the pilot program established under paragraph (1).

(3) NATURE OF ASSISTANCE- The assistance provided under this subsection—

(A) shall be available for use to plan for and finance the acquisition, construction, reconstruction, or moderate or substantial rehabilitation of a structure or a portion of a structure to be used as supportive housing for very low-income veteran families in accordance with this section; and

(B) may also cover the cost of real property acquisition, site improvement, conversion, demolition, relocation, and other expenses that the Secretary determines are necessary to expand the supply of supportive housing for very low-income veteran families.

(4) CONSULTATION- In meeting the requirement of this subsection, the Secretary shall consult with—

(A) the Secretary of Veterans Affairs; and

(B) the Special Assistant for Veterans Affairs, as such Special Assistant was established under section 4(g) of the Department of Housing and Urban Development Act.

(c) Forms of Assistance- Assistance under this section shall be made available in the following forms:

(1) Assistance may be provided as a grant for costs of planning a project to be used as supportive housing for very low-income veteran families.

(2) Assistance may be provided as a capital advance under this paragraph for a project, such advance shall—

(A) bear no interest;

(B) not be required to be repaid so long as the housing remains available for occupancy by very low-income veteran families in accordance with this section; and

(C) be in an amount calculated in accordance with the development cost limitation established pursuant to subsection (j).

(3) Assistance may be provided as project rental assistance, under an annual contract that—

(A) obligates the Secretary to make monthly payments to cover any part of the costs attributed to units occupied (or, as approved by the Secretary, held for occupancy) by very low-income veteran families that is not met from project income;

(B) provides for the project not more than the sum of the initial annual project rentals for all units so occupied and any initial utility allowances for such units, as approved by the Secretary;

(C) any contract amounts not used by a project in any year shall remain available to the project until the expiration of the contract; and

(D) provides that the Secretary shall, to the extent appropriations for such purpose are made available, adjust the annual contract amount if the sum of the project income and the amount of assistance payments available under this paragraph are inadequate to provide for reasonable project costs.

(d) Tenant Rent Contribution- A very low-income veteran family shall pay as rent for a dwelling unit assisted under this section the highest of the following amounts, rounded to the nearest dollar:

(1) 30 percent of the veteran family's adjusted monthly income.

(2) 10 percent of the veteran family's monthly income.

(3) If the veteran family is receiving payments for welfare assistance from a public agency and a part of such payments, adjusted in accordance with the veteran family's actual housing costs, is specifically designated by such agency to meet the veteran family's housing costs, the portion of such payments which is so designated.

(e) Term of Commitment-

(1) USE LIMITATIONS- All units in housing assisted under this section shall be made available for occupancy by very low-income veteran families for not less than 15 years.

(2) CONTRACT TERMS-

(A) INITIAL TERM- The initial term of a contract entered into under subsection (c) (2) shall be 60 months.

(B) EXTENSION- The Secretary shall, to the extent approved in appropriation Acts, extend any expiring contract for a term of not less than 12 months.

(C) AUTHORITY OF SECRETARY TO MAKE EARLY COMMITMENTS- In order to facilitate the orderly extension of expiring contracts, the Secretary may make commitments to extend expiring contracts during the year prior to the date of expiration.

(f) Applications-

(1) IN GENERAL- Amounts made available under this section shall be allocated by the Secretary among approvable applications submitted by private nonprofit organizations and consumer cooperatives.

(2) CONTENT OF APPLICATION-

(A) IN GENERAL- Applications for assistance under this section shall be submitted by an applicant in such form and in accordance with such procedures as the Secretary shall establish.

(B) REQUIRED CONTENT- Applications for assistance under this section shall contain—

(i) a description of the proposed housing;

(ii) a description of the assistance the applicant seeks under this section;

(iii) a description of—

(I) the supportive services to be provided to the persons occupying such housing;

(II) the manner in which such services will be provided to such persons, including, in the case of frail elderly persons (as such term is defined in section 202 of the Housing Act of 1959 (12 U.S.C. 1701q)), evidence of such residential supervision as the Secretary determines is necessary to facilitate the adequate provision of such services; and

(III) the public or private sources of assistance that can reasonably be expected to fund or provide such services;

(iv) a certification from the public official responsible for submitting a housing strategy for the jurisdiction to be served in accordance with section 105 of the Cranston-Gonzalez National Affordable Housing Act (42 U.S.C. 12705) that the proposed project is consistent with the approved housing strategy; and

(v) such other information or certifications that the Secretary determines to be necessary or appropriate to achieve the purposes of this section.

(3) REJECTION- The Secretary shall not reject any application for assistance under this section on technical grounds without giving notice of that rejection and the basis therefore to the applicant.

(g) Selection Criteria- The Secretary shall establish selection criteria for assistance under this section, which shall include criteria—

(1) based upon—

(A) the ability of the applicant to develop and operate the proposed housing;

(B) the need for supportive housing for very low-income veteran families in the area to be served;

(C) the extent to which the proposed size and unit mix of the housing will enable the applicant to manage and operate the housing efficiently and ensure that the provision of supportive services will be accomplished in an economical fashion;

(D) the extent to which the proposed design of the housing will meet the physical needs of very low-income veteran families;

(E) the extent to which the applicant has demonstrated that the supportive services identified pursuant to subsection (f)(2)(B)(iii) will be provided on a consistent, long-term basis;

(F) the extent to which the proposed design of the housing will accommodate the provision of supportive services that are expected to be needed, either initially or over the useful life of the housing, by the very low-income veterans the housing is intended to serve; and

(G) such other factors as the Secretary determines to be appropriate to ensure that funds made available under this section are used effectively; and

(2) appropriate to consider the need for supportive housing for very low-income veteran families in nonmetropolitan areas and by Indian tribes.

(h) Provision of Supportive Services to Veteran Families-

(1) IN GENERAL- The Secretary of Veterans Affairs shall ensure that any housing assistance provided to veterans or veteran families includes a range of services tailored to the needs of the very low-income veteran families occupying such housing, which may include services for—

(A) outreach;

(B) health (including counseling, mental health, substance abuse, post-traumatic stress disorder, and traumatic brain injury) diagnosis and treatment;

(C) habilitation and rehabilitation;

(D) case management;

(E) daily living;

(F) personal financial planning;

(G) transportation;

(H) vocation;

(I) employment and training;

(J) education;

(K) assistance in obtaining veterans benefits and public benefits, including health and medical care provided by the Department of Veterans Affairs;

(L) assistance in obtaining income support;

(M) assistance in obtaining health insurance;

(N) fiduciary and representative payee;

(O) legal aid;

(P) child care;

(Q) housing counseling;

(R) service coordination; and

(S) other services necessary for maintaining independent living.

(2) LOCAL COORDINATION OF SERVICES-

(A) IN GENERAL- The Secretary shall ensure that owners of housing assisted under this section have the managerial capacity to—

(i) assess on an ongoing basis the service needs of residents;

(ii) coordinate the provision of supportive services and tailor such services to the individual needs of residents; and

(iii) seek on a continuous basis new sources of assistance to ensure the long-term provision of supportive services.

(B) CLASSIFICATION OF COSTS- Any cost associated with this subsection shall be an eligible cost under subsections (c)(3) and (i).

(i) Financial Assistance for Services-

(1) IN GENERAL- The Secretary of Veterans Affairs shall, to the extent amounts are available for assistance under this subsection, provide financial assistance for the provision of supportive services, and for coordinating the provision of such services, to very low-income veteran families occupying assisted housing. Such assistance shall be made through payments to owners of such housing for each resident of the housing based on the formula established under paragraph (2).

(2) FORMULA- The Secretary of Veterans Affairs shall establish a formula to determine the rate of the payments to be provided under this subsection. The formula shall determine a rate for each resident of the housing assisted under this section (which shall be adjusted not less than annually to take into consideration changes in the cost of living).

(3) AUTHORIZATION OF APPROPRIATIONS-

(A) IN GENERAL- There is authorized to be appropriated for the Department of Veterans Affairs to carry out this subsection amounts as follows:

(i) For fiscal year 2008, $1,000,000.

(ii) For each fiscal year after fiscal year 2008, such sums as may be necessary for such fiscal year.

(B) AVAILABILITY- Amounts authorized to be appropriated by subparagraph (A) shall remain available until expended.

(j) Development Cost Limitations-

(1) IN GENERAL- The Secretary shall periodically establish development cost limitations by market area for various types and sizes of supportive housing for very low-income veteran families by publishing a notice of the cost limitations in the Federal Register.

(2) CONSIDERATIONS- The cost limitations established under paragraph (1) shall reflect—

(A) the cost of construction, reconstruction, or moderate or substantial rehabilitation of supportive housing for very low-income veteran families that meets applicable State and local housing and building codes;

(B) the cost of movables necessary to the basic operation of the housing, as determined by the Secretary;

(C) the cost of special design features necessary to make the housing accessible to very low-income veteran families;

(D) the cost of congregate space necessary to accommodate the provision of supportive services to veteran families;

(E) if the housing is newly constructed, the cost of meeting the energy efficiency standards promulgated by the Secretary in accordance with section 109 of the Cranston-Gonzalez National Affordable Housing Act (42 U.S.C. 12709); and

(F) the cost of land, including necessary site improvement.

(3) USE OF DATA- In establishing development cost limitations for a given market area under this subsection, the Secretary shall use data that reflect currently prevailing costs of construction, reconstruction, or moderate or substantial rehabilitation, and land acquisition in the area.

(4) CONGREGATE SPACE- For purposes of paragraph (1), a congregate space shall include space for cafeterias or dining halls, community rooms or buildings, workshops, child care, adult day health facilities or other outpatient health facilities, or other essential service facilities.

(5) COMMERCIAL FACILITIES- Neither this section nor any other provision of law may be construed as prohibiting or preventing the location and operation, in a project assisted under this section, of commercial facilities for the benefit of residents of the project and the community in which the project is located, except that assistance made available under this section may not be used to subsidize any such commercial facility.

(6) ACQUISITION- In the case of existing housing and related facilities to be acquired, the cost limitations shall include—

(A) the cost of acquiring such housing;

(B) the cost of rehabilitation, alteration, conversion, or improvement, including the moderate or substantial rehabilitation thereof; and

(C) the cost of the land on which the housing and related facilities are located.

(7) ANNUAL ADJUSTMENTS- The Secretary shall adjust the cost limitation not less than annually to reflect changes in the general level of construction, reconstruction, and moderate and substantial rehabilitation costs.

(8) INCENTIVES FOR SAVINGS-

(A) SPECIAL HOUSING ACCOUNT-

(i) IN GENERAL- The Secretary shall use the development cost limitations established under paragraph (1) or (6) to calculate the amount of financing to be made available to individual owners.

(ii) ACTUAL DEVELOPMENTAL COSTS LESS THAN FINANCING- Owners which incur actual development costs that are less than the amount of financing shall be entitled to retain 50 percent of the savings in a special housing account.

(iii) BONUS FOR ENERGY EFFICIENCY- The percentage established under clause (ii) shall be increased to 75 percent for owners which add energy efficiency features which—

(I) exceed the energy efficiency standards promulgated by the Secretary in accordance with section 109 of the Cranston-Gonzalez National Affordable Housing Act (42 U.S.C. 12709);

(II) substantially reduce the life-cycle cost of the housing; and

(III) reduce gross rent requirements.

(B) USES- The special housing account established under subparagraph (A) may be used—

(i) to provide services to residents of the housing or funds set aside for replacement reserves; or

(ii) for such other purposes as determined by the Secretary.

(9) DESIGN FLEXIBILITY- The Secretary shall, to the extent practicable, give owners the flexibility to design housing appropriate to their location and proposed resident population within broadly defined parameters.

(10) USE OF FUNDS FROM OTHER SOURCES- An owner shall be permitted voluntarily to provide funds from sources other than this section for amenities and other features of appropriate design and construction suitable for supportive housing under this section if the cost of such amenities is—

(A) not financed with the advance; and

(B) is not taken into account in determining the amount of Federal assistance or of the rent contribution of tenants.

(k) Tenant Selection-

(1) IN GENERAL- An owner shall adopt written tenant selection procedures that are—

(A) satisfactory to the Secretary and which are—

(i) consistent with the purpose of improving housing opportunities for very low-income veteran families; and

(ii) reasonably related to program eligibility and an applicant's ability to perform the obligations of the lease; and

(B) compliant with subtitle C of title VI of the Housing and Community Development Act of 1992 (42 U.S.C.

SEC. 3. ASSESSMENT OF PILOT PROGRAM.

(a) In General- Upon the expiration of the 2-year period beginning on the date of the enactment of this Act, the Secretary of Veterans Affairs, in consultation with the Secretary of Housing and Urban Development, shall conduct an assessment of the pilot program carried out under section 2 to determine the effectiveness and limitations of, and potential improvements for, such program.

(b) Submission of Assessment to Congress- Not later than 180 days after the expiration of the 2-year period described in subsection (a), the Secretary of Veterans Affairs shall submit a report to the Congress regarding the results of the assessment required under subsection (a).

SEC. 4. TECHNICAL ASSISTANCE GRANTS FOR HOUSING ASSISTANCE FOR VETERANS.

(a) In General- The Secretary of Housing and Urban Development shall, to the extent amounts are made available in appropriation Acts for grants under this section, make grants to eligible entities under subsection (b) to provide to nonprofit organizations technical assistance appropriate to assist such organizations in—

(1) sponsoring housing projects for veterans assisted under programs, including any pilot programs, administered by the Department of Housing and Urban Development;

(2) fulfilling the planning and application processes and requirements necessary under such programs administered by the Department; and

(3) assisting veterans in obtaining housing or homeless assistance under programs administered by the Department.

(b) Eligible Entities- An eligible entity under this subsection is a nonprofit entity or organization having such expertise as the Secretary shall require in providing technical assistance to providers of services for veterans.

(c) Selection of Grant Recipients- The Secretary of Housing and Urban Development shall establish criteria for selecting applicants for grants under this section to receive such grants and shall select applicants based upon such criteria.

(d) Funding- Of any amounts made available in fiscal year 2008 or any fiscal year thereafter to the Department of Housing and Urban Development for salaries and expenses, $750,000 shall be available, and shall remain available until expended, for grants under this section.

US SENATE BILL 2347

TITLE: A bill to restore and protect access to discount drug prices for university-based and safety-net clinics.

SPONSOR: Sen Obama, Barack [IL] (introduced 11/13/2007) Cosponsors (31)

RELATED BILLS: H.R.4054

LATEST MAJOR ACTION: 11/13/2007 Referred to Senate committee. Status: Read twice and referred to the Committee on Finance.

SUMMARY AS OF:

11/13/2007—Introduced.

Prevention Through Affordable Access Act - Amends title XIX (Medicaid) of the Social Security Act to revise requirements for the best price component of the formula for determination of the Medicaid rebate for a covered single source outpatient drug or a covered innovator multiple source outpatient drug. (Under current law, best prices shall not take into account prices that are merely nominal in amount.)

Revises the list of entities to which sales by a manufacturer of covered outpatient drugs at nominal prices shall be considered to be sales at a nominal price, or merely nominal in amount (and thus excluded from computation of the best price for such drugs).

Adds to such list any entity that is: (1) operated by a health center of an institution of higher education, primarily for its students (university-based clinic); or (2) a public or private nonprofit entity that provides family planning services under the Public Health Service Act (safety-net clinic).

MAJOR ACTIONS:

¤NONE¤

ALL ACTIONS:

11/13/2007:

Read twice and referred to the Committee on Finance.

TITLES(s): (italics indicate a title for a portion of a bill)

¤NONE¤

COSPONSORS(31), ALPHABETICAL [followed by Cosponsors withdrawn]: (Sort: by date)

Sen Baucus, Max [MT] - 11/14/2007

Sen Bingaman, Jeff [NM] - 11/13/2007

Sen Boxer, Barbara [CA] - 11/13/2007

Sen Brown, Sherrod [OH] - 11/13/2007

444

Sen Cantwell, Maria [WA] - 11/13/2007

Sen Carper, Thomas R. [DE] - 12/3/2007

Sen Clinton, Hillary Rodham [NY] - 11/13/2007

Sen Collins, Susan M. [ME] - 11/13/2007

Sen Dodd, Christopher J. [CT] - 2/12/2008

Sen Durbin, Richard [IL] - 11/14/2007

Sen Feinstein, Dianne [CA] - 11/13/2007

Sen Harkin, Tom [IA] - 11/13/2007

Sen Kennedy, Edward M. [MA] - 11/13/2007

Sen Kerry, John F. [MA] - 11/13/2007

Sen Klobuchar, Amy [MN] - 11/13/2007

Sen Lautenberg, Frank R. [NJ] - 12/5/2007

Sen Leahy, Patrick J. [VT] - 11/13/2007

Sen Levin, Carl [MI] - 12/11/2007

Sen Lieberman, Joseph I. [CT] - 12/3/2007

Sen McCaskill, Claire [MO] - 11/13/2007

Sen Menendez, Robert [NJ] - 11/13/2007

Sen Mikulski, Barbara A. [MD] - 12/3/2007

Sen Murray, Patty [WA] - 11/13/2007

Sen Nelson, Bill [FL] - 12/11/2007

Sen Sanders, Bernard [VT] - 12/3/2007

Sen Schumer, Charles E. [NY] - 11/13/2007

Sen Snowe, Olympia J. [ME] - 12/11/2007

Sen Stabenow, Debbie [MI] - 11/13/2007

Sen Tester, Jon [MT] - 11/15/2007

Sen Whitehouse, Sheldon [RI] - 11/15/2007

Sen Wyden, Ron [OR] - 11/13/2007

COMMITTEE(S)

Committee/Subcommittee:

Activity:

Senate Finance

Referral, In Committee

RELATED BILL DETAILS: (additional related bills may be indentified in Status)

Bill:

Relationship:

H.R.4054

Identical bill identified by CRS

AMENDMENT(S)

¤NONE¤

IN THE SENATE OF THE UNITED STATES

November 13, 2007

Mr. REID (for Mr. OBAMA (for himself, Mrs. MCCASKILL, Ms. COLLINS, Mr. KENNEDY, Mrs. MURRAY, Ms. STABENOW, Mr. BINGAMAN, Mr. WYDEN, Mrs. FEINSTEIN, Mr. KERRY, Mr. HARKIN, Mrs. BOXER, Mr. LEAHY, Mr. MENENDEZ, Ms. KLOBUCHAR, Mr. SCHUMER, Mr. BROWN, Ms. CANTWELL, and Mrs. CLINTON)) introduced the following bill; which was read twice and referred to the Committee on Finance

A BILL

To restore and protect access to discount drug prices for university-based and safety-net clinics.

Be it enacted by the Senate and House of Representatives of the United States of America in Congress assembled,

SECTION 1. SHORT TITLE.

This Act may be cited as the 'Prevention Through Affordable Access Act'.

SEC. 2. RESTORING AND PROTECTING ACCESS TO DISCOUNT DRUG PRICES FOR UNIVERSITY-BASED AND SAFETY-NET CLINICS.

(a) Restoring Nominal Pricing- Section 1927(c)(1)(D)(i) of the Social Security Act (42 U.S.C. 1396r-8(c)(1)(D)(i)) is amended—

(1) by redesignating subclause (IV) as subclause (VI); and

(2) by inserting after subclause (III) the following new subclauses:

'(IV) An entity that is operated by a health center of an institution of higher education, the primary purpose of which is to provide health services to students of that institution.

'(V) An entity that is a public or private nonprofit entity that provides a service or services described under section 1001(a) of the Public Health Service Act.'.

(b) Effective Date- The amendments made by this section shall be effective as of the date of the enactment of this Act.

US Senate Bill 2392

Title: A bill to direct the Secretary of Education to establish and maintain a public website through which individuals may find a complete database of available scholarships, fellowships, and other programs of financial assistance in the study of science, technology, engineering, and mathematics.

Sponsor: Sen Obama, Barack [IL] (introduced 11/16/2007) Cosponsors (None)

Related Bills: H.R.1051, S.2428

Latest Major Action: 11/16/2007 Referred to Senate committee. Status: Read twice and referred to the Committee on Health, Education, Labor, and Pensions.

Summary As Of:

11/16/2007—Introduced.

National STEM Scholarship Database Act - Directs the Secretary of Education to establish and maintain, on the public website of the Department of Education, a database of information on public and private programs of financial assistance for the study of postsecondary and graduate science, technology, engineering, and mathematics.

Requires that such database: (1) provide separate information for each field of study; (2) be searchable by category and combinations of categories; (3) indicate programs targeted toward specific demographic groups; (4) provide searchers with program sponsor contact information and hyperlinks; and (5) include a recommendation that students and families carefully review application requirements and a disclaimer that scholarships presented in the database are not provided or endorsed by the Department or the federal government.

Requires the Secretary and the entity contracted to furnish and regularly update information to consult with public and private sources of scholarships and make easily available a process for the sources to provide regular and updated information.

Major Actions:

¤NONE¤

All Actions:

11/16/2007:

Read twice and referred to the Committee on Health, Education, Labor, and Pensions.

Titles(s): (italics indicate a title for a portion of a bill)

¤NONE¤

Cosponsor(s):

¤NONE¤

COMMITTEE(S)

Committee/Subcommittee:

Activity:

Senate Health, Education, Labor, and Pensions

Referral, In Committee

RELATED BILL DETAILS: (additional related bills may be indentified in Status)

Bill:

Relationship:

H.R.1051

Related bill identified by CRS

S.2428

Identical bill identified by CRS

AMENDMENT(S)

¤NONE¤

IN THE SENATE OF THE UNITED STATES

November 16, 2007

Mr. OBAMA introduced the following bill; which was read twice and referred to the Committee on Health, Education, Labor, and Pensions

A BILL

To direct the Secretary of Education to establish and maintain a public website through which individuals may find a complete database of available scholarships, fellowships, and other programs of financial assistance in the study of science, technology, engineering, and mathematics.

Be it enacted by the Senate and House of Representatives of the United States of America in Congress assembled,

SECTION 1. SHORT TITLE.

This Act may be cited as the 'National STEM Scholarship Database Act'.

SEC. 2. NATIONAL DATABASE ON FINANCIAL ASSISTANCE FOR STUDY OF SCIENCE, TECHNOLOGY, ENGINEERING, AND MATHEMATICS.

(a) Establishment and Maintenance of Database-

(1) DATABASE- The Secretary of Education shall establish and maintain, on the public website of the Department of Education, a database consisting of information on scholarships, fellowships, and other programs of financial assistance available from

public and private sources for the study of science, technology, engineering, or mathematics at the post-secondary and post-baccalaureate levels.

(2) PRESENTATION OF INFORMATION- The information maintained on the database established under this section shall be displayed on the website in the following manner:

(A) Separate information shall be provided for each of the fields of study referred to in paragraph (1) and for post-secondary and post-baccalaureate programs of financial assistance.

(B) The database shall provide specific information on any programs of financial assistance which are targeted to individuals of a particular gender, ethnicity, or other demographic group.

(C) If the sponsor of any program of financial assistance included on the database maintains a public website, the database shall provide hyperlinks to the website.

(D) In addition to providing the hyperlink to the website of a sponsor of a program of financial assistance as required under subparagraph (C), the database shall provide general information that an interested person may use to contact the sponsor, including the sponsor's electronic mail address.

(E) The database shall have a search capability which permits an individual to search for information on the basis of each category of the information provided and on the basis of combinations of categories of the information provided, including whether the scholarship is need- or merit-based and by relevant academic majors.

(F) The database shall include a recommendation that students and families should carefully review all of the application requirements prior to applying for aid, and a disclaimer that the scholarships presented in the database are not provided or endorsed by the Department of Education or the Federal Government.

(b) Dissemination of Information on Database- The Secretary shall take such actions as may be necessary on an ongoing basis, including sending notices to secondary schools and institutions of higher education, to disseminate information on the database established and maintained under this Act and to encourage its use by interested parties.

(c) Use of Vendor To Obtain Information- In carrying out this Act, the Secretary of Education shall enter into a contract with a private entity under which the entity shall furnish and regularly update all of the information required to be maintained on the database established under this section.

(d) Encouraging the Provision of Information- In carrying out this Act, the Secretary of Education and the contracted entity shall consult with public and private sources of scholarships and make easily available a process for such entities to provide regular and updated information.

SEC. 3. AUTHORIZATION OF APPROPRIATIONS.

There are authorized to be appropriated to carry out this Act such sums as may be necessary for fiscal years 2008 through 2012.

US SENATE BILL 2428

TITLE: A bill to direct the Secretary of Education to establish and maintain a public website through which individuals may find a complete database of available scholarships, fellowships, and other programs of financial assistance in the study of science, technology, engineering, and mathematics.

SPONSOR: Sen Obama, Barack [IL] (introduced 12/6/2007) Cosponsors (6)

RELATED BILLS: H.R.1051, S.2392

LATEST MAJOR ACTION: 12/6/2007 Referred to Senate committee. Status: Read twice and referred to the Committee on Health, Education, Labor, and Pensions.

SUMMARY AS OF:

12/6/2007—Introduced.

National STEM Scholarship Database Act - Directs the Secretary of Education to establish and maintain, on the public website of the Department of Education, a database of information on public and private programs of financial assistance for the study of postsecondary and graduate science, technology, engineering, and mathematics.

Requires that such database: (1) provide separate information for each field of study; (2) be searchable by category and combinations of categories; (3) indicate programs targeted toward specific demographic groups; (4) provide searchers with program sponsor contact information and hyperlinks; and (5) include a recommendation that students and families carefully review application requirements and a disclaimer that scholarships presented in the database are not provided or endorsed by the Department or the federal government.

Requires the Secretary and the entity contracted to furnish and regularly update information to consult with public and private sources of scholarships and make easily available a process for the sources to provide regular and updated information.

MAJOR ACTIONS:

¤NONE¤

ALL ACTIONS:

12/6/2007:

Read twice and referred to the Committee on Health, Education, Labor, and Pensions.

TITLES(s): (italics indicate a title for a portion of a bill)

¤NONE¤

COSPONSORS(6), ALPHABETICAL [FOLLOWED BY COSPONSORS WITHDRAWN]: (Sort: by date)

Sen Coleman, Norm [MN] - 12/6/2007

Sen Collins, Susan M. [ME] - 12/6/2007

Sen Durbin, Richard [IL] - 12/6/2007

Sen Johnson, Tim [SD] - 12/17/2007

Sen Lieberman, Joseph I. [CT] - 12/17/2007

Sen Nelson, Bill [FL] - 12/18/2007

COMMITTEE(S)

Committee/Subcommittee:

Activity:

Senate Health, Education, Labor, and Pensions

Referral, In Committee

RELATED BILL DETAILS: (additional related bills may be indentified in Status)

Bill:

Relationship:

H.R.1051

Related bill identified by CRS

S.2392

Identical bill identified by CRS

AMENDMENT(S)

¤NONE¤

IN THE SENATE OF THE UNITED STATES

December 6, 2007

Mr. REID (for Mr. OBAMA (for himself, Ms. COLLINS, Mr. DURBIN, and Mr. COLEMAN)) introduced the following bill; which was read twice and referred to the Committee on Health, Education, Labor, and Pensions

A BILL

To direct the Secretary of Education to establish and maintain a public website through which individuals may find a complete database of available scholarships, fellowships, and other programs of financial assistance in the study of science, technology, engineering, and mathematics.

Be it enacted by the Senate and House of Representatives of the United States of America in Congress assembled,

SECTION 1. SHORT TITLE.

This Act may be cited as the 'National STEM Scholarship Database Act'.

SEC. 2. NATIONAL DATABASE ON FINANCIAL ASSISTANCE FOR STUDY OF SCIENCE, TECHNOLOGY, ENGINEERING, AND MATHEMATICS.

(a) Establishment and Maintenance of Database-

(1) DATABASE- The Secretary of Education shall establish and maintain, on the public website of the Department of Education, a database consisting of information on scholarships, fellowships, and other programs of financial assistance available from public and private sources for the study of science, technology, engineering, or mathematics at the post-secondary and post-baccalaureate levels.

(2) PRESENTATION OF INFORMATION- The information maintained on the database established under this section shall be displayed on the website in the following manner:

(A) Separate information shall be provided for each of the fields of study referred to in paragraph (1) and for post-secondary and post-baccalaureate programs of financial assistance.

(B) The database shall provide specific information on any programs of financial assistance which are targeted to individuals of a particular gender, ethnicity, or other demographic group.

(C) If the sponsor of any program of financial assistance included on the database maintains a public website, the database shall provide hyperlinks to the website.

(D) In addition to providing the hyperlink to the website of a sponsor of a program of financial assistance as required under subparagraph (C), the database shall provide general information that an interested person may use to contact the sponsor, including the sponsor's electronic mail address.

(E) The database shall have a search capability which permits an individual to search for information on the basis of each category of the information provided and on the basis of combinations of categories of the information provided, including whether the scholarship is need- or merit-based and by relevant academic majors.

(F) The database shall include a recommendation that students and families should carefully review all of the application requirements prior to applying for aid, and a disclaimer that the scholarships presented in the database are not provided or endorsed by the Department of Education or the Federal Government.

(b) Dissemination of Information on Database- The Secretary shall take such actions as may be necessary on an ongoing basis, including sending notices to secondary schools and institutions of higher education, to disseminate information on the database established and maintained under this Act and to encourage its use by interested parties.

(c) Use of Vendor To Obtain Information- In carrying out this Act, the Secretary of Education shall enter into a contract with a private entity under which the entity shall furnish and regularly update all of the information required to be maintained on the database established under this section.

(d) Encouraging the Provision of Information- In carrying out this Act, the Secretary of Education and the contracted entity shall consult with public and private sources of scholarships and make easily available a process for such entities to provide regular and updated information.

SEC. 3. AUTHORIZATION OF APPROPRIATIONS.

There are authorized to be appropriated to carry out this Act such sums as may be necessary for fiscal years 2008 through 2012.

US Senate Bill 2433

TITLE: A bill to require the President to develop and implement a comprehensive strategy to further the United States foreign policy objective of promoting the reduction of global poverty, the elimination of extreme global poverty, and the achievement of the Millennium Development Goal of reducing by one-half the proportion of people worldwide, between 1990 and 2015, who live on less than $1 per day.

SPONSOR: Sen Obama, Barack [IL] (introduced 12/7/2007) Cosponsors (9)

RELATED BILLS: H.R.1302

LATEST MAJOR ACTION: 2/13/2008 Senate committee/subcommittee actions. Status: Committee on Foreign Relations. Ordered to be reported with amendments favorably.

SUMMARY AS OF:

12/7/2007—Introduced.

Global Poverty Act of 2007 - Directs the President, through the Secretary of State, to develop and implement a comprehensive strategy to further the U.S. foreign policy objective of promoting the reduction of global poverty, the elimination of extreme global poverty, and the achievement of the United Nations Millennium Development Goal of reducing by one-half the proportion of people worldwide, between 1990 and 2015, who live on less than $1 per day.

MAJOR ACTIONS:

¤NONE¤

ALL ACTIONS:

12/7/2007:

Read twice and referred to the Committee on Foreign Relations.

2/13/2008:

Committee on Foreign Relations. Ordered to be reported with amendments favorably.

TITLES(s): (italics indicate a title for a portion of a bill)

¤NONE¤

COSPONSORS(9), ALPHABETICAL [FOLLOWED BY COSPONSORS WITH-DRAWN]: (Sort: by date)

Sen Biden, Joseph R., Jr. [DE] - 2/12/2008

Sen Cantwell, Maria [WA] - 12/7/2007

Sen Dodd, Christopher J. [CT] - 2/12/2008

Sen Durbin, Richard [IL] - 2/7/2008

Sen Feingold, Russell D. [WI] - 2/13/2008

Sen Feinstein, Dianne [CA] - 1/23/2008

Sen Hagel, Chuck [NE] - 12/7/2007

Sen Lugar, Richard G. [IN] - 2/5/2008

Sen Menendez, Robert [NJ] - 2/11/2008

COMMITTEE(S)

Committee/Subcommittee:

Activity:

Senate Foreign Relations

Referral, Markup, In Committee

RELATED BILL DETAILS: (additional related bills may be indentified in Status)

Bill:

Relationship:

H.R.1302

Related bill identified by CRS

AMENDMENT(S)

¤NONE¤

IN THE SENATE OF THE UNITED STATES

December 7, 2007

Mr. OBAMA (for himself, Mr. HAGEL, and Ms. CANTWELL) introduced the following bill; which was read twice and referred to the Committee on Foreign Relations

A BILL

To require the President to develop and implement a comprehensive strategy to further the United States foreign policy objective of promoting the reduction of global poverty, the elimination of extreme global poverty, and the achievement of the Millennium Development Goal of reducing by one-half the proportion of people world-wide, between 1990 and 2015, who live on less than $1 per day.

Be it enacted by the Senate and House of Representatives of the United States of America in Congress assembled,

SECTION 1. SHORT TITLE.

This Act may be cited as the 'Global Poverty Act of 2007'.

SEC. 2. FINDINGS.

Congress makes the following findings:

(1) More than 1,000,000,000 people worldwide live on less than $1 per day, and an-other 1,600,000,000 people struggle to survive on less than $2 per day, according to the World Bank.

(2) At the United Nations Millennium Summit in 2000, the United States joined more than 180 other countries in committing to work toward goals to improve life for the world's poorest people by 2015.

(3) The year 2007 marks the mid-point to the Millennium Development Goals dead-line of 2015.

(4) The United Nations Millennium Development Goals include the goal of reducing by one-half the proportion of people worldwide, between 1990 and 2015, that live on less than $1 per day, cutting in half the proportion of people suffering from hun-ger and unable to access safe drinking water and sanitation, reducing child mortality by two-thirds, ensuring basic education for all children, and reversing the spread of HIV/AIDS and malaria, while sustaining the environment upon which human life depends.

(5) On March 22, 2002, President George W. Bush stated: 'We fight against poverty because hope is an answer to terror. We fight against poverty because opportunity is a fundamental right to human dignity. We fight against poverty because faith requires it and conscience demands it. We fight against poverty with a growing conviction that major progress is within our reach.'.

(6) The 2002 National Security Strategy of the United States notes: '[A] world where some live in comfort and plenty, while half of the human race lives on less than $2 per day, is neither just nor stable. Including all of the world's poor in an expanding circle of development and opportunity is a moral imperative and one of the top priorities of U.S. international policy.'.

(7) The 2006 National Security Strategy of the United States notes: 'America's na-tional interests and moral values drive us in the same direction: to assist the world's poor citizens and least developed nations and help integrate them into the global economy.'.

(8) The bipartisan Final Report of the National Commission on Terrorist Attacks Upon the United States recommends: 'A comprehensive United States strategy to counter terrorism should include economic policies that encourage development, more open societies, and opportunities for people to improve the lives of their families and enhance prospects for their children.'.

(9) At the summit of the Group of Eight (G-8) nations in July 2005, leaders from all eight participating countries committed to increase aid to Africa from the current $25,000,000,000 annually to $50,000,000,000 by 2010, and to cancel 100 percent of the debt obligations owed to the World Bank, African Development Bank, and International Monetary Fund by 18 of the world's poorest nations.

(10) At the United Nations World Summit in September 2005, the United States joined more than 180 other governments in reiterating their commitment to achieve the United Nations Millennium Development Goals by 2015.

(11) The United States has recognized the need for increased financial and technical assistance to countries burdened by extreme poverty, as well as the need for strengthened economic and trade opportunities for those countries, through significant initiatives in recent years, including the Millennium Challenge Act of 2003 (22 U.S.C. 7701 et seq.), the United States Leadership Against HIV/AIDS, Tuberculosis, and Malaria Act of 2003 (22 U.S.C. 7601 et seq.), the Heavily Indebted Poor Countries Initiative, and trade preference programs for developing countries, such as the African Growth and Opportunity Act (19 U.S.C. 3701 et seq.).

(12) In January 2006, United States Secretary of State Condoleezza Rice initiated a restructuring of the United States foreign assistance program, including the creation of a Director of Foreign Assistance, who maintains authority over Department of State and United States Agency for International Development (USAID) foreign assistance funding and programs.

(13) In January 2007, the Department of State's Office of the Director of Foreign Assistance added poverty reduction as an explicit, central component of the overall goal of United States foreign assistance. The official goal of United States foreign assistance is: 'To help build and sustain democratic, well-governed states that respond to the needs of their people, reduce widespread poverty and conduct themselves responsibly in the international system.'.

(14) Economic growth and poverty reduction are more successful in countries that invest in the people, rule justly, and promote economic freedom. These principles have become the core of several development programs of the United States Government, such as the Millennium Challenge Account.

SEC. 3. DECLARATION OF POLICY.

It is the policy of the United States to promote the reduction of global poverty, the elimination of extreme global poverty, and the achievement of the Millennium Development Goal of reducing by one-half the proportion of people worldwide, between 1990 and 2015, who live on less than $1 per day.

SEC. 4. REQUIREMENT TO DEVELOP COMPREHENSIVE STRATEGY.

(a) Strategy- The President, acting through the Secretary of State, and in consultation with the heads of other appropriate departments and agencies of the United States Government, international organizations, international financial institutions, the governments of developing and developed countries, United States and international nongovernmental organizations, civil society organizations, and other appropriate entities, shall develop and implement a comprehensive strategy to further the United States foreign policy objective of promoting the reduction of global poverty, the elimination of extreme global poverty, and the achievement of the Millennium Development Goal of reducing by one-half the proportion of people worldwide, between 1990 and 2015, who live on less than $1 per day.

(b) Content- The strategy required by subsection (a) shall include specific and measurable goals, efforts to be undertaken, benchmarks, and timetables to achieve the objectives described in subsection (a).

(c) Components- The strategy required by subsection (a) should include the following components:

(1) Continued investment or involvement in existing United States initiatives related to international poverty reduction, such as the United States Leadership Against HIV/AIDS, Tuberculosis, and Malaria Act of 2003 (22 U.S.C. 7601 et seq.), the Millennium Challenge Act of 2003 (22 U.S.C. 7701 et seq.), and trade preference programs for developing countries, such as the African Growth and Opportunity Act (19 U.S.C. 3701 et seq.).

(2) Improving the effectiveness of development assistance and making available additional overall United States assistance levels as appropriate.

(3) Enhancing and expanding debt relief as appropriate.

(4) Leveraging United States trade policy where possible to enhance economic development prospects for developing countries.

(5) Coordinating efforts and working in cooperation with developed and developing countries, international organizations, and international financial institutions.

(6) Mobilizing and leveraging the participation of businesses, United States and international nongovernmental organizations, civil society, and public-private partnerships.

(7) Coordinating the goal of poverty reduction with other development goals, such as combating the spread of preventable diseases such as HIV/AIDS, tuberculosis, and malaria, increasing access to potable water and basic sanitation, reducing hunger and malnutrition, and improving access to and quality of education at all levels regardless of gender.

(8) Integrating principles of sustainable development and entrepreneurship into policies and programs.

(d) Reports-

(1) INITIAL REPORT-

(A) IN GENERAL- Not later than 1 year after the date of the enactment of this Act, the President, acting through the Secretary of State, shall submit to the appropriate congressional committees a report on the strategy required under subsection (a).

(B) CONTENT- The report required under subparagraph (A) shall include the following elements:

(i) A description of the strategy required under subsection (a).

(ii) An evaluation, to the extent possible, both proportionate and absolute, of the contributions provided by the United States and other national and international actors in achieving the Millennium Development Goal of reducing by one-half the proportion of people worldwide, between 1990 and 2015, who live on less than $1 per day.

(iii) An assessment of the overall progress toward achieving the Millennium Development Goal of reducing by one-half the proportion of people worldwide, between 1990 and 2015, who live on less than $1 per day.

(2) SUBSEQUENT REPORTS- Not later than December 31, 2012, and December 31, 2015, the President shall submit to the appropriate congressional committees reports on the status of the implementation of the strategy, progress made in achieving the global poverty reduction objectives described in subsection (a), and any changes to the strategy since the date of the submission of the last report.

SEC. 5. DEFINITIONS.

In this Act:

(1) APPROPRIATE CONGRESSIONAL COMMITTEES- The term 'appropriate congressional committees' means—

(A) the Committee on Foreign Relations and the Committee on Appropriations of the Senate; and

(B) the Committee on Foreign Affairs and the Committee on Appropriations of the House of Representatives.

(2) EXTREME GLOBAL POVERTY- The term 'extreme global poverty' refers to the conditions in which individuals live on less than $1 per day, adjusted for purchasing power parity in 1993 United States dollars, according to World Bank statistics.

(3) GLOBAL POVERTY- The term 'global poverty' refers to the conditions in which individuals live on less than $2 per day, adjusted for purchasing power parity in 1993 United States dollars, according to World Bank statistics.

(4) MILLENNIUM DEVELOPMENT GOALS- The term 'Millennium Development Goals' means the goals set out in the United Nations Millennium Declaration, General Assembly Resolution 55/2 (2000).

US SENATE BILL 2519

TITLE: A bill to prohibit the awarding of a contract or grant in excess of the simplified acquisition threshold unless the prospective contractor or grantee certifies in writing to the agency awarding the contract or grant that the contractor or grantee has no seriously delinquent tax debts, and for other purposes.

SPONSOR: Sen Obama, Barack [IL] (introduced 12/19/2007) Cosponsors (None)

RELATED BILLS: H.R.4881

LATEST MAJOR ACTION: 12/19/2007 Referred to Senate committee. Status: Read twice and referred to the Committee on Homeland Security and Governmental Affairs.

SUMMARY AS OF:

12/19/2007—Introduced.

Contracting and Tax Accountability Act of 2007 - Prohibits any person who has a seriously delinquent tax debt from obtaining a federal government contract or grant. Requires federal agency heads to require prospective contractors or grantees to: (1) certify that they do not have such a debt; and (2) authorize the Secretary of the Treasury to disclose information describing whether such contractors or grantees have such a debt.

Defines "seriously delinquent tax debt" and an outstanding tax debt for which a notice of lien has been filed in public records.

MAJOR ACTIONS:

¤NONE¤

ALL ACTIONS:

12/19/2007:

Read twice and referred to the Committee on Homeland Security and Governmental Affairs.

TITLES(s): (italics indicate a title for a portion of a bill)

¤NONE¤

COSPONSOR(s):

¤NONE¤

COMMITTEE(s)

Committee/Subcommittee:

Activity:

Senate Homeland Security and Governmental Affairs

Referral, In Committee

RELATED BILL DETAILS: (additional related bills may be indentified in Status)

Bill:

Relationship:

H.R.4881

Related bill identified by CRS

AMENDMENT(s)

¤NONE¤

IN THE SENATE OF THE UNITED STATES

December 19, 2007

Mr. REID (for Mr. OBAMA) introduced the following bill; which was read twice and referred to the Committee on Homeland Security and Governmental Affairs

A BILL

To prohibit the awarding of a contract or grant in excess of the simplified acquisition threshold unless the prospective contractor or grantee certifies in writing to the agency awarding the contract or grant that the contractor or grantee has no seriously delinquent tax debts, and for other purposes.

Be it enacted by the Senate and House of Representatives of the United States of America in Congress assembled,

SECTION 1. SHORT TITLE.

This Act may be cited as the 'Contracting and Tax Accountability Act of 2007'.

SEC. 2. GOVERNMENTAL POLICY.

It is the policy of the United States Government that no Government contracts or grants should be awarded to individuals or companies with seriously delinquent Federal tax debts.

SEC. 3. PROHIBITION ON AWARDING OF CONTRACTS TO DELINQUENT FEDERAL DEBTORS.

Section 3720B of title 31, United States Code, is amended—

(1) in the section heading, by adding at the end 'or contracts';

(2) by adding at the end the following:

'(c)(1) Unless this subsection is waived by the head of a Federal agency, a person who has a seriously delinquent tax debt shall be proposed for debarment from any contract awarded by the Federal government pursuant to procedures established by regulation by the Administrator for Federal Procurement Policy.

'(2) The head of any Federal agency that issues an invitation for bids or a request for proposals for a negotiated acquisition shall require each person that submits a bid or proposal to submit with the bid or proposal a form—

'(A) certifying that the person does not have a seriously delinquent tax debt; and

'(B) authorizing the Secretary of the Treasury to disclose to the head of the agency information limited to describing whether the person has a seriously delinquent tax debt.

'(3) The Secretary shall develop and make available to all Federal agencies a standard form for the certification and authorization described in paragraph (2).

'(4) Not later than 270 days after the date of enactment of this subsection, the Administrator for Federal Procurement Policy shall issue revised regulations to incorporate the requirements of this subsection.

'(5) For purposes of this subsection:

'(A) The term 'contract' means a binding agreement entered into by a Federal agency for the purpose of obtaining property or services, but does not include—

'(i) a contract designated by the head of the agency as assisting the agency in the performance of disaster relief authorities; or

'(ii) a contract designated by the head of the agency as necessary to the national security of the United States.

'(B)(i) The term 'person' includes—

'(I) an individual;

'(II) a partnership; and

'(III) a corporation.

'(ii) A partnership shall be treated as a person with a seriously delinquent tax debt if such partnership has a partner who—

'(I) holds an ownership interest of 50 percent or more in that partnership; and

'(II) who has a seriously delinquent tax debt.

'(iii) A corporation shall be treated as a person with a seriously delinquent tax debt if such corporation has an officer or a shareholder who—

'(I) holds 50 percent or more, or a controlling interest that is less than 50 percent, of the outstanding shares of corporate stock in that corporation; and

'(II) who has a seriously delinquent tax debt.

'(C)(i) The term 'seriously delinquent tax debt' means an outstanding debt under the Internal Revenue Code of 1986 for which a notice of lien has been filed in public records pursuant to section 6323 of such Code.

'(ii) Such term does not include—

'(I) a debt that is being paid in a timely manner pursuant to an agreement under section 6159 or section 7122 of such Code; and

'(II) a debt with respect to which a collection due process hearing under section 6330 of such Code, or relief under subsection (a), (b), or (f) of section 6015, is requested or pending.'.

SEC. 4. PROHIBITION ON AWARDING OF GRANTS TO DELINQUENT FEDERAL DEBTORS.

(a) In General- The head of any Executive agency that offers a grant in excess of an amount equal to the simplified acquisition threshold (as defined in section 4(11) of the Office of Federal Procurement Policy Act (41 U.S.C. 401(11)) may not award such grant to any person unless such person submits with the application for such grant a form—

(1) certifying that the person does not have a seriously delinquent tax debt; and

(2) authorizing the Secretary of the Treasury to disclose to the head of the Executive agency information limited to describing whether the person has a seriously delinquent tax debt.

(b) Release of Information- The Secretary shall develop and make available to all Executive agencies a standard form for the certification and authorization described in subsection (a)(2).

(c) Revision of Regulations- Not later than 270 days after the date of the enactment of this section, the Director of the Office of Management and Budget shall revise such regulations as necessary to incorporate the requirements of this section.

(d) Definitions and Special Rules- For purposes of this section:

(1) PERSON-

(A) IN GENERAL- The term 'person' includes—

(i) an individual;

(ii) a partnership; and

(iii) a corporation.

(B) TREATMENT OF CERTAIN PARTNERSHIPS- A partnership shall be treated as a person with a seriously delinquent tax debt if such partnership has a partner who—

(i) holds an ownership interest of 50 percent or more in that partnership; and

(ii) who has a seriously delinquent tax debt.

(C) TREATMENT OF CERTAIN CORPORATIONS- A corporation shall be treated as a person with a seriously delinquent tax debt if such corporation has an officer or a shareholder who—

(i) holds 50 percent or more, or a controlling interest that is less than 50 percent, of the outstanding shares of corporate stock in that corporation; and

(ii) who has a seriously delinquent tax debt.

(2) EXECUTIVE AGENCY- The term 'executive agency' has the meaning given such term in section 4 of the Office of Federal Procurement Policy Act (41 U.S.C. 403).

(3) SERIOUSLY DELINQUENT TAX DEBT-

(A) IN GENERAL- The term 'seriously delinquent tax debt' means an outstanding debt under the Internal Revenue Code of 1986 for which a notice of lien has been filed in public records pursuant to section 6323 of such Code.

(B) EXCEPTIONS- Such term does not include—

(i) a debt that is being paid in a timely manner pursuant to an agreement under section 6159 or section 7122 of such Code; and

(ii) a debt with respect to which a collection due process hearing under section 6330 of such Code, or relief under subsection (a), (b), or (f) of section 6015, is requested or pending.

Printed in the United States
114151LV00002B/2/P